W9-AEU-792

Beyond the Darkness

BY THE SAME AUTHOR

Dame Cicely Saunders – Founder of the Modern Hospice Movement
The Changing Face of Death
The Gardeners
The World Walks By (with Sue Masham)
Tutu: Archbishop Without Frontiers
Teresa of Avila
The Road to Canterbury: A Modern Pilgrimage

Beyond the Darkness

A BIOGRAPHY OF BEDE GRIFFITHS

Shirley du Boulay

> I know that Great Person
> of the brightness of the Sun
> beyond the darkness.
> Only by knowing him
> one goes beyond death.
> There is no other way to go.

SVETASVATARA UPANISHAD
India, 800–400 B.C.E.

DOUBLEDAY

New York   London   Toronto   Sydney   Auckland

PUBLISHED BY DOUBLEDAY
a division of Bantam Doubleday Dell Publishing Group, Inc.
1540 Broadway, New York, New York 10036

DOUBLEDAY and the portrayal of an anchor with a dolphin are
trademarks of Doubleday, a division of Bantam Doubleday Dell
Publishing Group, Inc.

Library of Congress Cataloging-in-Publication Data
Du Boulay, Shirley.
Beyond the darkness : a biography of Bede Griffiths / Shirley du Boulay. — 1st ed.
p. cm.
Includes bibliographical references and index.
1. Griffiths, Bede, 1906– . 2. Benedictines — Biography.
3. Catholic Church — England — Clergy — Biography.
4. Catholic Church — India — Clergy — Biography. I. Title.
BX4705.G6226D8   1998
271'.102
[b] — DC21   98-30173
                                                CIP

Published by arrangement with Rider Books, a division of Random House U.K.

ISBN 0-385-48946-3

Copyright © 1998 by Shirley du Boulay
All Rights Reserved
Printed in the United States of America
November 1998
First Edition in the United States of America

1   3   5   7   9   10   8   6   4   2

In Memory of John

Contents

Illustrations

Acknowledgments

I would like to thank the following libraries and collections for giving me access to papers and letters concerning Father Bede Griffiths:

The Bodleian Library, Oxford, England
Christ's Hospital, West Sussex, England
General Theological Union Archives, Berkeley, USA
Kurisumala Ashram, Kerala, India
Osage Monastery, Oklahoma, USA
Prinknash Abbey, Gloucestershire, England
Shantivanam Ashram, Tamil Nadu, India
World Community for Christian Meditation, London
Magdalen College, Oxford, England
Wheaton College, Illinois, USA

I am greatly indebted to the following individuals, who took endless pains to send me tapes, letters and articles by Bede Griffiths: Fr Francis Acharya (Fr Mahieu) Peter Bentley, Father Douglas Conlan, Valerie Flessati, Fr Peter Milward SJ, Roland Ropers, Jyoti Sahi, Russill and Asha Paul D'Silva, Kathryn Spink, Br Wayne Teasdale, Christopher Venning, Judy Walter.

Also to Kate Nowlan and Daniel Skinner, for allowing me to use invaluable unpublished material written by their father Martyn Skinner, and by Hugh Waterman.

Special thanks are also due to the Bede Griffiths Trust for allowing me to quote freely from the works of Bede Griffiths and for all their support and encouragement.

Many people contributed to this book by sharing their memories and knowledge of Bede Griffiths. Some I have quoted verbatim, others have been woven into the tapestry of Father Bede's life. I would like to thank especially the members of the community at Shantivanam, the monks of Prinknash Abbey, Farnborough Abbey and Pluscarden Abbey and the following:

Fr Francis Acharya (Fr Mahieu), Fr Michael Amaldas, SJ, the late Dr Owen Barfield, Fr Michael Barnes, SJ, Fr Bruno Barnhart, OSB, Chuck Baroo, Peter Bentley, Fr Fabian Binyon, OSB, Phelina Bruce, Nigel Bruce, William Buchanan, Dr Fritjof Capra, John and Ingrid Careswell, Fr Christudas, OSB Cam, Milo Coerper, Sister Pascaline Coff, OSB, Fr Douglas Conlan, Mrs Margaret Croissant, Andrew Crowe, Sr Carla Curran, Russill and Asha Paul D'Silva, Professor Felicity Edwards, Sr Eustella, Fr Laurence Freeman, OSB, John Gale, Fr Clarence Gallagher, SJ, Michael Giddings, Judge and Mrs David Griffiths, Richard Griffiths, Lilian Griffiths, Ruth Harring, Andrew Harvey, Geoffrey Hayward, Jill Hemmings, Fr Hyrudayam, SJ, Fr M. Jeyaraj, SJ, Br John (Maarten Turkstra), Professor Ursula King, Professor Nicholas Lash, The Rt Hon. Lord Longford, Revd Dr Eric Lott, Br Martin, Fr Thomas Matus, OSB Cam, Jyoti Minor, Kate Nowlan, Professor Raimon Panikkar, Dr A. Pushparajan, Dorothy and Toby Rance, Adrian Rance, Karl Rohr, Roland Ropers, John Saccidanand, Jyoti Sahi, Sr Valsa Sannidhanam, Penny Savory, Ronald and Hilary Seex, A. Senthillkumar, Dr Rupert Sheldrake, Jean Shuttleworth, Daniel Skinner, Fr Tony Slingo, Br Wayne Teasdale, Joan Terry, Christopher and Sue Venning, Judy Walter, Fr Magnus Wilson OSB.

Finally, many thanks to Judith Kendra, the most meticulous and supportive of editors, and others who read the manuscript and gave valuable comments: Fr Cuthbert Brogan OSB, Sister Pascaline Coff OSB, Bridget Fann, Fr Laurence Freeman OSB, Andrew Harvey and Judy Walter. Responsibility for any errors remaining is entirely mine.

Prologue

O ne summer evening in 1924, a seventeen-year-old boy was walking
   alone near the school playing fields. He had walked this way many
   times before; he had seen other beautiful evenings; he had often
heard the birds singing with that full-throated ease which precedes the
dying of the day. But this was different:

> I remember now the shock of surprise with which the sound broke on my
> ears. It seemed to me that I had never heard the birds singing before and I
> wondered whether they sang like this all the year round and I had never
> noticed it. As I walked on I came upon some hawthorn trees in full bloom
> and again I thought that I had never seen such a sight or experienced such
> sweetness before. If I had been brought suddenly among the trees of the
> Garden of Paradise and heard a choir of angels singing I could not have
> been more surprised. I came then to where the sun was setting over the play-
> ing fields. A lark rose suddenly from the ground beside the tree where I was
> standing and poured out its song above my head, and then sank still singing
> to rest. Everything then grew still as the sunset faded and the veil of dusk
> began to cover the earth. I remember now the feeling of awe which came
> over me. I felt inclined to kneel on the ground, as though I had been stand-
> ing in the presence of an angel; and I hardly dared to look on the face of the
> sky, because it seemed as though it was but a veil before the face of God.[1]

This experience was to be the catalyst that inspired the lifetime's search of
Alan Griffiths, later to become Dom Bede Griffiths. He came to regard it as
one of the decisive events of his life. Until that moment he had been a normal schoolboy, content with the world as he found it, but that evening a veil
was lifted. Not only were his senses awakened as he felt he was seeing,

1

hearing and smelling for the first time, but he experienced an overwhelming emotion, a glimpse of the unfathomable mystery that lies behind creation. He began to rise before dawn to hear the birds singing, to stay up late to watch the stars, to spend his free time walking in the country. This sense of awe in the presence of nature began to take the place of the religion in which he had been brought up and which came to seem empty and meaningless in comparison; from that day he longed for these sacramental moments, always seeking a reality beyond the mind. Consciously or unconsciously, everything in his life was directed to that end.

It was a life that transformed him from an idealistic, highly intelligent, serious and sometimes irritable schoolboy into a man of profound wisdom, from whom emanated unconditional love and who came to be widely regarded as a holy man, even as a saint. He was to become a beacon of light for thousands of people from all over the world, many of them longing for a truth they could not find in their own churches. His own search eventually enabled him to express, with the simplicity and directness which can come only from experience, the underlying unity of religions. At the end of his life he attained a spiritual wholeness granted to few, but his journey was to be long, eventful and often filled with controversy, pain and anguish. His inner life and development have the excitement of space exploration and the passion of a great romance.

CHAPTER ONE

An Edwardian Childhood

1906–24

Т he family into which Alan Richard Griffiths was born was very English, very middle-class, very Anglican. The youngest of four children, he was born on 17 December 1906, five years into the Edwardian era, a time heady with the freedom which H. G. Wells felt came from the fact that Queen Victoria was no longer 'sitting on England like a great paperweight'. These years before the cataclysm of the Great War were a period of complacent prosperity, a time when the class system reigned unchallenged, when confidence in the British Empire was a source of national pride and when an instinctive love of the countryside was ingrained in every heart.

Alan's grandparents on both sides came originally from farming stock, but the industrial expansion of the nineteenth century drew them into business and one of his earliest memories was of a portrait of his mother's father, resplendent in court dress – he was an alderman of the City of London – that dominated the family dining room. Alan's father, Walter Griffiths, 'a handsome man with a fair moustache and clear blue eyes',[1] was a manufacturing chemist from Liverpool, taken as a young man into his uncle's paint business and made a partner. On the death of his uncle, Walter took another partner, but before long found himself ousted from the business. The story that has come down to his family is that Walter's partner asked him to sign a piece of paper, cunningly choosing to do this on a busy railway station, presumably when one of them was about to catch a train. Walter, a gentle, kindly man, with what Alan called 'the heart of a child', did not read the form properly, signed obediently and found he had signed away his job and lost all his money. Alan, only four at the time, did not remember the incident, but its repercussions overshadowed his entire childhood, for his father never recovered from the blow. Walter developed neurasthenia, a kind of nervous debility, and, though an intelligent and able man, never worked again but lived entirely in the past, completely losing touch with his family. He loved them, but he could not relate to them nor they to him. Years later, in his sixties, Alan wrote to a friend: 'My father, as you know, was a very frustrated man. Like you, I never had a real father and this affects one's whole life.'[2] Alan recalled how his father spent his time in endless arguments on religion, politics and society, and made life difficult for his wife by 'refusing to co-operate'. Yet though Walter was weak, he was generous to a fault, never saying or thinking ill of anyone – a characteristic inherited by his youngest son. He did summon up enough indignation to bring a law suit against his former partner, but once that had failed he refused to say a word against the man who had ruined him; indeed, he regarded him as a friend until the end of his life.

Alan's mother, Harriet Lilian Frampton-Day (called Lilian by his friends, Lily by her husband), came from a large and devoted family of doctors and lawyers who were related to the eighteenth-century novelist Henry Fielding, from whom Lilian inherited a pronounced 'Hapsburg' nose. She was as strong as her husband was weak and in the face of such ill fortune was determined to hold the family together, so the six of them, Dudley, Laurence, Barbara and Alan, aged at the time between eight and four, moved from Walton-on-Thames to New Milton, a village in Hampshire close to both the New Forest and the sea. Lilian, supported only by her own tiny private income, toiled ceaselessly. She was a model of unselfish love, caring for her family to the total exclusion of her own needs – sometimes she hardly left herself enough to eat – and doing all the household work herself. This was not something for which her privileged background could have prepared her, as before the First World War it was assumed that such people, even those living in what was known as 'genteel poverty', had at least one servant. The hard work must have taken its toll, for Alan's earliest memories of her were her strong face and deep-set brown eyes surrounded by grey hair, but she ran the household so smoothly that the children were not conscious of any deprivation; indeed, Alan remembered a 'wild, open-air life, which was for me of almost unclouded happiness in spite of our poverty'.[3] The children helped with everything, which was also unusual in those days for a middle-class family, and Alan not only took a pride in making his own bed, cleaning his shoes, helping prepare the meals and clean the house, but was later to be grateful that he had become used to manual work and poverty so early in life.

It is hard, from this end of the twentieth century, to imagine the safety and peacefulness of life in the English countryside before the First World War – 'Our world was like a little paradise, really', Alan recalled wistfully.[4] The Griffiths' life was stable and uneventful; indeed, when, in his eighties, Alan (then Father Bede) talked about his childhood to Kathryn Spink, his first biographer, he continually interrupted himself to say thoughtfully, almost in awe, that the ordinariness of those far-off days was 'extraordinary . . . extraordinary'. In fact, if there had been any problems the children would not have known about them, as the family was quite unable to discuss emotions, still less show them; black sheep and family skeletons were kept firmly out of sight. Though Alan had the normal childhood illnesses – measles, chicken pox, whooping cough and mumps – it seemed that no one was ever in serious trouble or even went to hospital; such things as the mental illness of one of his mother's closest friends or a cousin's divorce were not discovered by the children until years later. Sex was never mentioned; indeed, once their family was complete it simply didn't happen, for his mother later admitted to Alan that after his birth she lost any interest in sex she might once have had and banished her husband from the bedroom. This reserve was not unusual in those days. Young people were brought up never to discuss sex, religion or any matters that might lead to controversy and it was not long since the Victorian bourgeoisie were covering the legs of the piano ('legs' carrying a sexual innuendo that was thought to be offensive). In fact, Walter's constant talk of politics would have been quite unusual and it is not surprising that he received little response from his family.

Though religion was never discussed, it permeated their lives. Their regular Sunday visits to the village church, with the children dressed in sailor suits and hats, gave Alan a love and respect for the Church of England which never left him and he had vivid memories of the Rector, 'a tall, thin man with a pointed beard and no roof to his mouth, which made his utterance laboured but very distinct'.[5] Alan remembered him as a good man, a student of Shakespeare and a lover of poetry, who could have stood for a portrait of Chaucer's parson whose looks, readers of *The Canterbury Tales* may recall, gave the impression that 'he could knit mighty matters out of books'. The Rector also earned the gratitude of his congregation by preaching short sermons, though the Low Church services, with their emphasis on the spoken word, did not appeal to Alan as much as the more aesthetically pleasing High Church services he encountered in the parish church at Yaverland when, in 1920, the family moved to a flat in a house owned by an uncle in

Sandown on the Isle of Wight. He was not sure, though, whether the attraction he felt was religious so much as his delight in the beauty of the words and the singing.

Curiously, despite both his parents being devout Christians, the children seem to have received little religious instruction, though when Alan was about eight he was given two books to read, *Quiet Talks about Jesus* and *Line upon Line*. The piety of his mother, though, made a deep impression on him. Often when he went to say goodnight to her she would be kneeling by her bed in prayer and he was clearly very touched when, not long before her death, she told him how one day when the children were young, almost at the end of her tether with exhaustion, she caught sight of herself in the mirror surrounded by a light which did not seem to come from any natural source, a phenomenon that her son was convinced was a sign of God's blessing on her hard and unselfish life. The hymns of the Victorian evangelists Moody and Sankey would ring constantly round the house, for Walter, who had a pleasant tenor voice, never tired of singing them; in old age Alan recalled him singing 'Pull for the shore, sailor, pull for the shore'. The only remotely formal religious instruction Alan received was from mother's old friend Mimi, who was like a godmother to the children, and who made him learn the Beatitudes and the tenth and fourteenth chapters of St John's Gospel by heart when he was only six years old. They could not have meant much to him at the time, but they remained engraved on his memory and something must have percolated through to him, if only by osmosis, for by the age of eight he was sitting up in bed on Sunday nights, conducting the evening service, chanting the responses and saying the prayers to himself.

So Alan's early years were spent in an atmosphere of genteel poverty and well-bred restraint as Lilian fought gallantly to preserve the respectability of her family and Walter provided a kindly if ineffectual background. Alan was devoted to his mother and wrote to her every week of her life when they were apart. Their relationship does seem to have had a very special quality; only a few months before he died he said that, though he was not conscious of it at the time, he looked back on it as 'a relationship of total one-ness'[6] and appreciated his good fortune in the background his mother provided: 'We see many people whose lives are so full of tragedy because they don't have the mother's love. I realize more and more what a grace it was for me. I keep looking back on that and feel that the mother – and it's not only my mother, but "the Mother" – is behind me all the time.'[7]

Unfortunately, the relationship between his parents was at best cool, though the children seemed to have got on well together, accepting the differences that they knew very well existed between them. One of the most attractive images is of the four of them bicycling wildly round the garden, out of the front gate, round the house and in at the back. Another is of Barbara, the only girl and at home when her brothers went to boarding school, impatiently longing for their return as each term came to an end. Sometimes they went to tennis parties and dances, but somehow sex never came into it – or at least sexual feelings were never admitted – and girls were really 'just good friends'.

Dudley, four years older than Alan (whom he affectionately called 'Cupid'), became rather remote as he grew older and was distanced from the family, especially after he joined the Merchant Navy and became a wireless operator. He must have felt some responsibility towards his younger brother, for when Alan was sixteen it was he who supplied the information that their parents were too embarrassed to impart, giving him a small book called *What a Young Man Ought to Know*. Laurence, who considered taking Holy Orders before becoming headmaster of Salisbury Choir School, was the one with whom Alan had most in common and they were very close, from quite an early age discussing subjects like astronomy together. Alan had a deep admiration for his sister Barbara, a good and kind woman who had inherited something of her mother's nature and cared lovingly for anyone in need. According to her nephews, who were devoted to her, she 'had not a brain in her head and was very judgmental'. She was also said to be 'weird about sex', though just what that means remains unclear. Certainly she was unfortunate in that respect, for her marriage to a Church of England clergyman was annulled on the grounds of his homosexuality. There was another mysterious member of the family, Alan's imaginary friend 'Harold', who was a convenient scapegoat for any minor misdemeanours to which he did not want to admit. Recollecting Harold in his old age, Alan felt that though he was an ordinary little boy, he must have been a little odd to have invented Harold. It seems likely that the existence of this invisible figure suggests an inner loneliness, a need for a deeper relationship than he had with his siblings, though this was never something to which he admitted.

Alan was his mother's Benjamin, her youngest and most favoured; he was also the brightest intellectually. It says a lot for the harmony between the siblings that they seem to have felt no resentment in the face of this maternal favouritism; one gets the impression that they simply acknowledged, without jealousy or resentment, that he was not only the most intelligent of the four, but the best loved. Laurence's children (Laurence was the only one to produce grandchildren for his parents) felt that part of Lilian's fight for her family took the form of encouraging her talented favourite, even of

7

putting considerable pressure on him, and Alan's own account of his early years supports this. He remembered starting French when he was only four years old, taught by a local man from a nearby kindergarten who also sold ice-cream (no doubt an added incentive); at seven, despite their poverty, he was given a special teacher in Latin and two years later he started Greek.

Like many small boys he dreamed of his future. He had seen a steam-roller outside the family home and watched the man straddling the huge machine, from his small height apparently dominating the world. That was his first ambition: he would be the driver of a steamroller. Then a friend who was a midshipman and had become something of a family role-model gave him the idea of joining the Navy. Alan's intention was to become admiral of the fleet. Later he decided to join the Indian civil service and end his days as Viceroy of India. These ambitions of his childhood, this desire always to be at the top, shed a new light on a man whom humility was to become so marked a characteristic.

In 1915, when he was nine and the First World War had been raging for a year, he followed his elder brothers to a relatively new school called Furzie Close, a preparatory school at Barton-on-Sea, just over a mile from their home in New Milton. It was a small private school of no particular academic repute – boys there were not expected, for instance, to get scholarships to public schools – so there was tremendous rejoicing when one was accepted by Osborne, the naval training college. Coming from so poor a home Alan was allowed to be a day boy, the only one at the time. The unwanted distinction to some extent marked him out, but he enjoyed the life and received a good education, though he felt the couple who ran it presided over a sort of tyranny. 'I don't know which was worse,' he said, 'the man or his wife.'[8] Alan's contemporaries there included Henry Whitehead, later famous as a professor of geometry, the Trevelyan brothers, one to become the film censor and the other ambassador to Moscow, and Frank Pakenham, now Lord Longford. The school no longer exists and it is Lord Longford, with whom Alan had forged a lasting friendship, who recounted the only known incident of their time there. It concerns, amazingly considering the irenic men both schoolboys were to become, a boxing match between the two:

> After the third round I lay back happily on my stool in front of a large audience of wounded soldiers. Pointing to my adversary, I said to my second, 'It looks all right, he's covered with blood.' The second, an old hand, knew better. 'Wait till they wipe it off,' he said. And sure enough it was my blood, not his. The referee stepped forward and held aloft the arm of my conqueror, Alan Griffiths.[9]

This reference to the wounded soldiers back from the battlefields is a reminder of how remote the Griffiths family were from the Great War. When he came to write his autobiography, Alan remarked on 'the ordered peace and security in our lives, which seems to have passed away from life generally after the Great War. Even the war did not seriously disturb the peace for us, as we were living far away in the country and neither I nor my brothers were of age for military service.'[10] In fact, it was on 10 October 1918, with the Allied advance well under way and just a month before the signing of the armistice, that Alan went up to London to compete for a place at Christ's Hospital, where Dudley and Laurence were already pupils.

Christ's Hospital was an inspired choice for the sons of a family down on its luck but resolute in its ambitions. The school was one of three charitable foundations started in the sixteenth century by Edward VI, who is said to have been inspired by a sermon on charity given by Bishop Ridley, the Protestant bishop and chaplain to Henry VIII. It was known as the 'religious, royal and ancient foundation of Christ's Hospital' and was intended primarily for the relief of the poor; to Alan's delight there were no class distinctions, just the simple directive that payment should be made according to income. It was severely Protestant, and several years were to pass before Alan discovered that two famous Catholic converts, Edmund Campion, the Jesuit martyr, and Augustine Baker, the author and English Benedictine monk, were boys there during the sixteenth century.

Christ's Hospital owes its popular name, the 'Blue-Coat school', to the traditional Tudor dress: a long blue coat with silver-buckled leather girdle, knee breeches, yellow petticoat and stockings, neckbands and a blue cap. The petticoat and cap were given up in the middle of the nineteenth century, but in Alan's time the boys wore (as they still do) the coat, with its belt and silver buckle, the coarse yellow woollen stockings and, in the opinion of the boys, extremely uncomfortable black shoes. The belt has a special significance, as the younger boys wear a narrow girdle with a simple button, and only the more senior boys are allowed both a wider belt and the coveted silver button entitling the wearers to be known as 'broadies'. Anyone not fortunate enough to acquire such a belt from an old boy had to save up and buy his own.

Though the school was run as a charity, once it had been shown that the parents were sufficiently poor for the application to be accepted, the boys still had to sit a competitive entrance examination and the standards were high. The school archives reveal the finances of the Griffiths family in their stark simplicity. Walter's incapacity to work had to be admitted and Lilian's average yearly income over the last three years was entered at £150. They also record that Alan took the optional subjects of Latin, French and Mathematics as well as the compulsory papers in English, Arithmetic, History and Geography, but what they do not tell is that out of over a hundred applicants Alan passed first. How pleased Lilian must have been at her Benjamin's success. Years later Alan remembered how mother and son were on the train on their way to his first day at boarding school. Opposite them sat another woman with her son, who told them that her son had passed second into Christ's Hospital. Slightly self-conscious but unable to conceal her pride, a delighted Lilian said, 'My boy passed first.'[11]

Alan started at Christ's Hospital on 15 January 1919, his first two terms coinciding with the last year of Dr Arthur Upcott, a learned and respected man with a flowing white beard who regularly wore the red gown of a Doctor of Divinity. He was renowned for being a strict disciplinarian, believing that poor boys needed to be especially tightly controlled, and has been described as the last of the great Victorian headmasters. (It used to be joked that on Sunday he would preach about Jesus suffering the little children to come to him and on Monday the children went to see the headmaster and suffered.) The public school code of the time prohibited any demonstration of affection and the emotional atmosphere was as repressed as the life Alan had become accustomed to at home. He was outraged at having to call his mother 'The Mater' and surprised that families visiting their children were not welcome on the school premises, but had to take their children out to tea.

A vivid picture of life at Christ's Hospital under Dr Upcott's headmastership comes from Nigel Bruce, a contemporary of Alan's, though the two did not become friends until they met again when they were in their forties. The masters, Nigel says, were mainly 'superannuated types who had been winkled out of retirement when the young ones were serving in the war'[12] and they had an Edwardian sense of discipline. As the Great War had only just ended, rationing was still in force and the regime was harsh, even by the standards of public schools of the time. The boys slept on 'thin, thin mattresses' with 'bolios' (the current 'housey' slang for pillows) and they were permanently so cold that they all got chilblains. Two ex-Boer War sergeants carried out at least one public flogging every term, which took place in front of the whole school (then at least 800 boys), no one but the boy in question knowing the nature of the offence. There was also regular birching, which was distinguished from flogging by being done in private and by the use of twigs bound together rather than the cane. Nigel Bruce experienced this. He was cutting himself the regulation half-inch slice of bread, which used to be marked out on a long board with nails, when a crumb fell off; Nigel rolled it into a ball and flicked it across the room. For this he was reported to his house master, sternly reminded of the starving Russians and birched until he had deep score marks from neck to knees. Even the school matron, presumably accustomed to such sights, was shocked. Another boy was caught prancing around in his nightgown one evening, reported for indecent exposure and given a birching. The maths master must have been particularly strict, for the boys were beaten if they so much as made a mistake in his class.

Alan never complained of this harsh regime, though he did find the cruelty extraordinary. One of his first masters was asthmatic and Alan remembered how if any boy gave a wrong answer he would 'leap up and down and hit people over the head. If you made a bad mistake you lost ten marks. You lived in fear the whole time. The whole year I lived in perpetual fear.'[13] Another teacher was even worse: 'He was more systematic, he would make you stand outside – sometimes there were two or three people standing outside – then he would beat you. The fear was always there.' His characteristic determination to see the best in people led him to add: 'They were good men and they taught us well. They did it for our good. But you know I think I still suffer from that psychological fear.'[14]

Alan was luckier than his older brothers and did not have to endure Dr Upcott's reign for long. In September 1919, W. H. Fyfe (later to be given a doctorate and a knighthood) became headmaster and the whole spirit of the school changed. For Alan, 'It was a renaissance, a burst of new learning.'[15] Fyfe was the first headmaster who was not also a clergyman and he was a Christian humanist, a classical scholar, modern in his ideas and possessed of what Alan called 'a ubiquitous sense of humour'.[16] His influence on the boys was immense, particularly on Alan with whom he struck up a friendship that lasted until Fyfe's death in 1965. Thus Alan benefited from a liberal headmaster with 'a near genius for picking out the boy of character and giving him all he'd got'.[17]

Under Fyfe the religious life of the school continued as before, the boys going to the school chapel every weekday and twice on Sundays; Alan remembered sitting long hours in the chapel under a painting of St Stephen being martyred in a glowing orange robe. He learnt the catechism by heart for his confirmation, though he recalled that neither he nor the master who was listening to his recitation took much interest in it. Religion was just part of the routine of school life, holding little emotional charge for him, though he enjoyed the singing and admitted in later life that the daily readings from the Bible affected him more than he realised at the time. The only religious teachings that impressed him were Fyfe's sermons, delivered unconventionally from the lectern in the middle of the chapel rather than from the pulpit, and holding the boys spellbound. Fyfe did not believe in dogma and once, when challenged on the Virgin Birth, he simply replied, 'Does it really matter?' Such were the unconventional ways in which he introduced the boys to an ideal of the humanity of Christ that was to remain with Alan all his life.

Nigel Bruce remembers Alan as a solitary person, mature for his age, beautiful to look at, very tall, very charming. 'He was well above us all. You would immediately mark him out as being an exceptional person.'[18] Even if this description owes something to the exaggerated memory of an admiring contemporary, it is clear that Alan was unusually talented. He himself said: 'I probably reached the pinnacle of my intellectual ratings when I was about twelve. After that I began to decline'[19] Slightly older than most of the boys when he entered, he skipped the lower forms and went straight into the middle or 'broady' form and in his second year joined the sixth form, becoming what was known as a 'Grecian', in which role he was lent to various houses as a kind of assistant master, supervising prep in the evenings. In his final year he became captain of his house. His gift for leadership was already becoming apparent and he was regarded as both an intellectual and as disarmingly modest, though paradoxically his tendency to make friends only among other intellectually-minded boys led many to consider him something of a snob. In fact, he admitted to being accused of 'going about the school as though he owned the place'. One friend for whom he had a great admiration liked to quote one of the less attractive lines from Horace, 'I hate the profane crowd', and for a short time this boy became a model for Alan, who would strive to keep up with him.

Alan was, at least at first, an all-rounder. Though certainly more of an academic than a sportsman, he hardly deserved being brushed aside by his housemaster as 'one of those useless Grecians', for he was tolerably good at games, playing in the school rugby team and, though not a keen cricketer himself, following the test match scores. As Frank Pakenham could confirm, his long reach made him a good boxer. He discovered the visual arts through a book in the school library called *Six Centuries of Painting* and he was musical, singing in the school choirs as, in turn, treble, alto and tenor. He also played the violin and was an accomplished pianist, practising every day for ten years or more and learning a whole repertoire – Chopin, Schubert, Brahms, Bach's Preludes and Fugues – by heart. At school concerts he played violin solos, sang sea shanties and was understandably proud on one occasion when a member of the audience said his rendering of Debussy's *Clair de Lune* made it worth coming to the concert for this alone.

However, the significance of Christ's Hospital in Alan's life did not lie in its discipline, in sport, in music, religion or even in friendship, which was not at this stage in his life as important as it later became. It lay instead in the influence of W. H. Fyfe, someone to whom Alan was for ever indebted. It was Fyfe, he claimed, who taught him to think for himself and encouraged his interest in literature and art; Fyfe who excused him from games, a reprieve for which he was deeply grateful as he could spend the games periods cycling round the countryside; Fyfe who kindled his latent interest in politics by introducing him to Plato's *Republic*, where he began to see socialism as the modern expression of Plato's ideal. It was Fyfe too who encouraged Alan to read and whose first act as headmaster was to enlarge the school library, so the boys had access to a wide range of books including Alan's ancestor Henry Fielding, Jane Austen, Meredith, Conrad, Shakespeare and Milton. Reading became Alan's absorbing interest, so much so that his real life was in those stories far more than in the external world. At any time, when the school schedule did not require him to do anything else, he would be deep in a book, oblivious of the noise around him. He discovered that at night he could with impunity leave the bathroom light on and indulge in late-night watery reading, devouring *Paradise Lost* with the book propped up against a board across the bath.

Of all that he read at that time, Alan was most impressed by the novels of Thomas Hardy. Through them he discovered the beauty of the English countryside, 'the deep rhythm of peasant life in contact with the rhythm of nature',[20] for though he had always lived in the country he had never felt that he belonged to it. So moved was he by Hardy's descriptions that one holiday he made a walking tour of Wessex to trace the places mentioned in the novels. Even more significantly, he discovered through Hardy 'that tragedy alone can reveal the deepest human values'[21] and this realisation touched on something that was to be of crucial importance to him. So far in his short life he had known nothing of tragedy, indeed he had had no experience of any emotional depth; he was caught in a painful dilemma, on the one hand longing for direct, first-hand experience, on the other realising that in fact he was living largely through the intellect. For many years, indeed for much of his life, thinking, reading and expressing himself through reason were his emotional outlets, not life itself. So his reading not only led him to intellectual concepts (for instance, the Greek tragedians convinced him that life had never been lived so completely as in fifth-century Athens) but it was through reading Hardy's great novel *Tess of the D'Urbervilles* that he acquired the concept of God as 'a grim, impersonal power, to whom human life is a kind of sport';[22] he rejoiced in the sounds and rhythms of Swinburne's poetry and in the shock to the conventional morality of the time in his *Poems and Ballads*; the poetry of Wordsworth and Shelley resonated with his own deepest feelings and further fired his love of nature.

By 1924, Alan's last year at school and the year of the first Labour government, he was becoming politically aware, though again it was an awareness that owed more to reading than to any direct knowledge of the lives people led or of the injustices that were going on around him. Tolstoy's interpretation of the Sermon on the Mount in *Kingdom of Heaven* led him to see the Beatitudes as the ideal of conduct and to find the ideal of non-resistance to evil so attractive that he, together with three other friends, became pacifists. They were all supposed to join the Officers' Training Corps and heard that they were to be made lance-corporals. This they refused to do, tackling the subject with the uninhibited directness of bright, rebellious youth. They told the head of the Corps that they didn't approve of it and would not take rank. When he told them they should listen to him, as he was old enough to be their father, they replied: 'Tolstoy's old enough to be your father, you should listen to Tolstoy.' They won their point.[23] Indeed, with Fyfe's tactful intervention they were eventually released from the Corps altogether.

Time that might have been spent playing at soldiers was spent reading. The plays of Bernard Shaw, Ibsen and Galsworthy became a yardstick against which to judge the social order of the time; Shelley's political ideal-ism and his conception of the regeneration of mankind was almost a substi-tute for the faith of the Gospels. Perhaps, he admitted, it was just the rebelliousness of youth, but many of his contemporaries shared his views and when he wrote of this period he often referred to himself as one of a group of like-minded people: 'We were ardent socialists and pacifists. Ramsay Macdonald was our hero, and we were firmly convinced that nothing but militarism and imperialism stood between the world and uni-versal peace. These views were not popular in the school, and we had some difficulty in persuading the authorities of our sincerity.'[24]

So what did all this reading and thinking do to his feelings about Christianity? The teaching of his mother's friend Mimi and the regular services in the school chapel had given him the basic Christian under-pinning that was part of any child's education. More specifically, one term when he was confined to the infirmary with a poisoned knee, he read

Giovanni Papini's *Story of Christ* and this, together with Fyfe's sermons, filled him with a love of Christ which never left him. But it was a love felt at the level of Christ's humanity, the love of a perfect human being (rather as he revered Socrates) coupled with an appreciation of the moral teaching of the Gospel. His own assessment was that his view of life was essentially pagan rather than Christian. His religion was the love of nature, his imagination responding to the worship of the Spirit as expressed by one of his favourite passages in his beloved Wordsworth:

> And I have felt
> A presence that disturbs me with the joy
> Of elevated thoughts; a sense sublime
> Of something far more deeply interfused,
> Whose dwelling is the light of setting suns,
> And the round ocean and the living air,
> And the blue sky, and in the mind of man:[25]

While he was still at Christ's Hospital the family had moved again, this time to the village of Burghclere, near Newbury, and Alan used to spend the holidays walking in the woods and climbing the hills around. He learned the names of the birds and wild flowers and would spend whole days sitting by a stream and watching the wild life around him.

> I was seeking for something all the time, though I could hardly have said what it was. I liked the solitude and the silence of the woods and hills. I felt there the sense of a Presence, something undefined and mysterious, which was reflected in the faces of the flowers and the movements of birds and animals, in the sunlight falling through the leaves and in the sound of running water, in the wind blowing on the hills and the wide expanse of earth and sky.[26]

He sensed these feelings had 'something of a religious character'[27] but he had no interest in the formal religion of his upbringing; indeed, he had come to believe that Christianity was a thing of the past. He was influenced by Bernard Shaw's religious scepticism, and any residual faith he might have had was further shaken by reading Samual Butler's *The Way of All Flesh*, for he was swayed by its argument that the narratives of the Resurrection in the four Gospels could not be reconciled with each other. In fact, the difficulties he had in accepting Christianity were legion. Like many of his contemporaries he was prejudiced against any form of dogma, any belief in an authority beyond reason and any conception of an absolute moral law. He knew no one capable of answering his questions and curiously, given his inquiring mind and avid appetite for reading, he made no serious effort to study the problems this raised, simply accepting the sceptical attitude to Christianity taken by most of the books that came his way.

This, then, was the mind-set of the schoolboy, walking in the fields that summer's day and graced by an experience which, he felt, comes to most people at some time, but is too often allowed to fade into insignificance. The normal pattern of his thinking was disrupted and now he knew that there was another dimension to existence. He had experienced one of those moments in which people come face to face with reality: 'We see our life for a moment in its true perspective in relation to eternity. We are freed from the flux of time and see something of the eternal order which underlies it. We are no longer isolated individuals in conflict with our surroundings; we are part of a whole, elements in a universal harmony.'[28]

From that moment everything changed. Now his only pleasure lay in this mysterious communion with nature. It came to bear for him a kind of sacramental character. He felt he belonged to an immemorial past, in comparison with which modern civilisation was only a temporary aberration. He longed to be united with this spirit, though he did not know what he was seeking or what he would have to suffer in the search. Now he was convinced that 'the rediscovery of religion is the great intellectual, moral and spiritual adventure of our time'.[29] His search for God had begun.

CHAPTER TWO

Athletes and Aesthetes

OXFORD 1925–29

When Alan decided to go to Oxford his first choice was New College as it was considered to have the highest standard for Classics, the subject he had decided to read. After the brilliance of his schooldays it must have come as a shock to learn that he had not been accepted, and after hearing the news he wandered dejectedly down Oxford's High Street. As he approached the river he saw Magdalen College and immediately decided that this was the place for him. He was so impressed by the beauty of the tower and the cloisters, the Deer Park and the Meadows surrounded by Addison's Walk, that he went in; impressed further by the chapel and the singing of the choir, he applied and this time not only was accepted but was given an Exhibition of £50 a year. He went up in October 1925.

At first Magdalen seemed a curious choice for so intellectual and withdrawn a young man, for in those days its standing was not high and it was said to attract the dregs of Eton and Charterhouse, the frivolous and those who did not intend to take their studies too seriously. One of Alan's like-minded contemporaries was shocked at the company he found he was keeping: 'There was a band of those who set the tone, noisy, self-assured, sophisticated. They had no doubts or qualms; and did not, as I did, address dons as "Sir" . . . I hardly remember a single night of my first two years when yelling and singing and the sound of hunting horns or the breaking of glass would not have been heard somewhere.'[1] This noisy crowd was comparatively rich, they lived in luxury and did little work, shouting in the cloisters and preferring hunting, boating, drinking and playing polo or rugby to studying. There were numerous groups, cliques and coteries and the whole atmosphere gave substance to Chesterton's contemptuous description of

17

Oxford as 'the playground of the idle rich', though, unlike in most such groups, women hardly featured in their lives. Alan commented ruefully that the only woman they saw regularly was the matron and that segregation was almost complete, with Magdalen a monastery within the greater monastery of the university itself. On rare occasions when the men met girls from the women's colleges they found them dull and referred to them as 'les végétales', mocking the dutiful way they took notes with coloured fountain pens. If they invited a girl to the standard college tea of anchovy toast and honey buns she had to bring a chaperone, who would decide when it was time to go, indicating that the moment had arrived by firmly putting on her gloves.

There was another side to life at Magdalen, though, for at the time the undergraduates fell into two categories – the 'athletes' and the 'aesthetes'. The aesthetes, in contrast to the athletes, tended to favour a simple life, to work hard and to spend their time in more high-minded ways. Among these men Alan, earnest, industrious and poor, felt at home. He had his Exhibition, which Magdalen later increased to £150, and this was just enough to cover his college expenses. For clothes and pocket money he had to depend on his mother, and though the family was a little better off there was still very little to spare and he had to live as cheaply as possible. He was naturally ascetic and this never troubled him – though he admitted to looking wistfully sometimes at a green or purple shirt in a shop window – but the austerity of his life began to affect his health. His friend Geoffrey Hayward remembers him as rather sombre and repressed: 'In early days, despite his height and good looks, he looked "peaky" and blue-veined. I don't know why, for the food in Magdalen was very good. As an Exhibitioner he had very slender means, and looked it; he could not splash out in the fashionable dress of the day: he was and looked a "scholar". He was used to hard, concentrated work.'[2]

The first term at any new institution can be frightening and lonely, but Alan never admitted to loneliness or uncertainty and the impression that comes across from those who knew him at the time is that his inwardness and need for solitude protected him. He simply didn't seem to notice or mind things that disturbed some of the other freshmen. He was perceived as 'Someone who was not immersed in typical Oxford life. He was quite a distinctive character, an exceptional man. There wasn't anyone else quite like him.'[3] So he was not worried by the initiatory ordeals, for instance, when groups of college men, hunting in packs, tried to persuade freshmen to join their clubs and associations. Alan was visited by members of the Officers' Training Corps and impressed one of his contemporaries by his 'imperturbable self-possession'. He 'not merely refused to join, but gave as his reason that he had just joined the Pacifists Association. And having said, no doubt went on reading Walter Pater, oblivious of hostile looks.'[4]*

While at Christ's Hospital Alan had not made any deep or significant friendships, though it is hard to know whether this was due to his own reserve or some lack of compatibility with the other boys. Oxford, however, saw the flowering of his capacity for friendship and he met many men with whom he maintained long and close ties. Among his contemporaries were the poet John Betjeman, Oliver van Oss (who became headmaster of Charterhouse), Owen Barfield, the author of the renowned *Poetic Diction* (1928), Geoffrey Hayward and the critic Hugh L'Anson Fausset. Later, C. S. Lewis became a life-long friend. But there were two men at Magdalen, Martyn Skinner and Hugh Waterman, with whom he began to share his life. They went on walks and holidays together, shared ideas and, in the timeless way of students the world over, talked far into the night. Their friendship was to be a constant thread running through Alan's life and they kept in touch for over sixty years, corresponding regularly until the end of their lives; well into his seventies Alan wrote to Hugh that he believed they had become closer in friendship than ever before.

So what were they like, these men who became so close to Alan? Hugh's mother set great store on her son being a gentleman, 'courteous, reliable, sympathetic, and, above all, unselfish'. It seems that he fulfilled her hopes, for he had a gentleness of character that was reflected in his appearance: he was a fresh-faced young man with an innocent, good-tempered expression and a wholesome ruddy complexion. He was destined to follow the family tradition and become a lawyer, so he was entered at the Middle Temple and travelled up to London every few weeks to eat his dinners in hall, as a proof of law terms kept. On each trip he went to the National Gallery and sat in front of his favourite pictures – Leonardo da Vinci's *Madonna of the Rocks* and Antonio da Messina's *Crucifixion*. He could not understand why his parents wanted him to be a lawyer when he was 'too tongue-tied to say boo to a duck, let alone the proverbial goose'.[5] Alan was enchanted by him. Not only did they share a love for nature and for poetry, but Hugh was generous and affectionate, with a strong feminine side that was a welcome relief among the over-masculine surroundings in which Alan lived. 'He was altogether free from that habit of repressing all expression of affection from which I had suffered at school . . . He brought a kind of grace into my life which I had never experienced before.

*Walter Pater was one of the leading influences on the English 'aesthetic' movement of the 1880s.

There was something in him of the spirit of St Francis of Assisi.'[6] Alan called Hugh 'a typical English pragmatist',[7] and considered that it was he who 'first taught us [himself and Martyn] to be human'.[8]

For his part, Hugh valued the 'elder brotherly concern' he received from Alan and found his eager idealism compulsive. Two memories from Oxford capture something of the companionship they shared. One night they were sitting over the fire talking about Milton, when Alan began to read *Paradise Lost* aloud, not stopping until he had finished the entire poem – at three o'clock in the morning. Then there was the occasion when they visited Alan's home near Newbury, and walked down the Ox Drove at Burghclere and on through the woods, trying to identify the birds by sound rather than just by sight. They were on their way to visit Stanley Spencer, who was painting his Resurrection on the east wall of Sandham Chapel and who delighted them by talking of the simplicity and the sacredness of ordinary life, the appreciation of which was becoming one of the shared attitudes that bound them so closely together.

Like Hugh, Martyn Skinner came from a privileged background. He was a little shorter than Alan, an elegant, striking-looking, bespectacled man with piercing blue eyes and aquiline features. In later life his portrait was painted by Eric Kennington, who said that Martyn's was the most sensitive face he had ever painted. Martyn's father, Sir Sydney Skinner, was chairman of Barkers, one of London's first big department stores, but he had no illusions about himself or about what he was doing. As he and Martyn watched the huge building go up he remarked, 'Much of what people will buy in there they don't really need, and some they would be better without.' Martyn could not bring himself to follow his father into business and became a poet, admitting ruefully that while the love of nature, poetry and art were in his blood, he came from a home where 'there was no appreciation of any of those things, except the occasional admiration of a sunset'.[9] Before coming up to Oxford he remembered the family making a 5000-mile tour of Europe with no 'aesthetic knowledge or sensibility', yet it was then, in a negative way, that he first became aware of beauty, first realised how much he abhorred modern civilisation. This moment of truth struck him when he saw an enormous hoarding, the size of a small house, at the top of a pass on the Dolomites, 'outraging an otherwise glorious panorama of mountain and valley. I can see it still, and feel the shudder of abhorrence.'[10] This symbol of man despoiling the earth was to remain with him all his life; often he would share the memory with Alan.

While Alan was an Exhibitioner, and Hugh a 'gentleman commoner', Martyn won a Demyship (the word used at Magdalen for Scholarship) and, from a literary point of view, was to become the most successful; he was praised by the literary figures of his time and his poems were honoured, *Letters to Malaya* winning the coveted Hawthornden Prize in 1943. Like Hugh he was painfully shy, but Hugh considered that while his own shyness took the form of talking too much, Martyn's made him appear aloof. Their mutual friend Geoffrey Hayward wrote that they were both 'strong out-standing characters', singling out Martyn's steadfastness and Hugh's charm, tolerance and extraordinary courtesy.[11]

Soon the three were doing everything together, sharing their idealism, their socialism, their love of literature and nature and their hatred of modern civilisation. They were seriously inclined, drinking cider rather than beer or whisky, never gambling and attending no wild parties. They spent days on the Cherwell 'reading Spenser and Milton among the drag-onflies'.[12] They went to the poorly-supported Playhouse Theatre, where they saw a mixed bag of plays by Shaw, Strindberg, J. M. Barrie, Ibsen, Galsworthy and Chekhov. They spent long evenings listening to Beethoven's last quartets. Every week they attended the Union debate, occa-sionally hearing distinguished visitors such as the flamboyant Lord Birkenhead. More in youthful idealism than with any real interest they joined the University Labour Club; given their idealism they could hardly do otherwise, for Oxford in the 1920s was reacting against conventional morality and both socialism and pacifism were growing strongly. Alan helped to found the Peace Union, which subsequently linked up with the No More War movement, but though he considered himself a socialist and was becoming increasingly aware of social inequity, his political action never went further than supporting the miners in the General Strike of 1926 and offering to sell copies of the *Daily Worker* in the streets.

Martyn recalled that though he could not remember Alan 'romping or gallivanting', he was not invariably serious and had some reputation as a storyteller. A surprising side of the young Alan is revealed in an anecdote he liked to tell about Tennyson. The poet was spied writing alone, then rising and leaving his manuscript behind, so his watchers, thinking to find the latest masterpiece by the great man, stole a look. What they found was:

> When I want to wipe my arse,
> I always use a tuft of grass.
> When grass is bare and tufts are none,
> I wipe my arse upon a stone.
> And when there's neither grass nor stone,
> I leave my bloody arse alone.[13]

21

Despite moments of undergraduate high spirits, Alan emerges as a slightly reproving figure who was considered rather high-minded and straitlaced by some of his fellow undergraduates. On one occasion they were punting with Geoff Hayward and 'a distinguished aesthete'. Geoff had had rather too much to drink and, irritated by the high-flown conversation that had been going on between Alan and their aesthetic friend, ranted and roared in pugnacious mood. Geoff was doing the punting, and the situation became hazardous as the boat hovered on the edge of a weir while the water rushed past. Martyn rocked with helpless laughter, while Alan, angry and admonishing, could only say, 'Don't be a fool, Geoff. Geoff, pull yourself together.'

Though he was not at ease with the rowdy party-going clique at Magdalen, once Alan had formed his own circle of friends he was very happy at Oxford. He loved the place, then 'a quiet sleepy Barchester of dons and colleges, populous only during term and invaded by the traffic only of bicycles'.[14] He was fortunate in his lodgings, spending his second year in Magdalen's coveted eighteenth-century 'New Buildings', his third in the Iffley Road and his fourth at Laurel Farm, a house with a huge garden in Old Headington, then a remote and almost unspoilt village. And, at least to start with, he was content to be reading Classics. He did well in Honour Moderations, the first examination he had to take after five terms, gaining five alphas, only two short of the seven required for a first-class degree, but instead of continuing his intended course in Classics and going on to Greats, he changed to English Literature. This change was greeted with some disapproval by the college, for Classics was considered the best degree anyone could take, while English had only recently been given degree status and was regarded with some condescension. Alan was adamant. He insisted on changing, partly as he did not want to study philosophy, which pursuing Greats would have entailed, but even more because he had begun to lose faith in the intellect and in reason and wanted more beauty and poetry in his life. It is perhaps surprising that he had not chosen English in the first place, for years later he reminded Martyn of his youthful ambitions: 'Do you realise that when I was at school and at Oxford the one passion of my life was for English prose? I could never write poetry, but the study of English prose and the desire to write in the great tradition was the strongest motive in my life.'[15]

He was quite clear-sighted about what he was doing, admitting that he was 'oblivious of every aspect of truth except that which appealed to me'.[16] And the truth he felt he had grasped was that abstract thought, when it loses touch with the realities of life, was dangerous. He had discovered the value of experience, finding in it a deeper insight into reality than abstract thought could offer. With Keats he believed in 'the holiness of the heart's affections and the truth of the imagination' and reading English Literature would, he hoped, bring him nearer to living out this ideal; the poetic imagination might be the means by which he could regain control with the reality he had glimpsed that summer evening at school.

So more than ever he spurned the athletes and joined the aesthetes. He visited the British Museum and the National Gallery; under Laurence Binyon's guidance he acquired some Japanese prints and two Whistler mezzotints for his rooms. He continued to read, as he had always read, and he longed, as he had longed since his last year at school, to become a writer. Along with many of his contemporaries his patron saints were Walter Pater, widely acknowledged at the time as a master of English prose, and Pater's famous disciple Oscar Wilde. (It was Pater, incidentally, who coined the phrase 'Art for Art's sake'.) He would spend days drifting down the river in a punt reading Spenser's *Faerie Queene* and Sir Philip Sidney's *Arcadia* – always he sought beauty, whether through reading or through nature. During his year in the 'New Buildings', the view from his window was a nature-lover's delight:

> Outside my window there was an almond tree, which came into pink blossom early in the spring before any other colour had appeared, and in the river walks I could watch the procession of spring flowers coming out day by day from the snowdrops and crocuses at the end of January, followed by the small blue scylla and periwinkle in February, until the primroses and violets and daffodils came with March. There were nuthatches and tree-creepers and birds of all kinds nesting in the trees, and once I saw a kingfisher rise from the water just beneath me and fly into the sun, showing the first blood-red of its breast and then the blue glint of its wings.[17]

The prize in this bran tub of aesthetic pleasures was that by changing from Classics to English Alan acquired C. S. Lewis as his tutor. Lewis, only eight years his senior, had gained a triple First at Oxford and had become a Fellow and Tutor at Magdalen the year Alan came up. From the start they got on marvellously well together, the tutorial relationship soon ripening into a friendship which was very close for five years and which continued until Lewis's death in 1963. Later their meetings became infrequent, but they were in constant touch by letter, though unfortunately only a fraction of their copious correspondence survives.

The first impression of Lewis, with his heavy build and florid face, his country gentleman appearance with tweed hat, pipe, walking stick and dog, the man of the world who was known to make bawdy jokes, could hardly have been further from the spare and already ascetic Alan, who found it hard to reconcile this image, which he felt Lewis liked to project, with the man of great intellectual power and immense learning. It was this side of the man that Alan soon learned to admire and love, but there were many others. He had the deepest respect for him as a moralist, as a master of literary criticism, and for the depth of his psychological insight. He was thrilled by the romantic imagination shown in some of Lewis's early work, feeling at home with a tutor who had passed through a phase very similar to that in which his new pupil was determinedly remaining.

At their first meeting Alan tried to justify the loss of faith in reason and the intellect that underlay his wish to change from Classics to English, though he admitted that his new tutor could not possibly convince him he was wrong, as he was not open to reason on the subject. A tutorial with Lewis 'was a battle of wits, and it was through opposition that one came to friendship with him' wrote Alan.[18] Lewis himself said that their friendship 'began in disagreement and matured in argument'.[19] So they argued with the utmost freedom, in the way only those who are basically in tune with each other can argue. Alan claimed not to understand why Lewis liked him, but the fact that he had met a worthy opponent must have had something to do with it. Lewis was to have a profound and lasting influence on many of his pupils, but he had not at that stage achieved the fame that was to be his and though Alan found him formidable and unshakable, like many intelligent undergraduates he was not going to be cowed into instant submission and pursued his crusades, for instance against Dryden and Pope and the Age of Reason, which stood for all he despised, with a tireless fervour. Indeed, Lewis hinted that Alan was one of the more intractable of his pupils, turning implied criticism into compliment by admitting to many people, including Alan himself, that he was 'one of the toughest dialecticians of my acquaintance'.[20]

Neither of them was a Christian at the time; indeed, Alan felt Christianity had ceased to have any significance for the present day. He was beginning to flesh out the instinctive reaction of his schooldays, suggesting that contact with reality must be sought through sensation rather than through thought; that wisdom was to be found not in philosophy or any form of religion, but in an experience which gave a direct insight into the meaning of life. Consciously or unconsciously, he was always seeking the state of ecstasy that he had first glimpsed on that summer evening during his last term at Christ's Hospital. He argued that a new religion was needed and that its prophets were Wordsworth, Shelley and Keats. His religion was the worship of nature and he could see no connection between the God manifested in nature and the God preached in church.

In his third year Alan gave a paper on these views to the Michaelmas Club, a small group of Magdalen men of which he was a founding member and Lewis the president. He claimed that imagination was the real essence of our human existence and that reason was a destructive, nihilistic power, working as Anti-Christ in our human pilgrimage; we must find a new corporate faith to help us back to greater simplicity, to innocence, where true life could be found. The college archives record that this theory found favour with virtually everyone present and that as soon as he had finished speaking a host of speakers tried to make themselves heard. 'Mr Griffiths was ecstatic in his views . . . No conclusion was reached, and when the meeting was adjourned at an advanced hour, everyone felt more convinced and clear in his own views than he had been at the beginning of the evening.'[21]

Alan never became a member of Lewis's famous 'Inklings' set, mostly because he was not yet a serious author as were the regular members such as J. R. R. Tolkien, Charles Williams and Lewis himself (Alan's first book was not published until 1954), but Owen Barfield, one of Lewis's oldest and closest friends, suggested a rather different reason. The Inklings meetings, he said, were accompanied by drinking and laughing, something he was sure Alan would not have liked. He felt that Alan did not have much sense of humour, and recalled an incident when he, Lewis and Alan went for a two-day walk, the tradition on these walks being that serious talk was discouraged and permitted only in the ten-mile stretch they usually did before lunch. As evening approached, the norm was fooling and schoolboy jokes. Alan 'offended protocol by engaging Barfield in a lengthy and profoundly serious theological battle. Equilibrium was badly upset, nor was it restored until the party had him [Alan] cracking jokes along with the rest of them.'[22] The final straw was a discussion on whether or not all sins were forgivable. One of them must have suggested that some that were not, for Barfield never forgot that to his response, 'In that case I must be damned', Alan replied: 'But of course you are.'[23]

Alan was, however, completely at ease walking with Hugh and Martyn and it was something they took every opportunity to do. All three men shared a painful awareness of the conflict between the ugliness of the modern industrial city and their ideal of a life in harmony with nature. It was not that they condemned either science or reason in themselves; rather, it was the divorce they perceived between on the one hand science and the rational mind, and on the other the world of instinct, feelings and imagination. For this they blamed the Industrial Revolution, in their eyes the root of all evil:

It was when the human mind became separated from its roots in feeling and instinct that it became diseased, and the infallible mark of the disease was the ugliness of its productions. This was how we explained the ugliness of the modern city in comparison with the beauty of the Cotswold towns and villages which we visited. When the mind was in harmony with nature, as it had been in the past, then its products had a spontaneous beauty, which flowed from men's hands with the same certainty as ugliness passed from the machine into its products.[24]

Already they were questioning the nature and value of civilisation, a topic that was to preoccupy Alan and Martyn for the rest of their lives. Alan had gained some historical perspective from reading Spengler's *Decline of the West* and felt that 'every civilisation in the past had its periods of rise and decline, and that our civilisation bore all the marks of decay'.[25] He was seeing for himself how this process was happening in Oxford, already expanding into suburbia in the north, invaded by Cowley from the east, where a pressed-steel factory for car bodies was set up during Alan's second year at Oxford. They felt that 'human life' was being impoverished and degraded by being deprived of that beauty which belonged to it by right'.[26] Their reaction was flight. They sought the solitude of the hills and the sea and spent all their free days walking, talking, reading, or simply being silent, trying to find communion with nature. Martyn's father had given him a small car, and they turned a blind eye to their inconsistency in using it. Not only was the car paid for by money earned by the building of a modern department store, a symbol of everything they detested, but the car itself was a product of the Industrial Revolution they so despised. Nevertheless, whenever they could they took off to the Cotswolds, to the Chilterns, to the Berkshire Downs. They never took food, but would walk for at least twenty miles, returning lunchless in the evenings. In the vacations they could go further and one New Year's Day took the coastguard path round Cornwall to Land's End; another winter's day they walked from Salisbury to Stonehenge, crouching under the massive stones for shelter to watch the midnight sky.

Of all their holidays, the most adventurous, the one that for Martyn was the climax of their Oxford careers, and for Geoff Hayward one of the greatest events of his life, was their trip to Ireland in the summer of 1927. It was Geoff's idea. He had a passion for Irish mythology and hoped to be able to collect legends first-hand from the Irish people, particularly from school-teachers and innkeepers. Martyn organised the practical arrangements and, as ever seeking solitude, they decided they must go west of Cork. So the advance party, Geoff and Martyn, took a train and travelled the thirty-six miles to Dingle, a journey which, interrupted by a cow unwilling to leave the track, took three and a half hours. Just outside Dingle half the town gathered to race the train in to the station and they found themselves the centre of much curiosity and interest. Dingle was unfamiliar with tourists at the time – seventy years later it is still possible to lose your way and find no one able to give directions in English – and these strange young men, wearing shorts and carrying tents and baggage, without a word of Gaelic, caused quite a stir. No one could imagine what they could possibly be doing there or why they should want to come. But even this was too near civilisation for Martyn and Geoff and they set off round the peninsula, through villages so poor that 'they smelt of hunger'[27] eventually settling on Clogher Strand. They decided on a site under the dark mass of Clogher Head, the Atlantic Ocean only a few feet away, gulls, gannets, cormorants and curlews their only companions and nothing between them and America; a site that Alan described as perhaps the wildest and most primitive place they had ever found.

Martyn and Geoff returned to Dingle to meet Alan and Hugh, collect their tents and make practical arrangements. The Kennedy family (whose daughter, then aged ten, still remembers the famous campers) promised to provide them with milk, eggs, soda-bread and butter and to do their washing. The campers then let it be known that they wanted two donkeys. The words were hardly out of their mouths before the place was teeming with donkeys and they went off with three, one for 30 shillings, one for £1 and one for 5 shillings, to the sound of a woman shouting from her window, 'I see it's a gentleman donkey ye've bought'. Again, most of the inhabitants of Dingle seemed to be watching as four young men and three donkeys set off up the main street, but the 5-shilling donkey turned out to be more trouble than it was worth, so they asked the children from whom they had bought it and who were following in the straggling crowd that surrounded them, to take it home. The other two proved to be insufferable nuisances and soon broke away and disappeared; the last glimpse the campers had of them was on the clifftop, their silhouettes mating against the dawn sky. So the campers had to rely on their feet, taking scant consolation from the fact that their donkey purchase earned a paragraph in the *Daily Mail*.

They camped at Clogher Head for six weeks, the richness and vividness of the experience remaining long with them; Geoff Hayward still remembered it in detail over sixty-five years later. He recalled how their shorts led to them being taken for scouts, how their poverty made people think they were shipwrecked sailors, how their inability to understand a greeting in

Irish was met with such laughter that they turned the tables by replying '*Bon jour*' and '*Guten Morgen*'. One local was so impressed at their reaching this remote spot that he said to them, 'Eh boys, ye moost ha' wonderful coorage.' They couldn't see where courage came into it, but they were continuously touched by the kindness they met and by the fact that the curiosity was never more than polite.

They experienced the usual dramas that attend camping holidays. There was the night they were ragging around and the centre pole of the kitchen tent broke, knocking over the primus stove and setting fire to the tent; there were the curious meals concocted from whatever was available, like the rhubarb Mrs Kennedy brought them, which they stewed in a kettle and took turns to eat through the spout; the foraging expeditions to Ballyferriter, a small village about six miles away. Once again they were a male group, showing no desire that it should be otherwise, but just occasionally their monastic calm would be shattered. Geoff remembers with affectionate amusement how Alan reacted when a girl, partnerless at a local festival, approached the camp hopefully. At Geoff's warning, 'There's a girl coming', Alan said he was not interested. 'But he went inside, combed his hair, put on sandals and sat primly outside.'[28]

In their different ways, it was solitude they sought. Hugh was the most gregarious, working with the women who were twisting straw and tying up the sheaves behind the men cutting oats with sickles; sitting in a circle with them, sharing their midday soda-bread and cold tea as they passed round a broken-stemmed clay pipe. It was Hugh who met the rather simple character known as the 'Goose-man', who used to climb the headland every day to see if he could glimpse America. Martyn, captivated by the beauty of Clogher Bay and the nearby village of Graigue, spent most of the time 'just mooning around' and writing poetry; Geoff collected legends and tried fasting. He kept it up for four days and four nights, giving up only when his fellow campers threatened to break camp and go home unless he stopped.

It is perhaps significant that Alan, arguably the most inward-looking of the four of them, retained fewer memories of the details of that holiday. When Walter McGrath, an enterprising Irish journalist, wrote to him in 1980 asking for his account of the camp, he replied that their stay in Kerry remained always in his mind, but that as he could never remember details of names and places he referred the journalist on to his friends. For Alan most of all it was 'just the presence of wild nature which we sought and the sense of being alone between the hills and the sky and the sea'.[29] The seabirds, the violent winds, the Atlantic rollers tossing their spray seventy feet high, the savage fury of the elements – these answered, at least in part, the need for direct experience that was crying from his soul. He was not yet able to define exactly what they were seeking, but with hindsight felt that 'in an obscure way without knowing it we were seeking God'.[30]

And still he read. They used to try to match their reading to their environment, and Martyn could not understand how Alan could read *Hamlet* on the top of a cliff looking towards the Blasket Islands, in scenery of such absorbing wildness; he felt the appropriate reading would have been Yeats, the border ballads or Ossian. It was an unimportant, though significant, disagreement. Already for Alan the inner landscape, the landscape of the mind, drew him with a magnetism no surroundings could rival.

Hugh and Martyn did not sit for their degrees, Hugh because he became seriously ill with pneumonia, a dangerous illness in those pre-antibiotic days; Martyn because he didn't feel he had done enough work – the muse of poetry had, he felt, lured him away from the muse of history. There was some family pressure to complete the course on which he had embarked, though to go down without a degree was not uncommon in those days. So for Alan's last year he was without his two greatest friends, though they continued to meet for walking holidays. It was thought possible that he would get a First, but when the results came he found he had to settle for a Second. Later he was philosophical about this, saying that he had always recognised that academically he was just 'good second class', but at the time he was deeply disappointed. Martyn recounted how Alan was so disgusted with himself when he received his decree scroll that he threw it into the Thames. Nor did he ever apply for his MA. Lewis and Owen Barfield both thought that Alan's failure to get a First was due to the persistence of his attacks on Dryden and Pope who, unfortunately for Alan, were favoured by the examiners.

Alan came down from Oxford with no very clear idea what he was going to do with his life. He had no religious commitment, no firm philosophy of life; he was profoundly discontented with the world in which he found himself, in fact, so great was the turmoil in his mind that he felt it was beginning to have physical effects. But 'At the same time our minds began to undergo a transformation. We began to discard our romanticism and to give ourselves to more serious study and thought.'[31] They were beginning to see themselves as permanent spectators and were no longer content that this should be so; it was time for them to put theory into practice and a plan was forming in their minds.

CHAPTER THREE

'Like a Man Climbing a Mountain'

JULY 1929–APRIL 1930

Afiter Oxford Alan, Martyn and Hugh all felt profoundly discontented. They had no religion or philosophy of life to guide them and they did not know how to live in the world into which they had been born. Such was their disillusion with modern civilisation that Alan went so far as to say, some twenty years later, that they had met 'the disintegration of the human soul – of all human culture'. What was really at stake, he continued, was 'man's natural, human destiny in its right relation to nature, with mankind and with God'.[1] What way of life was open to them? For long hours they grappled with this question, eventually deciding to put their ideals into practice, to live less in their heads and more in practical, day-to-day life. They would try to live a self-supporting communal life, of the utmost simplicity, in a cottage in the country. For almost a year they lived in the light of this plan and though this light was sometimes flickering, sometimes glowing with strength and confidence, it absolved them from facing seriously the question of looking for a job. To live a life of leisure in the twenties may have been exceptional, but it was not freakish.

They had not, however, bargained for further illness. Within two months of leaving Oxford Hugh, barely recovered from his bout of pneumonia, discovered he had heart trouble and Martyn developed a limp, the cause of which was never discovered, but which to some degree affected him for most of his life. Once Hugh was well enough, the two spent most of their time together, sometimes in their parental homes, sometimes travelling. Occasionally Alan would join them, but mostly he was occupied on another sort of journey.

As the only one of the three to have no private means, Alan had had to give some thought to what he would do after coming down from Oxford. Lewis's friend Owen Barfield was among those who felt that if Alan had done more reading he could have become an academic, but he never made any attempt to do so and there is no indication that it was something he ever considered seriously. He did follow up the suggestion of his friend Hugh L'Anson Fausset, and applied for a job reviewing books on *The Times Literary Supplement*, but he was told that he was not ready for the position and should first obtain some experience. As he considered that art was his religion, the way he believed the meaning of life could be found, his own wish was to be a creative writer; however, in practical terms he felt that his only hope of gainful employment lay in teaching and the only money he earned was through private tutoring.

It was C. S. Lewis who determined the next few months of Alan's life by advising him to make up for what he had missed in changing from Classics to English Literature by reading some philosophy. During Alan's last year at Oxford the friendship between the two men had deepened, Alan often admitting how much he owed to their relationship. It says much for the high regard in which Alan held his former tutor that he was prepared to take his advice and embark on a subject he had previously sought to avoid, the very thing, in fact, with its emphasis on the intellect rather than experience, that was the complete opposite of the life he was planning. Just as at school he had lived more through stories than through actual relationships and at Oxford he had learned about politics through Tolstoy rather than from life, so to study philosophy could have taken him into the realms of pure academic thought rather than to the spiritual experience for which he longed.

He was determined that this should not be so. He approached the task wholeheartedly and methodically, clear in his own mind that he was not interested in systems and dogmas for their own sakes, but in finding a philosophy by which he could live. This is why his journey into philosophy proved to be such a profound and enthralling experience – it was about nothing less than the meaning of life. He was concerned only with what he could relate to personally, always half-consciously seeking a rational explanation for his experience in the presence of nature when he was at school, the moment when he had been given the end of 'the golden string' of Blake's poem. He knew he had to follow that string:

> I give you the end of a golden string
> Only wind it into a ball,
> It will lead you in at Heaven's gate,
> Built in Jerusalem's wall.[2]

Apart from a few suggestions from Lewis, with whom he was in constant correspondence, he was on his own, with little guidance, but this did not seem to have deterred him. If following the golden string meant reading philosophy, then read philosophy he would. It was a time in Alan's life when insights alternated with turmoil, when flashes of understanding were followed by periods of confusion. 'I was like a man climbing a mountain, whose vision of the peak is often cut off, who loses himself in ravines and frequently takes false trails, and to whom the summit, when it appears, is veiled in mist.'[3]

It is not often possible to record the inner development of a man in his early twenties with any accuracy, but we are fortunate in that Alan wrote two accounts of this period of his life, one in 1938, in an article for a Benedictine magazine, another in his autobiography, *The Golden String*, which he completed some fifteen years later. So although he admits that his thought did not develop with quite the logical consistency he gave it on mature reflection, we can have some insight into his reaction to the intense reading that was his main activity during these few months.

He started with Descartes, generally considered to be the founder of modern philosophy. The idea that the existence of God was capable of philosophical proof – which was new to him – interested him momentarily, but he was not impressed with Descartes' argument for proving it and did not linger long enough to see the implications of the Cartesian idea that mind was pure spirit and matter pure mechanism, though he was later to call this theory of the split between mind and matter 'the most disastrous error ever propagated, which was to put philosophy on a false trail for centuries and to vitiate all modern thought'.[4]

He went on to Spinoza, whose thinking filled him with intense excitement. Idealist as he was, he was delighted by the declaration in the *Ethics* that wealth, fame and honour were of no value compared to wisdom; encouraged that somehow Spinoza made wisdom seem an accessible goal. Already in revolt against his own romanticism, Alan appreciated the Dutch philosopher's clarity and precision, feeling he needed this 'dose of pure reason'[5] and in the concept of 'the intellectual love of God' he found 'the very expression of my desire for union with the God of nature'.[6] He had long been aware of the limitations of his own experience, resting solely on his fleeting adolescent insight; now he recognised that this awareness of a deeper reality behind the face of nature, real though it was, was only 'a confused intuition'[7] which he had never subjected to rational scrutiny. From that moment he began to criticise his experience of God, beauty and love and to try to give it a rational basis.

He also learned from Spinoza about himself. Alan had a passionate nature, something people who knew the mature man did not always realise. Unable, until extreme old age, to express his emotions freely, there is something touching about the restrained admission he made in *The Golden String* when, impressed with Spinoza's idea of self-knowledge as a means of controlling the emotions, he realised that 'It was not by running away from one's passions or by trying to suppress them that one could be free from their power: it was by learning to face them, to study them and know their source and their direction.'[8] With the benefit of hindsight he felt he had underestimated the difficulties, assuming that knowledge led naturally to control; nevertheless, for an intense yet inhibited young man it was a valuable insight.

That Alan's reading was more than an academic exercise (though it would almost certainly be found wanting by a professional philosopher) is shown in his reaction to every philosopher he tackled. Always there was something to which he responded personally. It might have been, as with Spinoza's idealism, an issue already alive for him which he found freshly illuminated, but often he exalted in the light of a new idea, sometimes to become part of his later thinking. For instance, the *Meditations* of Marcus Aurelius awakened in him a holistic concept of the universe, which appealed to both his imagination and his reason. The suggestion that the cause of suffering lay in individuals being in conflict through failing to see their place in the whole was to find a place in his mature thoughts. So too he was attracted by the idea that virtue is its own reward and that to be virtuous was to live according to the law of the universe. This is the first glimpse of the attraction that a life of virtue was to have for him, though it had entered his unconscious when, as a small boy, he read the *Beatitudes*. Now Spinoza and Marcus Aurelius kindled his interest in moral virtue, which he began to see as something that involved one's whole being, 'the flowering of one's whole nature'.[9]

As Alan continued climbing his philosophical mountain, his excitement increased. He moved on to Berkeley's *Principles of Human Knowledge*, charmed by the style and so overwhelmed by the recognition that struck him as he read that, in his eighties, he could still recite by heart the passage that inspired him at the age of twenty-three:

Some truths there are so near and obvious to the mind that a man need only open his mind to perceive them. Such I take this important one to be: *viz.* that all the choir of heaven and all the furniture of the earth, in a word all the bodies which compose the mighty frame of the world, have not any subsistence without a mind, that their being is to be perceived and known; that consequently so long as they are not actually perceived by me or do not exist in my mind or that of any other created spirit, they must either have no existence at all or else subsist in the mind of some eternal Spirit.[10]

Suddenly he saw that it was impossible to conceive of things existing without a mind to know them: 'God was a mind, a pure Spirit, and the universe was the thought of his mind, while our own perception of things was simply a limited participation.'[11]

A development of this moment of recognition came as Alan saw in the 'eternal spirit' the same presence that he had been seeking in nature, but now it was not only a presence, but a mind that could be known. There was a mind behind the universe, and it was God's mind; man simply played his small part within that mind. Almost as amazing, to a young man who held the Church in such low regard, was that Berkeley was a bishop of the Established Church. It says little for the religious teaching he had received that he was amazed to find that such thinking could come from a Christian: 'This was the first time that it had occurred to me that the doctrine of the Church had any rational justification. I felt that this eternal Spirit of Berkeley was one with that Presence which I had observed in nature and now for the first time I perceived that it might have some relation with the God of Christian orthodoxy.'[12] This realisation was, he knew even at the time, a momentous event in his life.

Alan felt that neither Hobbes's materialism, nor Locke's common sense, nor Hume's scepticism had much to offer him, so, keeping to his rule of reading only that to which he could personally relate, he went on to read Kant's *Critique of Pure Reason*, attracted by the distinction drawn between the world of the senses and the world of the understanding. Alan's constant preoccupation, though at the time he would not have expressed it thus, was with finding a unity beyond the opposites. In order to further his understanding of Kant's ideas, he turned to Coleridge who, as both poet and philosopher, he hoped might reconcile reason and imagination. Coleridge, he found, not only accepted Kant's distinction between the world of the mind and the world of nature, but used his philosophical powers in defence of Christianity, seeking to relate both natural forms and human ideas to their source in God. Reading Coleridge led him to a deeper appreciation of Plato, though he was outraged to find that in the *Republic* Plato excluded poets from his ideal state, on the grounds that they did not deal with reality, but only with the 'copy of a copy'. As Alan was convinced that the poet was nearer to the truth than the philosopher precisely because he was seeking to embody reality, this matter, the relation between the poet and the philosopher, was something that was to concern him for years.

So to the *Confessions* of St Augustine. When he mentioned to Lewis that he was going to read it, Lewis responded: 'Of course, you will read it in the original.' Alan had had no such intention, but thus challenged he said yes, he would. From then on he read in the original language whenever possible and found this brought him into such close contact with the mind of the writer that the author of his current book was often more real to him than the people with whom he was living. The emotion with which he read St Augustine was stronger than anything he had known before. He compared it to the ardour with which he used to read Shelley and Swinburne, but now it was no longer a vague emotionalism, a romantic ardour, but 'a passion of religious love of an intensity which I had never known before.'[13] Here was what he had been seeking, a record of a personal experience written with passionate intensity and imaginative power, yet engaging the intellect in its insistent search for truth. He rejoiced to find that imagination and intellect could exist together.

This fusion of imagination and intellect was taken further as he read Dante and decided that he was the greatest poet he had ever read, with an intellect 'immeasurably greater than that of Shakespeare or Milton'.[14] Even though he was an intensely moral young man, Alan had objected to 'morality' – at least theoretically – seeing it as extolling cold reason over the fire of life. Now he found his view of romantic love transformed and he was affirmed in his instinct that 'it was better to go to hell with the great lovers than to go to heaven with the moralists'.[15] He learnt from Dante that it was not the fires of love themselves that were evil, but undisciplined and uncontrolled passion; he considered Dante to be a greater poet than Shelley and Keats because he was a greater lover and he was a greater lover because his intellect reinforced the power of love rather than condemning it. He now saw Shakespeare's heroes – Hamlet, Othello, Lear, Macbeth – as the slaves of passion, while Dante showed him that victory over passion was won not by surrender, nor by suppression, but by its transformation.

The transformation of passionate feelings, especially those of a sexual nature, was something with which Alan had already been struggling during his time at Oxford. One vacation his elder brother Dudley decided to further his sexual education and together they went to Paris, visiting the cabarets and music halls of Montmartre in the (for the Griffiths family rather surprising) company of a man he refers to simply as Michael, a friend of Dudley's who lived with a prostitute. Alan, though he had had no personal experience of such things, was not shocked – after all, he knew about Parisian life through reading French novels, particularly Stendhal, and he had even written short stories in the style of Maupassant – nor did the situation give him any particular *frisson*, but it did satisfy his curiosity: 'I wanted to know what was to be known and to learn to face it, like the novelist who can only describe a scene of passion when he has learnt to look on it with detachment. It was no doubt a dangerous course to follow and I was still utterly ignorant of myself; but it forced me to face the problem of the true nature of love.'[16] He liked the prostitute, who confided in him her yearning to be married and have children, later saying of her, with the relative lack of inhibition that characterised his old age, that 'She was very good, I believe, and Michael enjoyed it with her.'[17]

His memory of attitudes to sex at Oxford do not accord either with normal human nature in early youth or with Oxford life as portrayed by, for instance, Evelyn Waugh or Grahame Greene. According to Alan: 'At Oxford everybody used sex language, everybody was a bastard or something like that, but human beings had no sex really. You never mentioned it.'[18] So it is not surprising that his deeper understanding of sex came, as with so much in his early life, through books. His friend Hugh L'Anson Fausset, who lived near the Griffiths family home at Burghclere, lent him D. H. Lawrence's *Fantasia of the Unconscious*, which had been published in 1922. For the first time he became aware of the idea of the unconscious, which he was later to explore more deeply through the work of C. G. Jung. He saw that on the one hand there was the conscious mind, with its powers of reason, on the other hand the unconscious, a storehouse of deep instinctive feelings and intuitive perceptions. Just as he learned something about self-knowledge from reading Spinoza, now through Lawrence he realised that the split between conscious and unconscious was not only in civilisation but in himself: 'I had been living all through my life at school and at Oxford on my conscious mind and the unconscious life of instinct had been habitually repressed. My awakening to the beauty of nature and my feeling for poetry had come as a merciful release for this repression, but it had still left me unbalanced.'[19] Thus, from both Dante and Lawrence he discovered the danger of repressing sexual feelings, though he did not come to the conclusion, as so many have done, that Lawrence was advocating sexual indulgence. Rather he absorbed from Lawrence what he came to believe himself – that sex is essentially a holy instinct. He and his friends at Oxford had had no problem with seeing sex as good in itself, but now he went further, regarding it as sacred. Immorality in sex is not just self-indulgence, it is the profanation of the sacred, 'the desecration of a holy instinct which arises from the depth of our unconscious being and is the bearer of life or death'.[20] From this insight came another that was to grow and influence his thinking for his whole life: that primitive man, however immoral or cruel he might seem from a twentieth-century viewpoint, retained a sense of the holy.

Thus, ancient civilisations were in contact with the deep source of life and had a beauty and a dignity that are lost to us today.

Anyone who thinks that the celibate who has forsworn sex becomes immune to its demands, need only listen to Alan, speaking in his old age after years of monastic life. He made no secret of the conflict that sex aroused in him, introducing the subject himself to interviewers who perhaps felt this was a subject they should not broach. Talking to one such interviewer he said: 'I always had very deep friendships and it always started in the spirit, then it became emotional and always the sex element came into it and how to deal with that? . . . I always felt I shouldn't fulfil it at the sex level – it was not my calling – but it was a struggle for years.'[21] He added that he felt that the chronic constipation which plagued him for much of his life was caused by the tension created by repressed sexual energy.

While for these few months Alan was engrossed in reading, he still found time for his friends. One of these was the painter Stanley Spencer, whom he had come to know while he was at Oxford. In his late thirties, some years older than Alan, Spencer at that time was working on his famous murals of army life for the oratory of All Souls' at Burghclere, close to the Griffith family home. Alan would walk over, sometimes to the church to watch him paint, sometimes to his home to talk. He found in Spencer's work, with its religious insight into everyday life, something of the quality of St Francis, and it was through Spencer that he came to appreciate the paintings of Giotto and the music of Bach. He began to find that in art as in literature he was being driven back in time, back from his youthful love of romanticism to an earlier and, he became convinced, greater art. This shift towards early, eventually to primitive, art was to continue and is vividly illustrated by his account of a visit he made to an exhibition of pictures in London:

> I remember now how in the room of the primitives I felt like spending half an hour in front of each picture and could hardly drag myself away. In the next rooms with Piero della Francesca, Botticelli, Bellini etc I was still deeply held; then as I moved on to the high renaissance, Titian and Tintoretto, I found myself admiring but not deeply moved, until I was soon walking quite rapidly through the succeeding rooms. I was only stopped by the post-impressionists – Cezanne, Renoir, van Gogh, who seemed to recover something of the early spirit.[22]

Once he had gone back as far as primitive art, where could he go then? Where was the source, the origin, of art? He began to feel that behind all great art – Bach, Dante, Giotto – stood religion; a religion that did not inhibit creativity as he had previously thought it must inevitably do but, on the contrary, was crucial to its full and highest development. Up till now art had been his religion, now it was being supplanted. Surely this should have been among the most momentous of his experiences? Yet he took this discovery very coolly, merely recounting it as another stage on his journey. It is as if the full significance of this insight had not yet hit him.

Alan was never out of touch with Hugh and Martyn for long, and though he could not afford to join them on their trips to Europe he often spent time with them when they travelled nearer home. Twice he joined them in a cottage they rented in the Quantocks, on one occasion starting a commonplace book, something he was to keep up, at least intermittently, for much of his life. Martyn remembered the first entry, written in 'his immaculate classical handwriting'. It was the description of the young wife in Chaucer's *The Miller's Tale*. Another year they visited Watchet, the home of Coleridge's Ancient Mariner, where an incident recorded by Martyn reflects the receptive mood they were in:

> We went up to the hill high above, and stopped to look at an area covered with wild roses, growing in thickets in a kind of white wilderness high over the sea. We thought we'd explore this – and all at once, emerging from a kind of cave screened by roses in flower, there he was, a bearded figure, white headed in nondescript garments that might have been those of a retired seaman. We turned and hurried back to the road without a word.[23]

Of all the trips which Alan made with his friends at that time the most memorable was a tour of English cathedrals. They started from Cambridge and visited Ely, Peterborough, Southwell, Lincoln, York and the abbeys of Fountain and Rievaulx. They were not the only visitors; cathedrals were already becoming tourist attractions, and they were both shocked and amused by comments from American tourists following a similar trail, such as: 'Oh, we're doing them all, and we've six more and I'm sick of it.' They were happier with the way they were accosted at Fountains, as a 'fat, tipsy Yorkshire Wife of Bath' climbed out of the coach asking, 'Which is way t' poob?'[24]

They were intoxicated by the whole experience. They decided Rievaulx must be the finest religious building in the whole of England and Alan and Martyn (Hugh was still not well and did not join them) determined to go a second time to see it by moonlight. They did not escape the watchful eyes of the curator, who firmly told them to go to bed, so they dodged round and succeeded in entering from the back. The sight of the nave against the hill behind, the full moon bathing it in light, was something they never forgot.

Just as he was becoming increasingly aware of opposites in life and thought, so Alan was more and more aware of contrasts between old and new, between the works of God and the works of man, whether it was the beauty of the great cathedral of Peterborough 'rising above the hideous smoky city like an apparition from another world'[25] or the partnership of the artist with God seen in the craftmanship of the Gothic cathedrals of Lincoln and York. Awed and astonished by the stained glass and the sculpture, he felt he was in the presence of an unfallen world, unutterably saddened by the thought of all that had been lost. There was more. He was working his way back through art, music, philosophy and he was finding what he sought – an almost unconscious union between man and nature: 'I saw that behind all this there lay the power of a vast intelligence, not merely of an architectural genius but of a whole philosophy of life.'[26]

Having feasted on Gothic glory, they continued to the Lake District, spending three August weeks at Ullswater. Hugh was still unwell, so Alan and Martyn left him wandering the gentle lakeside edges as they walked, rowed and climbed over three thousand feet to the top of Helvellyn. For Alan, though, the high point of the holiday was of a different order. There, in the landscape for ever associated with Wordsworth, he was once again fleetingly possessed by the experience for which he was always longing: 'I remember that I went out once alone among the hills, when a mist began to gather, and I felt myself alone in that mysterious solitude, as though I had been at the bottom of the sea, cut off from all the haunts of men; and once again the sense of that Presence which I had experienced at school took possession of me.'[27] He felt as if he were alone in the universe, 'a sort of total emptiness, and yet total bliss, was there. It was a wonderful experience.'[28]

The tastes and travels of these three young men might seem self-indulgent, remote from the concerns of their fellow men, but they had their own stars to follow, their own inner problems to face. In those days, self-examination and the constant probing of one's inner life were not taken for granted as they are today, so those rare moments when feelings are revealed had to be taken very seriously. There was a great depth of pain in the way Alan spoke for the three of them, lamenting the instability, the unrootedness, of their lives: 'We did not belong like Wordsworth to the Lakes. We did not belong anywhere. That was part of our misery; whether we liked it or not, we were uprooted like the rest of the world, and wherever we went we could not escape ourselves.'[29]

There was one further ingredient in the rich diet of intellectual and spiritual food which Alan was digesting during these few months, one that was eventually to give him a sense of belonging, and that was his first encounter with eastern thought. One of his mother's friends who, as a suffragette, a theosophist and – something rare in women in those days – a smoker, had been a delightful curiosity to the Griffiths children, introduced him to three great classics of eastern religious wisdom. They were the *Bhagavad Gita*, the supreme expression of Hinduism, a version of the *Dhammapada* called the Buddha's Way of Virtue, regarded by Theravada Buddhists as a synopsis of the central truths of Buddhism, and the Tao Te Ching, one of the most important texts of Taoism. He still held no Christian beliefs and these books had little direct effect on his thought other than giving it a wider non-Christian background, but it is significant that, far from finding anything unchristian about them, he felt they were expressing the same truths he found in Christianity. So the Buddha and Lao Tzu joined Socrates, Spinoza and Marcus Aurelius, along with the Christ of the Sermon on the Mount, in his panoply of great spiritual leaders. The influence of these books on his later life was to be immeasurable, but at the time he said only that they acted as 'a secret ferment in my soul'.[30]

All through this short period of his life Alan was referring to turning points, moments of intense excitement, times when he was touched and charmed and 'felt that a new light had dawned', times when he experienced what he called an intense and unfamiliar 'passion of religious love'. He had no idea where these moments of illumination were leading him, seeing them simply in the context of a secular culture to which religion was, though important, merely a background. He was certainly no nearer to Christianity, which he still regarded as a thing of the past, still less to Roman Catholicism. His was a journey into the unknown but, though he could not have known this, it was also a preparation for the future. He could hardly have spent the time more fruitfully than by this period of intense reading. A quarter of a century later he wrote: 'The effort of thought was so intense, the desire for a new life which I experienced was so fervent, the light which I received penetrated so deeply into my mind, that the marks of it remain in my soul like the grain of a tree, and I still feel it as part of a living process of thought which has never ceased.'[31]

By the beginning of 1930, plans for the simple life of which they had been dreaming began to crystallise. Alan had often stayed with Hugh and Martyn in a farm in the Cotswolds and in a cottage at Sutton Courtenay, a village near Oxford, where they discussed their ideas far into the night. At last the scheme took shape, acquiring a place and a name. The next stage of their lives, the 'great adventure', a stage so important that all three referred to it continually until the end of their long lives, was Eastington.

CHAPTER FOUR

Eastington

1930

The 'Plan', the 'Great Experiment', the 'Adventure in Living' or, as they usually called it, simply 'Eastington', was to influence the rest of their lives. Today it would not be considered a very remarkable venture, but this was nearly seventy years ago when words such as ecology, environment and conservation were not, as now, part of everyday vocabulary; when the car, far from being seen as a problem, was venerated. Apart from famous exceptions like Tolstoy, there were few precedents for a way of life that quite deliberately took a path in direct opposition to the norms of the day. While their contemporaries were starting on their careers, living full social lives, falling in love and getting married, moving politically to extremes of left or right, or taking the changes in civilisation in their stride and turning a blind eye to what many regarded as a time of crisis (unemployment was widespread and worsening, the great Depression already looming), they did none of these things but chose, with commendable courage, to put their ideals into practice and to embark on a way of life that, bold and imaginative a venture though it undoubtedly was, must have seemed quite extraordinary to their friends.

Martyn and Hugh had originally intended to explore the British Isles on foot before putting the plan into action, but by the time Alan had accepted their invitation to join them (and probably largely due to his influence), their resolve had become clarified; they intended to reject the civilisation they had come to criticise so deeply and live without machines or gadgets or any of the products of civilisation – in fact, they wanted to have nothing to do with anything made during or after the Industrial Revolution. At this stage they had no very definite ideas as to how they would do this beyond agreeing that they would have everything in common and live in great simplicity, as far as possible being self-supporting, but they were confident enough to begin to look for a cottage.

In the late summer of 1929 they went to Ford Farm, in the Cotswolds, intending to use it as a base from which to find somewhere suitable to live. They soon saw an advertisement for a pair of cottages some four miles away and Alan, already rejecting mechanised transport, walked there and back to view them. (Martyn wrote that he walked thirty miles, so he probably came from Oxford.) Eastington was then, as indeed it still is, a small unspoilt village on the river Leach near Northleach, and Alan, according to Martyn 'quite starry-eyed', reported favourably both on the cottages and on the tenant, Jim Holtom, who lived in the second of the pair. The price was £500, which Martyn, or rather the generosity of Martyn's father, provided.

Though Alan's account of Eastington is the fullest, Martyn and Hugh, in diaries, poems, letters and memoirs, also wrote about their time there. Their memories are broadly in agreement – in fact Martyn was 'astonished by his [Alan's] clarity and assurance and the summary, convinced and convincing, of the beliefs we then held, the fervours and abhorrences that directed us to a new way of life' – so between them they have left a clear impression of what their life was like. They do, however, differ in their memory of the month of their arrival, Martyn remembered arriving in September, Alan was in no doubt that it was the following April. Alan never claimed a good memory for facts, but in this instance it looks as if he was right.

Eastington is more a hamlet than a village, with a tiny church but no shop and no pub. Being at the end of a cul de sac it was, and remains, very quiet; in those days the only entry was a cobbled track too rough for cars or lorries and accessible only by horse, bicycle or on foot. The stream runs a few hundred yards from the track and a nearby meadow, known as Rotten Pot, gives a view up the valley. Their cottage was one of a small terrace, built of good Cotswold stone; the stone walls were whitewashed, the oak beams painted with creosote, the floors covered with coconut matting. There were four rooms. Downstairs the kitchen doubled as a living room and a second room served as a study; upstairs was a bedroom which the three of them shared, keeping the other one free for visiting friends. They slept on plain wooden trestle beds, the mattresses stuffed with straw from a neighbouring farm, the only furniture a table and four wheelback chairs they picked up locally. They do not mention clothes, though Alan's sister Barbara was persuaded to find a loom and weave them rough vests made from the wool of Scottish sheep. The simplicity was absolute, unrelieved by curtains, cushions or coverlets.

The cottage was solid and weatherproof, but, like most cottages at the time, it had no water, drainage or lighting. Until recently the villagers had walked a quarter of a mile to a spring in a neighbouring field to get their water, but by 1930 there was a tap, and every day one of the three took two huge pitchers to fill with water, sometimes in winter having to thaw the frozen tap by lighting straw underneath. At first they read by the light of an oil-lamp, but as they became stricter, trying ever harder to use nothing that savoured even remotely of the Industrial Revolution, they turned to candles. A local blacksmith made them a wrought-iron candelabrum and they bought tallow-dips, which had once been a local industry, for candles. To their great joy they discovered that not only did the four candles give a better light, but that the light, reflected on the bare white walls, flickering against the dark oak rafters, created a most beautiful and peaceful atmosphere. Already they were proving their theory: simple, natural means used for natural ends, however humble, are beautiful. This candlestick, with the slightly eccentric, off-balanced beauty of the artefact, is now a treasured possession of Martyn's son Daniel; it is touching to imagine the three of them, earnestly reading by its light.

The simple life has its less romantic side, however, and the absence of drainage meant the use of an earth closet in the garden; one of Alan's first jobs was to clean it out and spread the contents on the garden, where they immediately started growing their own vegetables. Far from regarding this as an unpleasant chore, this was precisely the life they wanted, just as rising at dawn was a delight, keeping their lives in the rhythm of the country, man and nature working together. They were living a primitive life, close to nature and as far as they could get from the 'civilisation' they abhorred. Industrialism was approaching, fast and steadily; they were consciously learning the secrets of a traditional way of life before it was totally destroyed, consciously resisting anything that might throw the shadow of modernity across their path. Sometimes their attempts to escape the twentieth century might seem a bit extreme; indeed, Martyn himself felt that their attempts to write with a quill pen and their refusal to use a safety razor were 'bizarre'. Even the inkwell was specially made by a local blacksmith. They shunned the gramophone and the wireless; they would not read modern books or newspapers, and another of their ideas ('perhaps the silliest', wrote Martyn) was the decision to read, as far as possible, early editions and folios in pre-industrial editions. They became so soaked in the past that when Alan went to stand by the main road two miles away watching the cars go by, the life streaming past him seemed 'as far removed from their lives as ancient Rome or Babylon'.[1] All this may seem obsessive, and perhaps it was, but it was an honest attempt not only to shirk no detail, but to recognise the relationship between the outer life and the inner. It would be hard to enter fully into the mind of a pre-Industrial Revolution countryman while using technology of which he would not even have dreamed.

As far as possible they were self-supporting – the purchase of the cottage included some stabling and a field – but if they had to buy food, they would buy only local produce. They drank no tea or coffee, used honey rather than sugar and did not smoke. Their breakfast porridge was made from Cotswold oats; their bread, baked in an old brick oven, from stone-ground flour from the old mill at Winchcombe, which was believed to have been working since the Norman Conquest; milk came from a cow they had bought and which one of them milked at dawn every morning. For lunch they had vegetable stew, made in a hay-box from their own produce, with slices cut from a great round of the local cheese, Double Gloucester; in the evening there were eggs from their own ducks, four Khaki-Campbells who faithfully laid four eggs every morning. At Hugh's suggestion they fasted on Fridays, taking nothing but some dry bread and cold milk throughout the day. Their only luxury was honey, and that of course was in the comb, made by the village beekeeper. To their surprise they found this life-style very cheap, the three of them living on the equivalent of £100 a year, allowing not only for living expenses, but even including books. Alan notes wryly that on occasional visits to their parental homes they would spend more in a day than they needed at Eastington for well over a week.[2] (The rent of most of the Eastington cottages – between three and four shillings a week – gives an idea of the cost of living in those days.)

When they visited their families there was no question of taking a train, for the train above all things was a symbol of that which had destroyed the peace and order of the countryside. At first Alan would bicycle the seventy-odd miles to visit his parents; later he walked, staying two nights on the way, thus every excursion from the village became an adventure, deepening his sense of belonging to the country. Walking was a large part of their lives as it had been at Oxford, but now Alan walked more for health than for pleasure, regarding it as an encroachment on the time he wanted to give to reading and meditation, and tended to sigh when he had to take some exercise. On the other hand Martyn, confined to the cottage by the persistent lameness that dogged so much of his life, yearned to accompany him. So it was in the first instance for Martyn that they bought a horse, a robust cob called Kit, which they all learned to ride, simply by jumping on and riding bare-back round the field. Later they acquired a pony trap, 'not of the governess-cart type, called a "tub", but a highly-perched baker's cart, good for seeing the scenery but bad for catching the wind'.[3] Thus Martyn was free to explore the countryside and sometimes Kit and the pony trap would take all three of them to places like Malmesbury, where they went to see the abbey.

Nobody has ever claimed that living in community is easy and as they worked out how to live this new life there were many things over which the three of them disagreed. But the one principle about which they never once argued, according to Hugh, was sharing their resources. There was no resentment about the fact that Martyn's father had provided the house, that Martyn and Hugh had small private incomes and that Alan had no money to contribute. Nor, it seems, did they argue about who did the various jobs. Most of the tasks were taken turn and turn about, but Hugh was responsible for growing the vegetables and every morning it was Alan who fetched the water and fed the ducks. This became quite a ritual. A visitor recalls Alan referring to them as his 'little sisters' and remarked on the kindness and gentleness with which, at dawn and again at dusk, he escorted them from their shed to the nearby stream.

Martyn, less mobile than the other two, did the sedentary jobs like washing the dishes. Forty years later Hugh was still moved to recall Martyn's labours: 'I was turned upside down to remember how we let you do, day after day without relief, that most unpleasant and futile of all Eastington chores – keeling the greasy iron porridge pot in almost cold water with a bunch of miserable sodden twigs.'[4] Martyn's lameness also deprived him of helping with the milking, and Alan, though eager to do his share, was not, according to Martyn, 'cut out for practical work of any kind'[5] and had to give up his attempts to milk their Friesian cow after a month's strenuous efforts failed to extract a single drop. Hugh was more successful. He had first milked a cow when they stayed at Ford Farm and found it 'one of the most inspiring experiences of my life'.[6]

The chores done, much of the day would be occupied with reading, as they spent several hours every day in the small fireless room which they used as a study. In winter Alan's feet were so cold that he would have to take a walk to restore his circulation, but, he claimed, the cold kept his brain clear. He read Aristotle, the historian E. H. Clarendon, John Donne, Jeremy Taylor, Milton and Sir Thomas Browne, coming to the conclusion that because it was a time when the traditional order of life was still preserved, the seventeenth century was the Golden Age in English history. Although it was a time of violent conflict, Alan argued that, because the battles were fought in the framework of tradition, 'it had the rich vitality of an ancient culture receiving new life from new ways of life and thought'.[7] He could not have known at the time how this insight, this combining of old and new, was to become so important a part of his later development.

Indeed, with hindsight it is possible to see the seeds of much of his later thinking taking root at this time, though Alan himself is unclear exactly when the ideas began to formulate in his mind. It was at Eastington that he began to think historically, rather than simply ideologically, about civilisation; to trace patterns in the rise and fall of great civilisations like Babylonia and Egypt, Greece and Rome. He began to see in each of them how primitive culture degenerated into material prosperity, how creative energy became monotonous uniformity. At a deeper level he saw the breakdown of morality and the exploitation of the poor by the rich. This was not the sort of moralising to which he had objected in the past and which he had considered an abstract system imposed on life, it was more that he was glimpsing the poetic vision of Tolstoy, Dostoevsky and Wordsworth. He saw that the errors of modern civilisation did not lie only in the split between reason and imagination, rather: 'The source of evil was to be found in the human mind rising up against God and seeking to build up its civilisation without reference to God, the supreme arbiter of destiny, whose will was the ultimate source of all human happiness.'[8]

Most of their reading they did alone and independently, but soon they began to read together. They each had an old Black Letter edition of the Authorised Version of the Bible and every morning, as the breakfast porridge was cooking and, in winter, the candlelight flickering, they would sit round the table studying the great tomes, reading every chapter from Genesis to Revelations. At first their interest was purely literary, for the Authorised Version of the Bible contains some of the most beautiful English ever written, even in the seventeenth century, the period to which they were all so attracted. Alan began to see in the encounters between God and Man in the Old Testament a reality deeper than anything he had known before. As he read of Job's relationship to the divine presence he was once again where he longed to be – in the realm of experience. The Hebrew prophets struck him with the force of a revelation as he saw in their words a more profound judgement on our civilisation than he himself had ever made. He realised that: 'Our civilisation was not merely an offence against beauty and truth, against that rational order of life upon which human culture is based. It was an offence against the moral order of the universe.'[9] And if his prejudices against industrialisation were confirmed, so too was his instinctive leaning towards all that was true and beautiful; for instance, he never forgot the emotion with which he read the words about wisdom: 'For there is in her a spirit quick of understanding, holy, alone in kind, manifold, subtil, freely moving, clear in utterance, unpolluted, distinct, unharmed, loving what is good, keen, unhindered, beneficient, loving towards man, steadfast, sure, free from care, all-powerful, all-surveying, and penetrating through all spirits that are quick of understanding, pure, most subtil.'[10] He found that the reconciliation of religion and philosophy which he had glimpsed in Dante and St Augustine had its roots in the Old Testament itself.

Soon Hugh and Alan passed from reading to praying, dropping to their knees on the bare stone floor, even, according to Alan, kneeling out in the cold at the back of the house, where 'the words seemed to pierce the soul'.[11] (It was many years before Martyn began to pray, and that was due to the influence of C. S. Lewis.) Living in this rural village their reading had a practical as well as a spiritual poignancy, the background of the Old Testament finding its parallel in their own lives as they read the stories of Moses tending his flocks, then walked round the fields at lambing time, seeing how when a ewe lost her lamb the shepherd would cover another lamb with the dead lamb's coat so the ewe might think it her own.

They talked, of course, they talked endlessly. It is hard not to wish that the tape recorder had existed in those days, though the very suggestion would have filled them with horror. As it is, we have only scant hints of the nature of their conversations, for instance Martyn writing, long after they had gone their different ways, of 'an Eastingtonian surmise about the benefits of the substitution of machines for men' and Hugh admitting that usually Alan had the edge on them, though recalling how the three of them laughed at the memory of a debate on the 'simple life', when Martyn and Hugh cornered Alan into a theory that the village blacksmith could make an X-ray machine. They would often discuss points arising from their reading. Geoff Hayward remembers them reading St Augustine in Latin and Alan shaking his head as they discussed it, saying, 'No, not that.' 'Slightly irritating', wrote Geoff, but he was forming his own particular philosophy: 'It was a stage in his life.'[12]

They were none of them Christians, any more than they had been at Oxford. As so often speaking for them all, Martyn wrote: 'Religion appeared almost something out of date: and the church part of the suburban life we found drab and uninspiring . . . we felt the need for a wider and more glorious reality.' And Hugh: 'Like many of our contemporaries after the First War we were shocked by the complacency of the Anglican Church as we saw it, and with the understanding we then had, we thought St Paul's insistent distinction between the spirit and the vile body had distorted the Gospels: it was not a distinction that we felt in the eagerness and vigour of youth.'[13]

Even though Alan had by now come to admire the philosophical and moral ideas of Christianity, he was still far from faith. Yet Christ was a figure that inspired them all with devotion and love, 'as a kind of greater Socrates, who had sacrificed himself by holding on to the truth'.[14] At the time it was not simple piety that compelled Alan to his knees; rather, it was that having studied the economic and political structure of the seventeenth century – the conflict between King and Parliament, between the new merchant class and the old aristocracy, between the new science and philosophy and the ancient tradition – he was led to study the religion which had underpinned social structures for so long. The inexorable hound of heaven was pursuing him, taking, for the moment, intellectual form, but his days of agnosticism were numbered.

What did the villagers, the men and women who lived naturally and unself-consciously a life that was for Alan, Martyn and Hugh a 'great experiment', think of these intruders in their midst? Eric and Ethel Holland, who live today in the cottage the three young men owned in 1930, remember them with affection. Alan used to come over from Prinknash, by which time he was 'Father Bede', and they still talk affectionately of 'Beady' and his visits. They remember Hugh, sitting on the stone wall round land that is now used as allotments, watching the stars – they called him 'the astronaut'. In short, with the tolerance and courtesy of the country-dweller, they did not regard them as curiosities. The Hollands were then, of course, young children, but unless their memories are mistaken, the three young men were on good terms with all the villagers who simply absorbed them into their lives and befriended them. Alan remembered the unmarried couple who lived in the only cottage considered an eyesore, the tiles having been sold and replaced by an asbestos roof (Alan, predictably, saw this as 'an example of greed and industrialism bringing disharmony into the ordered beauty of life').[15] Then there were the two brothers who had not spoken to one another for twenty years; one was an atheist and the other a devout Methodist. They were closest, though, to their next-door neighbours, the Holtoms.

Though Jim had been driving a coal lorry, the Holtoms were a farming family. Jim's father was a shepherd on a nearby farm and his brother worked on another; farming was in his blood and he spent his spare time working on a smallholding. So when the three young men bought some more land and another couple of cows, he gladly accepted the offer to work with them. Between them they soon had enough milk to supply their twenty-odd neighbours, for until then there had been no fresh milk in the village. Jim's daughter-in-law still remembers the three men with great warmth and Jim was to become a life-long friend, particularly of Martyn's, who went on to farm with him in Berkshire.

The austerity of their lives does not seem to have included a rigorous attitude to solitude; indeed, the room they kept for their friends was in constant use. One regular visitor who lived alone, once telling Alan that 'he could have howled through loneliness', was the potter Michael Cardew, whose work was later exhibited in the Victoria and Albert Museum and who made many of their pots and plates and tea-cups. (They were much relieved at this, as they had feared they might have to use cheap crockery made on modern machines.) Occasionally Cardew would bring his pipe and tabor to the cottage, to accompany the old English rounds which they used to sing. A motet by William Byrd moved Alan particularly, the words 'Non nobis Domine non nobis, sed nomini tuo da gloriam' (Not to us Lord, not to us, but to your name be the glory) seeming to him 'like so much else in our life . . . prophetic of events to come'.[16] Jim Holtom cannot have enjoyed these informal sing-songs as, when asked what they were like as neighbours, said 'All right, apart from the noise', which, given that they were mostly very quiet, seems rather an overstatement.

They would relax their rules when visitors came, though they had come to enjoy their vegetarian diet and did not welcome the cold ham or the scrags of mutton their guests put in the lunchtime stew, or the imported tea brewed in the Cardew pot. Alan's friend Hugh L'Anson Fausset was one Oxford friend honoured in this way, Oliver van Oss another; he brought a friend who was a history don at Magdalen, who both delighted and shocked them by cooking a steak and kidney pudding. There were visits from another friend, Noel Alexander, who, suspecting that he was not finding favour with the three, mocked their venture, and from Geoff Hayward, who did not mind if he found favour or not and whose levity went down into Eastington history. For instance, knowing that Alan still suffered from the constipation that had afflicted him since Oxford and noting the hours he would spend locked in the outside privy, named it 'the bog of Allan'.

The visit etched most firmly in Martyn's mind was one which in fact never happened. Alan and C. S. Lewis were still good friends and in regular correspondence, but the memory of the student–tutor relationship was too fresh for the friendship yet to be one of equals, and Alan was very excited at the prospect of his visit, postponing a projected walk in case it might overtire him and prevent him from doing justice to his distinguished visitor: 'So the Friday came, but no Lewis; and the Saturday followed, poor Alan expectant and anxious, gazing out of the window, walking up to the main road, all blank and Lewis-less.'[17] Apparently Lewis had never promised to come, but had just said he would call in if it proved possible. Alan, as Martyn admitted, was rarely put out, and this sad little incident shows a side of his character seldom in evidence. If in later life he had similarly looked forward to seeing someone, he would have concealed his disappointment; temperamentally he did not wish the world to see behind his controlled, reserved exterior and seldom allowed it to do so.

After less than a year the Eastington experiment was over and the three friends went their separate ways. They had been planning a 'New Experiment', intending to find a farm and to take the Holtom family with them – Jim was to be the manager, his father the shepherd and his brother a farmhand. They discovered that, owing to a defect in the title deeds, they could not complete the purchase of the smallholding at Eastington, so they began looking around for some land, once again relying on Martyn's father for money, though by then he had lost a great deal of it. This plan never worked out, but Martyn is adamant that Alan, though he never mentions it in *The Golden String*, was part of the scheme; indeed, he movingly recalls how he and Hugh returned from spending a few days with Hugh's family to hear of his decision not to join them:

> As we drove up we caught sight of Alan sitting alone and forlornly on the cottage step, reading St Augustine's *City of God*. He didn't get up to meet us at the stable, but gave a rather subdued smile of greeting as we greeted him. He asked about the trip and later discussed St Augustine. While we were away he had decided he would not come with us and the Holtoms. And then there were two. And the Great Experiment was over.[18]

Why did this experiment in living, so close to their hearts and so whole-heartedly undertaken, break up after so short a time? It would be unrealistic to expect any three people to live together in perfect harmony, and sometimes they had rows, as Hugh recalled:

> You may remember that in *The Golden String* Dom Bede says I suggested fasting and it was a mistake and we weren't ready for it. What he omitted to say is that I slammed out of the cottage in a fury and a frustration because it seemed to me that although we had simplified our lives it was sheer hypocrisy to pretend that we weren't really leading very enjoyable lives on money provided by your father and mine without depriving ourselves of anything so that it hurt, nor were we taking responsibility for ourselves . . . it was the most frustrating time of my life.[19]

Incidents such as this, however, are not usually cataclysmic, any more than had been their early disagreements about how the cottage should be furnished. There must have been more to it. Given their reserve it is hard to be sure of the exact nature of the problems that finally put an end to the experiment, but there are clues. 'We were three very close in friendship but far apart in temperament', wrote Hugh, as so often summing up things which Alan barely touched on and which even Martyn did not face so squarely. 'There was indeed both serenity and exhilaration, and a satisfaction in our daily work, but it was also a very tough time, tough not merely because of the austerity of our life . . . but tough intellectually and emotionally.'[20]

The more one reads their later writings and correspondence, the more it becomes clear that there were indeed deep emotional problems, a 'tremendous intensity of emotional life going on all the time'.[21] It also becomes clear that the problem lay in Alan's 'eager idealism', the very quality that the other two had found so attractive at Oxford. He was, wrote Hugh, 'over-eager that you should share his vision'. Alan recognised this in himself, recalling, 'Everybody said I was tremendously enthusiastic about everything and I talked and talked and expected everyone to share my enthusiasms.'[22] But the lightness of his tone does not match the seriousness of the problem it presented for his friends. Alan's idealism, the source of so much of his later strength, the characteristic that lay behind so much of his work, was central to their problems. On the one hand they found it compulsive, on the other it sometimes proved obsessive and overbearing. All three were gentle, kindly men, their relationship of such warmth and charity that they seldom indulged in criticism of each other, though in a burst of irritation Hugh wrote to Martyn in 1934: 'Would it ever be possible for Alan to live with tact and courtesy?'[23] Though Alan could never have been called selfish, Hugh and Martyn often felt they were being used to work out his life rather than being allowed room to work out their own.

> Seized of an idea every circumstance of life had to be slotted into his theory, squeezed in sometimes, and doubts were swept up like leaves – already perhaps, a Catholic mind in the making! Usually most inspiring, it could also be most infuriating to a mind that likes to see both sides before making itself up, and quite often I thanked the Lord that in the Cotswolds there was no shortage of hills to lift up my eyes unto.[24]

So wrote Hugh. Even Martyn, though probably closer to Alan's ideas, agreed that their lives began to differ, as Hugh spent more and more time with Jim Holtom, Martyn went for long rides on horseback and weeded the garden and Alan tirelessly read Aristotle, Plato, St Augustine and St Paul, his only recreation being their conversations and arguments. Sometimes, too, he wished Alan could be a little more moderate over matters that came to affect them all, such as fasting: 'Alan was becoming a glutton for abstinence; and no sooner had we agreed to one [diet] than he would propose another. Hugh who was never so heartedly a Great Experimenter as we were, began to jib at this; and I too came to see there would be no end to these new abstinences.'[25]

In *The Golden String* Alan says little of the way the experiment ended, other than to say 'a division began to take place among us'.[26] Even when asked near the end of his life if the break-up of the community was distressing to him, he simply said: 'Not really. We had been through a wonderful experience. There were stresses at times, especially with Hugh – there was a difficult period – tension between us, but we got over it.'[27] Certainly they got over it, but his memory had let him down, for in two letters to Martyn, written just two years after they had left Eastington, the extremity of Alan's emotion overcame his natural inhibitions and he reveals an altogether different picture: 'It seems to me that we were given at Eastington an insight into the soul which very few people have had. I do not believe that this mass of evil, which appeared there and made it a little hell (as I believe it really was a foretaste of what hell may be) was peculiar to you and me and Hugh.'[28] And a few weeks later:

> Oh Martyn, what torments I must have inflicted on you and Hugh at Eastington. I judge from those which I inflicted on myself, though they can be nothing compared with what you had to suffer. But you don't know what a diabolical spirit there is within me, and it is intolerably hard to fight because it constantly appears in the form of an angel of light. But I am beginning to know it better and to order my life accordingly.[29]

'This mass of evil', 'A foretaste of what hell may be', 'Torments', 'A diabolical spirit'. Tension there certainly was, but was there really a need for such agonising, such bitter self-reproach? Some of the anguish he expressed can be attributed to his suffering at the time he wrote those letters, but did they really reflect the truth of the situation? The one certainty is that the experience at Eastington, far from ending their friendship, bound them together for life. Hugh wrote, not long before his death: 'The give and take of that experience has kept us together for fifty-five years in, as it were, a community of thought.'[30]

It is clear that as a young man Alan was not easy to live with; that the saintly man he was to become was the result of his determination, the fruit of a life of prayer and meditation, rather than the path of a man born with a naturally easy temperament. The search for holiness, the journey on which he was already embarking, is a hard road. If he sometimes overrode the needs of his companions, it was the blindness brought on by the intensity of his own struggle and he certainly paid for it in the remorse that later swept over him. Much later Hugh summed up the way Alan had been and the man he became in a single phrase: 'He is much more now a pervasive light than a consuming flame.'[31]

The three friends were to reflect on the Eastington experiment, sharing memories of it, revisiting it, dreaming of it, for the rest of their lives. 'At the beginning', Hugh wrote, 'it was largely self-interest, to lead a decent life in the simplest, most self-sufficient way possible to ease my own social conscience about my privileged upbringing, to study more widely and to write.'[32] But they were well aware of the inconsistency of living such a life on money obtained by the very means of which they were so critical. Even at the time they knew they were escaping the responsibilities of what Martyn called 'the e-y-l world' (earning-your-living) while simultaneously depending on it, though they did acknowledge that they were at least seeking 'some sort of reality in its place, and one that imposed its own rules and rigours'.[33] He and Hugh also felt that they were motivated 'more by what we flew from than by what we sought'[34] though they explicitly exempted Alan from this criticism, knowing that for him it was 'a mile or two of his pilgrim's progress to his religious conversion'.[35] They were also very aware how easy it would be to romanticise the time at Eastington as idyllic, casting themselves as single-minded, idealistic young men, and this they resolutely refused to do; in fact, Hugh admitted to being uneasy about the success of Alan's book, fearing that it had given the venture a glamour that it did not deserve. He was also distressed (and it certainly would not, in his case, have been jealousy) years later when he revisited Eastington, to find middle-class residents referring reverently to *The Golden String* as 'The Book'. The most they would claim was that it was remarkable that it happened when it did, over thirty years before such experiments became commonplace.

The brevity of the Eastington experiment does not mean it should be regarded as a failure, either in terms of the relationships between the three men or in the effect it had on their lives. But in the light of the sad break-up of the little community, it is important to remember how much the three men shared: the vivid memories of healthy plain living, of intense cold, of endless discussions on the meaning of life, of 'early autumn days, winter dawns, and various sensory impressions; the draughts, taste of bread and cheese, candlelight'.[36] Even more to remember their shared motivation, particularly the sense of unity derived from their conviction that what was nearest to nature was good. 'The motives that took each of us there grew up with us as we lived together', wrote Hugh. 'How we grew each other up could be as valuable to anyone young, or at any rate young at heart, as the story of our daily round.'[37] Here perhaps is the key to why Eastington was to remain deep in their very souls. During those few months the effect they had on each other and the often painful things they learned about themselves became, as Alan said, 'the decisive event in all our lives'[38] and was to bind them together with hoops of steel. They were all to struggle to live out the ideals they had tried to live at Eastington, but Martyn handed Alan what must be, from one fellow Experimenter to another, the ultimate accolade: 'As for Eastington's aims and ideals, has not Bede followed them through?'[39]

So they parted, Hugh to marriage,* Martyn to farming and poetry, and Alan – Alan had yet further to go, more to suffer, in his journey into the deepest and darkest places in himself.

*Hugh had met Eileen, his future wife, on a visit to Oxford while they were living at Eastington.

CHAPTER FIVE

Dark Night

1931–32

After Eastington Alan was unsure of almost everything; he did not know what he believed or what he wanted to do with his life. He was more confident on his friends' behalf, convinced that they had made wrong decisions and not hesitating to say so. He told Martyn that he would not find the life he wanted in farming and writing poetry, and his reaction to Hugh's engagement was extraordinary. His letter telling him that in planning to marry he was 'missing his vocation', hurt Hugh so deeply that he felt unable to respond and asked Martyn to reply on his behalf. Alan did not disapprove of his friend's choice of partner; it is the phrase 'missing his vocation' that indicates his thinking. He was not yet a monk or even a Roman Catholic, he knew that Hugh was far too sociable to live the life of a recluse, yet he seemed to be assuming that the three of them, together or apart, had in some way been called to a particular way of life, that they would continue to live along Eastingtonian lines, austere, apart from their peers and spurning anything to do with the civilisation they abhorred.

For himself, the one thing of which he was certain was that he must continue his spiritual search, so he returned home to Burghclere and took a job tutoring a small boy for a couple of hours each day. This left him plenty of time for reading, as always his refuge, his stimulation and his emotional life. His reading had rarely been haphazard, but now it was becoming more focused, as if he was being drawn towards his destiny. Having spent many hours at Eastington reading the Old Testament, he progressed naturally to the New Testament and, as when he was reading philosophy, the doors of perception opened up before him as he read.

He started with St Mark, thinking to find in the earliest Gospel the most authentic portrait of Christ, and met a vibrant figure, free from the idealisation of Renaissance paintings or the simpering accretions of the Victorians. Here was truth and he could no more doubt the character and personality of this man than he had doubted that of Socrates or Marcus Aurelius. When he went on to St Matthew and St Luke and compared the different versions of the birth of Christ and the Resurrection he was again overwhelmed by this impression of truthfulness, the quality he had always sought in literature. Any discrepancies in the different accounts and the fact that no attempt had been made to iron them out increased rather than shook his belief, for it rang true. It was many years before his mind was clear on the subject, but now he accepted that there was an objective truth in the Gospels that had to be faced. St John's Gospel forced him to face this conviction at an even deeper level, for he was in no doubt that it was the record of an experience of unfathomable depth: 'I realised that to reject this would be to reject the greatest thing in all human experience; on the other hand, to accept it would be to change one's whole point of view. It would be to pass from reason and philosophy to faith.'[1]

There it was, stark and uncompromising. He was caught, as he was so often to be, between the polarities of reason and faith, intellect and experience, mind and heart. He had no intention of discarding reason, but it was wholeness, the inner truth, that he was seeking. At Oxford and at Eastington he and his friends had sought truth through imagination, especially through poetic imagination; now, as he went on to read St Paul, he realised that faith was the very thing they had been seeking. Hardly had he absorbed this revelation when, like waves crashing impatiently ashore, he found he had to revise his attitude to the Church. Perhaps the Church was not, as he had previously believed, an outdated institution of only social significance, perhaps it transcended this world, perhaps it spoke of a new humanity. He had been corresponding with C. S. Lewis on the text 'As in Adam all die, even so in Christ shall all be made alive', and now he realised that 'the Church was nothing less than this new humanity . . . it was a social organism of which Christ was the "head" and all men were potentially its members'.[2] He continued to read Richard Hooker, generally considered to be one of the Church of England's greatest theologians, and began to go to communion at his local church.

But this was not the happy ending of fairy stories; in fact, it was not an ending at all. His decision to attend church regularly provided him with a routine and a practice, he found constant delight in the beauty of the Church of England services, but still he had not found faith. He continued to read. He read the *Summa Theologica* of St Thomas Aquinas, finding in it 'the complete philosophical justification for Christianity'[3] and the

Ecclesiastical History of the English People by Bede, the monk known as the 'Father of English History' whose name he was later to adopt. Given his time at Oxford and the extent of his reading, it is hard to believe that, until he read Bede, he had not realised that the Church of England had been part of the Roman Church just as England had once been part of the Roman Empire. Such a gap in his knowledge reflected the prejudice felt towards Roman Catholics when Alan Griffiths was a young man. It was a time when top jobs were often denied to Catholics and when children at Church of England schools were known to throw stones at Catholic children.

It had never occurred to Alan that the old English village churches he so loved had once resounded to the Latin Mass. In fact, he had not really thought very much about the Roman Catholic Church at all; it was something foreign, strange and very frightening. He had known one Catholic family as a child, but had never spoken to any members of it; at school a small group went off to Mass on Sundays, but again the Griffiths family knew none of them; at Oxford he remembered someone pointing out a Catholic undergraduate to him, but it was simply a matter of curiosity. At home, as in society at large, the prejudice against Catholicism was emotional and unthinking, his father considering the Roman Church 'outside the pale', his mother saying that nothing would give her greater pain than that someone she loved should become a Roman Catholic. Deeper still, in Alan's opinion, was the prejudice that race memory had instilled into every English heart. 'The breach with Rome is a psychic event in all our lives, something which lies deep buried in the unconscious, but is ready to erupt into consciousness whenever circumstances force us to encounter it. It was this monster from the depths of my soul which I now had to face.'[4]

In the late 1990s, when the balance has switched, the ecumenical movement has been gaining ground and Roman Catholics are now the largest group of church-going Christians, this may sound extreme but, though few would have been as extreme as Alan in their reactions, his experience was not unique. The 'monster' had to be faced and Alan went on to read Newman, the Anglican clergyman who had shocked mid-nineteenth-century England by resigning as vicar of the University Church of St Mary's, Oxford, and being received into the Roman Catholic Church. He found that Newman, basing his thought on the Bible, the Fathers* and the Anglican divines of the seventeenth century, had followed a path very similar to his own and found it untenable. This disturbed Alan so much that he went to the Catholic Church in Newbury one Sunday morning to attend

*The writers on the Christian mystery in the first centuries of the Church.

Mass. He had read of Catholicism in Dante and St Thomas Aquinas, but to come face to face with it was another matter and the experience left him even more frightened of it than before. In the early 1930s, long before the changes of the Second Vatican Council, this would have been a Tridentine Mass and Alan was ambivalent in his reaction to the ringing of bells, the smell of incense and the muttering of unintelligible words. 'It attracted by its mystery, it repelled by its strangeness and uncouthness', he wrote.[5] Nevertheless, after the service he went to speak to the priest, who misjudged his young questioner and spoke contemptuously of Hooker and his doctrine of the mystical body of Christ, which represented the very heart of such religious conviction as Alan so far possessed. He left with a sense of injury and no respect for the wisdom of his instructor. Divided and torn as he was, this encounter tipped the scales back to the church of his childhood; he decided that Hooker's view of the Church as a mystical body without any fixed or definite form of organisation was as pure a form of Christianity as he could find. He rode to Oxford to see the principal of Cuddesdon College and, to his mother's delight, he decided to take orders in the Church of England.

If, having made this decision, Alan was allowed any peace of mind, it did not last for long. The principal of Cuddesdon College may have sensed some lack of certainty in his vocation, for he advised him to get some practical experience of work in the slums before starting his studies. It was not what Alan was expecting, but he decided that to submit to the Church's discipline was a test of his faith and in any case the idea of working in the East End of London appealed to him, so he went to the Oxford mission in Bethnal Green.

He found it intolerable. It was not the work itself, for he liked living among the poor. He enjoyed the nearby market, the fruit and vegetables displayed on the stalls giving him a reminder of the earth and the country for which he always longed. It was London and all that it represented that filled him with horror. He had been living very austerely, praying and fasting until he had become thin and weak, so perhaps he was even more sensitive than usual, but he could not find peace. He went to St Paul's Cathedral and Westminster Abbey, to the British Museum and the National Gallery, to try to recover his sense of values beyond those so evident in a great capital city, but to no avail. Everything that London stood for shocked him so much that 'I felt it as a giant force opposed to all that I loved, ceaselessly beating against the doors of my mind, breaking down my resistance and driving out the spirit of prayer . . . I felt this "world" around me, the world of time and flux and change and sensation, and I knew that it was at war with the world of that eternal order in which I believed.'[6] His deep unrest came to a climax as he realised how, despite his longing for experience, his religion had been external, involving his mind and to a certain extent his imagination but not his heart. He felt, as he had half-admitted to his Eastington companions, that 'Behind all my fervour and enthusiasm there had been an intense egoism'.[7] His discontent, until now projected on to the world, was turned on to himself. He was not clear what particular sins he had committed, he did not even really understand what repentance was, but he found himself repeating continually the words, 'I must repent, I must repent'. In this state of mind, fired by a resolution that had the force of a command and seemed to have nothing to do with his own will, he decided he must make an effort to break with the world that was destroying the peace of his soul. He would not go to bed that night; he would spend the whole night in prayer.

He went to the chapel at the top of the mission house, appalled at the irrationality of what he was doing, frightened of the isolation into which he was being driven, his reason revolting against this desire to repent. He was in many ways deeply conventional and though there was much about the world that he despised, he was still governed by its standards. To stay up all night in prayer seemed quite absurd, yet this impulse would not be gainsaid: 'Which was I to obey, this obscure instinct, this apparently irrational urge, or my reason and common sense?'[8] He followed his instinct, knelt down on the floor and remained there all night.

Though the urge to pray all night seemed irrational, it was will power that kept him there. The conflict he suffered during those long dark hours, the most intense he had ever endured, was about the place of reason in his life, yet it could not be answered by reason.

> The conflict went deeper than I could possibly understand. I had lived up till now by my own will. I had worked out my own philosophy and religion for myself and without knowing it I had made a God of my own reason. I had made myself the judge of everything in heaven and earth, and I acknowledged no power or authority over me. Even if theoretically I now acknowledged the authority of God and the Church, in practice I was still the ruler and the judge. I was the centre of my own existence, and my isolation from the rest of the world was due to the fact that I had deliberately shut myself up within the barriers of my own will and reason.[9]

Now the irrational had exploded into his life, instinct and common sense were at war; his reason could not control it and he knew no other way. He was literally and metaphorically in the dark, in a 'darkness which is outside the sphere of our consciousness, the abyss where all known landmarks fail'[10] and he was filled with horror. As the hours wore on he began to realise that he 'was being called to renounce the very citadel of my self'.[11] He had to surrender to a power beyond reason, yet this power appeared only as darkness, 'an utter blank'.

Alan had never before meditated on the passion of Christ, but now he felt that all he could do was to place himself in the Garden of Gethsemane, where Christ had faced the darkness of death and dereliction. Eventually, after long hours of agony, the thought came to him that reason was the serpent that was destroying his life and he determined to listen to it no longer. Immediately the conflict ceased. He resisted the almost overwhelming temptation to go to bed and stayed kneeling on the floor, his mind fixed firmly on the figure of Christ.

By the next morning he was weak and dazed, worn out and hopeless, almost in despair. He did not know what was to become of him; his long dark night did not seem to have led him to any conclusion or offered him any course of action. As he was leaving the room he heard a voice, an inner voice yet one that was not his own, say: 'You must go on a retreat.' As he barely knew what repentance meant, so he did not know what a 'retreat' was – he had a vague idea it might be some sort of clerical conference. He went to a nearby Anglo-Catholic church and asked the priest if there was a retreat to which he could go. There was. With the strange synchronicity that sometimes happens at moments of great crisis, it was not far away and it was beginning that morning.

The retreat was being given by the Cowley Fathers, the colloquial name for the priests of the Society of St John the Evangelist. An elderly priest talked of the fundamental doctrines of Christianity – of original sin and redemption, of the Incarnation and the Holy Trinity. He talked simply and personally and Alan realised with shame that, though he had studied philosophy and theology, knew some church history and doctrine, he had somehow never heard the simple truth of the Christian faith. Worse, he had rejected the Church and gone his own way without really knowing what it was he was rejecting. Now the repentance for which he had felt so blind a need swept over him like a flood. Tears poured from his eyes as he made his first confession and his whole being seemed renewed. After the agony and despair of the preceding night he had found the peace and joy he was seeking. He was in the kind of state for which it is almost impossible to find words, but he manages to convey something of his experience, which must surely have been one of those states variously called a 'peak experience', enlightenment, *satori* or *kensho*.

That eternal truth and beauty which the sound of London threatened to

banish from my sight was here the universal law . . . Everything seemed to
lose its harshness and rigidity and to become alive . . . When I went outside
I found that the world about me no longer oppressed me as it had done. The
hard casing of exterior reality seemed to have been broken through, and
everything disclosed its inner being. The buses in the street seemed to have
lost their solidity and to be glowing with light. I hardly felt the ground as I
trod . . . I was like a bird which has broken through the shell of its egg and
finds itself in a new world; like a child who has forced itself out of the womb
and sees the light of day for the first time.[12]

That evening, opening the Bible at random, he read St John's words,
'Not that we loved God, but that he loved us', and he began to understand
what had happened to him. All the time he had thought he was seeking
God, he had not realised that God was seeking him. His experiences at
school, reading poetry, studying philosophy, searching for the truth of
Christianity – in all these he had made himself the centre, studying the
reflection rather than the reality. Now he was on his knees before God,
acknowledging his own nothingness. 'I was no longer the centre of my life
and therefore I could see God in everything.' He was filled with love:

And now I felt that love had taken possession of my soul. It was as though a
wave of love flowed over me, a love as real and personal as any human love
could be, and yet infinitely transcending all human limitations. It invaded
my being and seemed to fill not only my soul but also my body. My body
seemed to dissolve, as things about me had done, and felt light and buoy-
ant. When I lay down I felt as though I might float on the bed, and I experienced such rapture that I could imagine no ecstasy of love beyond it.[13]

Such states do not last; on this earth they cannot. When Alan returned
home to Burghclere, thinking his troubles were over, it was to find the rapture fading and his troubles increasing. Now he was overcome by a compulsive asceticism, a course on which he did not intentionally embark and
which had little to do with reason. With the return of the old passion came
a new trial, as every night he was overwhelmed by the thought that he
should not go to bed but stay up in prayer: 'I seemed to see the darkness
opening up in front of me again, and something seemed to urge me to cast
myself into it.'[14]

He had not totally lost his grip on reality, but he knew that he was close
to breakdown and was restrained as much by fear as by reason. What lay
behind these extreme reactions, these overwhelming urges? He had been
reading the lives of the saints and knew about their ascetic practices – did

he unconsciously want to resemble them? It seems unlikely, for he knew that these practices were no longer in favour and, conventional as, at heart, he was, he was very conscious that people must find his behaviour odd, which was not something he wanted; indeed, he wrote wistfully to Martyn saying: 'I hardly know what my friends must think of me now.'[15] Whatever the psychological reasons for his obsession there seems no doubt that these impulses to fasting and excessive hours of prayer came uninvited and unwelcomed. Nor did he relish the thought of the exhaustion that he knew followed a night of prayer. He tried to live an outwardly normal life, but found that without asceticism his inner life became dull and empty.

He turned to the mystics, finding some comfort in Christians like Johann Tauler and Henry Suso, but was driven into further confusion by Hindu and Buddhist mysticism. Was God a person, as Christians believe? Could he be conceived impersonally, like Brahman? Might the Absolute Reality be a state, like the Buddhist Nirvana? His mind was in chaos; he must have thought that he was going mad. He decided to follow the example of the Desert Fathers and find a remote place where he could be absolutely alone, leading a life of prayer and meditation and waiting for God's will for him to be revealed. He had saved some of the money he had earned as a tutor and thought he should be able to find a small cottage and live on a shilling a week, so, putting all his worldly possessions in a knapsack, he left home to find a place he had once noticed while walking in the Cotswolds. His mother was, as always, sympathetic, but Alan admitted, though surely putting it rather mildly, that 'naturally she cannot understand altogether'.[16] Loving mother that she was, she must have suffered for her tormented son, but she probably knew that he did not understand what he was doing any more than she did.

Alan went to Ford Farm in the Cotswolds, where he had stayed before with Martyn and Hugh, and soon found the signpost he remembered, pointing up to a desolate place to which the postman had told him no one ever came. He followed the path and soon saw a little one-roomed thatched cottage by the side of a wood – the ideal hermitage. To his great disappointment the local farmer told him that it had been let that very day, but took him to some cottages further up the valley. There, on sheep-filled open pasture at the top of the hill, about 900 feet up, he found what he wanted: a two-roomed cottage with bare boards and rafters, no heating, lighting or sanitation, but warm and watertight. He agreed terms with the farmer and arranged for his next-door neighbours, a farm labourer and his wife, to do his washing and to provide him with some cooked vegetables at midday. He then wrote asking Martyn to bring over the bed and straw mattress he had used at Eastington and bought himself a sleeping bag, a table, a stool and a clock. 'Thoughts are all turned inward now', he wrote to Martyn, 'for it is there and not in nature that I believe the kingdom of heaven is to be found.'[17] He hung a crucifix over the table and began a life of continuous prayer and meditation.

Extreme asceticism once more had him in its grip, now made worse by his inability to find a way of life which satisfied him. He limited his recreation to an afternoon walk and cut out his midday meal, finding that the perfect basis for a simple life was bread, butter and milk, though periodically even this would be reduced to bread and water. If he went further and had no food for a whole day he found that 'a fountain of living water seems to open within me, and my soul seems to be marvellously refreshed'.[18] What should he do? On the one hand his spiritual life thrived on starvation, on the other he knew that if he followed this course too far he was in danger of becoming physically ill and mentally unbalanced. Though sometimes on the verge of some sort of insight as he read the Bible for hours or as he attended communion at the local parish church in Winchcombe, he could find no peace and after two or three months he could bear it no longer. Too weak and confused to get out of the hole into which he had dug himself, he wrote asking Martyn to come and fetch him. 'I have been a fool and a fanatic ever since I first led you to Eastington', he wrote.[19] He had thought he had renounced the world for ever, but he was wrong; he would go to Cuddesdon after all.

As soon as he had dropped the letter to Martyn into the box he felt ashamed; he had come to this remote spot in response to what he believed to be a call from God and already he was giving up. He went to bed in great distress, confused thoughts churning round in his head, and woke in the morning knowing what he had to do. The question was simple: was he going to live according to the values of the world or according to his faith in God? He had felt the power of God at school; at Eastington he and his friends had tried to break with the post Industrial Revolution world; in his painful night-long struggle at the mission house he had renounced reason; now he must hand over his will to God.

He was determined to pray without reserve; he resolved to cast himself on his knees before God and not to rise until he had found an answer. Once again he shut himself up in a tiny room with only a skylight to remind him of the world, he placed himself in imagination at the foot of the cross and began to pray without inhibition, pouring his heart and soul into a passionate plea for help. He was carried away by a great wave of prayer and almost immediately the answer came, an answer of such clarity and such astonishing simplicity that he couldn't understand why he had not thought of it before. He realised that his way of life, with its extreme asceticism and denial of the world, was not one in which he should continue. He saw quite clearly that he should stay where he was, but that he should take work on the farm and give up trying to order his life for himself. This simple solution left him feeling totally at peace.

Many people have had moments of this sort of clarity, a blinding simplicity that follows hours of wrangling, anguished questions and tortured explanations. But an added dimension to Alan's experience was that he had started praying at about eight o'clock in the morning and when he rose he thought, if he bothered to think at all, that he had been on his knees for perhaps two hours. When he sat down to write again to the long-suffering Martyn, telling him not to come, he looked at the clock and realised he had nearly missed the last post, for it was four o'clock in the afternoon. For eight hours he had virtually lost consciousness; he had been in a very deep place, beyond the world of space and time:

> It is here that the soul is at all times in direct contact with God. For behind all the phenomena of the world, behind the sights and sounds, behind the forms and energies of nature, there is the ever active presence of God, which sustains them in their being and moves them to act. It was into this region that I believe I was drawn at this time, and my will in the silent depths of its being reached out to the will of God.'[20]

He had struggled against every renunciation he felt was being demanded of him, yet once he had placed himself in the hands of a power beyond himself he knew then that he must stay governed by that will, not his own.

Alan's life began to take on at least a semblance of normality, though it was a long way from the lives that his friends and contemporaries were leading and it is easy to forget that he was only twenty-six years old. The next day he began to work on the farm and took regular meals with the farmer and his wife; once again he felt part of a human family and his life had some sort of pattern. Though he said that he was 'still as big a fool as ever in all work on a farm',[21] he had by now learned to milk, so every morning before breakfast he helped with the cows, then spent the day working with Ted, the shepherd. Ted was a Welshman who read the Bible in his own language, and as they worked, perhaps spending a whole morning searching for a lost sheep, both men were aware, as indeed Alan had been at Eastington, of the biblical background to the shepherd's life. At least partially back in the world, he no longer sought complete isolation and he renewed his friendship with Michael Cardew, who was still living nearby and who now had an assistant in his pottery, Barbara Millard. Alan took to her immediately. Barbara was a South African, brought up in a remote part of Southern Rhodesia (now Zimbabwe) and the two shared a love of the open countryside as well as a deep interest in religion. At the weekends they would spend whole days in the hills together, go to church at Winchcombe, and discuss their shared difficulties with the Church of England. Alan even wondered about marriage, but soon decided that theirs was a relationship of friendship, not love, though he told her when they parted that he would never really feel separated from her. This was indeed the case, for after Barbara returned to South Africa and married they corresponded regularly, until her husband wrote saying that she had been killed falling off a horse. 'I think I realised then for the first time', he wrote, 'the true nature of a friendship which is founded on the love of God, and which unites two people in such a way that even death cannot divide them.'[22]

Marriage was not to be Alan's way. Nor, though in later life he said thoughtfully to a homosexual man asking for his advice, 'When I was young I might have been a homosexual', did he ever have a sexual partner. His sexual feelings, which caused him great anguish and which he was eventually to speak about quite freely, were never to find physical expression; all his energy was directed towards his search for God. Now, with Barbara's departure, he once more had time for reading and, with no particular intention, he bought Newman's *Development of Christian Doctrine*, in which the author defends his change of allegiance from the Church of England to Roman Catholicism. Almost immediately Alan found himself drawn again to the question of whether he should join the Church of Rome. He had become convinced that the Church was founded on historical reality; his problem now was to find the connection between the primitive simplicity of the Gospels and the complex structure, the elaborate dogma and ritual, that was the Roman Catholic Church. Newman, by seeing that the Church is a living organism, beginning like a seed in the New Testament and gradually developing, gave him his answer: 'I realised then clearly that the Church was indeed the mystical body as I had believed it to be, but that it was no more possible for the Church to grow without a corresponding development of dogma and discipline than for the human body to grow without developing bones and muscles.'[23] At the same time he came to the conclusion that continuity, the thread running from the time of the Apostles to the present day, could be better found in the Roman Church than in the Church of England. He also felt affirmed by Newman's support of his own feeling that the New Testament, while first and foremost a record of facts, was also a poetic history: 'There were no abstract philosophical concepts; all was expressed in the richly symbolic terms of poetry and imagination.'[24]

As he worked on the farm, these thoughts turned endlessly round in his head and he remembered a moment when they were topping turnips in a frost, the cold so intense that it was an effort to take hold of the icy leaves, and thinking, 'If ever my life had been sane and my mind calm it was now'.[25] He had decided. He knew it would hurt his mother but it could not be helped. The force that had driven him remorselessly through so much pain for so long was now driving him to join the Roman Catholic Church.

This move from the Church of England to the Church of Rome is made by so many today that it is hard to realise just how significant a move it was for someone of Alan's time and background; just how great is indicated by the fact that he did not know a single Catholic priest to go to for instruction, or even where to go for advice. He did not even know if there was a Catholic church in the neighbourhood. He asked at the bookshop at Winchcombe and was surprised to learn that the Catholic Church of St Nicholas was just round the corner, so he went to see the priest, Father Palmer, who loaned him some books. Reading them confirmed Alan in his new thinking, but still something held him back; his mind was settled but he needed further assurance. He wrote to his mother telling her that he would do nothing until he had found the visible presence of Christ in the Church. The sign he was waiting for was to come very soon.

CHAPTER SIX

Love at First Sight

PRINKNASH 1933–47

Alan's questions to Father Palmer, searching, anguished and astute as they undoubtedly were, cannot have been easy to handle and perhaps this is why, on 5 December 1932, the priest took Alan to a nearby monastery in Gloucestershire, Prinknash Priory, a community of some thirty Benedictine monks. Perhaps, on the other hand, the priest discerned a vocation in this intense young man. Whatever the reason, his instincts were right, for this visit was to prove decisive in Alan's tormented spiritual life. One of the oldest monks at Prinknash, Father Alban, recalled Alan Griffith's first visit:

> I remember him arriving from Winchcombe in a country tweed suit with knickerbockers and thick woollen stockings, satisfied with the poor curtained cubicle we had to offer him, a tall, lanky and intellectual young man.[1]

> He was not a bit stylish or fashionable, he looked like an intellectual farmhand, a young Bernard Shaw without the beard.[2]

Alan's joy at discovering Prinknash knew no bounds. He had read about medieval monasteries, he had visited abbeys such as Rievaulx and Fountains, but he had thought of these ruined buildings as relics of the past; despite his wide reading his preference for anything written before the Industrial Revolution had left him unaware that monastic life still continued in the twentieth century. At that time the Prinknash community lived in an old Cotswold manor house on the side of a hill, the view stretching over the plain to the Malvern Hills; the beauty of this natural setting alone would have drawn him, but he was touched at an even deeper level, for he perceived a beauty not only of a natural, but also of a supernatural order: 'The presence of God had been revealed to me that day at school beneath the forms of nature, the bird's song, the flowers' scent, the sunset over the fields; but now it was another presence which I perceived, the presence of God in the mystery not of nature but of Grace.'[3]

It was love at first sight. Like many people before him, he was moved by the white habits of the monks, the chants and ceremonies, the order and dignity of the life, but above all he was impressed by the spirit of kindness and charity in the place, which he soon traced back to the Rule of St Benedict: 'Let all guests who come be treated like Christ himself, for he will say, I was a stranger and you took me in.' During the six weeks that he stayed at the priory enjoying Benedictine hospitality, he came to see that prayer did not have to be the source of pain and turmoil, as had been his recent experience; he saw that for these monks it was as normal as eating and drinking – it was the very breath of life. This was the life that, blindly and unconsciously, he had been seeking for years, though he had had no idea it was there to be found. He also saw his discovery of Prinknash as the sign he had been seeking and for which he had promised his mother he would wait. He hesitated no longer. After less than three weeks, on Christmas Eve, he was received into the Roman Catholic Church by the Prior, the Reverend Dom Benedict Steuart, and on a still moonlit evening, as he made his first communion at Father Palmer's church in Winchcombe, he knew that a new epoch had begun for him.

He was invited to stay at the priory for as long as he wished, and for the next month he attended the offices in church, spent hours in the library and was treated with great kindness and wisdom by the Prior. Father Benedict clearly understood very well the loneliness and suffering which his young visitor had endured; indeed, the legacy of excessive fasting was all too visible in Alan's pathetically thin and frail body. The Prior insisted that he ate every morsel of food that was put before him and, in daily conversations after dinner in the refectory, he answered all his questions, to Alan's surprised relief dealing with questions on sex as naturally as those on theology.

It did not take Alan long to decide that he wanted to become a monk, but, like many converts, his immediate wish was to preach the truth he had now discovered. Would he be able to do that better as a Dominican or a Franciscan? His reading soon led him to realise that just as preaching had occupied only a few years of Christ's life, the greater part being passed in obscurity in Nazareth, so a monk could follow this example – he could leave the world and lead a hidden life of prayer and work. Alan saw that Christianity was not just a doctrine to be preached but a life to be lived. On

15 January 1933 he was clothed as a postulant and entered the monastery to 'try his vocation'. The normal period of postulancy was six months, but because he had so recently been received into the Church, he was given a year.

Now known as Brother Alan, he started on his new way of life with the enthusiasm and total commitment with which he tackled every new venture. 'I am hoping by retiring into a monastery to withdraw my mind altogether from the wisdom of this world, and to give myself up to the contemplation of heavenly things,' he wrote to Martyn Skinner.[4] But, as always, nothing in his spiritual life was easy; hardly had he donned the black robes then worn by postulants than he encountered what he called 'the first great crisis of my monastic life'.[5] It was perhaps an unusual problem: the life was not austere enough for him. He was used to a far sterner regime – eating little, praying much, living as simply as it was possible to live and remain a human being. Now he had to eat meals that were admittedly simple, but which included fruit and vegetables, cheese, eggs and fish. The beds he could accept – they were made of wood, the mattresses of straw – the cells, furnished only with a desk and a chair, passed his litmus test of asceticism. The real shock to this ardent young man longing for a life of sacrifice was that he had to endure hot baths and central heating 'and other luxuries of that kind'.[6]

There was always reading in the refectory at meal times, and quite soon after he entered the monastery and encountered this problem of what seemed to him an insufficiently ascetic life-style, the reading was about the Cistercians and the greater austerity which they introduced into the Benedictine life. Immediately he asked permission to visit the nearest Cistercian monastery, which was on Caldey Island. The Prior had the good sense to let him go, and Alan discovered 'that what I had been seeking was a fantasy under which my own self-will was disguised'.[7] As they sat in formal rows at desks reminding him of his schooldays, he realised that, whatever the merits of the life, it was not for him. He would have returned immediately to Prinknash, but the Prior wisely insisted that he stayed a couple of weeks to be quite sure.

Though it is tempting to smile indulgently at this passionate search for a more rigorous way of life, at the way fantasy immediately diverted him, if only briefly, from a full appreciation of the place he had just discovered with such joy, there was, for Alan, a real and very serious message in this episode. He learned about the humility and obedience essential for the monastic life.

This is, I suppose, the hardest lesson which it is possible for anyone who has been brought up in habits of independence to learn. Neither humility nor obedience had had any meaning for me, and it was characteristic that I had never even recognised them as virtues to be found in Christ. Now I began to see that the whole life of Christ could be regarded as one long act of obedience to the will of his Father.[8]

Alan had been so independent for so long, following his own promptings, deciding for himself what he was to eat, how long he should spend in prayer and how long he would allow himself to sleep. However spiritual his intentions, he had been working out his *own* ideal, heeding no other person, still less any other institution; for him to submit to a way of life imposed from outside was a task of Herculean dimensions. It did not take him long to see that self-will, like the devil, could appear in many guises; it could be an inappropriate desire to preach the Gospel, to live an unduly austere life or indeed to crave any form of spiritual ambition. He had to learn to submit to the humility and obedience which are the basis of monastic life. And he did. Hard though this was, there was one great compensation: he had at last found a community and a way of life. This was a case of finding his life by losing it. He had been isolated for too long; now he wanted nothing more than to lose himself in the community and their long-tested way of life.

What, then, of this community to which Alan had been so mysteriously and so propitiously led? Attempting to re-establish Benedictine life in the Church of England, a group of monks settled in 1906 on the tiny island of Caldey, two miles south of the Welsh coast and the home of religious communities since the sixth century. In 1913 the whole community became Roman Catholics and in 1928, only five years before Alan's arrival, they moved to Prinknash Park and were affiliated to the Cassinese Congregation of the Benedictine Order.*

The Benedictines were founded in the sixth century by St Benedict of Nursia who has come to be known as the 'Father of Western Monasticism' and whose Rule reached Britain in the seventh century and became the norm of English monasticism. Unlike the other great religious orders they do not, strictly speaking, constitute a single order, but are a confederation of many congregations, alike only in that they all follow, respect and treasure the Rule of St Benedict. So Alan, in joining the Prinknash community, was becoming both a Benedictine and a member of what was then called the

*Congregation: A group of monasteries united by ties of doctrine and discipline.

Cassinese Congregation of the Primitive Observance, but which later became known as the Subiaco Congregation. It is the only congregation to have houses in every continent. It is also – and it is tempting to suspect that Alan rejoiced in this perversity – almost the only Benedictine congregation outside the tropics to wear white. The others are known as the 'Black Monks'.

The Rule of St Benedict is one of the great treasures of Christianity, praised by all, not least by the seventh-century Pope St Gregory the Great, for the clarity of its language and for its spirit of moderation. This was exactly what Alan, enthusiastic sometimes to the point of obsession, needed and he rejoiced in it. At first he could not understand that the community were living a contemplative life – to him it seemed a life of incessant activity and so, at one level, it was. The day was divided into three roughly equal portions; five to six hours of prayer, five hours of manual work and four hours spent reading the Scriptures and other spiritual writings. It was some time before he learned that contemplation does not necessarily mean spending long hours in total stillness and quiet, but is rather a habit of mind, a state of being continuously in the presence of God, not only in chapel but whether working, talking, eating or during the occasional periods of recreation.

The details of the timetable change over the years, but the principle on which it is built remains constant, the regular periods of prayer, work and study – one of St Benedict's great legacies – giving each day a balance that was balm to Alan's soul, at last allowing him some peace, absolving him from the need to make every decision himself as he had been doing for so long. As this was to be the structure of his day for over twenty years, and as this pattern was, in one form or another, to underpin the rest of his life, it is worth looking at in some detail.

The day is divided into periods of three hours, each one beginning with the chief task of the Benedictine monk, the saying of the Divine Office. When Alan joined the monastery the day began at 4 a.m. with the Night Office, a time when one might not expect to be feeling at one's most attentive. From the windows of the chapel they used at the time the view stretched across the plain of Gloucester and the Malvern Hills, in summer the song of the birds competing with the plainchant of the monks. 'I felt', wrote Alan, 'that we were joining our voices with the choir of nature in praise of the Creator.'[9] The Night Office was followed by Matins and Lauds, then there was a short break during which they washed, shaved and tidied their cells before returning at 6 a.m. for Prime and Mass, at which those who were not priests (and who would have already celebrated private masses) made their communion. So they would have been up, mostly in chapel, for three hours before 'pittance', which consisted of tea or coffee, bread or toast and butter, eaten standing up in the refectory. There was then a short break for reading before Terce and High Mass at 8.30.

At 9.30 the day's work began. The morning was usually spent in study, with a break for the midday office followed by lunch, eaten in silence as they listened to a reading, usually history, biography or travel. After lunch the monks had an hour off, known as 'Meridian', during which they could read or sleep, before changing into hooded blue cotton smocks for an afternoon of manual work. As a postulant Alan was given jobs like scrubbing the floors, keeping the boilers going, planting or lifting potatoes, helping in the laundry or, much of the time, doing building work. Soon after he entered, most of the community went down with 'flu and he found himself working in the kitchen. Some of the monks became skilled builders, but Alan, though willing, never acquired a particular skill and was employed in plastering, mixing concrete, breaking stones, perhaps building a new road or, later, digging the foundations of the new church. The afternoon would be broken by the office of None at 3 p.m. and 'caritas', or tea, like 'pittance' eaten in silence. Vespers at 5.15 would be followed by half an hour of silent prayer and a short period of recreation, the only time of the day in which they were allowed to talk freely. The last office was Compline, sung in the dark by the light of just two candles. At about nine o'clock they retired and after about six hours' sleep the whole cycle would begin again.

It could not be called an easy life, but Alan loved it. At last he was living out a vision of life in which there was nothing that was not holy and, crucial to his sanity, he was no longer an isolated outsider, struggling towards some barely formulated ideal with no one but himself and his reading to guide him. He had the support of a community, he had a pattern of life and he had the Benedictine Rule. He had found a life in which he was serving God at all times, whether eating, working, studying or in chapel, where he was deeply moved by the plainsong. 'I cannot tell you how deeply the chant affects me', he wrote to Martyn Skinner, 'it is the very voice of our prayer.'[10] He was also doing what he had tried to do since Eastington, living a life to which the rhythm of the seasons was a constant background: 'I was no longer a spectator merely, but taking my part in the universal plan, and I felt myself to be an element in an ordered scheme of existence.'[11]

At the earliest possible opportunity, exactly a year after he had been received into the Roman Catholic Church, Brother Alan was clothed as a novice and given the name of Bede. Though today monks usually keep their own names unless there is already someone in the community with the same name, it was normal practice in those days for the novice to be given a new, monastic name. It is quite possible that he was not consulted on the matter, but he was entirely happy with it, for the eighth-century Venerable Bede, the 'Father of English History', had been, and continued to be, important to him. The change of name is not without significance: for instance, Alan's feast day was no longer his birthday, but 27 May, the feast day of the Venerable Bede, and the date is honoured by the whole community.* Monks who may not be in regular touch write to each other on their feast days and at Prinknash it was a tradition that on the eve of a monk's feast day a bowl of flowers was put in his place in the refectory and everyone in the community embraced and congratulated him. On the day itself he was invited to take tea with the Abbot. (Nowadays it is usually something stronger.)

It was when he was clothed as a novice that Brother Bede, as he was now known, promised to observe the three vows of poverty, chastity and obedience, or, in the slight variation adopted by the Benedictine Order (which pre-dates the vows taken by the other religious orders), obedience, conversion of manners and stability. Conversion of manners – an acceptance of the continual call to repentance – embraces poverty and chastity, while stability means that the novice takes a vow to remain in a particular Benedictine community for the rest of his life.

To live a life of poverty was never a problem for Bede; as his fleeting interest in the Cistercian way indicated, he would have preferred a life of even greater asceticism. He had already decided that marriage was not for him. Stability was to become something with which he would have to wrestle, but for the moment the hardest of the vows for him, as for most new novices, was obedience. Bede was never a natural conformist, never found the path of obedience easy. He had spent so long in solitary study, struggling to faith almost unaided, that it did not come naturally to him to submit to authority and at first he found it hard to follow the guidance of his monastic superiors. He felt himself to be the polar opposite of St Augustine, who claimed: 'I would not believe the Gospel, were it not for the authority of the Church.' For Bede it was a case of accepting ecclesiastical authority only because he had come to believe in the truth of the Gospel. Though in later life he was to challenge that authority, it was, as other independent spirits had found before him, in accepting the authority of the universal church that his faith became secure; he came to realise that faith could not rest in individual experience alone. This did not exclude the exercise of his critical

*St Bede's feast day is now changed to 25 May.

faculties; in fact, the constant balancing of reason and faith added zest and stimulation to his studies. This was, after all, still the same man who had wrestled for so long with the great problems of faith; the same man who had gone to see Martyn Skinner in hospital and, after the briefest formal inquiry as to his health, had launched straight in: 'Now, Martyn, about papal infallibility . . .' Martyn loved to tell that story.

Any problems Bede may, indeed must, have encountered with this new way of life found generous compensation in his feeling of having arrived, of having found his true path in life:

> I had sought Him in the solitude of nature and in the labour of my mind, but I had found Him in the society of His Church and in the spirit of charity. And all this came to me not so much as a discovery as a recognition. I felt that I had been wandering in a far country and that I had returned home: that I had been dead and was alive again: that I had been lost and was found.[12]

Bede's spiritual suffering had been intense; he surely deserved this reward for his persistence in following so hard a path. He had, as any person with a true vocation would agree, quite simply fallen in love with the Benedictine life. More specifically he loved Prinknash. Just before he made his solemn profession he wrote to Martyn Skinner: 'I love this place so much that I simply don't know how I would live outside. I love every moment of the day, every stick and stone here, and every soul in the community, more than words can tell. And yet I find the life very hard in many ways, and I have a sense of the awful tragedy of life which almost overwhelms me.'[13] His passionate nature had found an object for his passion; his restless, avid curiosity had found a container, a context, from which to question the great issues of faith and life; his asceticism had found a balance that was simple and austere, but which allowed him to maintain physical health. His fifteen years at Prinknash, when he left the monastery only for the yearly community trip (for instance, in 1935 they went to Malmesbury by coach) or for visits to the dentist, were to be the most peaceful, in some ways the happiest, of his life.

At one level, certainly viewed from the outside, these years, with their regular rhythm of work, prayer and study, were outwardly uneventful and, especially in comparison to the turbulence preceding them, they were years when at last Bede found inward peace. But even a life withdrawn from the world has its highlights, and for Bede these were the ceremonies which marked the various stages of his monastic life. As a novice he would have had to go through the whole Rule, though Father Fabian Binyon, who has been a monk of Prinknash since 1950, remembers: 'At that time there was too much emphasis on what you were *supposed* to do and not enough on what you actually did.'[14] In 1934 Bede passed successfully through the three 'scrutinies', in which the senior monks decide whether or not a novice is suitable to continue, and on 21 December of that year he made his simple profession, becoming a 'Choir monk', that is a monk who has decided eventually to become solemnly professed. His solemn profession took place on 21 December 1937, by which time he was already studying with a view to becoming a priest. On 25 February 1940 he was made a deacon and on 9 March of the same year, at the age of thirty-three, he was ordained a priest.*

These events, stepping stones in the monastic life, concern a person's entire future both in the world and in relation to God and to humanity, and the ceremonies accompanying them reflect their significance. Bede was especially moved by the clothing and the symbolic prostration. The monastic habit consists of a tunic, a long undergarment reaching down to the ground, and a length of material with a hood attached called the scapular, which signifies the yoke of Christ. When a monk is given these clothes, he is symbolically 'putting on Christ'; Christ receives him into the community and he acquires a new status in society, marked off as a man of prayer. He then makes a solemn promise to observe the vows and walks up to the sanctuary, hands outstretched, repeating three times

> Uphold me, O Lord, and I shall live;
> And do not confound me in my expectation.

Next he is clothed in the cowl, a heavy outer garment with long sleeves, and kneels at the feet of the Abbot and all those who have made their profession, before they all exchange the kiss of peace. Then, for Bede the most significant gesture of all, the newly-professed monk lies prostrate on the floor of the sanctuary: 'He was offering himself as a living sacrifice to God in union with the sacrifice of Christ which was being enacted at the altar. From this time he had no power over himself either to possess anything or to do anything apart from the community to which he was joined. His life was entirely consecrated to God.'[15] At a half-conscious level this was what Bede had been seeking since his experience at school when he was seventeen years old. He expected it to answer his deepest needs.

---

*In *The Golden String* Bede anticipated these dates by a year in each case. The dates I have given are taken from the Prinknash archives.

Life in a monastery such as Prinknash Priory was, of course, concerned primarily with the life of the spirit, but during Bede's years a few events stand out, beacons in the regular routine of prayer, manual work and study. Most significant was that in 1937 Prinknash was made an abbey and the following year Dom Wilfrid Upson became Abbot. Abbot Wilfrid was the most extraordinary, versatile and dynamic man. He was remembered as a magician who could perform miracles with a pack of cards; a musician as at home accompanying a comic song as with plainchant; an expert illuminator; a producer of plays, whether religious or secular. He was renowned for his love of travel, once confiding 'that his idea of perfect bliss was sitting in a jet-plane hurtling over land and sea'[16] and his plans for Prinknash, for which he was unabashed in seeking publicity, were both ambitious and extravagant. Yet underneath it all was a shy and sensitive priest of great kindness, determined to see the good in everyone he met. After his death in 1963, Bede, feeling the obituary in *The Tablet* did not give a true picture, wrote from India:

> Those of us who knew him as an Abbot at Prinknash can witness to the fact that he was above all an abbot as St. Benedict portrays in his Rule, whose first concern was always for the souls entrusted to him . . . I would say that his greatest gift was as a spiritual father. He had a sympathy and patience, a humility and understanding of souls which was truly supernatural.[17]

This letter says as much about the writer as about the controversial Abbot, for Bede gives no inkling that the relationship between the two men was not always easy.

It was typical of the determined and impulsive Abbot Wilfrid that he could not wait to start working on his plans to develop the monastery. On the very day that he was blessed as Abbot he dug the first sod of the foundations of a new abbey church, expected to take thirty or forty years to build, to cost £100,000 and planned to be the most magnificent Benedictine abbey in the world. It was eventually finished in 1972, by which time the community had grown and Prinknash was attracting thousands of visitors, so Abbot Wilfrid's vision must be considered a success. But perhaps it was just as well that Bede was by then thousands of miles away, for he was always devoted to the old chapel and, though he spent long hours working on the site, was never enthusiastic about the new church. Indeed, one of his contemporaries remembers that while all the other monks were working away in a fever of excitement, preparing for Cardinal Hinsley to arrive and lay the foundation stone, Bede spent the morning in his study. It was not laziness, but simply that he had not been asked to do anything and could not muster up any enthusiasm over a project of which he had never approved. Nor did he like the famous pottery, which resulted from the building work, for in digging the foundations a rich bed of clay was discovered and the resourceful monks began to experiment with making and selling colourful ceramic ware. 'I think the whole thing was a mistake', he wrote, 'but the Abbot is commercially minded!'[18]

September 1939 was only a few months away, however, and hardly had work on the monastery begun than it was interrupted by the outbreak of the Second World War. For the next six years all human activity throughout most of the world was dwarfed by war, but it seems to have affected the life of the monastery surprisingly little, even though Prinknash, on the flight path to an aircraft factory near Gloucester and to an anti-aircraft base near Cheltenham, was considered to be a danger area. All the priests volunteered to become chaplains to the forces, but if the abbey were to continue and if the needs of the diocese, expanded by evacuees from London, were to be met, the Abbot could allow only one man to go to each force, so the remaining monks did air-warden service at the local vicarage. Bede took his turn manning the local air raid post through the darkest hours of the night, from 11 p.m. till 2 a.m., playing cards and giving yellow and red warnings when German bombers passed over on their way to Coventry. He found it all very interesting, though in later life he used to say wistfully that though he had lived through two world wars he had been completely unscathed by both; indeed, he often wondered at how little violence of any kind he had experienced at first hand.

His letters, particularly those to Martyn Skinner, indicate his reactions to the war and though, like everyone else, he was appalled by the hysterical character of Hitler's speeches and the utter monstrosity of his actions, unlike others he was convinced that Hitler would never invade Great Britain. Also unlike most people, he read *Mein Kampf* from cover to cover, approving of its exposure of the capitalist system. He had found the true centre to his life and approached everything from the point of view of Christianity, yet he seemed to forget that all over Europe Christian was fighting against Christian as he wrote that the crucial question of the war was 'Who was standing for Christianity?'[19] In April 1941, as Hitler was over-running Yugoslavia and Greece, his mind was firmly on other matters:

> My only real concern is with the grain of mustard seed which God has planted in our garden. It contains all my hope and joy and love; everything which wife and children and possessions mean to others. My whole happiness in this world and the next. I did not know that love could grow so strong (at least in one as weak as I am). It absorbs all my being and leaves room for little else.[20]

An admirable attitude in a monk, though Bede did not at that stage seem to share the idea that a Christian should have a Bible in one hand and a newspaper in the other. This was to come later.

Now that Bede had found the community for which he longed, what of his friends and family? In a very real sense he had, in becoming a Benedictine, acquired a new family; in fact, for some people giving up friends and family can be 'part of the thrill – it's as if you were jumping off a cliff.'[21] Bede, with his passionate nature and his tendency to live at the extremes of the emotional spectrum, would almost certainly have shared this view, would have regarded the sacrifice of all he had previously known and held dear as part of the challenge, his contribution to the way of life he was so grateful to have found. He was later to admit that he had not fully appreciated his mother's pain at, in a sense, 'losing' her favourite and talented son, at the time seeing it from his own point of view in the light of the Gospel text: 'Unless a man will hate his father and his mother and his wife and his children, and his own life, he cannot be my disciple.'

Nevertheless, for a man with such a gift for friendship it cannot have been easy, for Prinknash was one of the stricter of the Benedictine houses and it was normal for a novice to see his family only rarely and for friendships to be restricted to occasional visits and correspondence – and even that was further inhibited by the monks receiving their letters opened and being expected to hand over outgoing letters unsealed. As far as Bede's family was concerned, there is no evidence that they came to his clothing or to either of his professions, though he wrote regularly to his mother until her death in 1937. She died in a car crash shortly before his solemn profession and, despite the close relationship he had always had with her, his reaction to her death was surprisingly unemotional. 'I hardly felt any shock,' he wrote. 'The sense that the life of the body was over with all its trials and sufferings, and the life of the soul beginning to last for ever, was overwhelming.'[22] His brother Laurence must have reacted more strongly, for he was driving the car at the time and it was even suspected that the accident might have caused the heart defect from which he himself later died. Through the accident Laurence met Mary, who nursed one of the people hurt in the accident and whom he eventually married. When they were engaged he took her to see Bede at Prinknash and Mary, who recalls the occasion with wry amusement, remembers how she said to her fiancé, 'If I'd met Alan before I met you I would have married him. He's far better looking.' As for his father, he becomes a vague and distant figure, though Bede was constantly grateful for the devoted way in which his sister Barbara cared for him.

He never lost touch with his close friends, writing to Hugh Waterman and Martyn Skinner (though less frequently than he did later, when he had greater freedom), and occasionally friends would visit him at the monastery. One of the first was C. S. Lewis, who came to see him while he was still a novice. They had kept up a lively correspondence and, though Bede's letters are no longer extant, thirty-eight surviving letters from Lewis, written between the years 1933 and 1962 (the year before his death), and two articles written by Bede, give some idea of the friendship between the two men.

Well before he left Oxford their relationship had changed from one between student and teacher to the adventure of their shared search for faith, when, as Bede wrote, 'we were discovering the truth together and almost every day brought some new insight into the goal we were seeking'.[23] After they had been converted to theism, Lewis encapsulated their friendship in a rather charming line, curiously phrased in the third person: 'Both now believed in God, and were ready to hear more of Him from any source, Pagan or Christian.'[24] Together they had begun to appreciate the religious background to the English literature they read, which they called 'this Christian mythology', and together the idea that it might be true had began to dawn on them. They became Christians at almost the same time, both felt they were taking part in a Christian Renaissance and both published accounts of their conversions in the mid-1950s, Lewis dedicating his autobiography *Surprised by Joy* to Bede, whom he describes as his 'chief companion on this stage of the road'.[25]

Now they wrote to each other with intensity, mostly in affection though sometimes a note of irritation creeps in. Lewis once wrote to Bede that 'on the purely natural and temperamental level there is, and always has been, a sort of tension between us which prevents our doing much mutual good'.[26] This cannot have been the whole truth, for the two men would not have written at such length or shared so much had they not derived something from it, but after Bede became a Roman Catholic Lewis did not wish to discuss their differences and, an Ulsterman and a Protestant to his bones, felt that Bede was trying to convert him to Catholicism. He put his cards on the table soon after Bede had become a novice:

> I had better say once and for all that I do not intend to discuss with you in future, if I can help it, any of the questions at issue between our respective churches . . . I could not, now you are a monk, use that freedom in attacking your position which you undoubtedly would use in attacking mine. I do not think there is anything distressing for either of us in agreeing to be silent on the matter: I have had a catholic among my most intimate friends for

many years and a great deal of our conversation has been religious. When all is said (and truly said) about the divisions of Christendom, there remains, by God's mercy, an enormous common ground. It is only abstaining from one tree in the whole garden.[27]

On the occasion of Lewis's visit to Prinknash they seem to have had some disagreement, for Lewis wrote assuring Bede that he had no need to apologise:

My friendship with you began in disagreement and matured in argument, and is beyond the reach of any dangers of that kind. If I object at all to what you said, I object not as a friend or as a guest, but as a logician. If you are going to argue with me on the points at issue between our churches, it is obvious that you must argue *to* the truth of your position not *from* it. The opposite procedure only wastes your time and leaves me to reply, moved solely by embarrassment, *tu sei santo ma tu no sei filosofo!* [You may be holy but you're no philosopher!][28]

It sometimes seems as if Bede was determined to stoke the fires of the differences that Lewis had no wish to pursue. On one occasion Lewis reminded Bede that his last letter had included a line that had kept him chuckling ever since; it was 'You have no reason to fear that anything you say can have any serious effect on me.' Lewis responded with asperity:

The underlying assumption that anyone who knew you would feel such a fear is not only funny but excruciatingly funny . . . ask the Prior if he sees the joke: I rather think he will . . . You, in your charity, are anxious to convert me: but I am not the least anxious to convert you. You think my specifically Protestant beliefs a tissue of damnable errors: I think your specifically Catholic beliefs a mass of comparatively harmless human tradition which may be fatal to certain souls under special conditions, but which I think suitable for you. I therefore feel no *duty* to attack you: and I certainly feel no *inclination* to add to my other works an epistolary controversy with one of the toughest dialecticians of my acquaintance . . . as well, who wants to debate with a man who begins by saying that no argument can possibly move him? Talk sense, man! With other Catholics I find no difficulty in deriving much edification from religious talk on the common ground: but you refuse to show any interest except in differences.[29]

Lewis later apologised for being somewhat ill-tempered when he wrote this letter, which had riled Bede enough for him to recall it years later, admitting that his enthusiasm had been excessive. He explained that he had no wish to convert Lewis to Catholicism but simply enjoyed the debate, wanting it to continue.[30]

As we have only one side of the correspondence, Bede's contributions can only be surmised from Lewis's references to them, but it is clear that they sent each other their latest articles and books, giving appreciative though always outspoken reactions. It is clear, too, that the relationship between tutor and pupil had developed into one between equals, though there were occasions when Lewis rebuked Bede mildly, surprised, for instance, at the return of his 'anti-intellectualism' and questioning Bede's provocative suggestion that Jesus was 'essentially a poet and not at all a philosopher'. Over many matters they thought as one; for instance Lewis agreed totally when Bede wrote of 'escaping from the circle of morality into the love of God', adding, 'in fact you have written an excellent commentary on St Paul's view of the "Law".'[31]

Often they wrote of poetry. Both preferred American poetry to English, but Lewis, in disagreeing with his correspondent, summed up the changes in Bede's attitude from his time at Oxford, when he looked to poets and to poetry for the meaning of life, finding his greatest happiness in reading poetry and reflecting on nature and the world in its light, to later years, when he seldom opened a book of poetry: 'I think both your old attitude to poetry (when you looked for religion in it) and your present one (in which you reject it as a bridge you have now finally crossed) are equally based on an error common to all modern critics, that of taking poetry as a substantive thing like chemistry or agriculture. Surely the truth is that poetry is simply a special kind of speech.'[32]

Yet no account of their friendship would be accurate if it did not acknowledge that there were many areas in which they were far apart. Bede felt that Lewis was fundamentally conservative, one of the great defenders of the European cultural tradition; indeed, Lewis described himself as 'a dinosaur'. Bede, though steeped in traditional values, was essentially radical, soon to be seeking a new vision for the twentieth century. Lewis claimed not to attempt 'the precipices of mysticism'; for Bede, the experience of union with God was the goal of man's life on earth. Most of all they disagreed about the importance of the Church. Lewis had little interest in the Fathers, while for Bede they were the bedrock of western monasticism. Lewis was quite unconcerned about the Church as an institution, believing in 'mere Christianity', which he considered to be common to all committed Christians from the followers of the Salvation Army to Roman Catholics, and describing religion as 'a matter of good men praying alone, and meeting by two's and three's to talk of spiritual matters'.[33] Though Bede

81

was to become very critical of it, the question of the Church was all-important to him; indeed, it was the concept of the Church as the mystical body of Christ that had led him to embrace the Roman Catholic faith.

This dialogue between two minds, mutual respect allowing room for fervent disagreement, held a specially important place in the life of a monk with only limited opportunities for this sort of exchange. Bede never wished to exaggerate the differences between them – indeed, he felt that what they shared grew rather than diminished as the years rolled by – and certainly their disagreements never shook their friendship. Despite Bede going to India in 1955, the two men never lost touch and at their last meeting, just a month before Lewis's death in 1963, Lewis reminded Bede that they had been friends for nearly forty years. Looking back over these years, Bede wrote of his debt to Lewis's critical mind and his kindness, saying: 'There are not many things in my life more precious to me than that friendship.'[34]

In one sense, Alan Griffiths, in becoming Dom Bede and retiring to a monastery, had left the world behind, yet any leanings he still had towards the solitary life (being torn between a purely eremitic way of life and a life that included contact with people was a tension he found difficult to resolve as he grew older) were not to be encouraged, for soon after his solemn profession he was made guest master and began to acquire a continually expanding circle of friends from all classes and professions and from every sort of religious background. Monasteries have always been magnets for visitors, St Benedict's Rule stating that a monastery is rarely without guests and that they should be welcomed as Christ himself. At Prinknash there were usually five or six guests at the weekend, in the summer as many as fifteen, some seeking faith, some in spiritual crisis, some simply needing a rest.

Being guest master has its problems as well as its pleasures. Father Fabian Binyon, who has been guest master himself, says: 'You have to see Christ in the guest and it's not always easy. How you deal with nut cases, for instance. Some people think you have to put up with almost anybody, that you can't show them out, but you've got to consider the community and you can't encourage people to sponge on the community.'[35] The Rule says that there should always be someone at the door, and that would normally be the porter, but visitors would immediately be passed on to the guest master, who would have to deal with confidence tricksters and travelling salesmen as well as people in real trouble needing help. Sometimes there were visitors like Haile Selassie, the Emperor of Ethiopia, who was staying locally just after the outbreak of war and decided he would like to see the monastery.

Everyone who remembers Bede as guest master at Prinknash always speaks highly of him in that role. People were impressed at the way he would perform humble tasks, such as bringing guests hot water in the morning and drawing their curtains, as well as talking with them and helping them in their spiritual lives. He himself valued most the freedom his position gave him to meet people at a deep level. He recognised the value of offering kindness and a listening ear, but in the last resort felt it was only prayer that could give the sort of help people were seeking:

> Behind all words and gestures, behind all thoughts and feelings, there is an inner centre of prayer where we can meet one another in the presence of God. It is this inner centre which is the real source of all life and activity and of all love. If we could learn to live from this centre we should be living from the heart of life and our whole being would be moved by love. Here alone can all the conflicts of this life be resolved and we can experience a love which is beyond time and change.[36]

Bede was beginning to be seen as a man of deep prayer, a natural leader, even a possible abbot. It came as no great surprise to the Prinknash community when, in April 1947, Abbot Wilfrid Upson sent him to Farnborough to be Superior. Ironically it was his open-hearted attitude to people, the very qualities that had served him so well as guest master, that was to lead him into one of the most difficult situations of his monastic life.

CHAPTER SEVEN

Shattered Dreams

FARNBOROUGH 1947–51

In April 1947 Bede left Prinknash, its huge new abbey once more under construction now that the war was over, for St Michael's Abbey, Farnborough, a Benedictine foundation with a curious and rather romantic history. It was originally made by Premonstratensian canons, the building having been commissioned by the Empress Eugenie, wife of Emperor Napoleon III. Unfortunately, the Empress and the canons disagreed so badly that, eight years later, she persuaded the Abbot of Solesmes to replace them with a small community from France. The Empress was born in 1826, just eleven years after the defeat of her husband's famous uncle at Waterloo, and was a devout Roman Catholic favouring a strong papacy. With the end of the Second Empire, her family was exiled to Britain and, after the death of both her husband and her son, she assumed the role of *grande dame* in exile. She is proudly remembered, the monks referring to her affectionately simply as 'Eugenie'. The imperial crypt below the abbey contains the tombs of the Emperor Napoleon III, his son the Prince Imperial and the Empress herself.

St Michael's Abbey, a magnificent Grade I listed building whose French Gothic silhouette dominates the skyline for miles around, is her most lasting memorial and for some years the monastery had an international reputation for studies in liturgy, Gregorian chant and Church history. However, by 1946 depleted French numbers prompted Solesmes to offer the monastery to the Subiaco congregation under Prinknash Abbey, so Abbot Wilfrid, always eager to accept a challenge, sent twenty-five of his best monks, 'the cream of the community' according to Dyfrig Rushton, himself later Abbot of Prinknash,[1] paying Bede the compliment of appointing him as the Prior.

84

The new foundation was made on 29 April 1947, a short ceremony at which the Abbot symbolically handed the new Prior a cross, a copy of the Rule of St Benedict and a psalter. Bede was ecstatic. Less than two months after the move he wrote to Martyn Skinner: 'I have never been so happy in my life. It's like the fulfilment of all my dreams since we were at Eastington.'[2] This eagerness over new beginnings was to mark every change in Father Bede's life; he was a natural enthusiast. 'One of the things about Father Bede was that he would see his life in chapters', said his old friend from Prinknash, Father Fabian. 'The chapter comes to an end and you turn the page and the past is forgotten and everything is all coloured with roses again.'[4] There is no indication that his initial happiness at Prinknash was fading, but once the opportunity for some autonomy was offered to him he seized it gratefully. He must have known that he had leadership potential, that there were things he would like to do if he had the power base from which to do them. It is clear, however, in a letter from C. S. Lewis, that he also foresaw the difficulties in such a position, for Lewis wrote:

> I offer you my congratulations on your new office: my prayers you know you already have. There will certainly, as you anticipate, be a cross somewhere in it, but one mustn't assume crosses any more than consolations. You remember in the *Imitation* 'the devil does not mind in the least whether he snares us by true or by false pictures of the future.' In my experience it seldom comes where it is anticipated.[4]

At first everything seemed to go well. Bede's job was to administer the farm, the estate and the monastery; he was also Master of Studies and had responsibility for the smooth running of the monastery, the spiritual welfare of the monks and, with the help of a guest master, of the numerous visitors. He made a good impression on the other monks, who still remember his striking appearance and his punctilious attendance at every office, always one of the first to be waiting 'in statio' for the office to start; they appreciated the way he always took on his share of the manual work, however humble. They knew that he could be naive and gullible – he would not notice, for instance, if one monk played him off against another – but they loved him for his genuineness, his sincerity, his integrity and the way he practised what he preached. Father Magnus Wilson,* later Prior of Farnborough himself, said: 'He was a marvellous man. What he *did* meant that he didn't need to say. He taught by example rather than by words, as a monastic superior is supposed to do. He was always there. He was manifestly a man of prayer.'[5]

---

* Bede was Father Magnus's Novice Master at Pluscarden in the early 1950s.

They were impressed, too, by his learning and by the conviction with which he spoke, whether as a preacher or when giving the regular 'Conferences'. Those who knew how gentle he was in later life may be surprised that at this stage, in his early forties, the monks found him a strict superior, though always just.

It was, however, a tough assignment, for not only was it the first time that Bede had held an administrative position or indeed exercised power of any kind, he also had to cope with the problems inherent in starting what was essentially a new foundation, at the same time taking into account the feelings of the four monks, three French and one German, left from the Solesmes congregation. How, for instance, do you adapt a church to the taste of the newcomers, when that means offending the French by 'removing all the excrescences from the High Altar and the two side altars and making them more simple and dignified'?[6] And there was the constant problem of numbers. By the time that Bede had settled in and they had made the place their own, they were already losing men to Pluscarden, another new foundation Prinknash was making at the same time in Scotland. For the most part he remained determinedly optimistic, in 1949 writing to Father Aelred Carlyle (who had been Superior in the original days at Caldey Island) to tell him how happy they were at being a growing community and that the Juniors were 'the best group he had ever known' and will they please send some more. Yet the following year he had to admit that hopes were dashed when only one postulant decided to stay and the conclusion was reached that the community was not yet strong enough to fulfil Bede's ambition of starting a noviciate. The problem lay partly in Abbot Wilfrid's ambitions in starting two new houses at the same time, for, as Bede soon realised, they did not have enough young and able solemnly professed monks to man all three houses.

Though in this new position Bede was kept very busy, he always found time for books; indeed, one of the threads that runs consistently through his life is his intellectual curiosity. At Prinknash he had always read during the afternoon siesta and at night was known to disturb his neighbours by keeping on his bedside light to snatch reading time after the official 'Lights out'; he maintained this habit during his time at Farnborough and for the rest of his life. During this period he read Jane Austen, whom he considered 'a sound moralist' (he once said of her: 'I believe that she was the greatest moral theologian England ever produced').[7] He also read Dickens, George Eliot, Tolstoy, Lewis's friend Charles Williams and some of the books that were beginning to flow from Lewis's own pen, though the author modestly felt that Bede took *Perelandra* too seriously. He read the *Aeneid*, Aristotle, his favourite philosopher Jacques Maritain and Walter Hilton's *The Ladder of Perfection*. In spite of his now ambivalent feelings about poetry he continued to read Dante and especially enjoyed Gerard Manley Hopkins, T. S. Eliot and Coventry Patmore; he also studied German, Italian and Hebrew. While at this stage of his life his choice of books leaned towards the classical, even the predictable, as he got older he became more curious, eager to learn about new directions of thought.

A characteristic which was beginning to become apparent and which was influenced by his reading was the humility that kept him constantly reassessing his own opinions. In articles, books and correspondence, his views on, for instance, civilisation and industrialism, changed and developed over the years. Unlike so many people with strong convictions, he was as eager to hear other points of view as to express his own. One of the issues which had already begun to absorb his attention was the relationship between Christianity and other religions.

The tormented searching of his twenties, culminating in his conversion to Christianity, was over. He was never to regret becoming a Christian, never to falter in his belief in Christianity or in his devotion to Christ. Nor, in reading his correspondence with his fellow monks, can one easily detect any other strand in his thinking. But in his letters to his friends he is more open, more ready to explore tentatively the new avenues that were being revealed to him as his reading widened to include eastern religions. His exchanges with C. S. Lewis on the subject never got very far, mostly because of Lewis's lack of enthusiasm, but as early as 1937, the year in which he was solemnly professed, he had written to Martyn Skinner telling him how he was beginning to explore Buddhism, Hinduism and the writings of Lao-Tzu and to recognise their value. It was a matter of great urgency, he thought, that their relationship to Judaism and Christianity should be understood. Just before he moved to Farnborough he had discovered a translation of the *Upanishads*, made by Yeats with the help of an Indian swami and published in 1936, and for the first time he began to study eastern spirituality in depth. The great achievement of eastern religions was, he was discovering, 'to have seen that beneath all the flux of phenomena there is one infinite unchanging reality'.[8] This insight, still only at an embryonic stage, was to become central to his thinking.

Alongside his growing interest in eastern religions came a disillusionment with some aspects of western Christianity. At the time, and for many years, he was to remain convinced that, whatever the value of other religions, they could be fulfilled only in Christianity, yet he was critical of the

Church, longing to see the church of his dreams. In those days people did not openly criticise the Church and in even entertaining such thoughts Bede was in a minority; for the most part he kept his thoughts to himself, but he did confide in Martyn Skinner. In 1938 he had written that the Index of Forbidden Books (a list of books considered by Roman Catholic authorities to be dangerous to faith or morals, compiled in 1557 and not suppressed until 1966) was 'a survival of the old world which is an unconscionable time a-dying. I don't think anything can be done until it is dead.'[9] But poet and optimist combined as he maintained that there were 'seeds of life in the rotten apple' and that 'Soon you will see her [the Church] rising from the waves like Botticelli's Venus – but not the Venus this time of a pagan renaissance but the bride of Christ. It looks to me as though there will be a century or more of persecution for the church in which all rottenness will be purged away, and then, well, either a new Christianity or the end of the world.'[10]

Two years later he aimed his epistolatory guns at Rome: 'The Vatican is one of the best organised bureaucracies in the world, with wireless, telephones, central heating and everything up to date. But I always have the feeling that it is clogged and bound by the chains of tradition, so that really new life cannot develop . . . The old order of Christianity must go.'[11]

Some of this thinking emerges tentatively in his articles, as from his early days as a monk he had written regularly for PAX (the quarterly review of the Benedictines of Prinknash), becoming one of its most sought-after contributors. In the 1930s his articles, for the most part, inhabited uncontroversial ground – poetry in St Benedict and in the Bible, an enthusiastic piece about the second-century Christian apologist St Justin, whom he argues may be called the first Christian philosopher, an account of his own conversion, the mysticism of the English novelist Mary Webb, a long article welcoming the possibility of a reunion between the Church of England and the Church of Rome – but here and there a line creeps in hinting at issues that were to concern him more and more passionately. His preoccupation with industrialism, something about which his views were to change and develop throughout his life, found expression as early as 1938:

> The present industrial system compels the great majority of men to work in a manner which is incompatible with a fully developed Christian life, and often makes any kind of Christian life impossible. The condition of a worker in modern industry can only be compared with that of a slave in the Roman Empire: it involves a human being in a manner of life which is fundamentally inhuman; for it treats him not as a human person but as a unit of labour.[12]

In some of these early articles he put forward ideas that were unusual in coming from a monk at that time. For instance, he suggested that the West had much to learn from the East and that contact between the Church and the philosophical and religious minds of India might lead to a development of Christian thought; that the philosophy of the Buddha, though it might have the appearance of atheism, had a moral and mystical power which has hardly been surpassed; that the writings of the sixth-century Chinese philosopher Lao-Tzu revealed 'a most profound mystical intuition of reality, which comes at times very near to a true understanding of the Divine nature'.[13] Though he referred constantly to ancient wisdom, his concern was not simply to return to past times (as they had tried to do at Eastington) so much as to incorporate traditional values into the present, and indeed the future. For instance, he argued that in a world which can no longer claim to be Christian the task of the church of the future must be to reconstruct the whole order of society.

As with the Eastington experiment, it is sometimes hard to remember that Bede was writing, not in the 1960s but before the Second World War. Though the first English translation of the *Bhagavad Gita* had been made as early as 1793 and though travellers and colonial administrators had picked up some knowledge of eastern thought and brought it back to a small circle of their countrymen, such ideas were far from being common currency; in fact, to many they would have been shocking. For a monk to have come to these conclusions in his early thirties solely through his own reading, before he had known any other life than that of the English countryside, places him arguably ahead of his time, certainly at its cutting edge.

At Farnborough, however, it was not so much the dialogue between the different faiths that concerned him as the dialogue between Christians, though his arguments in favour of ecumenism tended to lead on to a recognition of all that Christians hold in common with Jews and Muslims, Buddhists and Hindus. He was delighted to read in *The Times* on 1 March 1950 that the Vatican had made a new pronouncement urging talks between Catholics and non-Catholics and followed closely the resulting correspondence, which indicated a deep and widespread desire for Christian unity. He wrote about it both to Father Carlyle and for *PAX*, maintaining that in an age when many believed in the values of materialism, even of atheism, the conflict was no longer between Christians, or even between people of different religions, but between those who believed in a spiritual reality and those who did not.

He was adamant that, despite divergences of doctrine, a study of the first five centuries of the Church must lead to a clear view of all that is held in common by Christians of East and West, by Protestants and Catholics. Though he had left his own Anglican roots behind and was convinced that the fulfilment and completion of every form of Christianity, as of every form of religion, lay in Roman Catholicism, he was (though C. S. Lewis would not have agreed) concerned with similarities rather than with differences: 'We have first of all to show ourselves in sympathy with every form of truth wherever it may be found, and this means that we must seek out the truth in every form of religion and try to relate it to the truth of Christianity. It requires of us also great discernment to discover what must be preserved in each case and what must be rejected.'[14] He longed, with a yearning more acute than was generally expressed by Christians at the time, for unity of faith among Christians and his belief that a start could be made by fostering friendly relationships between the denominations led him to pursue his own contacts. For instance, he had been in correspondence with Dr Selwyn, the Dean of Winchester, who brought a group of Anglicans to Farnborough for discussions; he was also in regular touch with various Anglican priests, including the Superior of the Cowley Fathers, perhaps remembering his first confession, made to a Cowley Father in London all those years ago.

One task which comes the way of many priests, particularly of religious superiors, is of instructing people in the Roman Catholic faith. Many will testify to Father Bede's ability to present Catholicism in a way acceptable to Anglicans brought up to fear 'bells and smells' and the papacy, and who were reluctant to join a church which was still a misunderstood minority. One group of people to whom he was particularly important in this way was the Taena community, a group of pacifists and anarchists started in 1942 by George Ineson and living at the time in the Forest of Dean. George Ineson came to see Father Bede at the suggestion of Toni Sussman, a pupil of the psychologist C. G. Jung and an analyst herself, whom Father Bede had come to know in the 1940s. She was a remarkable woman, described as 'Tiny and indomitable, relaxed yet glowing', who was known to say, 'Go home and meditate on the difference between the Important and the Essential'. Her interest in the unity of religions was visibly demonstrated by the Buddha placed at one end of her mantelpiece and the Mother of God at the other. She had a great influence on Bede, not only introducing him to Jung's thinking, but also encouraging his interest in eastern meditation.

In 1948 George Ineson took Toni Sussman's advice and stayed at St Michael's Abbey in order to receive instruction from Bede, mentioning the experience in his book *Community Journey*: 'Father Bede, who came to see me about three times a day, was extraordinarily patient; there was no preaching of the "take it or leave it" kind, he gave me instead the guidance of a native to a stranger in a far country.'[15] So impressed was Ineson by Father Bede that many members of the Taena community followed his example, and eventually the whole community became Roman Catholics. In 1950 Ronald and Hilary Seex, who had joined the community two years earlier, came to Farnborough to talk to Bede. Ronald was curious to meet him, though having heard that he was interested in Jungian psychology and eastern religions was not very hopeful that they would find any common ground, for these were things of which he had no particular knowledge.

> As it was I found he could talk about the Church equally in terms of Rilke and Wordsworth and I soon found that I could talk more freely to him than to any other priest I had ever met. We got on like a house on fire, he was the beginning of something quite different. My family were very much against Roman Catholicism but he made us realise it was human.[16]

Both Ronald and Hilary remembered long conversations in the garden of the abbey, with Bede sitting with his legs up after a recent operation for piles. He endeared himself to them by talking about Turgenev, Jane Austen and George Eliot; by not emphasising the catechism or talking much about dogma; telling them not to worry too much about doctrines like the Immaculate Conception, simply saying, 'Wait. That will come to you. Once you've got the kernel of it, it will be all right.' They were particularly impressed by the way he talked of the 'new creation', weaving his thoughts around St Paul's: 'If anyone is in Christ, he is a new creature: the former things have passed away; behold all things have passed away.'[17] In a moving, if slightly repetitive, article he suggests that Paul was thinking: '"To be in Christ, why it is nothing less than a new creation!" . . . it shows the utter transformation which is wrought in the world by the gospel. Something new has come into the world, something as new as when the first star shone in the firmament or the first living cell moved on the face of the waters.'[18] Hilary Seex remembered these periods of instruction with delight: 'He made it so warm and encouraging and positive. We responded to his inner conviction. You could give him your trust.'[19]

Such was Bede's success in communicating his faith that people flocked to see him, but while the response of Ronald and Hilary Seex shows something of the effect he had on lay people, the view from inside the monastery was rather different. The monks felt that his boundless charity and kindness to everyone who came to the abbey was excessive, that for the guests to outnumber the monks (as often happened) was disturbing to the life of the monastery. They were also concerned that a personality cult was developing round Father Bede and joked, only half affectionately, at what they called his 'apostolate of the parlour'.

There were a dozen guest rooms and Bede filled them with anyone who chose to come. Monks who were there at the time recall one visitor who would talk to an imaginary friend sitting next to him at meals, offering him forkfuls of food. He frightened the other guests so much that they would lock their doors at night, until eventually he was certified and taken away. Then there was a drunk who used to serenade the monks outside the windows. Bede would get out of bed to let him in and the whole monastery would be woken by the sound of the unfortunate man being sick as he sang his way up the stairs.

As one monk put it: 'Everyone who met Bede wanted to meet him again.' He was becoming a cult figure, attracting a mixed following which included young people, people with psychological problems and, as is often the case with charismatic priests, women. Some of these women wanted to advise him on the running of the house, and this worried members of the community who felt that Bede tended to be ruled by them when he should have stood his ground. And though there was never any suggestion of sexual impropriety, there were some whose devotion became embarrassing. One who left her mark on the community was Dr Mary Allen, who so idolized Bede that she modelled her life on that of the monks: she kept the same timetable; during the office she would cover her head with the hood of her white duffle-coat when the monks put up their hoods; she asked if they had crosses on their counterpanes because, if they did, so would she; once she hid behind a curtain in the chapel to hear a talk by a visiting priest intended for the monks alone. Bede did nothing to encourage her, in fact one story suggests he did his best to dampen her ardour. Apparently he would always call her Dr Allen while addressing another friend, Dorothy Rance, as 'Dorothy'. Why? asked the offended lady. 'Because she is special,' said Bede, with a remarkable (but perhaps deliberate) lack of tact. Dr Allen must have forgiven him, for when she died she left him a legacy which he put to good use in India.

The balance between obeying the Benedictine principle of welcoming the stranger as Christ and, as a monastic Superior, looking after the interests of the monks in his care, was not easy. It is tempting to take a romantic view of Christian charity and find Bede innocent of the charges later laid against him, though every monk who remembered his time at Farnborough was agreed that his hospitality was too indiscriminate; the only verdict that can be given, nearly half a century later, is 'not proven'. In any case his open-handed hospitality was only one of the reasons why he was not universally considered a success as Prior; another was that he was not a good administrator, which comes as no surprise, for apart from his lack of administrative experience he was by nature too impractical to succeed in a role that demanded at least a minimal understanding of plumbing, finances and the running of a sizeable community. Despite his time at Eastington it was said that he could not even light a fire, so he must have been slightly at a loss when, for instance, lead was taken from the church roof and he had to deal with the police and see to the repairs. These shortcomings in practicality were made worse by the fact that, as he once said to Ronald Seex, 'The trouble with communities is that they lead to irresponsibility because people join to find support.' Bede did not easily find people to take responsibility, nor did he have a good relationship with the one person who might have proved helpful, the bursar, especially because unlike previous incumbents, this Prior had the courage to stand up to him.

The real difficulties that were to decide his future lay deeper, in the complex area of autonomy (which Bede had welcomed on his appointment) and dependence. The Superior of a dependent community, as Farnborough then was, has very specific problems. On the one hand the abbey was insufficiently endowed and there was pressure to make the abbey, the farm and the estate financially independent; on the other hand a dependent house is just that – dependent on the mother house. In this case Bede was responsible to an exceptionally strong Abbot who wanted Farnborough and Pluscarden to be clones of Prinknash (for instance, over Christmas Abbot Wilfrid would visit the two dependent houses and identical celebrations would be held three times over). The Prior was there to represent the Abbot and he had to do what he was told 'at the nod of the Abbot'. 'Prior' was really only a courtesy title, he was in fact little more than a local Superior. It could be argued that the Abbot's intention was that the dependent communities should not feel different or neglected, that they should be confident that they were members of the same family, but all accounts agree that he did not give the priors of the dependent communities enough freedom. Father Magnus Wilson, who knew Abbot Wilfrid well, said: 'You couldn't move a salt cellar in the refectory without the approval of Prinknash – and that is a serious example.'[20] Bede was in an impossible position: for instance, it is not possible to run a farm when immediate decisions, such as how to treat a sick animal, have to be referred to a distant authority.

Abbot Wilfrid was becoming more and more dissatisfied with the new Prior of whom he had had such high hopes. On 18 December 1951 he came to Farnborough, saw the Chapter members and told them there was to be a change. Two days later Dom Basil Robinson arrived to take over and the very same day Bede left for Pluscarden. The official reason given was that Bede did not have the experience needed to cope with the difficult financial situation at the monastery.

It was a brutal way to carry out a decision that must have been hard for Abbot Wilfrid to make and traumatic for Bede. Opinions were, and still are, divided as to why he was sent away so abruptly and, even if his dismissal was justified, as to what the true reasons were. There were some who thought he had been an excellent prior and regretted his dismissal, others who felt he had filled the house with too many laymen, unemployed people and social misfits. Though his lack of administrative skills was the reason given and resentment at the 'apostolate of the parlour' the reason suspected, there was also the feeling that he had failed as Master of Studies because he exercised too strong an influence on the young postulants, teaching them about eastern mysticism, a subject which had not found approval on the Benedictine syllabus. And there was the sub-text, the possibility that Bede was too much of a leader, too independent, not sufficiently willing to do what he was told.

There is no definitive record of Bede's reaction to his ignominious dismissal, for by the time he spoke about it his natural optimism had taken over and he had forgotten how hurt he had been, but his friends were in no doubt, for Bede had written about the matter at length to Hugh Waterman, though Hugh, out of protective loyalty, told Martyn that the letter was so personal he had destroyed it. Years later Martyn and Hugh would still refer to what they called the 'Farnborough trouble' and the danger of a similar situation arising again. In 1970 Hugh wrote: 'I have always understood that what happened at Farnborough was what the Communists call a Personality cult of Dom Bede by the people round, and too much free discussion for Prinknash, which as a community that was converted always wanted to be Right by Rome.'[21] Martyn's response was that he had often wondered what happened to Bede at Farnborough and that he was still 'at a loss to know why he was so bitter about it', or why he had indicated a 'deep disillusionment about the monastic set-up'.[22] He suggested that Bede had been the victim of something like the intrigues in the university colleges of C. P. Snow's novels, but that there was 'No tinge of green in his apple'. In another letter to Hugh, recalling that Lewis had said that Bede had 'improved more than anyone else he knew and was a wonderful advertisement for the monastic life', Martyn wrote: 'You mention his recklessness, but he was no more reckless than Christ, Buddha, St Francis, Newman or even Albert Schweitzer . . . without being "ruthless" in this way, and giving pain to someone, it is impossible to achieve anything. I think he had a lapse at Farnborough, and a second lapse in resenting the correcting of it: but since then he seems to have done well.'[23]

Hugh Waterman, gentle, affectionate and valuing the friendship of Bede and Martyn above others in a life filled with friendship, could occasionally be surprisingly outspoken, almost harsh about his friend. In his exchanges with Martyn about the 'Farnborough episode' there is a passage which shows the way in which Bede matured and developed; the holy man he was to become emerging from the young man they had known for so long:

> I am sure largely unconsciously – he has got his own way with the ruthlessness of a tycoon. In fact, I didn't like to say this even to you when I last wrote, I think his bitterness at Pluscarden was the result of for the first time in his life not getting his own way and feeling caught in the System. He has never had to keep himself, or worry where next month's money is coming from and like many priests with good physical appearance and great charm he has always been powerfully assisted by women falling for him. I often think he is like St Paul (in case you think I am running down one of my two best friends) not only for his clarity of thought and expression and masterful disposition, but also – and particularly – the way he has become more tolerant with maturity: that is, tolerance which is a natural disposition with most people he has had to acquire with an effort and keep up with a discipline.[24]

The astonishing thing was that, disappointed, humiliated, even embittered, Bede never once criticised his Abbot personally, either his decision or the way in which it was implemented. Father Magnus is deeply impressed by this, for 'if anyone has a reason for feeling bitter against Wilfrid Upson Bede did, but I never heard him criticise the Abbot'.[25]

Bede honoured his vow of obedience in practice and in spirit as well as in theory; he learned from the experience, as Martyn realised when, again writing to Hugh of this painful episode in their friend's life, he reminded him of one of Bede's favourite sayings; it was undoubtedly a case, he wrote, of 'God drawing straight with crooked lines'.

CHAPTER EIGHT

Pluscarden

1951–55

Pluscarden Abbey is the most northerly Benedictine abbey in the world and one can only guess at Bede's feelings as he made the long journey to Elgin, a market town in the north-east of Scotland six miles to the east of the abbey. He had, in the words of one of the more forthright monks, been 'reduced to the ranks' and the physical distance (nearly 600 miles) that he was putting between himself and his old monastery, coupled with the cold, wet climate, must have added to his feelings of banishment.

Nevertheless he had come to a beautiful place, lying remote and quiet in a peaceful valley, in many ways a contemplative monk's dream. The monastery had originally been founded by King Alexander II of Scotland in 1230 and after 200 years as the home of a strict, though little-known, order called the Valliscaulians, the decision was taken to unite the house of Pluscarden with that of Urquhart Priory, so the white habits of the Valliscaulians gave way to the black dress of the Old Benedictines of Dunfermline and Urquhart. It continued as a Benedictine priory until the end of the sixteenth century, when the estate passed into lay hands and for nearly 400 years the priory buildings stood untended in the teeth of the elements, the roofs collapsing, ivy covering the walls, woodwork rotting and the beautiful old cloisters slowly filling up with rubble.

This was the abbey that the intrepid Abbot Wilfrid took over in 1948. He deputed twenty Prinknash monks to move to Pluscarden and one by one they came up, took a look and declined. (As the vow of stability is taken to a place, in their case Prinknash, they were under no obligation to go.) Eventually five monks, who became known as the 'Pluscarden Pioneers', decided to take the risk. One of them, Father Maurus, remembered the group arriving in the dark after being given a five-course lunch by some nuns in Aberdeen, followed by a five-course dinner at a convent in Elgin. Clearly the nuns knew what would greet them when they arrived at their new home. It was indeed chaos, and the work of restoration was to go on for years. Now, returned to something approaching its former splendour, it is serene and peaceful, welcoming 20,000 visitors a year.

Bede had, in fact, been there before. In September 1948, when monks from Prinknash and Farnborough travelled up to join the founding members for the formal opening ceremony, he had written about the occasion. In this unaccustomed role of news reporter he recorded how people flocked to the partially restored and only just habitable monastery from all over Scotland, many of those from the nearby towns and villages looking on the event as a kind of local festival. An altar had been erected on the site of the original altar, protected from the open skies by a canopy, and on either side were thrones for the archbishops of St Andrews, Edinburgh and Glasgow and several bishops of the Scottish hierarchy; the place was so packed that late-comers climbed up to sit in nooks and crannies in the walls. After the High Mass there was a procession, lunch, tea and another procession round the buildings, then the crowds went home and the monks were left to start their life of prayer and work. Bede sounded relieved that the place had become a monastery again: 'As evening drew on, we sang Vespers alone in the sanctuary, quietly carrying out the work of God as it had been done hundreds of times before, and then more than ever we felt that Pluscarden was once again a house of God, a living temple.'[1]

Pluscarden may be cold – it is on a level with Hudson Bay to the west and St Petersburg to the east – and Bede disliked the cold more than most people, but it is certainly a place of prayer and he loved the contemplative atmosphere. Nevertheless, although he never complained – indeed, it was not in his nature or in his vocation to complain – nothing that he has written or said suggests that he felt drawn to the place or that he was particularly happy there. Towards the end of his time at Pluscarden he broke his normal reserve and admitted to Martyn Skinner that, yes, he did find problems in monastic life:

> I think your criticism that too little is made of the stresses and strains of monastic life is very just. It is quite true that it came as the fulfilment of all my desires and satisfied my deepest instincts, but the stress and strain has often been appalling. In fact I often look on it as a kind of crucifixion and my prevailing sense is of profound disillusionment – I mean the sense that nothing in this world can ever give real and permanent satisfaction, and that everything – and everyone – betrays. But this is too much involved in my personal feelings for me to write about it with detachment.[2]

He had reservations, too, about the ecclesiastical side of monastic life. He did not regard himself as a pious person, more an *anima naturaliter Christiana* (a naturally Christian soul) and admitted that piety, in the sense of ecclesiastical ways and thoughts, never appealed to him: 'I still find many forms of piety in the church extremely tiresome and my instinct is always to flee from clerical functions to the hills!'[3] Too much should not be read into these admissions, for such moments of dissatisfaction come in every walk of life; given his natural reserve and determined optimism, together with the fact that he had to maintain a contented front in his day-to-day monastic life, there is some relief in knowing that he could face his negative feelings and admit that life was not always easy.

His fellow monks held him in high esteem, affectionately dismissing his interest in the East with, 'Oh that was just barmy – that was just him',[4] or, 'It was all quite beyond me'.[5] He was initially Master of Studies and was a great success in the role, remembered as an outstanding teacher, though one monk found him 'very intellectual, up in the clouds. We didn't always know what he was talking about.'[6] On the other hand, Father Maurus speaks enthusiastically about the way he made the scriptures live: 'He was nearer Thomas Aquinas than anyone I have met. He could have passed any exams in theology, he knew the texts inside out, he had that kind of memory. He lived the theology, his theology was prayer. After hearing him expound a sentence from the scriptures all you wanted to do was to go to the Chapel and pray.'[7] Father Maurus also recalls how he and Bede together asked if an extra period of *lectio divina* (a meditative reading that leads to personal prayer) could be inserted into the daily routine before Vespers. This was eventually granted.

More and more Father Bede was seen as a holy man with outstanding pastoral gifts. In May 1953, when the first novices were clothed, he became Novice Master as well as Master of Studies. John Ogilvie remembered him so warmly that he admitted to being almost in tears the day Bede left Pluscarden; his story is a touching example of how Bede's support affected his life. When John Ogilvie arrived at Pluscarden as a choir novice there was a general feeling that he was not suitable, partly because he suffered from very bad epilepsy, but he was desperately keen to stay and with Bede's encouragement he became an oblate. For forty years he worked as the sacristan, looking after the altar and the vestments, cleaning the sacred vessels, until eventually, well into his eighties, he was allowed to take vows and become Dom John Ogilvie. He never forgot the part Bede played in his life.

There was plenty of manual work to do in a monastery that had been a ruin for over 400 years and which was surrounded by nearly nine acres of grounds. Bede took his share, loving to work in the fields and to look after the poultry, enjoying garden work and 'pushing heavy weights about in a barrow'. His particular delight was making compost for the garden, arranging it methodically in layers, and he was remembered as someone who took real pleasure in showing visitors around, no doubt delighted to find new people with whom to exchange ideas. He continued to read voraciously during the afternoon break, re-reading Dickens, whom he had always found lovable, if sentimental, discovering Marcel Proust and Henry James, with whom he felt a particular personal bond. In a revealing glimpse of his own estimate of himself, he later said that this was because James was 'terribly intellectual yet getting into the emotional and the very subtle psychological world, observing the whole emotional world, in a way entering it and yet keeping away from it'.[8] He admired Carlyle and Ruskin, but preferred Hardy, whose 'roughness and uncouthness has a much stronger hold on me'. Again his reaction gives an insight into the passionate nature he tried so hard to conceal and control: 'I suppose it is that one learns to be afraid of being carried on the stream of one's emotion, and wants to be exact and truthful and sincere.'[9] He also continued to write, his growing reputation leading to invitations to contribute not only to *PAX* but to religious periodicals such as *Life of the Spirit*, *Blackfriars* (the monthly review of the English Dominicans), the American magazine *Commonweal* and the international Catholic weekly *The Tablet*.

Considering the full life of the Benedictine monk, with almost every moment accounted for, it is a miracle that he managed to write as much and as well as he did, for at this stage of his life the only time he could give it was half an hour after dinner. People who have lived with Bede often comment on the way he wrote, saying that he would sit thinking for some time, quite still, looking out of the window. Then he would simply write without pausing and without correction. This rings true, for his writing is always remarkable for its lucidity and, especially considering the complexity of some of his subjects, is easily accessible, but though he was a gifted writer he was too concerned with what he wanted to say to spend much time thinking of a telling image or a striking metaphor. A weakness in his writing, its occasional repetitiveness, which his friend Martyn Skinner remarked on and which can sometimes be mildly irritating, is typical of someone who writes fluently but who does not feel it is important to check his work thoroughly.

It was while he was at Pluscarden that he wrote his first book, an autobiography up to his time at Prinknash but, perhaps significantly, not covering the Farnborough period. The suggestion to write it came from an old

Oxford friend, Richard Rumbold, who, as a Catholic homosexual, felt himself rejected by the Church and perhaps empathised with the isolation that Bede had experienced in his early struggle to find his faith and his direction in life. It is surprising that someone as humble and reserved as Bede should have been able to write so freely at a deeply personal level, but he loved writing and longed both to do it and to do it well. He found he was able to regard his own story quite objectively, as if he were writing about someone else; as he was writing largely about experiences that had happened some twenty years earlier, in a way he was.

He called his autobiography *The Golden String*, from Blake's *Jerusalem*, feeling that with his early experience at school, his first intimation of immortality, he had been given the end of this 'golden string':

> It is the grace which is given to every soul, hidden under the circumstances of our daily life, and easily lost if we choose not to attend to it. To follow up the vision which we have seen, to keep it in mind when we are thrown back again on the world, to live in its light and to shape our lives by its law, is to wind the string into a ball and to find our way out of the labyrinth of life.[10]

In retracing the years in which he had followed up this vision, the often painful journey during which he had discovered first God, and then Christ and eventually the Church, he produced a book which was an immediate bestseller and is still regarded as a spiritual classic, remaining continuously in print for over forty years. It was well received critically. Philip Toynbee, writing in the *Observer*, called it 'A book of extraordinary and positive truthfulness . . . his experience is both genuine and very important'[11] and *The Tablet* regarded it as 'one of the profoundest, as it is certainly one of the best-written, spiritual documents of our time'.[12] It also – and this must have pleased its author as much as the reviews – had a powerful effect on individual readers; one, Abbot Aldhelm of Prinknash, became a Benedictine monk as a direct result of reading it. By the end of the book Bede had committed himself unequivocally to Christ and his Church, and in a moving passage he wrote of the Church for which he had such love, such high expectations and hopes:

> Thus the Church herself is the great sacramental mystery. Her hierarchy, her sacraments, her dogmas, are nothing but signs and instruments by which the divine mystery is manifested to mankind. If we stop short at the sign, then it becomes a wall which separates us from the truth: but if we enter by the gate of faith through the wall, then we discover the City of God.

We shall never rebuild our civilisation until we begin to build up again the walls which have been pulled down, and accept the Church as the guardian of the divine mystery. Then science and philosophy and art will once again recover their significance by being related to the true end of human life. Without the recognition of an end which totally transcends this world, science can only become a system of idolatry, philosophy can only contemplate the meaninglessness of human existence, and art can only disintegrate into fragments. But once we place the Church at the centre of existence as the guardian of divine truth and divine love, then the whole world recovers its meaning.[13]

When he wrote *The Golden String* he thought he 'had reached the end of his journey, at least as far as this world is concerned'.[14] But by the time it was published, in 1954, the golden string was tugging again and a new era was about to begin in his life, opening up ever widening horizons and bringing changes as profound as any that had gone before.

This new chapter in his life had had its roots at Farnborough, where he had met Father Benedict Alapatt, an Indian Benedictine who wanted to introduce the monastic life to the Church in India. Bede had taken a lively interest in the idea and when, in 1954, Father Benedict asked if he would join him in making a foundation, possibly under the auspices of Prinknash, he was eager to accept. Though at Pluscarden he had been very discreet about his interest in eastern religions – perhaps his experience at Farnborough had taught him that it was wiser to keep quiet about this side of his life – his first, almost instinctive, attraction had grown into a belief that from a Christian point of view the importance of Indian philosophy could hardly be over-estimated. Indeed, he felt that 'It marks the supreme achievement of the human mind in the natural order in its quest of a true conception of God.'[15]

He was reading and learning about other religions and was rejoicing in the similarities he found, pointing out how the idea of God in the Vedas* is almost identical with that of St Thomas Aquinas, and that if we can see the *atman*** in Christ, uniting God with Man, then Vedantic philosophy can be seen to form the basis for a Christian view of life. Again he observed how the Chinese idea of the Tao means simply 'the way' and was used in early Chinese texts to mean 'the way of heaven'; he had been reading a Chinese translation of the New Testament made by a Catholic convert, Dr Wu, and

---

*The ancient holy books of the Hindus.
**From the Sanskrit 'to breathe', so 'soul' or 'self'.

found that the opening lines of St John's Gospel had been translated, 'In the beginning was the Tao, and the Tao was with God and the Tao was God': 'In thus substituting the Chinese Tao for the Greek Logos, which we translate the "Word", Dr Wu has placed Chinese philosophy in the same relation to the Gospel as Greek philosophy was placed originally by St John's use of the word Logos.'[16]

Bede felt that in the Hindu conception of the *atman* and the Chinese conception of the Tao, mankind had gained the most profound insight into the mystery of God and that if these ideas could be seen in the light of the revelation brought by Christ there could be a development of theology as significant as its original development through the influence of Greek philosophy. He was very aware that many people have never encountered the Judaeo-Christian tradition, yet he was resistant to the idea, commonly held at the time (indeed still held by an ever-decreasing number of traditionalists), that one could only find salvation by becoming a Christian; it was urgent, he felt, that Christians should understand the relationship between the faiths. He was embarking on a difficult path, trying to hold the balance between appreciating the truth in all religions yet, in his confidence that they found their fulfilment only in Christ, implicitly laying claim to the supremacy of Christianity over all others.

Bede's interest in eastern religions was, however, far more than academic, it was deep in his bones, in his psyche, in his whole personality. It was not simply a desire for new ideas that made him long to accept Father Benedict's invitation; something deep in him was excited by the thought of a new way of life, by the need, as he wrote to a friend at the time, 'to discover the other half of my soul'.[17] It was also a disillusionment with western Christianity:

> I had begun to find that there was something lacking not only in the Western world but in the Western Church. We were living from one half of our soul, from the conscious, rational level and we needed to discover the other half, the unconscious, intuitive dimension. I wanted to experience in my life the marriage of these two dimensions of human existence, the rational and intuitive, the conscious and unconscious, the masculine and feminine. I wanted to find the way to the marriage of East and West.[18]

He wanted to go to India for his own interest and his own spiritual development, but he also felt that the prospect of helping in the foundation of the monastic life in India was of such infinite worth that he would be prepared to make any sacrifice for it. He was not blind to the risk he was taking. He later wrote to Father Michael Hanbury, a fellow Benedictine with whom he frequently corresponded, that even though the opportunity of going to India with an Indian monk who knew and loved his people was unique, it was a hazardous venture: 'I know that many people have no confidence in Father Benedict and it may be that we shall not succeed in doing anything, but I would gladly risk everything even to make a small beginning which might yet end in failure.'[19] The seeds of his thinking and of his changing personality were ready to be planted in Indian soil; no wonder he was so keen to accept Father Benedict's invitation.

It was not, however, up to him; he had taken a vow of obedience. He had to ask permission from his Abbot, the very same Abbot who had caused him so much pain by removing him from Farnborough. There is something immensely endearing, almost comic, about the way he wrote to his monastic Superior, knowing he should honour his vows of obedience and clearly wishing to do so, but passionately wanting to find that they need not conflict with his longing to go to India.

When he met with refusal he accepted immediately that the Abbot had reservations about Father Benedict, who was known to be a difficult man with a strong dislike of authority. He accepted too that Prinknash could not be responsible for another foundation – he knew from his own experience that having two dependent communities was already too much – but he could not let the matter go as easily as that:

> Does this mean that you don't want me to have anything further to do with it? If this is so, I am perfectly willing to accept your decision. But I talked the matter over with the Visitor, and he suggested that though it would not be advisable for me to do anything now, it might be possible later on, if Father Benedict succeeded in making a foundation under the archbishop, for me to be sent to assist him.[20]

All through the letter his readiness to accept the Abbot's decision seesaws with his wish to go. He is 'quite willing to give the whole thing up altogether, if you wish', but could he at least stay in touch with Father Benedict, who he admits is a 'very difficulty character', with a view to assisting him later on? He insists that he is not 'wedded to this in any way' and wants to do exactly as the Abbot wishes, but he would value the experience for himself and he believes that 'we have much to learn from the east about the monastic and contemplative life, but that is entirely secondary and does not affect my attitude'. Finally he thanks the Abbot for the consideration he has shown and plays what in a more devious man might have been considered his trump card: 'my desire to serve God in this way and the sense that it might be a genuine vocation was so strong. But it has helped me to realise how much I am attached to our community life and how much one must be guided by everything by obedience.'[21]

The Abbot was away at the time this letter was sent, and before he had received an answer, Bede wrote again, saying that Father Benedict wanted him to explain to the Archbishop of Bangalore why he, Father Bede, could not go to India. Would Abbot Wilfrid have any objection if he did so? And then he returned yet again to the substance of his previous letter: 'If you don't want me to have anything more to do with the matter I am quite willing to accept it: but if you think that at a later date, if Father Benedict could start a foundation, I might possibly be allowed to go and assist him for a time, I would like to keep an open mind about it.'[22]

Eventually Father Bede's polite persistence prevailed and the Abbot succumbed and wrote saying that Father Benedict's Abbot had given him permission to go to India and that he too would allow Bede to go – or rather to apply to the Abbot General in Rome for permission to go for a limited period. He admitted later that he felt that Bede had tried to 'force his hand' and was very clear about the terms on which he was giving his permission. He insisted that neither he nor the community could hold any responsibility in the matter, that Bede should get official permission from Rome, that the Indian Archbishop must accept full responsibility for the two monks and that it should be made very clear that the new foundation was not being made either from Prinknash or from St André, Father Benedict's monastery in Belgium. Bede had got his way in the end, though such was his determination not only to honour his monastic vows, but to be seen to have done so, that he described this permission as 'being sent to India'.

Bede had tried to avoid talking about the Indian venture at Pluscarden; nevertheless, by the beginning of 1955 word had got around and one or two of his fellow monks had very definite views on the subject, suggesting that his going was 'absolutely contrary to the Abbot's frequently and publicly stated wishes'; even that in going to India Bede was guilty of an act of disobedience. A more measured understanding comes from Father Maurus, who was at Pluscarden at the time and saw both sides of the question, the Abbot's and the monk's. He had the greatest affection for Bede, the sort of affection that allows for robust criticism:

> He would always go his own way in the long run and he wouldn't know he was doing it. The point was you couldn't do anything with him. If you have a monk like that you let him go off, because he'd be in the community like a piece of grit in the machinery of it, wanting to do something else. He was

charming and lovable, but at bottom, when you wanted him to go your way he'd bow out gracefully; but he wouldn't go your way. There was no violent opposition, he just slid through and the next thing was he was away . . . The Abbot was wise, he saw that he must say 'yes' to this fellow if he was going to keep him.[23]

Father Maurus's understanding of the Bede of the 1950s highlights aspects of his personality which were to affect much of the second half of his life. He understood, too, that despite Bede's love of community life – and indeed his need for it – he was essentially a loner. Father Maurus even went so far as to say: 'He never made a monk, unless you mean a monk meaning *monos*, a single person. He *couldn't* be a member of a community – he was just Bede, he was unique and he was a lovely character. He wasn't a cell in the body, he was a wandering cell. He was a loner.'[24]

Father Maurus also saw the unused potential in this immensely gifted man: 'It was like looking at a power engine that wasn't switched on. You could feel the power in him waiting to be used. It was inside him, it wasn't conscious but it was there.'[25] The curious and sad thing was that this power had not so far been satisfactorily harnessed. Abbot Dyfrig Rushton saw that 'From the word go you could see there was something special about him'[26] and Abbot Wilfrid's resistance to the Indian venture was partly because Bede was such a talented man, who had already had experience as Guest Master, Master of Studies and Novice Master and could be useful in many ways. He was even seen by some as a future abbot. Yet the Abbot had shown his high regard for him by sending him to Farnborough as Prior and it had not been a success. It is as if Bede's time had not yet come. Perhaps he knew it, for soon after he received permission to go to India he wrote to Martyn Skinner: 'I feel that somehow I am destined to go. There is something in me which will not be fulfilled till I have been there.'[27]

It only remained for Bede to get formal 'exclaustration' from Rome. He had initially thought that an exclaustrated monk was no longer able to wear the habit, in a sense ceasing to be a monk, and was adamant that he did not want anything of that kind. In fact exclaustration, literally 'out of the cloister', is simply the term used for a monk who is going to live for a while away from his monastery; in all other ways his status is the same, he is not released from his vows, he has not been laicised, he still continues to wear his habit. If there is any shadow over the exclaustrated monk it is only that it is considered a pity if he dies while still exclaustrated.

Once the Abbot had given his permission there was no problem in obtaining the indult of exclaustration,* which was dated 4 January 1955 and granted in the first instance for three years, but there was the further question of accountability. Neither the Abbot of St André nor the Abbot of Prinknash were prepared to assume responsibility for the project – that would be up to the Archbishop of Bangalore. He, in turn, though agreeing to the foundation, would not take any responsibility, spiritual or material, for the project; the two monks must obtain, from the Sacred Congregation for the Affairs of Religious in Rome, the authorisation to proceed by themselves alone. In February 1955 Father Benedict duly received this authorisation, which presumably covered them both, and they were free to make plans to go to India.

The next month Bede travelled from Pluscarden to join Father Benedict, only to find one more obstacle in their way: a telegram had arrived from the Archbishop of Bangalore telling them not to come. But he was not going to be deflected now. He ignored the telegram and, on 9 March 1955, Father Bede and Father Benedict set out for the three-week journey from the Port of London, via the Straits of Gibraltar, Suez and Aden, to Bombay.

*Indult: literally 'permission'.

CHAPTER NINE

Discovering India

1955–56

Though Bede was forty-nine when he set sail for India, he had travelled very little; as a young man he did not have the money, as a monk it had not been appropriate or possible. Apart from the short trip to Paris he had made with his brother when he was twenty, he had only been abroad twice: once to make a pilgrimage to Rome during the Holy Year of 1950 and once, in 1952, to Switzerland, where he had spent two weeks after an operation. His only experience of meeting Indian people was during the First World War when Indian soldiers were sent to a convalescent camp in the village where he lived. One particular Sikh became a great friend of the young Alan. Bede was by temperament, and at this time also in experience, very British.

Even before he reached India he began to find the dimension of life for which he had longed. When they reached Port Said he and Father Benedict went ashore for a couple of hours, where he was fascinated by the colour and exuberance that surrounded him; his enthusiasm was even greater when they reached Bombay. For the first time it was not the beauty of nature that entranced him so much as the sheer beauty and vitality of the people, of the human form. Like anyone visiting India for the first time, he was overwhelmed by the smells, the noise, the exuberant swarming masses, children running around naked, women in saris, men in turbans, cows wandering the streets, even sleeping, disdainful of danger, in the midst of the traffic. Almost immediately he felt at one with the Indian people and began to discover, as had hoped he would, the dimension he had found missing in the West, 'the other half of his soul':

Whether sitting or standing or walking there was grace in all their movements and I felt that I was in the presence of a hidden power of nature. I explained it to myself by saying that these people were living from the 'unconscious'. People in the West are dominated by the conscious mind; they go about their business each shut up in his own ego. There is a kind of fixed determination in their minds, which makes their movements and gestures stiff and awkward, and they all tend to wear the same drab clothes. But in the East people live not from the conscious mind but from the unconscious, from the body not from the mind. As a result they have the natural spontaneous beauty of flowers and animals, and their dress is as varied and colourful as that of a flower-garden.[1]

Yet amid this colour and life, so different from anything he had hitherto known, were the familiar Gothic and baroque churches built by European missionaries; the statues and pictures, altars, candlesticks and stained glass speaking of another culture. He had long been aware that Christianity's theology was Greek, its organisation Roman and its cultural expression European; during his first few weeks in India he realised that if Christianity was ever to speak to the Indian people it had to undergo a radical transformation and learn to express itself in Indian terms. Originally a religion of the Middle East, Christianity was now so westernised that it had to learn from Hinduism, Buddhism, Taoism and Confucianism before a real meeting between East and West could take place.

For Bede to fully appreciate that was to be the work of years, but for the moment he was dazed by the discovery of India as he saw how eastern and western culture, ancient and modern, live alongside each other; how two ways of life meet as in the midst of modern civilisation – airports, hotels, factories, cinemas, busy roads and traffic – people go about barefoot, squat and lie on the ground, eat with the hand and wear the simplest clothes; how beggars stand outside international banks and bulldozers work side by side with women in saris, carrying earth away in vessels on their heads for a pittance: 'You feel yourself in the presence of a mode of life which scarcely differs from that of earliest man . . . what is so overwhelming is the coincidence of the utmost modern luxury and display with life in its barest simplicity.'[2] He was so overwhelmed by the grace and simplicity of the people, by the realisation of his dreams of a timeless life, unchanged for thousands of years, that he was not, as are most people on a first visit to India, shocked by the unspeakable conditions in which the great majority live, by the beggars, by the visible disease, by the sight of whole families living under a sheet of canvas on the street. It was as if he was blinded to the extremes of their poverty by his joy in finding the spontaneity, the vitality, the colour, for which his reserved British soul had longed.

For the first six months he was based in Bangalore, making arrangements for the ashram and seeing something of Indian life. Shortly before he left England he had been invited by an Oxford friend to have lunch at the House of Lords, an invitation which had been quietly dropped when he asked if he could bring Father Alapatt; the House of Lords was not then a place where an Indian could be a guest, even if he was a Christian priest. How different now, as he was warmly received in the homes of the Indians who lived nearby. He saw the way they lived in one room with earth walls and floors; that they had no furniture, no crockery, knives or forks, but slept and ate on the ground, a palm leaf for a plate, their hands for cutlery. He watched them work in the fields with 'a kind of gaiety and leisureliness',[3] the ploughing still done by oxen and bullocks. It seemed to him that the basic pattern of life had not changed since palaeolithic times and he compared it to the way Christ must have lived in Jerusalem or Socrates in Athens. As he met more people he became aware that living a life of poverty and simplicity beyond anything he had imagined need not lead to a matching poverty of culture. He learned about traditional Hindu wisdom from an old man in the village who was a Sanskrit scholar; he became friendly with a student studying at the university, delighted to find that though in many ways very western, he quite naturally sat on the floor and ate with his hands, regularly conducting the worship at the nearby temple of the monkey god Hanuman. An early and unforgettable experience was an invitation to a tiny two-roomed cottage, where Europeans and Indians together sat cross-legged on the floor while two boys played Indian musical instruments, the mother sang and the father explained the meaning of the songs, all of which were religious. In these humble surroundings he knew he was face to face with one of the most profound religious cultures in the world.

Bede spent his first months in India living in a clergy house in Bangalore, where all the priests were Indian, yet the atmosphere was very western. There he met the distinguished scholar Raimon Panikkar and the two men took to each other instantly. Panikkar embodied in a unique way the meeting of East and West, as his mother was a Spanish Catholic, his father came from a well-known Hindu family and he himself had been brought up in Europe where he had taken degrees in science, philosophy and theology. He in turn had great respect, admiration and love for Bede: 'He and I were both fish out of water in that clergy house . . . Immediately we met it was a meeting of hearts and a meeting of everything.'[4] Though, like C. S. Lewis, Panikkar did not feel Bede had a philosophical mind, they agreed on most subjects, particularly on the importance of establishing Christian contemplative life in India, both men feeling that it was a scandal

that in India, the land of contemplation, there was not a single contemplative order and that when Christians came from the West they usually
became involved only with teaching and social work.

The two men became close friends, and together studied Sanskrit, the
ancient language of India in which the sacred Hindu texts are written. Their
teacher was a Carmelite nun, a professor of Sanskrit who taught in
Bangalore. Bede was never good at languages, but within six months he was
reading, albeit slowly, the great epics of the *Bhagavad Gita*, the *Ramayana*
and the *Mahabharata* in the original language. They also travelled together,
hiring bicycles to explore locally; Panikkar is still amused to remember how
he had to translate Bede's Oxford English into the 'babu' English with
which the people they met on their travels were familiar. They also went to
Mysore, where they visited the temples at Belur, Halebid and Somnathpur,
the cream of what remains of the most artistically exuberant period of
Hindu cultural development. Bede was enchanted, writing to his Oxford
friends that they reminded him of the abbeys of Fountains and Tintern.
Standing in the cruel heat of South India and seeing the sculptured friezes,
representing in ascending order the animal world, the human world of the
Hindu epics and finally the world of the gods and goddesses, was for him (as
indeed it is for the Hindus) a manifestation of the cosmic mystery in stone.
And as they went inside, as close as non-Hindus are allowed to the inner
shrine, he marvelled at the great throngs of worshippers: 'It is very impressive, with mantras chanted in Sanskrit, offerings of fruit and flowers, waving
of lights and incense sticks, and beating of drums and sounding of conches.
It is all done in a rather matter of fact way like Catholic ritual, but there is
real piety in the worshippers.'[5]

In the first flush of discovering a new culture Bede was eager and receptive, becoming aware of 'the power beyond both man and nature which
penetrates everything and is the real source of the beauty and vitality of
Indian life'.[6] He saw this power most clearly when he visited the cave of
Elephanta outside Bombay. As he walked through the mystery and immen-
sity of the forest of pillars protecting the figure of the Great God, the Siva
Maheswara, suddenly the three faces representing the benign, the terrible
and the contemplative aspects of God loomed out of the darkness from a
recess in the wall, colossal and overwhelming at first, but when he looked
closer at the front face he saw that it was in deep contemplation, full of
peace, solemn, gentle and majestic.

> Here carved in stone is what I had come to India to find, this contemplative
> dimension of human existence which the West has almost lost and the East

is losing. Here engraved in stone one could encounter that hidden depth of existence, springing from the depth of nature and the unconscious, penetrating all human existence and going beyond into the mystery of the infinite and the eternal, not as something remote and inaccessible, but as something almost tangible engraved in this stone. Here was the secret I had come to discover.[7]

Two other early and lasting impressions were made by a giant statue and a tiny shrine. When he was in Mysore he visited one of the oldest and most important Jain pilgrimage centres, Sravan Belgola, the site of a seventeen-metre-high statue of a naked man known as the Monk on the Top of the Hill and said to be the world's tallest statue carved from a single piece of stone. Bede believed this statue to be the figure of Purusha, in Vedantic thought the 'primal being' or archetypal man, who is said to contain the whole of creation in himself. He saw in this great statue a parallel with the first Adam of Jewish tradition and the Universal Man of the Muslims, going further and suggesting that when Jesus called himself the Son of Man he was relating himself to this primeval tradition and revealing the underlying unity of religions.

He was equally impressed when one day they sat down at the river's edge beside a little shrine, containing nothing but a roughly carved lingam and yoni, the male and female organs. If he was at first rather surprised (as indeed were many westerners in the 1950s) by the overt sexual symbolism so common in Indian visual arts, by the time he wrote about this period of his life for publication he had completely accepted it, rejoicing that Indians, unlike Europeans and Americans, have integrated sex and life. The way he wrote about it is reminiscent of the way he reacted to reading D. H. Lawrence all those years ago:

> A European would be inclined to regard this as 'obscene' but for a Hindu it has no such significance. For the Hindu sex is essentially 'holy'. It is a manifestation of the divine life and is to be worshipped like any other form of the divinity. God manifests himself in all the works of nature, in earth and fire and air and water, in plant and animal and man. Sex is one of the manifestations of the divine power – the Sakti – which sustains the universe and has the character of a sacrament.[8]

His instinct that in the East he would find the vision of cosmic unity for which he longed was being confirmed and his contacts with Hinduism were already supporting his long-held conviction that man and nature are sustained by an all-pervading spirit. It was this belief, he felt, that explains why in India every created thing is regarded as sacred. The earth is sacred, so it cannot be tilled before some religious rite has been performed; eating is sacred, and every meal is seen as a sacrifice to God, indeed the image of the household god is symbolically fed before the meal is begun; water is sacred, and to bathe in the Ganges, or any holy river, is regarded as auspicious and purifying; fire and air, plants and trees, animals, especially the cow, are sacred, but most of all man is sacred, a manifestation of the divine. He saw this attitude movingly demonstrated in a remark by Vinoba Bhave, for whom he had great admiration. (Vinoba was a disciple of Gandhi's who tried to persuade wealthy landowners to donate land to the poor.) Bede was very impressed when, after a day interviewing villagers, Vinoba said: 'To-day I have been visited 2,000 times by God.'[9] Though this attitude, this aware-ness of God in everything, was once found among Christians (for instance the Celts would not even milk a cow without first saying a prayer), Bede felt that the vision of the universe as sacred has been completely demolished by the western scientific world: 'Every trace of sacredness has been removed from life so that Western man finds himself in a world in which both man and nature have been deprived of any ultimate meaning.'[10] He was confi-dent that the West could learn to share this eastern vision of cosmic unity, but his great concern was how long the East, falling more and more under the influence of the West, could resist its impact.

Bede has been accused of using the terms 'East' and 'West' too simplis-tically and, in seeing the sacred everywhere, of having an over-romantic atti-tude to India. It is argued that even in 1955 India was becoming desacralised and that though Bede was often seeing the authentic sacred, he was some-times seeing what he wanted to see, what he so badly needed to see. Panikkar argues that there are 'levels of consciousness of the sacred' and that sometimes there are remnants of a sacred tradition only honoured in exter-nal ways, not really understood. For instance, he had found that when he asked people the meaning of the kolams* the villagers paint every day in front of their doors, 90 per cent of them did not know what they signified.[11]

Even if Bede was swayed by such an argument, nothing ever changed his conviction that India had a deep sense of the sacred which has been lost in the West and that underlying this was one of the great differences between the Semitic religions (Judaism, Christianity and Islam) and the religions of the East (Hinduism, Buddhism and Taoism). The Semitic tra-dition sees God as 'separate from and above nature, and never to be con-fused with it',[12] the distinction Christian theologians refer to as the unbridgeable gap between the Creator and the created, while in the eastern

*Kolam: traditional drawings invoking divine blessing.

tradition 'God – or the Absolute, by whatever word it may be named, is immanent in all creation. The world does not exist apart from God but "in" God; he dwells in the heart of every creature.'[13] Even in the first flush of his enthusiasm for India he was not blind to its limitations; he was not simply extolling the East in favour of the West, he was commending what he frequently called a 'Marriage of East and West', that the two should come together, each one supplying the dimension missing in the other. He was very aware of the dangers of the eastern attitude, realising that it can lead to pantheism and that in seeing God as present in everything there lies the risk of losing the distinction between good and evil. He was also critical of the idea of the material world as an illusion, as *maya*, though he came to think that this doctrine, which he continually encountered among educated Hindus, was a misunderstanding of the far more subtle and profound teaching in the *Upanishads*, the *Bhagavad Gita* and in the great Sankara himself.* Bede became convinced that the authentic Hindu tradition does not deny the reality of the material world; rather it sees the whole creation as pervaded by one eternal spirit – a spirit that creates and sustains the world and is both transcendent and immanent. In this first year in India his pleasure in the way of life and his recognition of the sense of the sacred pervading everything prevailed over any reservations. Already he was finding something of what he sought.

On 14 August Bede and Father Benedict moved into their new home, about ten miles from Bangalore, near a village called Kengeri; they called it Nirmalashram, the Monastery of the Immaculate, Nirmala being a recognised Sanskrit title of Our Lady. It was a small brick bungalow of seven rooms, whitewashed, with red tiles and concrete floors, pleasantly situated about 250 feet above the surrounding plain and sheltered by a grove of mango trees. Nearby was a small building which they intended to use as a chapel. They had all the water they needed from an artificial lake, known in India as a 'tank'. Despite Bede's joy in discovering India, he was still so steeped in the resonances of England that he was reminded of the places he had visited in his youth such as Somerset and Gloucester, and he described Kengeri by saying it was 'about the size of Painswick'. The day after they arrived, the Archbishop of Bangalore, Monsignor Thomas Pothacamury, in his role of Protector of the new foundation, with the Vicar-General and several members of the local clergy, came to bless the house and the two

---

*Sankara: a ninth-century Indian philosopher of the school of Advaita (non-dual) Vedanta.

monks were left to start the foundation of which they had dreamed for so long.

They settled down to monastic life, observing a timetable similar to that of Prinknash, except that they rose even earlier, saying the first office at 3 a.m. In common with most Catholic seminaries and religious houses in India, they continued in a western way of life. Apart from the heat – in April the temperature went up to 95 degrees F most days, which as a newcomer to India was about as much as he could stand – it was rather as if a little piece of England had been transferred to South India and there was little difference in the daily pattern of their lives. They had been given some furniture and a local craftsman had made them a refectory table and chairs; they continued to wear shoes and their white Benedictine habits and to use crockery. By November they had two postulants and a new noviciate block of four cells and seemed set fair to continue. Unfortunately it was not long before one of the postulants disappeared with all the bicycles, then returned at 3 a.m., knowing the community would be at Matins, and took everything he could lay hands on – typewriters, watches, clocks, fountain pens, some shoes and a suitcase. He was soon caught by the police and found to have a bad record; it was not the last time that Bede, endearingly gullible as he was, would be taken in by a man he readily admitted he had found charming.

After many years of reading eastern texts, Bede was at last in direct touch with Hindu culture and religion. How did it affect his thinking? It should never be forgotten that he had come to India not only to start a contemplative foundation but to find 'the other half of his soul', to find the feminine, the intuitive, the unconscious – dimensions that he felt were missing from western Christianity. He was not a missionary and being a Christian in India was not for him a question of imposing Christianity on the 'heathen', as people not Christians were still widely called; nor was it a matter of taking certain elements from Hindu culture and philosophy and building them into Christian thought. He wanted East and West to learn from each other; he wanted the different faiths to understand each other at the deepest possible level. It was more than a search for his own soul; in following his instinct and travelling to India he was at the cutting edge of his time, carving out a route that would lead to a new way of understanding religion and a spiritual enrichment for thousands of people. Years later he wrote to Judson Trapnell, an American scholar who wrote his dissertation on Bede's theory of religious symbols and practice of dialogue: 'From the earliest time I can remember I have always had the conviction that what I was experiencing was being given not for me alone but for others, in a sense for humanity.'[14]

Bede was at the centre of a kaleidoscope of new impressions. After twenty years of comparative intellectual and spiritual stability his mind was undergoing a sea-change and for some time this made it very hard for him to write. There are, however, a few indications of how he was thinking at this time. One was an article for *The Tablet* in which he began to develop his ideas on how Hinduism and Christianity could enrich each other. He granted that many would find the very idea of being a Hindu Catholic a contradiction in terms, that it seemed to be a choice between direct opposites, but he had come to a different conclusion, based on the answer to the question 'What does it mean to be a Hindu?' He argued that if, as was widely accepted, Hinduism is regarded as essentially a social system rather than a religion, then the position of Catholicism in India would be revolutionised. Immense practical differences would remain, but the change of attitude would mean that India could hear the message of the Gospel and Christianity could be spiritually enriched by the influence of Hindu culture. Despite all western missionary efforts, fewer than 2 per cent of Asians had become Christians and this was at least partly because Christianity had always been presented in European dress and, apart from a few notable exceptions, no effort had been made to adapt Christianity to the countries to which it was being brought – a process later known as 'inculturation'. Daily contact with Hindus and their culture were confirming him in thinking that a deeper understanding of Hinduism revealed that:

> . . . beneath the immense profusion of Hindu philosophy there is to be discerned a continuous metaphysical tradition of a most remarkable character. It is no longer possible to speak of 'pantheism' or 'Monism' or 'idealism' in regard to this philosophy . . . this Hindu philosophy is a genuine part of the 'perennial philosophy', which came to us in the West through Plato and Aristotle and Plotinus and was incorporated in Catholic theology by St. Thomas.[15]

The concept of the 'perennial philosophy', also referred to as the 'universal tradition', the 'metaphysical tradition', the 'eternal philosophy' or the 'traditional order', was something which had been part of Bede's thinking for some time and was to concern him all his life. At its heart is the contention that the perception of reality revealed in mystical experience is the same for all human beings; that through the symbols of different religions it is one reality that is perceived, independent of culture and faith. While he was at Kengeri, Bede wrote to Martyn Skinner that the 'traditional order' had been occupying his mind for a long time, that it had become the basis of all his thinking and that he was engrossed in the writings of exponents of the tradition such as Frithjof Schuon, René Guénon and Ananda Coomeraswamy.[16] His attitude to this subject was to undergo shifts of emphasis, but even before he came to India he was convinced that the tradition should be taken seriously. He argued that both religion and archaeology show that there are common elements in all the great religions and that the idea of God as the 'sacred mystery' is made known by means of symbols and takes shape in the primitive myths. Further, that while Indian philosophy recognises the validity of discursive thought, it has always maintained that there is a higher mode of thought which is not rational and discursive but direct and intuitive.

Bede was sometimes ambivalent about the perennial philosophy. For instance, just before he left England he had found it 'unacceptable to Catholics, though deserving serious study'[17] and at almost the same time he was writing that it represented philosophy in its purest form and was 'the divine preparation by which the people of the ancient world were prepared for the coming of Christ'.[18] Later he was to become convinced of its importance, writing to Hugh Waterman that 'the future of the world today depends on our recovery of this ancient tradition',[19] and to Martyn that it was, he was convinced, 'the path we must follow in the meeting of religions'.[20]

Though Bede's own experience was his touchstone and though his early experience of God in nature influenced the whole course of his life, he was always ready to submit his convictions to intellectual analysis. His belief that one transcendental reality underlies all religions is crucial to his thinking and was to become a source of debate and disagreement with modern theologians, many of whom are critical of it. They suggest that it is patronising and naive to claim that it is possible from one particular vantage point, of whatever religious standpoint, to discern what is true of all religions; that seeking for common elements in the different faiths runs the risk of rendering religion meaningless; further, that no observer, by virtue of his humanity part of the action, is able to stand above it in order to make such an evaluation. This debate about one of Bede's central beliefs was later to colour reactions to him, even among those who held him in love and admiration.

Another indication of his thinking in the mid-1950s was an important paper he read at an All India Study Week in Madras, which, rather to his surprise, was received with great enthusiasm. In it he tried to relate Hinduism to Christianity and the Church, in particular to consider how the Mass should be celebrated in India. He argued that while the Mass contains certain elements that are common to all religions, it is unique in being instituted by Christ himself, at a particular time and in a particular place;

further, that the structure of offertory, consecration and communion must always remain the same. But, he continued, it is important to distinguish between the parts of the Mass which must be unchanging and those which can be adapted to different cultures and customs. Apart from the crucial question of language, can Indian forms of expression and art be used in Christian liturgy and in particular in the Mass? At this stage he was convinced that it could not. Indian religion has been for the greater part of its history Hindu, and Hinduism is immensely rich in symbolism, but 'all these forms are charged with the genius of Hinduism and it is obvious that they cannot be simply transposed into a Christian form'.[21] Indian culture could not be brought into the Mass without a serious study of Hinduism and its symbolic expression, for man's relation to God is expressed through symbols. The way to start the process was to recover both our sense of the Christian mystery and our appreciation of symbolism.

In reaching this conclusion Bede touched again on the perennial philosophy. He quoted Newman saying that 'there is something true and divinely revealed in all religions all over the earth',[22] and continued:

> It seems to me to be of incalculable importance, when we are discussing the relation of Hinduism or any other form of religion to Christianity, that we should recognise that these religions are not simply 'false' religions to be rejected as a whole; but that on the contrary *they are all in their different ways forms of the one true religion, which has been made known to man from the beginning of the world*, (author's italics), though they are all in their different ways corrupted or distorted. What we have to do is not simply to condemn the 'errors' of these religions, but to study them humbly and sincerely and with deep sympathy, recognising them as divine in their origin and seeking to discover the pattern of that original divine truth in their present shape.[23]

His views on how Indian symbolism could be brought into Christian worship were to change and develop; his thoughts on different religions being different forms of the one true religion were to be challenged, seriously and frequently. But that debate lay in the future; his immediate problems were of a bureaucratic rather than a theological nature.

Though Father Bede and Father Alapatt had obtained the necessary authorisation to proceed in setting up the foundation by themselves, independent of either the Archbishop of Bangalore or the Abbot of Prinknash, they had not yet got the official document from Rome, the *nihil obstat**, which

---

Nihil obstat: literally 'nothing hinders'.

would give them the authority to be constituted as a diocesan institution. So as soon as they had dealt with the practicalities of living and had embarked on a monastic way of life in their new setting, they were faced yet again with obtaining official authorisation. At the end of October 1955, the Archbishop of Bangalore applied to the Sacred Congregation of Propaganda, the department of the Vatican concerned with missions to countries where there is no properly established hierarchy, for the necessary document, only to be told that the foundation was considered to be *'non opportunum'*. The opposition came mainly from the intervention of the Internuncio, the Pope's representative in Delhi, who argued that there was already a similar monastery nearby, the St André foundation at Siluvaigiri, and that (despite the fact that there were over five million Catholics in India) one Benedictine monastery was enough. He also did not approve of the way the foundation was being made, having no 'mother house'; he considered that it should be made from an existing monastery, with the novices being sent back to Europe to be trained. Bede drafted a reply, which the Archbishop forwarded to Rome. In it he pointed out that they were planning a strictly contemplative foundation, quite unlike St André, which envisaged work outside the monastery and appealed to different types of people; also that there was no other monastic community in India for men dedicated exclusively to the contemplative life. In his most persuasive style he argued that they were already established, with a monastery and land, with every prospect of more vocations and the wholehearted support of the Archbishop of Bangalore. He also appealed to the Abbot of Prinknash to intercede on their behalf.

They waited for a response with increasing anxiety, and by June 1956 they were expecting daily to receive news from Rome. It was not until September that they heard that their request to make a new foundation was rejected – quite definitely. Remembering this period, Panikkar said that he was 'probably one of the few people who witnessed his [Bede's] dark night of the soul, of his years of trial and not being understood'.[24] Whatever his feelings, Bede had written to his Abbot in June saying he was quite detached about the matter and ready for any decision that might be made and that his time in India had already been of 'such immeasurable blessing' that it was worth coming even for the short time he had had.[25] He also came up with suggestions as to how they might continue, for though he was striving for the detachment demanded of a monk, his wish to remain in India was too strong for him to give up easily. Could they form a *'pia unio'*, that is, an association without regular vows, which a bishop can establish in his diocese without recourse to Rome? Perhaps they could start a community of

Benedictine oblates (lay members of the community, again without vows)? A third suggestion was that the Archbishop had asked if he might remain and work in the archdiocese for the remaining eighteen months of his exclaustration. Abbot Wilfrid replied by return, clearly shocked. How, he wrote, could a solemnly professed Benedictine monk become a member of a community of oblates? Did that mean he would ask for laicisation? As for working for the Archbishop, that would mean consultation with the Abbot General in Rome, for he was released for the purpose of assisting in the foundation of a Benedictine community, not for general diocesan work.

Bede's fourth suggestion was more practical. He had become friendly with a Cistercian monk, Father Francis Mahieu, who was also trying to make a foundation in India. He asked the Abbot for permission to work with him, assuring him that he himself would never consider becoming a Cistercian. Father Francis was hoping to start a foundation in the Trivandrum diocese, the extreme southerly point of India, where they would be under the Congregation of Oriental Rites rather than under the Sacred Congregation of Propaganda, the department of the Vatican which had proved so intransigent over the Kengeri foundation. Another advantage was that, being in a different part of the country, there would no longer be a question of competition with the St André foundation at Siluvaigiri. Once again he had to convince Abbot Wilfrid, who was concerned at him working with a Cistercian and, knowing his monk and appreciating the beauty of the Syrian rite that they were hoping to use, pointed out: 'I think you have to be very careful not to allow yourself to be influenced by your own personal desire to work in India or by the attraction of the Syrian rite.'[26] Bede, genuinely anxious not to 'act irregularly in any way' but determined to continue what he had started, argued that the foundation would be a 'diocesan institute', strictly speaking neither Benedictine nor Cistercian, and that the only difference from their original plans at Kengeri would be the use of the Syrian rite, which, being the rite used in that part of South India, was entirely appropriate. Abbot Wilfrid gave his permission and on 21 November 1956 Bede left Kengeri to start again in Kerala, some 300 miles further south.

CHAPTER TEN

A Monastic Experiment

KURISUMALA 1956–63

I f Bede was dispirited by the bureaucratic trials and tribulations that led to the failure of his first foundation he kept it to himself, only allowing himself to admit that it was 'rather a blow' after all the work they had put into the place. As always his reaction was to look forward to the next phase in his life, and his cool reaction to the dashing of his hopes deeply impressed Father Francis, giving him great hope for their future partnership. It cannot have been easy for Bede to accept that he would not be in charge of the new foundation, but there had never been any question that Father Francis would be Prior or Acharya (spiritual guide) and Bede the sub-prior. For years Bede had been consciously seeking to surrender his ego to the will of God; this detachment indicates that he was winning the fight. While planning the move to Kerala he wrote to Father Francis: 'If God should think that it was his will, I would be prepared to stay out here for the rest of my life. On the other hand, if it is clear that there is nothing I can do, I am prepared to go back to Prinknash at any time.'[1] He was no dissembler and there is no reason to believe that he did not mean exactly what he said.

It was, however, a different matter for Father Benedict Alapatt, and Bede knew it. Father Benedict desperately wanted to be involved in the establishment of monastic life in India, but his reputation for being unable to live under religious obedience had preceeded him. Though Bede had shown commendable patience and loyalty, he had no option but to accept Father Francis's decision that this ardent but difficult monk could not be included in the Kerala venture, certainly not in its initial stages. So, with mixed feelings, Bede left Father Benedict behind and set off from Kengeri with Father Francis, travelling by lorry for the whole night and most of the next day, arriving in Kerala to a great welcome from their new bishop, Mar

120

Athanasios. Father Francis was delighted to find that 'for Father Bede it was the discovery of a new country and it won his heart without delay'.[2]

Who, then, was Father Francis, the Belgian monk with whom Bede was to spend the next ten years of his life? Born in 1910 he was a few years younger than Bede, but he had wanted to be a monk in India for even longer. In fact, his choice of Scourmont, the Cistercian Trappist monastery in Belgium which he entered in 1935, was prompted by the desire eventually to work in a foundation the Abbot was planning in India, but which in the event was diverted to Africa. He was, however, given permission to make a foundation by himself and after three unsuccessful applications for a visa he was eventually granted one by the Prime Minister himself, Pandit Nehru, who was so impressed by Father Francis's wish to work for the encounter of Christianity and Hinduism and by his determination to start a Christian foundation rooted in the monastic tradition of India, that he gave the application his personal support. Father Francis sailed to India just four months after Bede, arriving in Bombay on 12 July 1955. A year later he was invited to start his work in Kerala and, after several long and intense conversations to ensure that they shared the same ideals, he invited Bede to join him, writing to their mutual friend Toni Sussman:

> His assistance will be more valuable than any help we could get here as his own views fall in with the main features we are aiming at: a strictly contemplative life on the basis of the primitive observance of the Benedictine Rule, the use of the Syro-Malankara rite, a mind wide open to Indian religion and culture as well as to sound adaptations to the Indian ways and customs.[3]

In accepting an invitation to Kerala, a long narrow strip of land on the south-west coast of India, Father Francis had chosen one of the richest and most densely populated states in the country; it is also the state which boasts the most graduates and has a literacy rate of over 90 per cent. The fact that a third of the population are Christian owes something to Kerala's history, for it is probable that Christianity was established here as early as A.D. 52, when St Thomas the Apostle, or 'Doubting Thomas', is believed to have landed on the Malabar Coast. Local tradition claims that seven churches in Kerala were founded by St Thomas and some families, known as 'Malabar Christians' or 'Thomas Christians', believe they are descended from converts made by the Apostle himself. The denominations in Kerala are exceedingly complex, but whether or not the connection with St Thomas is historically accurate, what is certain is that from at least the fourth century the Church in India was connected with the Syrian Church and that for a thousand years it was subject to the Metropolitan of Persia. The arrival of the Portuguese in the fifteenth century led to a disastrous schism, the Portuguese finding it impossible to conceive of a Catholicism other than their own Latin brand and starting a campaign to force the Syrian Church to accept the jurisdiction of a Latin bishop and to change its rites and customs. While some Christians remained faithful to Rome, others broke away and placed themselves under the jurisdiction of the Patriarch of Antioch, suffering yet further fragmentation.

One of the brightest stars shining in this complex constellation was Mar Gregorios, the Archbishop of Trivandrum, whom Bede found the most understanding and sympathetic bishop he had ever known. He was a 'Jacobite' bishop (Jacobites being a group of Christians using the west Syrian rite derived from Antioch) and belonged to the Order of the Imitation of Christ, a congregation founded in the 1930s and reunited with the Roman Catholic Church, while still permitted to preserve the rite and customs of the Syrian Church. Mar Gregorios, who had a strong desire for the contemplative life himself, longed to see Christian monastic life established in India and was so anxious to see the foundation started that he let the two monks have a house, previously the Bishop's residence, free of charge. It was a large house with twenty-eight acres of ground just outside Tiruvalla and about seventy miles from Trivandrum, the capital of the state of Kerala. Though it was only a temporary arrangement they lost no time in cleaning, sweeping and whitewashing the inside of the house and clearing two patches of ground, one for a vegetable garden and the other for seventy-five banana trees they planned to plant before Christmas. They wrote to Rome for permission to transfer to the Syrian rite and began learning Syriac, which Bede found easy, and Malayalam, the local language, which he found very difficult. This time their bureaucratic exchanges went smoothly and speedily. On 12 August 1957 they received permission to start the new foundation and to use the Syro-Antiochene rites of the Malankarese Church; three months later the bishop signed the foundation charter. By then they had moved from Bishop's House to a nearby ashram in order to become familiar with the new Syrian liturgy before settling into the permanent home they hoped to find.

Eventually they were successful and on 20 March 1958, the eve of St Benedict's day, Bede and Father Francis, with two aspirants who had joined them, travelled the few miles to the hill country of the Western Ghats where, high up on the holy mountain of Kurisumala, a broad mass of granite rock shaped like the back of an elephant, they had been given 100 acres of land. The name Kurisumala means the 'hill of the cross', the cross dating from the nineteenth century when the mountain was a place of pilgrimage, but it was only after they had been there for a few weeks that they discovered that originally this cross had been erected in honour of St Benedict and that two medals of the saint were buried beneath it. They took this as a good omen.

Was this the site of their dreams? It was high, surrounded by hills which only fifty years earlier had been the forested haunt of tigers, elephants and bison. It was so remote that the only access was a rough track. The views were spectacular, the quiet all-pervasive. Their nearest contact with civilisation was a small tea-factory a mile and a half away but to reach even this entailed crossing a stream, which became a torrent during the monsoon, climbing a hill and following another rough country track. An Englishwoman living nearby at the time remembered the locals saying that the land was given to the monks only because its rocky grassland was unsuitable for growing tea and that it was hardly a kindness, for they could not hope to found a monastery there because of the rain (twenty inches a week during the monsoon) and the ferocity with which the wind broke over the ridge. For the three months of the monsoon, from June to August, the sun never appears at all, there is no way of keeping dry and everything turns mouldy and white with damp. However, the new arrivals were well pleased: it would have been hard to find a better place, thought Bede, and Father Francis wrote lyrically of the rocky, wind-swept and rain-drenched mountain where nature was at her fiercest and most elemental:

> In the midst of this great fearfulness the light has been shining. Indeed the light of Kurisumala is wonderful. Not only the blazing light of the dry season when the sun warms up the coldest days of the year in December and January, or the glorious sunsets over the Arabian Sea, but also the dawning light that every morning wakes up the clouds seeping in the valleys and makes each drop of dew in the grass shine like a diamond. Still more remarkable perhaps is the play of the evening light in the mist, when it is carried away by the wind. Its projection in swiftly moving patches of shade and light over the hills and meadows is a most inspiring image of the darkness–light battle that is waged within us.[4]

Their high spirits must have been somewhat dashed when they discovered that the stone building in which they hoped to live was not completed. They had to spend the first two weeks in an abandoned tea-factory and the next few months in a hut made of bamboo and plaited palm leaves, with no sanitation, no furniture and the floor covered simply with cow dung to keep off insects, as was the custom in India at the time even in the houses of the comparatively rich. They faced the full fury of the monsoon in this fragile hut, simply putting planks on the floor to protect the priestly vestments and books. It says something for traditional methods of building that while the hut proved a protection against the 200 inches of rain which descended on them in that first season, the iron roof of the stone building under construction – a long bungalow with wide verandas forming a kind of cloister – was lifted off by a violent gale one night, folding in two as easily as paper. Bede called these the most primitive conditions he had ever known: 'Eastington was luxury compared to this,' he wrote to Martyn Skinner, 'but I find it suits me very well.'[5]

Even living so simply, they needed money. Bede had contributed his share of the sale of the house at Kengeri, some 8,000 rupees, which together with the hospitality they had received from the local church saved them from serious financial problems. Even when the Palai Central Bank crashed and they lost all their savings, Bede remained unfazed, writing: 'Father Francis always seems able to get more and we haven't suffered from it.'[6] This does indeed seem to have been the case. After the crash, Father Francis begged 500 rupees from a local convent; two years later, when they were again badly in need of funds, the writer Louis Evely sent them the royalties of his first book, a bestseller; later still, a letter arrived from a London solicitor informing them of an unknown benefactor who had died, leaving his estate to be divided between the monastery and the Cheshire Homes. Their share was 300,000 rupees.

In embarking on this monastic experiment, Bede and Father Francis were attempting a delicate balance, not only living as contemplatives in the modern world, but travelling in virtually uncharted territory as they simultaneously lived a Cistercian interpretation of the Benedictine Rule, practised the liturgy of the Syrian Church and honoured the ancient tradition of the Indian sannyasi.* (Some of the more conventional Christians of Kerala might have been surprised by the opening lines of the Memorandum of Association written by the founders: 'To all rishis, brahmacharis, sannyasis of India, ancient and present, who dedicated themselves to the search for Truth, for the Paramatma, the Supreme Lord of the Universe . . .') The complexity of living in a combination of traditions affects every detail of behaviour, but clearly the most immediately obvious is dress. Father Francis and Bede had been given a lead in this matter before leaving for Kurisumala

---

*The traditional way of life of a holy man in India, from the Sanskrit word for one who has renounced the world.

when Mar Athanasios, the Metropolitan of Tiruvalla, gave them the *kavi*, the saffron-coloured robes of the sannyasi, a gesture which at the time surprised Bede; his acceptance proved a turning point in his approach to the way a Christian monk should live in India.* People who knew him in later life became so accustomed to him wearing the *kavi* habit that it comes as a surprise to realise that at Kengeri he had not only worn the white Benedictine habit himself, but when other priests visited, for instance Father Francis, had asked them to do so as well. Now he came to share Father Francis's wish to identify with the Hindu sannyasis and thus to identify also with the poor people of India. So they went barefoot, sat and slept on mats, took their meals of rice, curry, vegetables and pineapples (no meat, fish, eggs, cheese, bread, jam or pudding) from plain earthenware dishes sold locally, squatting on the floor and using their hands. Bede admitted that this was not at first easy for a European, though 'it has the attraction of a beautiful simplicity'.[7] For Father Francis it was an immediate source of pleasure:

> I can truly say, for instance, that I enjoy a good vegetarian meal, a simple meal of rice and curry, more than meat and gravy. Enjoyable also it is to live without arm-chairs, high and soft beds, yes, without all the gadgets of the city dweller. I enjoy walking barefoot. It gives a good grip on slippery roads and helps to walk without fear. It gives a pleasant contact with mother earth which brings joy, a joy which the man wearing socks and shoes cannot have.[8]

So, well content with their mountaintop home, they began to establish their new community. While the centre of their lives was the prayer of the Church and the celebration of its feasts and mysteries, they had to find a way of supporting themselves and they soon decided on cattle-breeding. This was a natural choice, for the cows could graze freely on the grasslands around the monastery and Father Francis, coming from Belgian farming stock, was well able to manage such an enterprise; though Bede's experience of cattle was limited to his time at Eastington, he gave it his whole-hearted backing. For both monks a particular attraction of this way of life was that, without involving themselves in activity outside the monastery, they could enter into the lives of the people around them.

There were, however, considerable problems, largely because of regular epidemics among the cattle and the lack of veterinary help. After their first

---

*It was probably at this time that Bede, following Hindu custom, took the additional, though rarely used, name 'Dayananda', 'the bliss of compassion'.

two cows died they sought the help of the State Animal Husbandry Department, only to find that a veterinary surgeon could not be put at the disposal of a private institution. However, Pandit Nehru had just launched a project to upgrade the 250 million head of cattle of the country – about one cow for every two people – of which about half were unproductive, owing to the sacred status of the cow in India and the prohibition on slaughtering even an old and sick animal. Father Francis and Bede were told that if they could import two pedigree bulls, preferably Jersey, and if these bulls could be used for the insemination of all the cattle in the area, they could be established as a pilot farm, or 'Key Village Farm' as they were commonly known. This would mean not only that they would have expert advice whenever it was needed, but that they would also be taking part in the community development plan for the whole of India. Both Father Francis and Bede appealed to their monasteries for help and in November 1961 two young Jersey bulls landed at Cochin harbour and were brought up the mountain to Kurisumala Ashram. Eventually it became a centre of insemination for the whole area and some hundred families settled nearby, living at least partly on the cattle-breeding started at the ashram.

In making a living from the land, the new community was following well-established monastic tradition, as did the daily programme which was similar to that of their brethren all over the world. The day was divided almost equally into periods of common worship, study and meditation and manual labour. They rose at 3 a.m. for the office, meditation and Mass (known as Kurbana), staying in church for four hours, with just a short break half-way through. Then, as at Prinknash, they had 'pittance', which consisted of bread and milk and an hour's free time, during which Bede often wrote letters. At 8.30 there was Terce and then manual work. The ashram employed outside labour only if it was unavoidable and Bede would help to clear the scrubland, fell trees, carry wood up the hill and, less strenuously, weed their flourishing pineapple trees – they were soon harvesting more than a hundred a week. From 10.30 till noon there were lessons for the young aspirants in scripture, Church history and philosophy. A vegetarian lunch of rice, vegetables and fruit was followed by a siesta, the office of None and two-and-a-half hours of work, a time which Bede used for writing and studying. Tea was followed by a bath – if pouring a bucket of water over the head can be so called – and at six o'clock there was Vespers, prayer and supper, again rice and vegetables, before Compline. They retired at 8.30, after a hard, but typically monastic, day. Bede admitted he found the hours of sleep rather short, but otherwise found the regime suited him well.

There were, however, important ways in which they were making new beginnings, the most significant being their use of the Syrian rite, translated into Malayalam. As the majority of Christians in Kerala belonged to the Syrian Church and knew all the chants by heart, this was entirely appropriate, but it had far-reaching consequences for it opened up the whole world of eastern Christianity. Both men loved the rite for its sheer beauty – Father Francis said that 'our office takes us back to heaven every three hours' and Bede spent long hours working on a translation into English – but for Bede it was also a reminder that before the Church used Greek or Latin it used Aramaic and that while most people think of Christianity as a western religion that spread through Greece and Rome to the whole of Europe, at the same time it was also extending eastwards through Palestine and Syria to Mesopotamia. Crucially, the Syrian rite, while far from the culture of India and the Far East, served as a bridge between western Christianity and the culture of India, China and Japan. In discovering Syrian monasticism, Bede was not drawn to the extremity of asceticism (for instance the famous case of St Simeon Stylites, who spent thirty-six years on top of a pillar), for him the real basis of Syrian spirituality was a deep concept of repentance, known as a 'second baptism'. This awareness of sin infuses the liturgy, as does the other pole of Syrian spirituality, perpetual prayer.

Bede was convinced that the great task of the Church in the East was to enter fully into the cultural inheritance of its people; he wanted to develop a Christian theology based on Indian and Chinese thought and drawing on the resources of eastern spirituality, Hindu, Buddhist, Taoist and Confucian. This did not mean a dilution of any tradition, but rather a new synthesis. His aim was for the Indian Church, while remaining totally Christian, to be open to the authentic values of Hinduism and be totally Indian; it was to be a two-way process, each tradition learning from the other. Wearing the *kavi* and living as far as possible like the Hindus was one step, the use of the vernacular in the liturgy another, one which the monks saw as an important turning point in the attempt to present the Gospel free of its usual western clothes. But there was a long way to go:

This is a task which has hardly begun. In India we need a christian Vedanta* and a christian Yoga, that is a system of theology which makes use not only of the terms and concepts but of the whole structure of thought of the Vedanta, as the Greek Fathers used Plato and Aristotle; and a spirituality which will make use not merely of the practices of Hatha Yoga, by which most people understand Yoga, but of the great systems of Karma, Bhakti and Jnana Yoga, the way of works or action, of love and devotion, and of knowl-

*A system of Indian philosophy based on the Vedas.

edge or wisdom, through which the spiritual genius of India has been revealed through the centuries.[9]

Bede and Father Francis were not the first to make this attempt, that honour goes to the Jesuit missionary Robert de Nobili, who adopted an Indian way of life in the seventeenth century and whom Bede regarded as a hero, the one missionary who really understood India. Much later, in 1950, the French monks Jules Monchanin and Henri le Saux founded Saccidananda Ashram in Tamil Nadu and began to adapt the monastic life to Hindu traditions and to initiate a dialogue with Hinduism. Nevertheless, the monks of Kurisumala were early pioneers at a time, well before the Second Vatican Council, when the Catholic hierarchy could only conceive of the religious life in India as a carbon copy of western orders. Predictably they met the opposition that is the fate of all pioneers. Father Francis was repeatedly told that the great need of the Church in India was a prosperous and well-organised monastic congregation from Europe or America. He later told a western journalist: 'Indianization was considered as a kind of apostasy in the eyes of those who could think of religious life only in terms of Canon Law, and for the broadminded it was something unpalatable or sheer eccentricity.'[10]

Bede's theological position at this time was that, while he had the highest respect for the great world religions, he regarded them as a preparation for Christianity, by which people can be led to their fulfilment in Christ: 'The trinity, the incarnation, grace and redemption, sacrifice and sacrament, all these ideas are properly revealed only in Christ. Rama, Krishna, Siva and the Buddha, all the mysteries and sacraments of Buddhism and Hinduism, are types and shadows of the mystery of Christ.'[11] Though his thinking about the 'fulfilment' theory was to change, his desire to establish a pure form of the contemplative life in India, something that was universally agreed to be lacking as yet in the Church in India, remained constant. He never forgot one of the sayings of the monastic fathers, 'A monk is one who separates himself from all men in order that he may be united with all men', and he knew that it would not be possible to enter into a real dialogue with the Hindu tradition until they had established their own tradition of the monastic way and deepened their own contemplative lives. The experience of Christ as the ground of all being was the inspiration of Christian monasticism and was the point where all faiths could come together:

For this means that in Christ we not only discover the centre or ground of our being, but we also find a meeting point with all other men and with the whole world of nature. There is a necessary separation from the world in a monastic life, a discipline of silence and solitude which is necessary for the discovery of this inner centre of being. But this separation should not divide a monk from the world but on the contrary enable him to meet the world at the deepest level of its being.[12]

With this emphasis on liturgy and contemplation, what of the charitable and educational works normally associated with Christians living in India? It would be a mistake to think that these men simply shut themselves away at the top of a mountain and forgot the world, though that is a charge often made against contemplatives. When Bede went to India his only idea was to help establish a contemplative monastery, but the Syrian Christians flocked to Kurisumala and the community grew quickly – after only eighteen months the numbers had risen to sixteen. Bede began to feel that in the face of the appalling poverty of India the contemplative life alone was not enough. He was constantly shocked by the conditions in which the average villager lived: whole families in small mud huts, usually with two rooms, each about six feet square, rarely getting milk, meat, fish or vegetables and sometimes so poor that they could not even afford rice. The farm work at Kurisumala was providing jobs locally and helping to raise the standards of cattle-breeding in the area, but Bede's energies were soon to find another outlet, inspired by spending the Easter of 1960 giving a retreat to a group of oblates in Kodaikanal, about 100 miles away. One of the oblates was a young India, Brother Stephen, who was working for the Sarvodaya movement.

Sarvodaya means literally 'service of all' and was the name given by Mahatma Gandhi to the movement he started in India, which was taken up after his death by Vinoba Bhave. By walking from village to village asking landowners to give part of their land to the landless, Vinoba had redistributed over five million acres of land and had also inspired the people with the idea of service and of raising the standard of life in the villages. Bede was keen to start a Christian centre for Sarvodaya work, but he immediately encountered a problem that was, in the context of his own expressed ideals, rather ironic. Gandhi and Bhave were both deeply religious, both Hindus, and it was the custom of all Gandhian groups not only to read from Hindu and Christian scriptures alike, but to address their prayers to both Hindu deities and to Christ. For the Hindu this presents no problem, for they have little sense of religious differences and regard all religions as essentially the same, differing only in their external expression, but Bede found it impossible to join in such prayers, feeling that Christians should not be asked to compromise their faith or act against their conscience. So he travelled to the far north of India to see Vinoba, finding him encamped in a village near Agra, wearing a loincloth and a shawl and showing that he was not totally averse to modernity by sporting a strange American-style green cap. He was surrounded by some 500 people, but Bede managed to secure his attention and as they walked together they discussed the matter, Bede insisting that there were real and essential differences between the different religious traditions and that these must be respected. Vinoba was at first unwilling to see his point of view, but Bede could be a persuasive man. In his own account of the conversation he recalls urging that the time for dialogue between the different religious traditions had come and that the object of this dialogue should be not to convert but to understand one another and to penetrate more deeply into the ultimate principles of each religion. What was needed was an ecumenical movement corresponding to that which was already taking place among Christians: 'We have to recognise that ultimately there can be only one religion for mankind, but that we cannot reach this one religion by ignoring the essential differences which exist. What we have to do is to strive to understand these differences and through mutual understanding to work towards a reconciliation.'[13] Eventually they agreed that Christians should be able to have their own prayers, in which others of course could join, but which would be exclusively Christian.

So Bede was free to set up a centre for Sarvodaya work near Madurai, where an American gift enabled them to acquire ten acres of land. The plan was to have a small ashram where Brother Stephen and a group of oblates could live and which would be a base from which they could work in the surrounding villages. Inevitably the question of money arose and Bede turns out to have had some success as a fund-raiser. He lost no time in writing to the oblates at Prinknash, encouraging them to contribute by saying that it would not be just another charitable donation, but would be spent on constructive work in the villages: making roads, digging wells, building houses, providing seeds and manures for cultivation and improving stock and village industries. Apologising for writing a begging letter, he asked them to raise £500 to begin the work. However, before they could organise their first fund-raising event, Bede was given £4,000 by a group of German bishops he had contacted through the Archbishop of Madurai. Immediately he began to develop a poultry farm to provide both much-needed eggs and an income for the ashram. Through Sarvodaya he could put the Christian Gospel into practice in modern India; further, he felt that Vinoba Bhave was the one person who, by following Gandhi and building up Indian life on the basis of the village, was working on the right lines. The movement was very much in accordance with the ideals Bede had held for so long; indeed, while he was at Kurisumala he wrote to Martyn Skinner: 'It is amazing the way what we were all groping for at Oxford has steadily grown and matured.'[14]

By any standards Kurisumala Ashram was a success. By 1960 they had formed a council and a working committee to run the ashram and in less than three years a wing of the monastery had been turned into a dairy, the morning and evening home of twenty-four milking cows, while the room above had become a weaving hall with two hand-looms. An acre of rough land, enclosed and levelled, was used for the intensive cultivation of tropical fodder grasses; a well was dug in the ashram garden; there were a banana grove and an orchard with mango, orange, guava and lemon trees. A field of pineapples yielded some 8,000 pounds of fruit a year which, together with the milk from their cows, brought them sufficient income to support their simple life-style. The work was done by members of the community who, in between classes in scripture, the Fathers, liturgy, monastic history and spirituality, and Indian thought and culture, cared for the cows, tilled the soil and tended the fruit trees.

Two important ways in which life at Kurisumala tried to assimilate the ascetic and the contemplative traditions of India were in the training of the new monks and a daily meeting known as the *satsang*. The first three novices to be trained there were clothed as monks in 1961 and their formation followed the traditional pattern common in India, with three stages; first the *sadhaka*, or learner, then the *brahmachari* or student of spiritual knowledge, finally the sannyasi, the one who has renounced all and commits his life to the quest of the Absolute. The common ground they sought between Hinduism and Christianity was, in at least some ways, already there, for Father Francis and Bede were delighted to discover that the ceremony for the Clothing of Monks in the Syrian tradition is identical to the *sannyasa diksha** of the Hindu monks. Both ceremonies consist of a reading of the scriptures of their respective traditions, followed by a series of sacramental initiations: tonsure, stripping bare in a holy bath and finally clothing in a monastic garment.

The *satsang* means literally 'the company of good people' and has a long tradition throughout India. The poet Tulasidas wrote:

> Without the *satsang* there can be no salvation,
> and without the grace of God there can be no *satsang*.

*The initiation as a renunciant.

> The *satsang* is the root of all goodness and the source of all joy, the real fruit of all spiritual exercises.[15]

At Kurisumala the *satsang* was the last meeting of the day. The community, together with any resident guests, gathered to sing *bhajans* (hymns), to listen to a reading from a holy book and perhaps to hear a spiritual discourse. They then all went to the church where they chanted psalms of protection for the night and the Acharya gave a blessing from the altar. Finally, one by one, every person walked up to kiss the Bible, bow to the altar and the Blessed Sacrament and took *arati*, the sacred light, from the oil-lamp burning before the icons.

The *satsang* was often well attended, for the community was beginning to attract many visitors. Most frequent were the locals, who came to the small dispensary the monks had opened seeking remedies for snake-bites, accidents sustained at work and the skin diseases caused by under-nourishment. There was also a small guest house for retreatants and occasional guests from all over India. One of these was J. A. Cuttat, the Swiss Ambassador to New Delhi and a former lecturer in comparative religion in Paris. Dr Cuttat was to become a good friend of Bede, who felt he had a deeper insight into Hinduism and its fundamental differences from Christianity than anyone else he knew at the time. Dr Cuttat's entry in the Kurisumala guest book must have delighted the founders, for he was clearly much moved by the experience, writing:

> An immense future seems to be promised to the wonderful synthesis realised in seed – but very really, on this Mountain of the Cross. I believe that on the day of Judgement the monks of Kurisumala will hear Christ saying to them, 'I was a stranger in the heart of my people and you received me. I was naked and you clothed me.' And Benedict and Bernard will add, 'What we did for the West you have done in the East.'[16]

It was Dr Cuttat who invited Bede to take part in an important conference in Rajpur, at the foot of the Himalayas, in April 1962. The intention was not so much to have an academic exchange as to share personal experiences, entering as deeply as possible into both Hindu and Christian experience and trying to distinguish their differences and relate them to one another. The view of the conference was that Hinduism was a religion based on a unique experience of God, 'which is India's gift to the world. It is for him [the Hindu] the culmination of all religion, the ultimate truth to which all religion, Christian included, must ultimately lead.'[17] Too often, Bede claimed, Christians have opposed this experience and thus been accused of dogmatism and intolerance and of refusing to bring their religion to the test of experience. The conference was following a path opened up in Dr Cuttat's book *The Encounter of Religions*, in which he placed the meeting point of the two religions at the point of the experience of God: 'to confront the two religions not in opposition from without, but from within at the point where they meet in the experience of God.'[18] As this was precisely Bede's view it is no surprise that the two men became such good friends.

The conclusions reached by the conference and summed up by Bede give a fair picture of his position in 1962, after seven years in India:

> Our task in India is not so much to bring Christ to India (as though he could be absent), as to discover Christ already present and active in the Hindu soul. After these centuries of preparation, Christ awaits his birth in the Hindu soul. It is for us to recognize his presence, to enter with deep sympathy into the movement of Hindu thought and experience which is leading it to Christ; to make contact with the Hindu in that inner depth of his being where he has so constantly sought God, and there to act as a midwife, in the manner of Socrates, to the birth of Christ.[19]

This conference also gave Bede the opportunity to see more of India. He travelled round the country in a complete circle – up via Bangalore, Poona, Bombay and Delhi; back by Benares (now Varanasi), Calcutta and Madras. He saw the Himalayas, he visited Rishikesh and was at Hardwar when the famous Kumbh Mela, the greatest of the Hindu pilgrimage festivals, was in progress. He also stayed at the ashram of Sivananda, then the most famous guru in India. Bede found something genuine in Sivananda and felt he had had real mystical experience but was not, on the whole, impressed: 'He is surrounded by devout ladies (mostly German) who worship him as a divine incarnation . . . [he is] smothered by adulation. It is the great weakness of Hinduism.'[20] As he travelled, Bede found that he himself was beginning to experience Indian adulation, and was deeply touched, though he recognised that it was partly because he was wearing the *kavi* habit and that in European dress he would probably have been seen, as were most western priests, as a worldly man. There is no doubt, however, that his reputation as a saintly person was growing and people who knew him at Kurisumala say that he was thought to be 'translucently holy'.

CHAPTER ELEVEN

The Other Half
of the World

1963–68

B y the 1960s Bede's name was becoming widely known; in fact, Father
Francis considered that he was becoming an international figure.
This was largely due to his writings: his autobiography *The Golden
String* was still selling well and he was writing articles and book reviews for
a variety of periodicals in England, America and India, a collection of which
was published in America in 1966 under the title *Christ in India* and in
Britain as *Christian Ashram*. His translation of the Syrian liturgy had met
with critical appreciation and he was regularly being invited to speak at conferences on religious subjects. He showed no particular pleasure in this public recognition, however, and when he was invited to meet the Queen and
the Duke of Edinburgh during their visit to Madras in the early 1960s, he
refused, remarking that though it might have been rather fun, he wasn't too
sure what their reaction would be if he turned up in his *kavi* habit and that
it was 'altogether too grand for him'.

In 1963 he did, however accept an invitation to go to America, where he
was awarded the Gold Medal of the Catholic Art Association for his work on
the ecumenical approach to non-Christian cultures. Receiving this award
entailed giving a talk in Santa Fé, New Mexico, and he also spoke at New
York's Carnegie Institute, the two lectures entitled 'The Meeting of East and
West' and 'The Church and Hinduism' covering many of the subjects about
which he had been thinking so deeply for so long. While he was in America
NBC Radio invited him to give four broadcasts in Washington.

On hearing that their friend was going to America, Martyn Skinner and

Hugh Waterman shared an affectionate and wry concern as to the effect it would have on him. They were right. Even before he boarded the plane, Bede wrote to Martyn that his ideas had been taken on more enthusiastically in American than in Europe or India and that he wanted to go there 'more than anywhere else in the world'.[1] Just as he had come to India seeking 'the other half of his soul', so he now felt that America and India represented two halves of the world; that he had to bring them together in himself by coming to terms with everything that America stood for. So enthusiastic was he about this first visit to America that he was convinced that it marked a new stage in his life.

Preparing these important talks also forced him to assess where, after eight years in India, he stood on some of the complex issues with which he had been wrestling, one of which was the question of industrialism and civilisation. Ever since Oxford, he and Martyn had carried on a debate over the question, 'Is industrial civilisation a good thing?' Martyn decided early on that it was not, and he never moved his ground, but Bede continued to pick at the bones of the argument almost obsessively, probing his own views and shifting his position this way and that, but never coming to a conclusion that satisfied him. He justified his ambivalence by explaining his deep conviction that in this world good and evil are inextricably blended: 'This is why I cannot stand with you against modern civilisation. I agree with all you say and am just about to go over to your side, and then I see the other side again. One must go beyond reason if the world is to make sense.'[2]

Then the kaleidoscope would shift and he would see the question from another perspective; for instance, soon after he settled in Kurisumala he had written that the simplicity of their way of life raised the question of civilisation in a new way: 'Should one be content with an earth floor and a thatch roof? I don't know . . . I can do without television and wireless and telephones etc . . . but not without books. Still I am dependent on civilisation for my books and the post.'[3] On the one hand he felt that industrialisation uprooted people from the land and from nature itself and that modern civilisation was essentially profane; that the town created an illusion of independence and made a person forget God, while in the wilderness one was continually dependent on God. On the other hand he admitted that, though the simplicity of their lives in Kerala was near to a pure state of nature and had a beautiful natural rhythm, he could not say he was satisfied with it, admitting that, 'Somehow their lives seem rather empty – so many people simply do nothing – there seems no creative impulse in them.'[4]

As he became more familiar with Indian life, so the issue became even more complicated for him. Daily seeing the appalling poverty around him, he was forced to modify his views and to begin to think there was no hope of relieving poverty except through civilisation. The pragmatist in him argued that we need both, the advantages of modern civilisation together with the simple life of the country. He did not agree with those Christians in India who felt that a Marxist analysis of society was the answer to India's needs. For Bede, Marxism's fatal defect was that it took the present industrial system for granted and did not seek to change the actual means of production. He was a convinced disciple of Mahatma Gandhi, the great pacifist's faith in non-violence and truth, the spinning wheel and the village community, standing for all he admired. He could no longer doubt that modern civilisation, with its science and technology, its democracy and humanism, 'has lost sight of the goal, which all ancient cultures held steadily before their eyes, and therefore beneath all its external achievements there is a growing sense of emptiness and of the meaninglessness of life',[5] but as he prepared to leave for America he felt he had to face the fact that modern civilisation was necessary and that the only thing that could save India was American aid. He even went as far as to say: 'There is no hope for mankind – I mean even for survival – apart from modern civilisation . . . but we must mitigate the evil effects.'[6] After all, he argued, 'Science is not wrong in itself – it is a gift of God – but it is misused owing to sin.'[7] On another occasion, arguing again that industrialisation as such was not necessarily evil, he wrote: 'Surely we must admit that the use of steam and electricity and atomic power by man is not intrinsically wrong. These powers are present in nature and presumably the Creator intended them to be used. It is the way in which they have been used which is wrong, and this alone constitutes the "sin" of industrialisation.'[8]

Seeing the American machine in action modified his views yet again, so much so that he found the problem insoluble and was in state of such confusion that he felt he had to turn down an invitation to write an article on the subject: 'India rather threw me off my balance, as it became clear that there were no resources in the country which could save it and that one had to accept industrialisation. But that does not mean industrialism at least in its present form is right. It only means that at present there is no alternative.'[9] He had, he admitted, been carried away by the sheer efficiency of American society, but he soon realised 'how unstable this society really is . . . it seems to me that it is *radically* wrong'.[10] It says much for his open-mindedness and his passionate desire to find the truth rather than simply to come to conclusions, that this argument, both with himself and with anyone who would tangle with him, was to go on for the rest of his life. His only consistent view on the subject, one from which he never deviated, was: 'All that really matters is that the sense of the sacred should be preserved.'[11]

Industrialism and traditional life, science and religion, West and East, masculine and feminine, reason and intuition, the contemplative life together with practical and pastoral care for those around him – all the time Bede was trying to reconcile opposites, seeking to find a synthesis, a whole, in the confusion and a multiplicity of life on earth. While he regarded it as one of the great tasks of religion in the twentieth century to confront the secular scientific culture that was affecting almost every corner of the world, he saw the meeting of East and West, in particular between Hinduism and Christianity, as the particular challenge of the Church in India. Just as in the West the ecumenical movement between different Christian denominations was taking shape, so 'There is need now of an ecumenical movement in religion, by which we seek to discover what is the common ground in the different religious traditions of mankind and then in the light of this understanding to comprehend all these different religious traditions in their vital relationship to the living Christ.'[12] He never ceased to stress that it should be a two-way process. Though, just as he had fallen in love with the Benedictine life at Prinknash, he had now fallen in love with India, he was not blind to its faults; and just as he wanted the West to learn from the East – for instance, he felt that there was nothing in Catholic theology which would not receive light from being studied in relation to the Vedanta – so he felt the East had something to learn from the West. Once again it was Martyn with whom he first shared these thoughts:

> The tragedy of the modern world is that reason has taken charge and driven imagination underground. But of course it only forces it into the unconscious where it sows the seeds, as you say, of revolution. This seems to me to be the problem of both East and West. The East must learn the use of reason, in science, industry, in politics and I would say above all in *moral* life (the absolutely universal dishonesty in India is paralleled, I believe, in almost every country in Asia and the Middle East.) But the West has to recover its lost imagination, not only in art, but in economic and social life (not least in sex.)[13]

India also affected Bede's views on sex, something which concerned him greatly and about which, given his Edwardian upbringing, his celibacy and his natural reserve, he wrote with a surprising freedom and lack of inhibition. As long ago as 1949 he had recognised that 'the sacred and the sacramental character not merely of marriage but of sex and the organs of sex has not always been fully recognised or given its proper place in Christian

Theology'[14] and had been critical even of the Church Fathers, to whom he was so devoted, for the disparaging way they spoke of marriage, regarding it as little more than a concession to human weakness. Now life in India and his study of Kundalini Yoga had deepened his understanding. Kundalini, the cosmic energy that is believed to lie within everyone, is seen as a coiled serpent at the base of the spine and the skilled practitioner can awaken this force, bringing it through the body's centres of psychic energy, known as the *chakras*, till it reaches the seventh, at the top of the head, where the masculine power of Shiva (the supreme Godhead) is united with the feminine power of Shakti (spouse of Shiva, the Divine Mother) bringing total integration and a feeling of bliss. He maintained that few people seem to realise the extent to which sex is the key to the spiritual life, or to appreciate that Kundalini is the driving power of our being; if this force is centred in sex, as it usually is, our whole nature becomes dominated by sex, which, though it can bring ecstatic pleasure, leads to the loss of our centre in God, the loss of our true life.

Bede never lost his admiration for D. H. Lawrence – indeed, he made a point of visiting his grave in New Mexico while he was in America – and his thinking on sex and Kundalini shows striking echoes of his early reaction to reading Lawrence as he wrote to Nigel Bruce:

> India has released in me the forces of the unconscious, which were previously submerged, and I have sometimes been terrified to find the demonic power which is in me. This is the 'dragon', as you say, which is in all of us. The spiritual life consists in the *conversion* of this power. We cannot destroy it or suppress it. It is not evil in itself, it is rather a holy power (as the Hindu genius has so well discovered) coming from God. But it has become subdued to our own selfish interest and so perverted. We have to turn this energy back to God, to withdraw it from sex and all selfish interest and to allow God to take possession of it. This is, of course, a tremendous battle, but all spiritual disciplines are ultimately concerned with this. I have been finding myself lately engaged in this battle as never before.[15]

Seeing western Christianity from a distance, Bede was feeling more and more that it 'needs a larger vision of life, which includes more consciously the whole evolution of nature and history to its fulfilment in Christ to be adequate to the needs of the modern world'.[16] In his personal letters he revealed his criticisms of western Christianity in a way that, at the time, loyalty and tact restrained him from admitting publicly. He wanted radical change in the Church, admitting that he was 'feeling very much the total inadequacy of Christianity to-day', finding modern Roman Catholicism an 'extremely decadent religion, a kind of fossilisation of what had once been a great tradition'[17] and the control of the Roman Curia 'rigid and disgusting – the spirit of the Inquisition was always – and still is – there'.[18] Unusually for those days, he even suggested that the Roman Church might have to moderate some of its views on the papacy, writing to a fellow monk that they must be prepared for great changes in the Church:

> The vernacular will eventually transform everything. It is the end of the whole Roman system set up at the Council of Trent. As you know, no doubt, a revolution is already taking place in theology & the Roman theology is on the way out. The next session of the Council will probably see a further phase in the revolution. If the Collegiality of the Bishops is established, the whole conception of the place of the Pope in the church will have to be revised. The teaching and governing authority of the church is *not* the Pope, but the bishops with the Pope at their head. This puts it in a different light altogether & bring us much nearer to the Eastern Church (& all ancient tradition.)[19]

He was, however, to draw some hope from the conclusions reached by the Second Vatican Council towards the end of the 1960s, feeling that it might lead to a thorough reconsideration of the place of the Pope in the Church, which he felt should be much more modest, and that it had opened the way to a renewal of the Church which could bring the main Christian churches into unity. In particular he delighted in the Council's admission that God might be found in non-Christian religions and in its decision, for the most part, to replace the Latin Mass with liturgies in the vernacular. Optimistic as ever, he believed the Council had opened the way to a complete renewal of the Church and released it from 'a bondage which had to go'.[20] For him the decisive point in the evolution of the Church was in the age of Constantine; it was then that the Church became a worldly power, adopting all the trappings of the Roman Empire, evolving a Greek theology and a Roman law. He longed for a new Church, appropriate to the second half of the twentieth century, for now, he argued: 'We are entering a new age, social, political, economic, a new phase of history, and the old forms are no longer adequate. We have to go back to the roots of our religion – as the Vatican Council has tried to do – to the Gospel, the early Church, even the Old Testament, and in Hinduism and Primitive religion.'[21]

One way in which Bede's thinking was infused by early and primitive religious traditions was in the importance he ascribed to symbols, an essential ingredient of his spirituality. Later he was to give his theories concrete expression; for the moment, while he was at Kurisumala, he was concerned mainly with theory. He felt an urgent need to recover the meaning of symbols in every sphere of life, in politics as well as religion: 'The Shepherd, the King, water, wine . . . these are deeply symbolic figures based on archetypal figures of the unconscious and therefore profoundly significant. Whereas modern figures like the President, the Probation Officer, Cornflakes etc, have been emptied of all symbolic meaning.'[22]

His ideas about symbols began to be formed early in his life, as he and his friends sat on the cold floor of their cottage at Eastington reading the Bible. Later, as a young monk at Prinknash Abbey, they were deepened by his experience of the liturgy and his wider reading of scripture. An even earlier influence was *Poetic Diction*, which C. S. Lewis had encouraged him to read when he was at Oxford. In this book, the great work of their mutual friend Owen Barfield, the writer shows that a word like 'spirit' (*spiritus* in Latin, *pneuma* in Greek, *ruah* in Hebrew) could originally mean wind, air, breath, life, soul or spirit, for in primitive speech a word contained a multiplicity of meanings. This theory, supported by philology, for the Greek word 'symbol' means literally 'thrown together', left an indelible impression on Bede's mind, as it reflected his constant concern with the balance between reason and intuition and corresponded with his conviction that 'primitive thought is intuitive; it grasps the whole in all its parts. The rational mind comes later to distinguish all the different aspects of the word and to separate their meanings.'[23] Nor did he cease to be influenced by Coleridge, who, as both poet and philosopher, he regarded as eminently qualified to state that though both poetry and philosophy imitate the truth, the philosopher represents it as a concept, the poet as an image. Further, that the image 'is concrete not abstract, and clothed in all the richness of sensual and emotional colouring which belong to it in reality'.[24]

In later life Bede continued to read widely on symbolism, notably Karl Rahner and René Guénon, but most crucial in his formulation of a theory of symbolism were the French philosophers Raissa and Jacques Maritain, whose ideas, greatly influenced by Aquinas, coincided precisely with his own. The Maritains contended that the symbol is a catalyst to the experience of a mystery that goes beyond understanding, that it can lead to the depth of the experience which it expresses. The American scholar Judson Trapnell is in no doubt about their significance to Bede's thinking:

In the works of the Maritains Griffiths found a contemporary and psychologically sophisticated interpretation of the origin of symbols within human consciousness and of the manner in which symbols guide the conscious mind back to its own sub-liminal depths in an experience of intuitive know-ing. These writings supported Griffiths' own emerging theory concerning the origin of symbols in an area of human consciousness secluded from rational activity and receptive to the divine; and they informed his own experience of how symbols may mediate an experience of knowledge.[25]

Bede would surely have agreed with Paul Tillich, who said that all lan-guage about God is symbolic except the statement, 'all language about God is symbolic'. He certainly found theological backing from Karl Rahner, whose thinking he greatly admired and who argued that 'the symbol is the reality, constituted by the things symbolized as an inner moment of itself, which reveals and proclaims the thing symbolized, and is itself full of the thing symbolized, being its concrete form of existence'.[26] Even before he went to India, when he was at Pluscarden, Bede felt that every word is a sym-bol, even the sacraments and the dogmas of the Church, such as the Trinity, the Incarnation and the Eucharist, 'do not define the mystery properly speaking, they only express in human terms what he [God] has chosen to reveal concerning himself' and are 'nothing but signs and instruments by which the divine mystery is manifested to mankind'.[27] Though he never strayed from his conviction that all religions seek to approach the reality of God through symbols, and that these symbols point to the mystery of human life, pushing us beyond ourselves, beyond our limits, he was very aware of the danger of stopping short at the sign, which would then become 'a wall which separates us from the truth'.[28]

What of Bede the man? How was life in India affecting him? For at least his first ten years in India he assumed that he would soon be back in England, simply asking for (and obtaining without difficulty) the extensions of his period of exclaustration he and Father Francis felt were necessary for the monastery to be firmly established. His initial enthusiasm for India never left him and it becomes increasingly clear that the country was claiming him – he was not the first to find that in discovering India he was discover-ing life. He had to a large extent found the life-style for which he had been searching for so long and the passionate man beneath the reserved exterior was finding expression:

> In the West life has been confined within certain limits – it is civilised and
> rationalised. Here it is still unconfined – beneath the surface of civilisation
> the world of nature, primeval, elastic, violent, evil, but also sacred, holy,
> passionate, pure and lovely is always present. It is in many ways a terrifying

experience – you feel that you cannot trust anyone or anything, everything is unstable. But as soon as you have ceased to rely on it, it reveals its other side, its beauty and tenderness and always its essential holiness.[29]

India was revealing him to himself in new ways and he knew there were parallels between his own feelings and the country in which he was living; that the lack of trust he was experiencing in his surroundings was mirrored in his inner life. The combination of British reserve and monastic training ensured that Bede's inner life remained largely hidden, but sometimes his correspondence gives hints as to how he was feeling. His sympathy with Jung's psychology, in particular his theory of the collective unconscious, was apparent when he wrote that he had learned a more and more deep distrust of himself: 'I can see that this must go on till there is no self left, and one finds the Self alone.'[30] He longed for his ego to dissolve, longed to be able to surrender completely into the hands of 'something infinitely greater than ourselves', but was conscious of being held in the grip of the past, 'not only one's conscious past, but the unfathomable hold of the unconscious, and of past generations, affecting one's physical make up, and still more, one's psychological structure'.[31] This desire for surrender, which he had first faced in the mission house at Bethnal Green, was to grow as he discovered the hard truth behind the Gospel injunction that 'whosoever will save his life shall lose it: and whosoever will lose his life for my sake shall find it.'[32] 'We can only gain our soul by renouncing it. I have found this again and again in different things that it is only by complete renunciation that one can reach truth and happiness.'[33]

At the physical level there is no doubt that the climate of Kerala affected him; his first experience of the monsoon – eighty-six inches of rain and not a glimpse of the sun for four weeks – led to quite a serious attack of fever, but he found that the less comfort there was outside, the more he found within, the more intense his spiritual life grew. The crucifying anguish of the spiritual battles and crises of his twenties might have been behind him, but though his manner seldom revealed his suffering, he was still tormented by inner struggles, striving always 'to *realise* this infinity in which we live': 'I must confess that though circumstances favour me now so much, progress is very slow. Or rather in a sense seems to go backward. The past comes up more violently than ever, and inumerable (sic) small weaknesses continually recur . . . but there are wonderful glimpses of something better – a sense of freedom, a light in the mind, which transfigures everything.'[34]

Living in the extremes of heat and rain also changed his feelings towards nature, the romanticism of his youth changing to a tougher realism. After enduring the monsoon continuously from 18 May until the end of November, he wrote: 'You realise out here how heartless and inhuman nature is. Nothing seems to be done for the benefit of man. If it rains it falls in torrents and nothing can grow, when the sun comes out, everything is dried up.'[35] At the same time he also rejoiced in the unbroken silence and the endless, ageless, timeless hills stretching to the peak of Mount Anai Mudi, the highest mountain south of the Himalayas:

> We are away among the hills with the great mountain mass of Kurisumala opposite us. There is beauty on every side. But so often everything is covered with cloud and mist. The rain comes and beats on the roof in torrents, everything disappears and one feels *submerged*. But then the storm passes and the mountain and the hills are there again with the sun shining on them, and larks singing in the air, and lovely purple flowers at one's feet. So much beauty, and yet so subject to change – that is our life on this earth.[36]

So, too, his feelings towards the Indian people were becoming less purely adulatory and more ambivalent, as he became increasingly clear-sighted about the people among whom he was living. He found them a joy to live with, particularly the Malayalams of Kerala, yet exasperating. Like most Europeans he was distressed by the lack of sanitation – even the rich had no lavatories at that time – and the consequent lack of elementary decencies, yet he was drawn by the simple humanity around him. He was impressed at how hard the people worked for exams, but saddened at the lack of deep or original thought. He was constantly touched by the way people shared their food and drink and immediately treated each other as friends, yet he admitted that 'they have terrible faults also – especially universal dishonesty'.[37] He still rejoiced in the awareness of the sacred he found all around him, yet his various remarks about the Indian attitude to prayer were curiously contradictory. Sometimes he wrote that they have 'a deep insight for prayer',[38] on another occasion that prayer was very superficial and that 'of contemplation I have found hardly a trace'.[39] Most surprisingly of all, he wrote: 'I am of the opinion that there is not very much deep spiritual life to be found in India to-day.'[40] Perhaps these contradictions were just part of the process of becoming familiar with a new country; or perhaps the key lies in a tantalising line, which he does not develop (perhaps he did not yet feel able to): Hinduism, he wrote 'is a deep undercurrent of life, sometimes almost hidden, and sometimes leaping to the surface, but sustaining the spiritual life of India'.[41] Such is the complexity of India that he had not yet fathomed her secrets.

In most ways the community at Kurisumala continued to flourish. When Bede and Father Francis first founded the monastery they had decided not to exceed twenty in number and within ten years the community had grown as large as they wished; the cattle-breeding and milk production were contributing to the material prosperity of the region and at their initiative a number of co-operative dairy farms had started nearby. The community was established in an unusual way of life in which its three monastic currents – the Cistercian daily pattern, the Syrian liturgy and the monastic tradition of India – merged to give it a unique identity. Yet all was not well between Father Francis, the Prior, and Father Bede, the sub-prior. 'I loved Father Bede and respected him', said Father Francis, 'but I could not agree in meetings and I expressed my disagreement.'[42] These disagreements were made even harder to reconcile by the younger monks' tendency to play the two men off against each other. Father Francis admitted: 'When I took a decision, you see, some of the monks would go to him and he would allow things which I would not allow . . . He could not but be a head, by nature he was a leader . . . people had great reverence for him and they went to him naturally.'[43]

Just as Father Francis thought of Bede as a natural leader, some people, probably including Bede, found Father Francis 'a very dominating character who was reluctant to devolve authority'.[44] Another area of tension was that Father Francis was trying to make a community which would merge with the local church, while Bede was filling a larger canvas as he became known across the world. Hugh Waterman, writing later, when Bede was in charge of his own ashram, thought that the friction between the two monks was because 'Father Francis's vision was of a place regenerating its neighbourhood by an example of good life and vigorous practical activity and Dom Bede's ashram is mainly devoted to study and discussion with a succession of people coming and going, which is of course the life Dom Bede is best at.'[45] Father Francis admired Bede's work and appreciated the theological teaching he was able to give to the young monks, but felt that though he and the monastery profited from his sub-prior's reputation, he regretted that his public writing and speaking was addressed largely to westerners and that Bede had little influence on the Church in India. Though it would be naive to assume that because this disagreement was between two monks there were no ordinary human emotions involved, equally it would be cynical to suggest that there was jealousy between the two men. There is no evidence of that. It seems that it was simply the common problem of authority when two strong-minded and talented people try to work closely together.

Father Francis had never thought their association would be permanent, and in 1965 he warned Bede that 'a body with two heads is not healthy'.[46] Two years later he told him of his intention to take a sabbatical year and leave Bede in charge, then, when he returned, they must make a decision. They could not both stay at Kurisumala. If Bede wished to remain then he would go somewhere else; if Bede wished to leave then he, Father Francis, would remain. He returned to find that Bede had decided to go back to Prinknash, but before he had even written to England fate intervened. Abhishiktananda, the French monk originally known as Father Henri le Saux, had decided to retire to the Himalayas and had asked his friend Father Francis to take over the ashram in Tamil Nadu where he had been living since 1950. Father Francis persuaded Bede to go, so on 15 August 1968, after just over ten years in Kerala, he left for Shantivanam, on the banks of the sacred river Cavery.

CHAPTER TWELVE

Lonely Years

SHANTIVANAM 1968–75

Bede's delight at Shantivanam knew no bounds. As ever filled with optimism, he rejoiced at the beginning of a new chapter in his life and only weeks after his arrival he was writing of the extraordinary effect the place had on him, that he had found something final and complete, even that it was like a resurrection. More and more he had come to feel that he belonged to India in a very deep sense, that the people and the country seemed to be in his blood. Now, deep in the southern state of Tamil Nadu, the home of Dravidian art and culture and the part of India least touched by British and Muslim influence, he wrote that 'the Tamil Nad corresponds with my unconscious – it is a kind of marriage in which I meet the other side of myself'.[1] Even the heat – the temperature sometimes rose as high at 105 degrees F – was not too much for him. He felt in tune with the life around him, just as he had felt in tune with the countryside all those years ago at Ford and Holcombe and, most of all, at Eastington. 'I have never known a place where I have felt so perfectly at home,' he wrote to the Abbot of Prinknash; 'It seems like the culmination of my pilgrimage.'[2] Far from being the end of his journey, he was in fact embarking on the most eventful and challenging period of his life.

Shantivanam which means 'forest of peace', is only a short distance from Tannirpalli, a village on a busy main road, along which bullock carts and buses from the nearby town of Tirachirapalli (usually known simply as Tiruchi or Trichy) pass regularly. There are villagers washing their clothes in the river and the endless noisy bustle of Indian life is today even noisier as loudspeakers blare out Indian music. But once down the short lane and in the ashram's grounds among the mango trees and palmyra palms, with the sacred river Cavery meandering gently along the boundary, there is a

deep, enveloping, almost tangible peace. It is not hard to see why it glad-
dened Bede's heart, or why it was the choice of the two Frenchmen, Father
Jules Monchanin and Father Henri le Saux, who settled there in 1950.
These two remarkable priests, who became Swami Paramarubyananda
(The Bliss of the Supreme Spirit) and Swami Abhishiktananda (The Bliss of
Christ), were pioneers in the dialogue between Hinduism and Christianity,
following the path hitherto trodden only by Robert de Nobili in the seven-
teenth century and Brahmabandhab Upadhyaya, a Brahmin convert to
Catholicism, at the turn of the nineteenth century.

They called it Saccidananda Ashram (the Hindu name for the
Godhead, from the Sanskrit words *sat* 'being', *cit* 'awareness', *ananda*
'bliss'), the implicit message being that the Hindu quest for God, enshrined
in this ancient word, finds a parallel in the Christian Trinity. In the early
1950s, before Bede and Father Francis had settled in Kurisumala, the two
French monks were already wearing the *kavi* habit of the Hindu sannyasi,
going barefoot, living in the utmost simplicity in small thatched huts, sleeping on the ground and eating with their fingers. They worshipped in a little
chapel built in the style of a Hindu temple, using both Sanskrit and the local
Tamil, alongside the Latin of the Roman liturgy. In their attempt to live as
Christians in the tradition of the Hindu sannyasi, entering deeply into the
whole tradition of Hindu thought, they were making the boldest experiment
yet in monastic life in India, but it was too far ahead of its time to meet with
any real success and not a single Indian found his vocation to their way of
life. In 1957, when Father Monchanin died, the experiment virtually came
to an end and eventually Abhishiktananda decided to retire to the
Himalayas, where he wrote several books of quite extraordinary insight.
Though the two monks had not realised their dream in the sense of forming
a new community, the seed of a new life in the Church in India had been
planted in Shantivanam's soil.

Bede felt immediately at home in his new surroundings, so very different from the mountaintop in Kerala where he had spent the last ten years.
The mango and palmyra trees are set off by tall straight ashoks; there is a
beautiful neem tree, used by the locals from time immemorial for anything
from medicine to toothbrushes; a pipal, or Bodhi tree, sacred to the
Buddhists, for it was in its shade that the Buddha found enlightenment; the
Bedam tree from which the bell that called the community to prayer still
hangs. Bede was no naturalist, it had always been the spirit of nature that
touched him rather than detailed observation; indeed, Martyn Skinner
once observed: 'He always used to be concerned more about the inward and
spiritual grace than about the outward and visible sign, even of a tempest off

Clogher.'³ So at Shantivanam it was the patterns of the trees against the sky that delighted him, the setting sun, the gathering darkness, the broad spreading leaves of the young banana trees, the singing and the flight of the birds: kingfishers, crows, green parrots, golden orioles, the pariah kite, so-called after its habit of living off garbage, the Brahminy Kite, known as the holy bird, for it is found only in places believed to be sacred. Occasionally he might have glimpsed the long white tail of the paradise fly-catcher high in the trees and was enchanted by a young mongoose that used to trot gently in front of his cell.

Bede's predecessors had lived very simply and the newcomers arrived to find only a chapel, a small refectory, a guest house and three thatched huts almost hidden in the jungly undergrowth. The two acres of land were over-grown with thorns and infested with snakes and scorpions, so Bede, who liked tidiness, immediately set to work clearing the thorns and planting coconut trees, bananas, plantains, frangipani and vegetables. He bought cooking vessels and, pragmatically, if inconsistently with his views on modern civilisation, installed electricity, running water and lavatories. He was still in many ways a westerner and admitted that he did not like bathing at an outside pump or in the river, nor could he get used to using the fields as a lavatory. His efforts met with the unreserved appreciation of Stephen, who had come with him from Kerala and was for a while the gardener before becoming the ashram's manager, though there were some who felt he took tidiness too far, making the place 'not so much the Upanishadic idea of the sacred forest but more an English garden'.⁴ Bede's ambivalence about anything savouring of modern technology and his ceaseless theoretical questioning on the subject now became particular: how far should he allow civilisation to intrude on the wild paradise he had inherited? He delighted in living among people whose rituals and customs had changed little in the last 2,000 years, feeling close to 'a sort of basic humanity', but he argued that even though the 'demonic dynamism' of modern civilisation destroyed all basic patterns of human society, it was not possible to go back to a pre-industrial state; the important thing was to learn to use what is good and reject what is bad. Yet he admitted to Martyn Skinner that he was now nearer to his friend's consistent opposition to civilisation than ever before, only months after arriving in Tamil Nadu writing:

What I am discovering is the intimate relation between nature and God. God is *present* in nature, in every created thing . . . Nature comes into being in the Word and expresses the mind of God to us, and nature is moved by the Spirit, which brings all things to maturity in Christ. This creation is in

1. Alan Griffiths' father, Walter Griffiths

2. Alan with his mother, Harriet Griffiths

3. Alan Griffiths c. 1926

4. The cottage at Eastington, where Martyn, Hugh and Alan lived in 1930

5. (Below) Hugh Waterman

6. (Above) Martyn Skinner, pastel portrait by Eric Kennington

7. (Right) C. S. Lewis in his study at Magdalen College, Oxford 1950

8. (Right) Bede Griffiths working on the foundations of the new abbey at Prinknash c. 1938

9. (Below) The Prinknash Community in 1942. Bede Griffiths second row from back, fifth from right. Michael Hanbury second row from front, second from right. Abbot Wilfrid Upson in the centre

10. Pluscarden Abbey, where Bede was a monk between 1951 and 1955

11. (Above) The Western Ghats – the view from Kurisumala Ashram

12. (Left) Fr Francis Mahieu, Prior of Kurisumala Ashram, 1995

13. (Below) The River Cavery at Shantivanam

14. (Above) The temple at Shantivanam

15. (Right) The dome of the temple

16. (Left) 'Christ in the lotus'. A figure in the grounds of Shantivanam before which people meditate

17. Father Bede's hut at Shantivanam, where he lived for 25 years

18. (Below) Father Bede working in his hut

19. Father Bede celebrating Mass in the Indian rite at Shantivanam, 1989

20. Brother Martin giving a talk in the meditation centre at Shantivanam

21. Russill and Asha Paul D'Silva

22. Father Christudas and Father Bede, 1992

23. Father Bede with His Holiness the Dalai Lama, Australia 1992

24. (Below) Father Bede with Cardinal Hume, London 1992

evolution towards the new creation, and man is the mediator, the high-priest, who unites nature with God.[5]

He was forced to be realistic, not least because the community needed to be self-supporting. He had been left £3,000 by Dr Allan (the woman whose attentions had mildly embarrassed him at Farnborough), and on that they had to live and pay for any improvements they made until the crops they planted brought in a small but regular income. Should he be ashamed of possessing an oil engine to water the coconut trees? It is clear that he was, but, 'What can one do? It disturbs the peace, but it enables us to live.'[6] He also started work on a meditation centre and a library, which he proudly told people he had designed himself and which he invested with great symbolic importance. It is octagonal with a wide veranda and a roof made of old rounded country tiles, and it was for him more than a collection of books. 'I want it to be a symbol of the unity of mankind and of all religions,' he wrote just before its opening in March 1970.[7]

Despite his optimism, Bede's early days at Saccidananda Ashram were not easy. In the first place the crucial matter of establishing a community of brothers proved harder than he had expected. He arrived with two brothers from Kurisumala, but one soon returned to Kerala and the other, after completing a course in theology at a local seminary, decided to get married. Father Francis sent another brother, who stayed for only six months. Later, another gave so much trouble, 'causing strife and dissension in the ashram and trying to make things difficult for me'[8] that Bede encouraged him to return to Kurisumala, which he did, though not before denouncing him to the Bishop, who mercifully paid no attention. There were times when he was almost alone, with no brothers or postulants at all, though a few visitors were beginning to come and he had the company of Stephen, who looked after all practical affairs such as contacts with government officers, organising the workmen and keeping good relations between the people of different castes working in the ashram. At the time Bede found him 'a wonderful person – very capable and absolutely devoted to me',[9] and Stephen's love for Bede was emotional and intense; he wrote to Hugh Waterman with an enthusiasm that made the recipient uneasy, though Martyn Skinner, to whom Hugh forwarded the letter, found it impressive and moving:

> After Monchanin's death the ashram was shaken and darkened in its atmosphere. Here came light and lit the place instead of the darkness. Within the short stay of his in this place, he has captured the hearts of these Tamilians

– why the whole of India, I am not mistaken if I say the whole universe . . .
Boys, girls, men and women flock around him to share his love, simplicity,
kindness and generosity. He is simple, kind and loving – the love which is
in him radiates straightaway – we venerate him and love him and people say
he is a living saint.[10]

Despite the hyperbole of this letter, there is no doubt that the magnetism of Bede's personality was already attracting people, both short-term
guests and people such as the artist/theologian Jyoti Sahi, whom Bede
described as 'a bit of a genius'[11] and who became a close friend, living at the
ashram for two years and staying on after his marriage to an Englishwoman,
Jane, whom he had met there. But a community needs monks, and
although Bede never wanted a large community, he had not envisaged
being alone. The comings and goings of his companions disturbed him, as
did the problems he found with the Indian temperament: 'Everybody is so
terribly emotional – very affectionate but easily turning to hatred and
jealousy and causing endless trouble.'[12] After two years he admitted to Hugh
Waterman that he was suffering from a kind of nervous exhaustion which
kept him awake at night.

> The life at the ashram here is not going too well, and I sometimes wonder
> whether I can cope with it. I don't seem able to keep people together and
> enable them to live at peace. Stephen is a dear person but he is very tem-
> peramental and easily gets upset, so that there is always some trouble going
> on . . . Probably it is largely due to my temperament which you found at
> Eastington. I don't seem able to change myself.13

Stephen had little sympathy with the contemplative life and the trouble
Bede refers to included a growing tension between Stephen and the other
brothers, which led to Bede helping him and his wife to buy some land and
build their own house near the ashram. Stephen's reaction to this act of
kindness was to claim that he had been rejected by Shantivanam and to conduct a campaign against Bede, denouncing the ashram as an immoral place
and spreading calumny around the neighbourhood. He somehow won the
ear of the Bishop of Tiruchi and even went so far as to take up the matter in
Rome, claiming that he intended to take over the ashram himself. Matters
came to a head when Bede felt that the very existence of the ashram was
threatened and he was forced to write to Cardinal Parecattil, the President
of the Catholic Bishops Conference of India, to defend himself against the
man who had once loved, indeed worshipped, him.

150

Bede was also not well physically. While he was still at Kurisumala he had been in hospital with a suspected gastric ulcer and Martyn Skinner had feared then that he might have a breakdown in health. After eighteen months at Shantivanam he admitted to 'feeling desperately weak and hoping that if he had to die he could die in the quiet of his own cell with the door open to the sound of the birds and insects'.[14] At the beginning of 1970 he had more stomach trouble, due to acidity (surely another sign of his nervous state), and another visit to hospital revealed that he had slight tuberculosis. He was urged to eat more protein – an instruction he interpreted by eating four eggs a day, hardly good for his chronic constipation. Later that year he spent another month in hospital with heart trouble and arteriosclerosis. By the beginning of 1971 his heart trouble had improved and the tuberculosis was cured, though he still suffered from continual lethargy due to arteriosclerosis. Looking back on the previous two years he again blamed himself and his temperament for his poor health. First there was his strained relations with Father Francis at the end of his time at Kurisumala, then the problems he found not only with the Indian temperament but with his own: 'It is, as you say, a matter of emotional tensions. Indians are very emotional by temperament and seem incapable of dealing rationally with any problem. We found it very difficult at Kurisumala and here with just two or three of us it became unbearable. I am too emotional myself and the strain of it made me ill.'[15]

By the end of 1970 he was deeply lonely, clinging as never before to his friendship with Martyn and Hugh, probably the only people at that time to glimpse into his heart. He wrote to Hugh that he and Martyn were in many ways closer to him than anyone else, 'apart from you two I have very few friends left now – so many have died and others have ceased to write. Your letters are so full of feeling and make me feel one with you more perhaps than ever before.'[16] Though he confided – as much as so reserved a man could confide in anyone – in both these men, at this stage it was Hugh to whom he most freely admitted his unhappiness, apologising for this untypical preoccupation with himself. Indeed, two letters were so desperate, so revealing, that the loyal Hugh told Martyn that he felt Bede would later regret saying so much and so he had destroyed them.

It was a three-way correspondence and the letters Hugh and Martyn exchanged in their concern about their old friend led to a discussion on the way he had changed in the long years – almost half a century – since they had first known him. 'Bede has made good, hasn't he, for once in the literal sense of the word', wrote Martyn[17] and, referring to C. S. Lewis's observation that Bede was a great advertisement for the monastic life, compared the man now in his sixties to the young man they had lived with at Eastington: 'What I have noticed particularly is his increasing tolerance and gentleness and forbearance. I am thinking in terms of "disputing" – you remember the endless "disputes" we used to have when these qualities weren't always apparent.'[18] A later letter, saying that Bede had had a wonderful life and would 'go straight through Purgatory like lightning through a furze bush'[19] led to a speedy riposte from the gentle Hugh:

> I still think it was a wonderful experience at Eastington that I wouldn't have missed, but I have often wondered if you and I didn't get our own purposes tangled and knotted in Dom Bede's string. Please don't misunderstand me: I admire Dom Bede intensely and value your friendship and his more than any other I have, but I still can't help being sceptical about the pursuit of holiness and I find the very special value attached to it very perplexing. I know he must have put up with intense physical discomfort since he has been in India, but he has always liked it that way . . . As for celibacy, from what he has told me, I think it was a giving up of what he never really wanted or was fitted for.[20]

Martyn responded that 'whether Bede was a saint or not we will never know' but that holiness should not be judged either by physical hardship or by living a celibate life: 'The whole art of spiritual living is to want to do what we ought to do. Bede had his call and answered; and from the evidence one would say that he has achieved his vocation.'[21]

In October 1971 Bede was in England and visited both Martyn and Hugh, talking for hours as they had in their Oxford days. After he had returned to India their discussion of his sanctity continued, with the tough honesty of true friendship. Hugh remembered that a friend of his, who admired Bede greatly, had judged him as 'A great man, yes, but not a saint, definitely not a saint . . . he gets what he wants.' Hugh, who seems to have been riled by any mention of holiness, added that he 'certainly didn't want the extended Senior Common Room type of life of dialectical holiness that Dom Bede was after',[22] while Martyn, questioning whether someone who gets their own way is automatically disqualified from saintliness, responded: 'I don't think of Bede as a "saint" – he may have some of the qualities of one – and for someone who was so self-assertive he seems now to be the opposite. This conflicts with your friend's views that he can't be a saint because he always has his own way . . . perhaps Bede has succeeded in doing it (getting rid of the ego) and all *has* been added.'[23]

The very fact that they were discussing Bede in this way indicates that he was now regarded as a holy man, attracting followers as holy people do;

nevertheless, it was beginning to seem as if this new venture, when at last he was in charge of his own ashram, was doomed to die before it was born. There is no doubt that he faced enormous difficulties and that he was deeply depressed, though in later years he made light of these early growing pains, but despite the emotional chaos he revealed to Hugh, he had his own way of dealing with the situation. 'More than once I have surrendered the whole thing', he later admitted. 'That's the secret. If you really renounce somehow it comes itself.'[24] And it did. After about two years, at a moment when he was quite alone and must have been feeling utterly deserted, he received a letter from two young monks from Kurisumala, Amaldas and Christudas, asking if they might join him at Shantivanam. He replied that he would care for them as if they were his own sons. Both were to be devoted to Bede and to the ashram and were to commit themselves to him for life.

Amaldas had been drawn early to the contemplative life, his particular interest in yoga and meditation leading him, soon after his first profession at Kurisumala, to spend forty days in solitude in the forest. After this he suggested to Father Francis that he should follow normal community life until noon, but he should then be free to spend the afternoon and night in private meditation in a hut set apart from the community. Father Francis had responded with indignation, saying that if he did not like the rules of the ashram he should start one of his own. As Amaldas was barely twenty, this was clearly not feasible, so, when Bede left for Shantivanam, Amaldas asked if he might accompany him; permission was at first refused, but eventually, hearing that Bede was alone, he asked again and was allowed to go for a short period. The fact that he never returned to Kurisumala was, strictly speaking, an act of disobedience and cannot have helped the strained relations that still existed between Bede and Father Francis.

The attraction Christudas felt towards Bede had a strange origin. His father had died when he was very young, and at the age of twelve he had a dream in which he fell into a deep well from which none of his family or friends was able to rescue him – a poignant image of a fatherless child. At last a man with very long arms reached down into the well and lifted him up saying, 'Come, my son.' Some years later Christudas went to Kurisumala on retreat and there, in the tall figure of Father Bede, he recognised the saviour of his dream. His devotion was immediate and total. 'Without knowing anything about him I was attracted to him, then when I came to Shantivanam I came even closer to him. I have never seen such a person in my life as Father Bede, so holy, so simple and prayerful. I felt, "Father, you are a saint."'[25] The relationship between Bede and Christudas was to become ever closer and to last until Bede's death. In Christudas Bede had found a son who loved him and a practical man who would look after him and later would administer the ashram; Christudas had found a loyal and devoted father, a spiritual guide and a man of whom he could say: 'I was the cloud of Father Bede, Father Bede was the shining sun . . . I knew everything practical, when people were cheating, things like that, but if I worried about money, he would say "No, try to live day by day, moment to moment, under the providence of God." Until his death I will stay with him. I believe he is a saint.'[26]

At last, after more than two years of a lonely life in a turbulent and constantly changing group, Bede had a loyal and committed, if small, community around him and was able to concentrate on developing the ashram. It is a great mistake to see the work of Bede in the context of the Christian missionaries, whose avowed intention was to convert Hindus to Christianity; this was never his aim, nor was it the aim of his two great predecessors at Shantivanam. Their vision of a deep meeting of Hindus and Christians, at a time when the ecumenical movement even among Christians was only just beginning, was far ahead of its time and its leaders are now accepted as spiritual giants. After Bede's death the theologian Professor Panikkar, who knew all three men well, wrote that he saw the leadership of the ashram as trinitarian, with 'Jules Monchanin, the founder, Abhishiktananda, the transformer, and Griffiths, the reformer. The three were so different that the friends of the first were rather critical of the second, and the followers of the second were not 'tuned in' by the third. And yet the three were great and holy. As a friend of the three I can vouch for this.'[27]

Both Father Francis and Bede had known Shantivanam for many years, as Father Francis had spent his first year in India there and Bede had visited more than once, writing to Father Francis: 'As you know I have very deep sympathy with what Père Monchanin and Père le Saux are attempting, though I don't feel I could adopt their methods.'[28] But that was twelve years earlier and Bede, always open to change, never again referred to this early resistance to their life-style, which he was not only to embrace but to take further.

How then, did Father Bede change and revitalise the ashram whose leadership he had inherited? In what way was he, as Professor Panikkar claims, a reformer? His broad aim was identical with his predecessors': to establish a form of contemplative life based alike on the traditions of Christian monasticism and Hindu sannyasi, renunciation of the world in order to seek God; his wish was, as had been theirs, for the monks to unite themselves to this tradition as Christian sannyasi, living a life based on the rule of St Benedict and the eastern Fathers of the Church, while studying Hindu doctrine and methods of prayer and meditation. Many of the externals of this life were also the same: the monks continued to wear the *kavi* habit, to go barefoot, to sit on the floor and eat with their hands – in short, to live with the simplicity and poverty of life normal for a sannyasi. Despite tensions between him and Abhishiktananda (Father Francis went so far as to say: 'Abhishiktananda could not *bear* Bede'),[29] Bede was intensely loyal to his predecessors, venerating their memory and often remarking on the depth and insight of Abhishiktananda's books. He was convinced that Monchanin's early death was brought about not only by the life of poverty and abnegation he had led, but even more by the spiritual suffering, 'which arose from the discovery of the gulf which separates the Christian from the Hindu and the crucifixion which must take place before they can effectively come together'.[30] Bede's work at Shantivanam was both a continuation and a development of his inheritance.

New leaders bring change, however, and by 1968, when Bede took over the ashram at Shantivanam, the spiritual climate was very different from that of the 1950s; young people were pouring eastwards in search of a God they could not find in the West, and the Second Vatican Council had opened the windows of the Church to new life and a new attitude to other religions. The *Declaration on the Church's Relation to Non-Christian Religions*, considered by Karl Rahner to be possibly one of the most significant acts of the Council, stated:

> The catholic church rejects nothing of those things which are true and holy in these religions . . . It therefore calls upon its sons and daughters with prudence and charity, through dialogues and cooperations with the followers of other religions, bearing witness to the christian faith and way of life, to recognise, preserve and promote those spiritual and moral good things as well as the socio-cultural values which are to be found among them.[31]

Bede frequently quoted this passage, clearly appreciating the licence it gave him as he became increasingly confident about the meaning and purpose of life in a Christian ashram. He sought not only to establish a contemplative life, but for Shantivanam to be a place of meeting between Hindus and Christians, between people of all religions or of none, between all people who are genuinely seeking God. He longed also to bring Indian spirituality, with its emphasis on interiority, to Christian life and to contribute to the development of a genuine Indian Christian liturgy and theology. Thus Christianity could be enhanced by the riches of Hinduism and Indian Christians would be able to bring their familiar cultural practices to their faith. It was not about conversion or triumphalism, but about exchange, respect, giving, sharing; Bede was convinced that one religious tradition should never be considered better than another, simply a different way to God. By the early 1970s the life-style which was to remain essentially the same for twenty years – indeed, it has continued after Bede's death – was firmly established.

Christudas remembers that Bede became far less strict at Shantivanam, both over small things – such as whether or not they always wore their *dhotis* or were sometimes allowed to go bare-chested, as indeed Bede came to do himself – and over larger things, like the daily schedule. Now they rose at 4.30 or 5 a.m., rather than the earlier start to which they had become accustomed at Kurisumala. They preserved the Benedictine model of manual work, study and prayer, but the emphasis between public worship and private prayer changed, with more time being given to private prayer and meditation. 'Here we were able to start our monastic life again in a more radical way,' wrote Bede.[32] While the Benedictine model is of a community of monks leading a common life of prayer and study, supporting themselves by manual work, the life of an ashram centres on personal prayer. Liturgy remained important to Bede, but after his move to Shantivanam his longing to follow the mystical tradition was given free rein and the balance shifted. The two hours of meditation, at dawn and sunset, became the framework of their lives, their common prayer an overflow of this silent communion with God. So their lives were balanced between solitude and community, the monks living in separate thatched huts in the forest, joining the guests for meals in the refectory, for the morning, midday and evening offices and for the evening *satsang*. They were searching for a supreme reality beyond religious differences.

'In order to know this supreme reality the human mind normally needs the support of a symbol,' Bede wrote in 1990,[33] and symbolism, crucial to an understanding of his thought, is outwardly evident in the chapel and its furnishings, just as inwardly it permeated his thought. Before one even enters the chapel it is apparent, for over the entrance to the ashram is a three-headed figure representing, in the Hindu tradition, the three aspects of the Godhead, the Creator, Preserver and Destroyer of the universe. It is also understood as a symbol of the three persons in one God of the Christian Trinity. It is significant, too, that the founders who built this entrance in the 1950s already considered the traditional depiction of the Trinity as too masculine, and showed the right-hand figure, the Holy Spirit, as feminine. Between the entrance and the outer court or *mandapam*, where the congregation assembles, Christianity and Hinduism are symbolically joined by Buddhism: the cross of Christianity is enclosed by a circle representing the wheel of the law of both Buddhist and Hindu traditions. At the centre of the cross is the word *Om*, the word from which, in the Hindu tradition, the whole creation comes and through which humankind can come to knowledge of God; here is a fitting symbol for Christ, the Word of God. The cross rests on a lotus, the symbol of the self.

The idea that there is one supreme being common to all religions continues into the outer court, where a cross is inscribed in Sanskrit with the words 'Worship to Saccidananda', again, given the parallel drawn between the Hindu Godhead and the Christian Trinity, uniting Christianity and Hinduism. The theme is continued over the doors to the inner sanctuary, with a line from the *Upanishads*: 'You alone are the supreme Being; there is no other Lord of the world.' Underneath, the words 'The Lord Christ' are written in Greek and Tamil. Only in the inner sanctuary, the 'cave of the heart' kept dark to signify that God dwells in the darkness, is the symbolism confined to Christianity. In this, the holiest place in the temple, there is simply a stone altar with a tabernacle, in which is the Blessed Sacrament, signifying the mystery of the death and resurrection of Christ.

Just as the outer form of the chapel bridges, indeed transcends, the divide between different religious traditions, so, over the years, the community sought to develop an Indian liturgy. They sit cross-legged on the floor in two facing lines (Father Bede used to sit at the centre, also cross-legged and wearing a prayer shawl rather than Roman vestments). Visitors and guests leave their shoes at the door of the temple and sit facing the altar, mostly on cushions or prayer stools, a few on chairs. The basic prayer and the Bible readings remain in English, widely spoken in India and by most visitors, but, in their gradual movement towards an Indian liturgy, readings from the Hindu religious writings such as the Vedas, the *Upanishads* and the *Bhagavad Gita*, as well as from the Tamil Classics and other scriptures, are included. They also sing Sanskrit and Tamil *bhajans* and chant *slokas* (Sanskrit verses).

All three offices end with the ancient Hindu blessing *arati*, a way of consecrating something to God. A light is waved before the Blessed Sacrament, symbolically revealing the hidden Christ, and then taken round the congregation, each person putting their hands to the flame and carrying the light of Christ to their eyes – a deeply moving gesture reminiscent of a similar practice found in Judaism. Another custom from the Hindu tradition which has been incorporated into the prayer of Shantivanam is the use of various pastes and powders, which are taken round to people after the

157

arati. At the end of morning prayer sandal paste is used – sandalwood, as the most precious of woods, being seen as a symbol of divinity; after midday prayer the purple powder known as *kumkumum* is placed between the eyebrows on the spot known as the 'third eye'. Here the symbolism is that the two eyes are the eyes of duality, while the third eye is the inner eye, the eye which sees the inner light according to the Gospel. In the evening, ashes, *vibhuti*, are used, signifying that sins and impurities have been burned away, just as ash is matter from which all impurities have been burned away. All the offices end with everyone doing a full prostration before the altar.

Every day the morning prayer is followed by Mass (at Shantivanam they belonged once again to the Latin rite, rather than the Malankara rite to which Bede had become accustomed at Kurisumala) where, as in a Hindu *puja*, the elements are offered to God as a sign of his creation. So in the offertory the four elements of earth, air, fire and water are offered as a sign that the whole creation is being offered to God, through Christ, as a cosmic sacrifice. The priest then drinks a sip of water to purify himself within, fruits of the earth are offered in the form of bread and wine, and eight flowers, placed in the eight directions of space and signifying that the Mass is offered in the centre of the universe and relates to the whole creation, are offered, one by one, accompanied by Sanskrit chants. *Arati* is then done first with incense, representing air, then with camphor, representing fire: 'Thus the mass is seen to be a cosmic sacrifice in which the whole creation together with all humanity is offered through Christ to the Father.'[34]

Though most people who have experienced an Indian liturgy find that these symbolic acts, far from taking one away from Christianity, draw one deeper into its mystery, there is always resistance to changes of this sort and Bede was following a dangerous path, littered with sharp pebbles, dangerous turns and unexpected hazards. As so often ahead of his time, he had sparked a controversy with an article written as early as 1960, well before the Second Vatican Council published its findings. He felt that, despite the wearing of *dhotis* and the use of Indian music, what was then called 'Indianisation' had hardly begun, something far deeper was needed; an authentic Indian Christian art could emerge only if the culture entered into the very thought and life of the Church. 'It is not a matter of copying the external form of Indian art but of penetrating into the inner spirit of the Indian genius and of transforming it by a genuine Christian inspiration,' he wrote in an article in *The Examiner*.[35] Later the Vatican Council's *Declaration on the Church's Relations to Non-Christian Religions* led to the recognition that faith must be a part of culture if it is to be fully lived, and thence to the coining of a new term, Inculturation Theology, which tries to share the whole cultural tradition of a people and was to be a way to approach a multicultural church. Bede felt this *Declaration* was a welcome attempt to deal with one of the most pressing problems of religion in the modern world:

> We have to recognise that the human race is essentially one, 'one in its origin' and 'one in its final goal', and the plan of salvation extends to the whole of this human race . . . Thus the way is now open to an 'ecumenical' approach to people of all religions, and, what is no less important, to those who are without religion and yet seek for truth and justice. This should mark the beginning of a new era in the history of the Church. No longer need we have a negative attitude to other religions and philosophies; we can welcome the truth to be found in all alike and co-operate in common tasks for the welfare of mankind.[36]

The *Declaration* led to the hierarchy of the Catholic Church attending two All-India Seminars. The second, held in 1969, just a few months after Bede had arrived at Shantivanam, expressed the need 'to establish authentic forms of monastic life in keeping with the best traditions of the Church and the spiritual heritage of India'.[37] and declared their intention to foster liturgical renewal in India. The guidelines ranged from the need to maintain a deep respect for the Christian message, through suggestions about the use of readings from the sacred books of other religions, to encouragement for adopting Indian gestures, vestments and forms of veneration. At the Seminar a Mass incorporating these ideas was hailed enthusiastically by the 600 participants. It must have seemed that the atmosphere was ripe for change, but liturgy evokes strong feelings and no sooner was the Seminar over than controversy arose, the laity in particular raising many objections and airing their views in both the national and foreign press. Soon Bede himself was to come under attack.

CHAPTER THIRTEEN

International Guru

By the middle of the 1970s Shantivanam was becoming famous, drawing people from all over the world, and Bede, who would never claim more than to be reaping where the founders had sown, was seen as a wise and holy man, a prophetic figure in tune with his time as few churchmen were, an inter-faith spokesman who could not be ignored – in short, a sort of international guru.

Inevitably his fame brought controversy and if it was a time of crowning, of achievement and recognition, it was also a time of personal trial, as his opponents made their voices heard. The most significant events of this period are curiously linked. The publication of his book *Return to the Centre* encouraged even more visitors to find their way to Shantivanam, and the ashram's silver jubilee in 1975 led to vicious attacks from the press and, eventually, to a severe reprimand from the local bishop.

The celebrations themselves were innocent enough and indeed there was much to celebrate. The ashram had struggled and triumphed, the last year particularly being what Bede called 'a year of consolidation'. Not only were there now eight members of the permanent community – two priests, two brothers studying for the priesthood and about to take their final profession and four aspirants – but they were a settled and harmonious group. Their three acres and small herd of cows provided for most of their needs and they had electricity, running water, guest rooms, a library and a meditation centre; the ashram was accepted as part of the local community and kept in close contact with the villagers through a dispensary, two spinning units employing sixty girls and a nursery school which they helped to establish and where they provided a daily meal for some fifty children. There was also another ashram being developed by some sisters who had stayed at

Shantivanam for a year; their eight acres were adjacent to Saccidananda and initially Bede was cautious, writing that 'It remains to be seen how it will work out'.[1] Most importantly, Shantivanam was fulfilling its intention of becoming a place where people came to pray and to experience the reality of God in their lives. In the words of an Indian Jesuit, Bede 'provides opportunity for anybody, man or woman, religious or lay, Christian or non-Christian, believer or atheist, to find with him [Bede] a haven of spiritual rest and recollection'.[2]

On 7 December 1975, several thousand people, mostly Hindus, came from the neighbouring villages to celebrate the jubilee, which culminated in the *Kumbabhishakam*, the 'anointing' of the *vimana*. This elaborate dome in the style of a Hindu temple was the idea of Bede and Jyoti Sahi, for whose understanding of the cultural situation in India Bede had the most profound respect. It represents the new creation in Christ and is a perfect blend of Hindu and Christian art. The brilliant colours and the sheer fun are typical of traditional Hinduism, while the figures covering the dome represent aspects of Christianity. At the base of the dome are the four beasts of the Apocalypse (the lion, the ox, the man and the eagle) showing the whole creation redeemed by Christ; above are four saints, including St Benedict, founder of contemplative life in the West, standing for redeemed humanity. The Virgin Mary is shown as Queen of Heaven and higher still there are four figures of Christ – Christ as King, as Priest, as Prophet and Teacher and as Contemplative. Crowning the *vimana* is the throne of God, covered with peacock feathers, and the lotus, supporting the *kalasam*, an ancient symbol of the four elements pointing to the infinite space in which God dwells. So 'the mind is finally turned to the ineffable mystery of the Godhead beyond name and form to which all earthly images are intended to lead us'.[3]

Bede was most moved by this contribution he had made to the ashram's symbolism, writing: 'Whenever I look up at it I think of Wordsworth's lines: "My heart leaps up when I behold a rainbow in the sky." It really raises the heart and mind to heaven.'[4] In the course of the jubilee celebrations he climbed to the top of the dome, consecrating it by pouring water on to the pinnacle and then sprinkling more on to the crowds below. This was followed by a procession round the temple and a Mass concelebrated by seventeen priests from different religious orders. It was a great day and, in Bede's words, 'a demonstration of what the ashram stands for'.[5]

Though many were moved by the celebrations and though the liturgy and life-style of Shantivanam has touched the lives and deepened the spirituality of thousands of people, there were some who were enraged by everything

161

Bede was trying to do at the ashram. Inculturation is, in Bede's words, 'trying to share the whole cultural tradition of a people'[6] and that only 2.5 per cent of the Indian population were Christians was, he felt, largely due to this cultural gap, as for a Hindu to become a Christian involves a change of culture as well as a change of faith. But inculturation in practice is a complex issue, raising endless questions and upsetting many people. For instance, adherents of the local religion, in this case Hinduism, may feel that their symbols are being misappropriated, even insulted, while some Christians fear that their church is being 'Hinduised'. The theologian Gavin D'Costa, though largely sympathetic to Bede, asked: 'Can Christianity really be stripped of all its trappings without also losing a sense of its own truth? For example, should not the Nicene Creed be determinative for all Christians? If all formulations are purely cultural and thereby disposable, will not the Bible itself eventually be subject to the same corrosion of authority?'[7]

The ashram had been under attack for some time, both from the local press and from extreme conservative Catholics who felt that it was undermining the Church. Some of these articles were aggressive and unscrupulous, causing absurd stories to circulate about the ashram. Stephen, his resentment still raging, stoked the fires by circulating 'first-hand' stories of immorality. Unfortunately, but perhaps inevitably, some of the local priests and the Bishop were influenced by these tales, and the local Vicar-General preached a sermon 'denouncing the ashram as unChristian and a scandal to the diocese'.[8] The Bishop remained friendly, though he didn't really approve of the ashram, his ambivalence perhaps shown in his plea of indisposition when asked to be the chief celebrant at the jubilee celebrations; he sent Father Irudayaraj in his place.

Many of these articles were of the brand of uninformed, hysterical journalism which should be consigned immediately to the waste-paper basket, but they do indicate something of the opposition which Bede faced. One journalist was so shocked that the name Saccidananda should be used to symbolise the Christian Trinity that he invited his readers to judge 'where we should pack off this Britisher turned purhoit.* We make no suggestions, for the place he should be packed off to is obvious.'[9] (Had this journalist done his homework he would have known that this parallel was first made by the original founders of Shantivanam, not by Bede.) So too, this 'Trichirapalli Correspondent' was offended that the word *Om*, sacred to Hinduism, is taken as a symbol for Christ: 'Only the absurdity of the ascetic of the Cavery can comprehend it.' Oblivious to the poverty and simplicity

---

*Usually *purohita – a Vedic priest.*

of the Shantivanam life-style, clear on the briefest visit, he accused Bede of being a foreigner in search of novelty, suggesting that 'some think that with a white skin and plenty of money they can do anything they like'.

At the root of these childish insults is a resistance to any form of inculturation, a failure even to attempt to see the universal truth contained in different religions. This journalist found the idea of the Virgin Mary depicted in a sari so blasphemous that he claimed he did not wish to print a photograph of it – though of course he did, asking all who saw it to 'please say a Rosary in reparation of the insult that Bede Griffiths has heaped upon the Mother of God'; and as for the consecration of the *vimana*: 'There is nothing, even by the wildest stretch of imagination, to serve as an analogy to this pot ceremony in Christian literature, rituals or approved Christian ceremonies.' Crucially, he ignores the fact that Indianisation of the liturgy had already been approved for the whole Church by the Vatican Council and for India by the All-India Seminar, aiming his darts not only at Bede personally, but at the National Biblical, Catechetical and Liturgical Centre in Bangalore and at those in authority who 'know about all this tomfoolery that goes on in the name of religion and yet keep quiet. This is more shocking than Bede's own gimmicks.'

Two further attacks in an Indian magazine called *The Laity* (now defunct) are particularly interesting in that Bede's reaction to them sheds light on his character. While the desire to defend one's position, even if not oneself personally, is natural enough, somehow one expects a man in Father Bede's position to maintain a dignified detachment. In fact, though he claimed not to be worried by these articles, confident that his position was theologically sound and that the ashram had many friends both locally and in Rome, he could not resist responding. He wrote an open letter to one of his attackers, Fr Anastasius Gomes, and a letter to *The Laity*, which they refused to publish but which appeared in another Indian periodical, *Vaidikamitram*. This letter opened with the observation that the editor of *The Laity*, looking for material for a public attack on the ashram and its Prior, pretended to be a friendly Sunday morning visitor. In passing Bede commented on some of the factual inaccuracies of the article, but his real concern was to point out that Shantivanam was a place of prayer and that their life was based on principles laid down by the Vatican Council itself – namely that the young churches should 'assimilate all the riches of the nations given to Christ as his inheritance', that 'The church rejects nothing that is true and holy in these religions', and that the task for Christians working in India was 'to recognise, preserve and promote the spiritual and moral values to be found in Hinduism, while all the time bringing them into the

ᴉe teaching and example of Christ'. Only by following such guide-
ld the Church in India be, as Father Monchanin had originally
both authentically Indian and authentically Christian. He
..d out that the rite which they used for Mass had been approved by the
Holy See and the Catholic Bishops Conference of India, and ended with a
question which contains the essence of his thinking on liturgy:

> Is it not possible for those of us who differ in our understanding of the exter-
> nal forms in which the mystery of our faith should be expressed, should
> recognise that the faith which we share is more important than its mode of
> expression, and that we strive rather to understand and respect those who
> differ from us and be reconciled in charity, than to judge and condemn
> them? Does the kind of article which Mr Kulandai wrote really further the
> cause of truth and charity in the Church?[10]

In his letter to Father Anastasius, a more informed correspondent, he
went further, questioning his attacker's appeal to the 'magisterium' (the
teaching authority of the Church), for there is always the question of interpretation:

> You do not seem to realise that a Roman document is just as much in need
> of interpretation as any other document of the Church, including the Bible,
> and this interpretation is the work of theologians. Every document, whether
> religious or secular, has to be interpreted in the light of its linguistic and
> cultural and historical background. The documents of the Church are
> couched in the language of their historical environment. There are many
> statements, which though acceptable in context of their historical setting,
> are quite unacceptable when taken out of it, and require to be re-inter-
> preted to-day.[11]

Questions of interpretation of the Bible or of Roman documents lead to
disagreement as surely as night follows day and, like any pioneer, Bede was
also to be criticised, usually with sympathy and understanding, by thinkers
and theologians in genuine pursuit of the best way to contribute to the
Hindu–Christian dialogue. His first taste of criticism from inside the
Church came eighteen months after the silver jubilee, when the Vicar-
General sent him a copy of the Bishop of Tiruchi's Pastoral Letter in which
he forbade the use of four of the points concerning the Indianisation of the
liturgy already agreed by the All-India Seminar. The Tamil Nadu bishops
had decided that the priest must not be welcomed by *arati* and by the washing of his feet; Mass must not be celebrated sitting on the floor, the practice
of *panchanga pranam* (kneeling in veneration, with the forehead and palms

on the ground) should cease; 'normal dress' should be worn, rather than the prayer shawl Bede was in the habit of wearing. An involved and highly technical correspondence followed, the kernel of the disagreement being whether or not a local bishop had the authority to over-rule a national decision and, if he had, whether the ashram could be considered a special case. The situation did not appear to be officially resolved and Shantivanam did not change its ways, Bede maintaining that, as an independent ashram, Shantivanam was not subject to diocesan control. However, the Bishop, whom Bede felt at the time of the jubilee 'remained friendly', became distinctly unfriendly, as is clear from an extraordinary letter he wrote to Bede at the end of 1979 in response to the news that he was back from a trip to America.[12] 'I trust your tour was pleasant and profitable', he wrote. 'But the people of this land may not be happy about your return. You were mentioned at the Ranchi meeting of the CBCI, but not in praise of you.' He went on to say that though Father Bede passed for a theologian, he did not know enough about the teaching of the Catholic Church and that, as Shantivanam was not canonically established, in matters of teaching and liturgy the ashram and its Prior came under his authority: 'Therefore kindly replace the cone on the Kalasam of the Vimanam of the chapel you have built in Thannirpalli with a suitable cross; and stop saying Mass squatting. Have an altar for celebrating Mass standing. I hope you will do this for the edification of our people and the glory of God.' If the tone of this passage is peremptory to the point of rudeness, there were also personal barbs. He doubted if the ashram could succeed, because:

First, you are, as those placed over me in authority have told me, by temperament (to use the expression of one of them) 'a lone bird' who cannot stick a community. Secondly, this ashram will have to be in an indianised fashion and particularly in a Tamil way as I have already told you more than once. But this is not possible with you who doesn't know the language of this region inspite of living here for many years and your present disciples are not the right persons for it . . . I think you would do well to go back to the West and start an ashram there in which you could be the Guruji and with your knowledge of 'Indian Spirituality' and Yoga exercises help the Westerners obtain the Peace of Christ and save the trouble and expense of travelling to and staying in this country.

Bede's reaction to this letter is not recorded but he must have received some comfort from the support he received from, among others, the National Biblical, Catechetical and Liturgical Centre in Bangalore and the Archbishop of Ernakulam, who wrote saying that he realised Father Bede's difficulty in ploughing a lonely furrow and that he was 'an apostle of Indianisation and hence a real missionary, with a correct outlook'. With surprising outspokenness, the Archbishop also sympathised with the 'adverse circumstances prevailing in Tamil Nadu, especially at the episcopal level'.[13]

It can only be surmised whether Father Bede's critics would have understood him better if they had read *Return to the Centre*, for its publication in 1976 brought a mixed reaction. Now, though, it is considered to be one of his most important books, selling for over twenty years not only in the English-speaking world but also in Portuguese, Polish, German and Italian translations. The book consists of a series of meditations on such themes as detachment, the nature of the true self, sin and redemption, the mystery of love and the one spirit in all religion: 'We have to try to discover the inner relationship between these different aspects of Truth and unite them in ourselves. I have to be a Hindu, a Buddhist, a Jain, a Parsee, a Sikh, a Muslim, and a Jew, as well as a Christian, if I am to know the Truth and to find the point of reconciliation in all religion.'[14]

Through all these essays runs the underlying theme, explicit in the title, that different religions are distinct manifestations of one underlying principle, that beyond all differences lies one transcendent reality:

> What is this 'transcendent Mystery', this 'ultimate Truth', this 'universal Law'? These are words we use to express the inexpressible. This is the whole problem of life, which continually baffles our reason. The ultimate meaning and purpose of life cannot be expressed, cannot properly be thought. It is present everywhere, in everything, yet it always escapes our grasp. It is the 'Ground' of all existence, that from which all things come, to which all things return, but which never appears. It is 'within' all things, 'above' all things, 'beyond' all things, but it cannot be identified with anything. Without it nothing could exist, without it nothing can be known, yet it itself is unknown. It is that by which everything is known, yet which itself remains unknown.[15]

This mystery is variously called Brahman, Atman, Nirvana, the Godhead, the Tao – indeed Lao-Tzu expressed the same idea when he wrote: 'The Tao that can be expressed is not the eternal Tao.' Christianity has also covered the same ground, St Augustine positing in the fourth century that 'If you understand it, it isn't God', Dionysius the Areopagite advocating a process of 'unknowing' and Aquinas enigmatically suggesting that 'the only thing we can say about God is that he is not what he is' and declaring that all that he had written was 'but straw' when compared to the great moment of illumination he experienced towards the end of his life. It is also found in Judaism, with the twelfth-century philosopher Moses Maimonedes saying that God can only be described in negative terms, an idea not unlike that expressed by St John of the Cross and contained in the Hindu description of the inexpressible mystery of Brahman as *neti, neti* (not this, not this). In short, Bede was not saying anything original, nor was he claiming to; he was simply exploring, from his own lived experience, an age-old insight, though in a time dominated by discursive reasoning it was not one that found easy acceptance. For Bede this understanding was crucial to man's very survival and he maintained that a total change of heart was needed; science must be subordinated to wisdom and discursive reason dethroned in favour of an acknowledgement of our dependence on a mystery that is beyond rational consciousness. In making the main thesis of his book this idea that ultimate truth is beyond reason and cannot be expressed, he knew that he was likely to face criticism, writing: 'I suppose I shall be accused of obscurantist mysticism, but isn't it strictly and logically true?'[16] He expected conservative Catholics to be shocked by it, admitting before the book's publication that he suspected it might be denounced to Rome, though confident that his point of view was accepted by broad-minded theologians.

How, then, was *Return to the Centre* received? If it *was* denounced to Rome, the authorities took no action, but *The Tablet* gave it what Bede called 'a shattering review, just pulling the book to pieces and saying nothing good at all . . . the man had obviously not understood it at all'.[17] Though Bede professed not to have been disturbed by it, reading this review cannot have been a pleasant experience. The reviewer (who courageously admitted twenty years later that 'had he been writing now he would have written rather differently') was unhappy with Bede's 'pre-occupation with the mystical' and, with some exceptions, found it 'an unhappy amalgam of what can only be described as opaque statements, confusions of thought and superficial generalisations'.[18] Other reviewers, however, took a very different view, *The Times* describing it as 'a modern classic, leading the reader to the foundations of the spiritual life',[19] *The Aryan Path* describing it as 'rich and comprehensive',[20] and the theologian David Edwards, writing in the *Church Times*, finding it 'a spiritually beautiful book' and, recognising that it was written from experience as much as from theory, saying: 'When he writes about the inexpressible, we soon realise that he lives in communion with it.'[21] These positive reactions were shared by the reading public, who felt that at last someone was articulating what they were thinking. Bede was finding, in his constant contacts with visitors to the ashram, that 'Everywhere to-day I find this concern to re-discover the symbol, to recover the whole, to return to the One.'[22] Among such people the book was received so favourably that the ever-increasing numbers drawn to the ashram have been attributed in part to the impact it made.

From the 1970s the ashram was filled to overflowing and Bede's experience as a Benedictine guest master stood him in good stead; he was, it was said, 'the perfect guest master to the end', personally welcoming guests, always available if they wanted to talk to him and alert to their needs, whether spiritual or practical. (For instance, Kathryn Spink was touched that, when she was staying at the ashram to write her biography, he worried that she found the vegetarian diet insufficient and was losing weight, so he insisted that she was offered eggs.) People of all religions and of none, of all nationalities and all ages, poured into the ashram at Shantivanam, sleeping on the balconies when the guest rooms were full. Why? The answer lies in Bede's personal holiness and charisma, in the unconditional love he gave to everyone he met; 'Love just poured out of him' was a typical comment made by visitors. It lies too in the depth of Bede's experience of God, which he tried to express in words, but which was perhaps even more apparent in his person. 'He was in touch with something that transcended words and we knew he was our friend,' said an Australian priest.[23] It lies in Bede's ability to listen, really to hear what people were saying; in his radical thinking and the simple life-style in which his theories were incarnated. It lies in his openness to new thinking and the way he never, up to the moment of his death, stopped learning. At nearly seventy he was able to say that not only was he 'surprisingly well', but that, 'I always feel about 21, just beginning to explore life and always finding new things.'[24] The needs and aspirations of people yearning to find God, but unable to feel at home in their traditional religions, were being met and they responded in their thousands.

In the 1970s more and more people were discovering the richness of eastern spirituality, in the form of Yoga, Zen, Buddhist Vipassana meditation, Sufi prayer and dance, Taoism, the teachings of Ramana Maharshi, Ramakrishna and Sri Aurobindo, the Transcendental Meditation of the Maharishi or the various gurus, both genuine and fraudulent, whom these spiritual travellers would visit. The East was becoming a magnet to those who were seeking experience rather than doctrine or ritual, those who had given up practising their own religion but could not give up their search for God; those who longed for the sense of the sacred lost to the West. Bede understood this need very well, he had after all been on a similar search himself since his experience of God in nature as a schoolboy over fifty years earlier. He found that many Christians, especially Catholics, 'seem to find their religion an obstacle to their search for truth and reality. For most of them Christianity is deemed to be identified with a formal, dogmatic, moralistic religion, which is a positive obstacle to their interior growth.'[25]

Bede identified a new movement in spirituality, a new era of consciousness. In 1966 he had written: 'We are in a stage of transition between the break-up of the ancient cultures and the birth of a new civilisation . . . a new structure has to be found and this will necessarily be universal, as we now belong irrevocably to one world.'[26] Now, in the 1970s, his letters and articles are peppered with this awareness. 'I feel that we are on the eve of a new breakthrough in consciousness, of a new wave of civilisation,' he wrote to Hugh Waterman,[27] and, 'One of the most remarkable phenomena in the world today is the awakening of a new spiritual consciousness, especially among the nations of the West, who have been subjected to the full impact of science and technology.'[28]

Among those who thought this way, who felt part of this new awakening, Bede stood as a beacon, for he represented hope for Christians, in that while identifying with their concerns he never deviated from his Christian faith. He invested new significance in the liturgy by encouraging it to expand to meet the needs of ordinary people in language, music and art; he longed for the Church, and in particular Christian monasticism, to respond to the needs of those new seekers after God: 'I feel that an ashram should be "open" to the world, not closed. A monastery is not based on "flight from the world", but on a withdrawal from the world in order to become a new creative centre of life in the world.'[29]

Bede was not blind to the fact that some of his visitors were simply seeking adventure or that many had tried drugs in their search for an alternative way of life, but in opening its doors to all comers and sharing the interiority of eastern religion, Shantivanam witnessed profound changes in many disillusioned people seeking for meaning in their lives. Writing in *The Tablet* of the many Catholics he had known who had not practised their faith for years but had undergone a profound conversion, rediscovering their faith in a new way, not from without but from within, he made a heartfelt plea to the Church:

> Could not the Church be more aware of the tremendous search for God, for a new consciousness beyond the mental consciousness, for a new age of spirituality which many believe is now dawning? The Christian experience of God is of unfathomable depth, but it is locked up in words and formulas, which have for many lost their meaning. Only when the Catholic Church opens itself to the immeasurable riches of oriental religion shall we be able

169

to answer the need of the new generation which comes to India and other parts of Asia every year in search of God.[30]

In the light of his understanding of the criticisms of the Church expressed by many of his visitors, what were Bede's own feelings about the institution of which he had remained a faithful member for so long? As truly as St Teresa of Avila considered herself a daughter of the Church, so was Bede one of its loyal sons, finding there the Christ to whom his devotion never wavered. 'I can honestly say', he wrote to a friend, 'that this is what the church means to me. It is the place where I can find this total Christ and give myself totally to him. All the human defects I can put up with because of this over-riding reality.'[31] Nevertheless, he was very aware of its 'human defects' and though loyalty largely restrained him in articles and public talks, he voiced his concerns in conversation and in letters. As the lover is often the sternest critic of the beloved, so Bede was sometimes, for so gentle a man, surprisingly outspoken.

In 1971 Hugh Waterman expressed his surprise that 'He takes a lot of contemporary thought which I thought the Church considered heresy as accepted and for granted',[32] and, though today there are many who would agree with Bede's ideas, in the 1960s and 1970s these views were voiced only by a minority. Since the 1930s he had been wanting radical change in the Church, and now he saw signs that it might be coming. In 1964 he had written that letter* to his brother Benedictine Dom Michael Hanbury, in which he said that the end of the whole Roman system that had been set up at the Council of Trent was in sight. He never denied the need for a Petrine Office, for him the basis of Roman Catholicism, but 'The whole concept of the place of the Pope in the Church will have to be revised. The teaching and governing authority of the Church is *not* the Pope, but the bishops with the Pope at their head.'[33] So too he was appalled by the bishops' backing of *Humanae Vitae*, the encyclical banning all forms of birth control:

> The spectacle of all these bishops supporting the Pope, like a lot of Communist party leaders toeing the party line, is sickening. Still it helps to bring out the conflict between an authoritarian view of the Pope and the Church, which makes human freedom impossible, and the new view of the Church as the People of God, guided by the Holy Spirit, and exercising its judgement at every level of laity, clergy, bishops and Pope.[34]

In a later letter he wondered if he had shocked his old friend by the vio-

*See Chapter 11, page 139.

lence of his views, but went on to ally himself with the liberals who were increasingly making themselves heard, and some of whom were finding themselves in trouble with the Vatican: 'I find myself almost wholly with people like Karl Rahner and Cardinal Suenens, & much in sympathy with Hans Kung (whose book on the Church impressed me immensely), and on the other hand, rather strongly opposed to the Roman Curia, (with its voice in Osservatori Romana, which has been called the Pravda of the Catholic Church) and a good number of the bishops.'[35]

He became increasingly worried by the attitude of Pope John Paul II, fearing that he would stop the growth of the Church and precipitate a crisis. 'The Roman Church is still far too authoritative and I don't like the treatment of Schillebeeckx and Kung. I don't altogether agree with either of them . . . but they have the right to write as they do. They have to be judged by their fellow theologians not by a little group in Rome.'[36] It is a curious fact that, though both he himself and his liturgical practices were criticised by his Bishop and despite the public criticism of the Vatican he was later to make, Bede was left in peace by Rome. One reason given is that he did not hold a teaching position at a seminary, another that his personal sanctity protected him and that the Vatican did not feel able to touch a man so widely regarded as a saint, but Bede himself felt that the explanation lay in geographical distance. There is a story of an English couple visiting Shantivanam, being much moved by the liturgy and asking Bede if they could take away a copy of the words. No, he replied, that could not be allowed. Understanding what lay behind this refusal, they asked, 'What do they think of what you are doing in Rome?' 'We are a very long way from Rome,' he replied with a smile.

If Bede's worries about the authoritarian nature of the papacy were in tune with a strong strand of Catholic thinking, so too were his views on some of its teachings. He was arguing in favour of married clergy as early as 1966,[37] certain that there was no necessary connection between celibacy and priesthood and that the only obstacle to change was the whole system of Church government. He regarded Christianity's difficulty in conceiving God as Mother as one of its greatest defects, writing in *The Tablet*: 'Perhaps it is only when we have learned to recognise God as Mother that woman will find her rightful place in the Church.'[38] In favour of allowing inter-communion, he distinguished between a shared faith and the divisions of doctrine and argued that the early form of the creed – 'I believe in one God, the Father Almighty, and in one Lord Jesus Christ, in the Holy Spirit and in the Holy Catholic Church' – was sufficient for membership: 'Admission to communion would be open to all who profess this faith and who intend to do in communion what Jesus said, "Do this in remembrance of me." All further development of Christian doctrine and of church organisation could then be left to the different churches to work out among themselves.'[39]

In all this he was broadly reflecting the thinking of the people who came to Shantivanam, but probably the single thing that most attracted them was the opportunity to meditate regularly in an atmosphere that encouraged it and with the guidance of someone for whom meditation had been a way of life for over fifty years. In his time at Prinknash, Farnborough and Pluscarden, Bede had valued the meditative reading of the Scriptures and the Fathers, saying that in the Mass and the breviary was 'a perfect method of prayer and contemplation'[40] but increasingly he came to find that this was not sufficient and that the ideal of contemplation, of a direct experience of God in prayer, had been lost. He accepted that western methods of prayer and meditation have a deep supernatural foundation, that the goal of a deeper level of consciousness in which the soul experiences its own centre was well known among Catholic mystics, but felt that it had become obscured by the emphasis on philosophy and theology: 'Even in our prayer and worship we tend to remain on the level of rational consciousness, and "meditation" becomes little more than an exercise in discursive reason. But the aim of all meditation should be to pass beyond the limits of the rational consciousness and awake to the inner life of the Spirit, that is to the indwelling presence of God.'[41] He was also saddened that western Christianity paid scant attention to the position of the body in prayer and that so few Catholics taught methods of contemplative prayer, though he regarded technique as only a vehicle which has to be transcended: 'It is, as the Buddha says, like a raft to carry you across the river, but you don't need to carry it on your head once you have crossed.'[42] He recognised that people were no longer satisfied with theories *about* God, but longed for direct experience; longed too to learn a method of prayer, a way to reach the centre, the point beyond thought. He was interested in the Transcendental Meditation taught by the Maharishi Mahesh Yogi, who, it is believed, has been responsible for teaching some four million people to meditate. 'It is to me completely convincing,' he wrote. 'It seems to me to be a method that is physiologically, psychologically & spiritually sound.'[43] Initially he was doubtful whether it could take one to really deep levels of experience, never trying it himself, declining opportunities to meet the Maharishi and regarding it only as a useful preliminary stage, but on reading more his position shifted: 'There is nothing in his theory of the states of consciousness which a Catholic could not accept. In fact, it agrees very closely with the teaching of St Teresa & St John of the Cross. I found myself perfectly at home with it. I had not realised before that Mahesh Yogi had gone so deep.'[44] Bede was also aware of the danger of spiritual movements becoming caught up in psychic phenomena such as levitation, which he regarded as secondary and unimportant, aware too that they can (and that some do) fall into the trap of becoming too involved with money.

Bede much admired the work of two American Cistercians, Thomas Keating and Basil Pennington. They too were concerned that Christianity had lost both the method and the true meaning of contemplative prayer and felt that this accounted for its failure to meet the needs of modern people. They appreciated that many Christians were cut off from the possibility of experiencing God within themselves; that there was a tendency to '"serve God," rather than to "taste God".'[45] Bede felt that total enlightenment must be very rare, but that *glimpses* of enlightenment, a kind of growing awareness, were not uncommon, and he was impressed by their method of 'centring power', which is in many ways remarkably like Transcendental Meditation.

The twentieth-century teacher he most admired, however, was John Main, a fellow Benedictine he met only once, in 1979, but whom he considered to be one of the most important spiritual guides in the world at the time and whom he credited with being the person responsible for bringing Christian contemplative life to lay people.[46] He was later to study this method of Christian meditation, based on the repetition of a mantra, at some depth and if anyone asked his advice on how to meditate, this was the method he most frequently suggested. Bede's own practice was the repetition of the Jesus Prayer ('Lord Jesus Christ, Son of the Living God, have mercy on me, a sinner') which, after many years, he had come to find 'goes on almost always when my mind is not otherwise occupied'.[47] He explained his own practice of meditation with such clarity that it is worth quoting at length:

> To answer your questions 1) My meditation period is normally an hour in the morning & an hour in the evening, but it is sometimes shortened slightly (3/4 hour) & sometimes lengthened to 2 or 3 hours, but not commonly.
>
> 2) I find that the words of the Jesus Prayer normally repeat themselves. Sometimes it goes on rather mechanically, the mind wanders; sometimes it seems to gather strength & one prays in a concentrated manner.
>
> 3) Sometimes the words 'fade out', but rarely completely so. They seem to go on in the 'heart'. One may not notice them, but one finds them going on, as it were.

4) If thoughts really intervene and cut off the prayer, then I renew the mantra again – or it renews itself, as soon as I realise what has happened.

5) Yes, I regard the concentration on the person of Jesus as very important. I feel that it puts on in touch with the concrete reality of his person, & 'focuses' the mind. To me this is the difference between Christian & Buddhist & Hindu prayer. Christian prayer reaches the Centre in & through Christ.[48]

The beginning of the 1980s saw a further development of Bede's spirituality. 'For me all his writings are footprints, which he left for us. But he is still beyond anything. We cannot reduce him to footprints, he was always on the move,'[49] said Brother Martin, a remarkable Indian monk who first met Bede in 1975 and has been a member of the Shantivanam community since 1984. Brother Martin sees four stages in this development which, like all such progressions, overlap each other and cannot be precisely dated. First was Bede's discovery of the love of Christ, so total that it led him to become a Benedictine monk. Then, in the 1930s, came the period when he began to discover other religions, though never doubting that, though all religions contain some elements of the truth, 'there is only one absolutely true religion . . . Christ is the Way, the Truth and the Life and without him no man comes to the Father'.[50] By 1973, however, he found that this statement needed qualifying: 'Christ is the ultimate fulfilment of all religion, the final and definitive word of God, but the same cannot be said of Christianity. Christianity, as an organised religion seeking to express the mystery of Christ, the divine Word, in human terms, suffers from the same defects as other religions.[51] Two years later he went further, writing: 'I am so tired of the childish pretence that Christianity is the only true religion and must be shown to be superior to others.'[52] He was moving gradually to the third stage, a conviction that all religions are complementary:

> Saivism, Vaishnavism and Shaktism, and the different schools of Vedanta in Hinduism; Hinayana and Mahayana Buddhism, with their different schools; the Sunni and Shia sects in Islam, and their different schools of philosophy; Catholicism, Orthodoxy and Protestantism within Christianity, with their different expressions of the one Truth of revelation, each with its particular insight. But one must learn to discern among these conflicting and partial views the principle which unites them, which transcends these differences and reconciles their conflicts.[53]

In the early 1980s came a glimmering of the final stage, the idea that there is one reality beyond all, a reality found in all religions. Bede became more and more interested in the advaitic experience. Much ink has been spilled in defining the word '*advaita*', but it would be hard to improve on Abhishiktananda's definition for clarity and brevity: 'Advaita means precisely this: neither God alone, nor the creature alone, nor God plus the creature, but an indefinable non-duality which transcends at once all separation and all confusion.'[54] While the word comes from the Vedas, there can also be a Christian *advaita*: 'In reality advaita is already present at the root of Christian experience. It is simply the mystery that God and the world are *not two*.'[55] The latest development in his own thought, Bede wrote to Nigel Bruce, was that he had become more and more 'advaitin':

> It seems to me that we have ultimately to go beyond all forms of thought – even beyond the Trinity, the Incarnation, the Church etc. All these belong to the world of 'signs' – manifestations of God in human thought – but God himself, Truth itself, is beyond all forms of thought. All meditation should lead into silence, into the world of 'non-duality', when all the differences – and conflicts – in this world are transcended – not that they are simply annulled, but that they are taken up into a deeper unity of being in which all conflicts are resolved – rather like colours being absorbed into pure white light, which *contains* all the colours but resolves their differences.[56]

CHAPTER FOURTEEN

The Marriage of Opposites

I t is entirely in keeping with Bede's nature that the concept of non-duality should have attracted him so strongly and that meditation should
have been central to his life, for he had always, in one way or another,
been caught in the tension between the opposites: in meditation he found
the still point beyond the world of duality, the reconciliation of opposites for
which he longed. While this reconciliation of opposites found practical
expression in the hours he spent daily in meditation, it was also something
in which he had a theoretical interest. Since meeting Toni Sussman in the
1940s he had been impressed by C. G. Jung's thinking on the subject and
he was also drawn to the idea of the '*coincidentia oppositorum*' posited in the
fifteenth century by the German cardinal and philosopher Nicholas de
Cusa. For de Cusa, whose thinking was so in tune with his own, the road to
truth lay beyond reason and contradiction; only by intuition could God,
where all opposites meet, be discovered. Writing of the German philosopher Bede said: 'Theology only advances through conflicting views. Perhaps
the human mind is so made that it can only obtain a partial view of reality,
and every view has to be corrected by another . . . All opposites are eventually reconciled in the universal truth, since all are partial expression of the
one reality.'[1]

We all live in duality, caught between opposites, but for Bede, more
than for most people, it was a matter of often bitter experience. Now in his
seventies, had he reached the reconciliation for which he longed? In his
twenty years in India he had found western emphasis on the conscious mind

balanced by a greater awareness of the unconscious, intuition taking its place beside reason and the feminine given more expression; to some extent he had found 'the other half of his soul' he came to seek. So too he had reached an understanding of the one reality behind all religions which enabled him to have on the mantelpiece in his hut not only Christian images such as the Rublev Trinity, crosses, icons and a statue of St Benedict, but the Hindu Nataraj (the dancing form of the god Shiva), statues of Buddha, the *Om* sign and a figure of a hermaphrodite. Nevertheless, there were opposites that tore him apart. There was some substance in his reputation as a 'loner', and his love of independence still fought with the longing to surrender his ego, something he had been seeking ever since he felt called 'to surrender the very citadel of myself' all those years ago in the mission house at Bethnal Green. He was still caught between detachment and engagement, claiming to be indifferent to criticism but unable to resist responding to his attackers. Perhaps most acutely of all, the contemplative and the communicator in him co-existed uneasily; his need for solitude would lead him to declare that he had 'foresworn all further travel', yet only a few weeks later he would be on a plane heading for a conference in Pakistan, Europe or America. Indeed, the trips to America reflected his feeling that America and India were two halves of himself that he had to bring together. Martyn Skinner, who never ceased to deplore dependence on modern technology, would often take him to task for his inconsistency in making constant use of the aeroplane and the media in his desire to communicate. For instance, soon after Bede's death, writing a tirade against television, he reflected: 'But at least I haven't appeared on it, as Bede did. This goes with jet travel – doing good by doing ill, ends and means . . . though when he wrote that jet travel didn't disturb him, he found it possible to meditate, I replied, "It ought to disturb you."'[2]

The opposites are full of potential. Just as male and female produce the next generation, so the marriage of any pair of opposites can bring new life, as the power and beauty of the liturgy at Shantivanam, a fusion of old and new, traditional and modern, East and West, bear witness. Bede sought balance, the 'middle way' beloved by the Greeks; for instance, he found the views of Martyn Skinner and C. S. Lewis on culture and religion too weighted towards conservatism:

I am trying to find a middle way between conservatism and modernism. I agree ¾ with you and Lewis, but I think that there is an aspect which you miss. I would say that growth of any kind, whether in nature, in culture or in religion, consists in *change in continuity*. Without change there is no life, but without continuity there is disintegration. Everything (& every person) in this world has to change if it is live, yet it (or he or she) has to preserve its identity.[3]

This awareness of the tension between continuity and change enabled him to respond to the needs of the twentieth century and both reflect and lead his age. He loved tradition and was steeped in it, but he was also, in the profoundest sense, a child of his time, never ceasing to be open to new developments, whether it was Schumacher's 'appropriate technology', organic farming, health foods and holistic ways of life, many forms of alternative medicine, themselves based on ancient methods of healing, and of course the various forms of meditation that were increasingly becoming known to westerners: 'One cannot simply go back to the past, nor would it be altogether desirable. We have to look forward to a new science and technology which will free us from some of the disasters which accompanied human life in the past – plague, famine, infant mortality and many forms of disease – but will at the same time be in harmony with nature and create a world of beauty.'[4]

Many elements in Bede's life, if not in opposition, contained enough differences to sow seeds of conflict within him. He wrote and studied widely, he spent hours in the role of pastor and spiritual counsellor – was he first a scholar or Superior of a community? He lived in a community, but often he satisfied his cherished desire for greater solitude, spending days in a hut some way from the ashram – was he monk, hermit or coenobite?* He was both Benedictine monk and Hindu sannyasi – did the two conflict? And, a question that sometimes concerned the authorities, did he run an ashram, with its roots in the first millennium before Christ, when the *rishis* retired into the forest to meditate, or a monastery, rooted in western Christianity?

Some people have questioned whether, in living this unusual life and in not belonging to a Benedictine congregation, he could still call himself a Benedictine. Bede himself was in no doubt that the Benedictine Rule governed his life and visitors to Shantivanam remarked that in the regularity of its life-style and in the sense of stability that saw it through storms and periods of peace alike, it was very Benedictine. An exclaustrated monk does not cease to be a Benedictine. Indeed, confirmation of how deeply he remained a Benedictine came from no less a person than the Abbot Primate himself, writing after Bede's death:

*Coenobite: a monk who lives in a community.

The Rule of Benedict has inspired and continues to inspire many forms of monasticism over the centuries, from enclosed communities of monks and nuns to the open communities of missionaries and teachers. It was in this tradition that Dom Bede Griffiths assumed the values of the Rule and gave them flesh in the culture and customs of India. Benedictine monasticism is indebted to him for his integrative work of joining East and West in both meditation and practice.[5]

There are, however, many ways in which an ashram and a monastery differ and this was a subject to which Bede gave much thought. Clearly, any Christian community is centred on Christ, while in ashramic life disciples gather round a guru in their search for God. A monastery has an institutional framework and is based on a Rule; an ashram is more a way of life than an institution. Monastic life centres on the liturgy and *lectio divina*; the ashram gives central place to contemplative prayer. Though there are exceptions, western monasticism usually takes the form of community life, its members living in one place; in India greater stress is laid on the solitary life, the Hindu sannyasi often wandering from place to place, unburdened by possessions, food or money. St Benedict attached great importance to withdrawal from the world and although Benedictines are rightly famed for their hospitality, their houses are single-sexed, while an ashram is essentially an open community, receiving men and women without distinction.

How, then, does a Christian ashram – and there are now at least fifty in India – reconcile these differences in practice? Shantivanam draws on both traditions, though this may not be immediately apparent. The impression of a visitor arriving for the first time, glimpsing the colourful temple through palm trees, palmyras and coconuts, seeing the saffron robes and the cross-legged postures, hearing the Sanskrit chants, may well be that they have wandered into a Hindu ashram by mistake. Explore the grounds and find, under the neem trees by the river Cavery, a statue of Christ sitting in the lotus position with the cobra, a sacred symbol of Hinduism, protectively curved over him; approach the temple and see the *Om* sign in the centre of the cross, and the newcomer might become a little confused. But come closer, look and see the Christian figures on the dome of the temple, attend the *'puja'* and find it is a Christian Mass, meet the Superior, and find he is a British Christian, and those impressions need to be reassessed. Even in externals it is indeed a Christian ashram, blending the symbols and life-style of both traditions.

So was Father Bede guru or Superior? Again, he was both: Superior in his relationship to authority, guru to the visitors. Some have questioned his wisdom in accepting the veneration normally accorded to a guru, but how, in India, could he not? It is true too, and rather uncharacteristic, that he allowed photographs of himself to be sold as postcards. There is, however, little evidence that he saw himself in the role of a guru and it is only very rarely that he refers to a guru–disciple relationship between himself and someone else. The word derives from two Sanskrit words *gu* and *ru* and indicates the removal of darkness. Bede was always available to talk to visitors, to try to help them in their journey from darkness to light, but they found he listened rather than taught, encouraged people to seek the experience of God rather than to ally themselves to any particular religious tradition or denomination. They found too that there was never any doubt that Christ was the centre of his life, that for Christians the guru is Christ, not a person, however spiritually advanced.

Then, though the community is rooted in Tamil Nadu and the life-style is Hindu, though it is open to all and encourages contemplative prayer, everything takes place in the context of the Benedictine Rule and it is the Benedictine pattern of prayer, study and manual work that structures the day. Unlike the normal Benedictine monastery, however, people studied both Hindu and Christian doctrine, striving always to relate the Hindu experience of God to the Christian doctrine of Creation, the Trinity and the Incarnation. Bede was in no doubt that this is central:

> A Christian ashram, if it is to be worthy of the name, must be a place where a meeting can take place in 'the cave of the heart' between the Christian experience of God through faith in Jesus Christ and the Hindu experience of 'Brahman' the One 'without a second,' the Ground of all creation and the 'Atman,' the Spirit, dwelling in the heart of every man. This meeting has to take place in the depth of contemplative experience, which is only possible in a life dedicated to the search for God, the quest of the Absolute, that has always been the goal of monastic life.[6]

Can this way of life be reconciled with the Benedictine Rule? Bede maintained that St Benedict was not attempting to fashion a fixed rule binding future generations, but was writing for his own time and circumstances, insisting that the Abbot was free to make changes according to circumstances. He argued that St Benedict's Rule was open-ended, that it both looked back to the Bible and the Fathers and ahead to changes relevant to different situations. 'Can we therefore find a place for an ashram in the Indian tradition within the context of the *Rule of St Benedict*? I would be inclined to say "yes," but it would require a drastic revision of the *Rule*.'[7] He supports this rather startling suggestion by noting that Cardinal Pignedoli, visiting India as the representative of the Pope in 1969, spoke in strong terms of the need for the monastic life in India, adding that 'attention must be given to adaptations and reforms that correspond to the signs of the times and their needs'.[8]

Bede's chief concern was that there should be a renewal of the 'charisma' of monastic life. The search for God may take many different forms – eremitic, wandering or in community, open or enclosed, ashramic or monastic – but nothing can be allowed to stand in its way. The real pilgrimage is 'the journey through the inner space of the heart, and this inner space can be found no less in the midst of a community than in solitude. It is this inner space within the heart which we all seek and that is the goal of all monastic life in the East as in the West.'[9] He knew that you cannot reconcile opposites in any sphere of life if you have not reconciled them in yourself. For Bede, seeking union, going beyond this world, beyond time and history, was central, but this did not mean losing touch with ordinary human life; here again it was balance he sought. He felt that to close oneself away in a solitary world of contemplation might lead to profound experience, but it misses a dimension of life and can deplete your relationship with God. The experience of contemplation led him to be more in touch with people, not less. Once again he was reconciling opposites – the active and the passive, the solitary and the communal. A telling example of this is that one of the first things he did when he took over the ashram was to take out a subscription to *Time* magazine, and his prayers of intercession were so wide-ranging that one visitor found them 'better than a news bulletin'.

Central to Bede's life and work was the relationship between Hinduism and Christianity. 'To me Eastern wisdom gives the key to Christianity. I cannot conceive of Christ now except in terms of Vedanta,' he wrote to Martyn Skinner in 1971.[10] Again, when courteously declining an offer to meet the Maharishi because he placed himself in the line of the gurus and his basis was Hindu, Bede explained: 'I am afraid that this might draw me from my Christian basis which is the deepest thing in my life, instead of enriching my life with the Hindu experience, which is what I want.'[11] So he sought exchange and interaction, sharing and mutual enrichment, in short dialogue, a means of communication which appealed to him in his old age as it had always appealed to him, though his manner had changed. 'He has substituted what he calls dialogue for the old habits of disputation, and he is as skilled a dialoguer as he ever was disputant,' wrote Martyn Skinner to Hugh Waterman,[12] ruefully recalling their endless and sometimes frustrating discussions at Oxford and at Eastington. Now, clear in his own mind what he sought, Bede could confront the opposites of East and West with passionate concern yet with equanimity.

From his early days at Shantivanam Bede had wanted to establish an intellectual tradition there, to make it a research centre where both the theory and the practice of Indian spirituality could be developed. This was balm to the hearts of the twentieth-century seekers who were drawn to Shantivanam. Many of them rubbed shoulders every day with people of other faiths, they ate at their restaurants, wore 'ethnic' clothes and listened to their music. Why should they make an exception when it came to religion? So Bede's wish that Shantivanam should become a centre for dialogue found a ready audience and an accomplished leader. To this end he put a lot of energy into building up the library, always keen to be given books and frequently asking friends to send him copies of things that had come to his attention.

By the 1980s Shantivanam often had over a hundred visitors at any one time and, as it acquired a place on the map of India, it was also visited by members of the Church. For instance, when the Catholic bishops of India met in Tiruchi in 1982, nearly half of them came to visit the ashram; hard on their heels came half a dozen German bishops. Bede arranged meetings between Hindus and Christians (one of the first and most successful was a three day Hindu–Christian dialogue in 1974), and travelled widely to attend conferences himself, whether the Monastic Conference for all-Asia held at Bangalore, a conference on 'Western Science and Eastern Mysticism' in Bombay or a meeting of the C. S. Lewis Society in California. He was also a frequent correspondent to the religious press.

How then did he see this process of dialogue? Bede expressed his position with characteristic clarity. He was in no doubt that to enter into dialogue it is essential to be faithful to your own tradition: 'You are not expected, in dialogue, to give way to the other. You are expected to say what is my faith, what is my relation to God and our understanding. Then to listen to others. Through that real confrontation there is a great hope.'[13] He considered that dialogue and mission are indivisible and that the great mistake made by the missionaries was to think they could preach the Gospel and receive nothing themselves. 'It was all on one side, and nobody likes to be simply on the receiving end. You are not being recognised as a person.'[14] So Indians came to see Christianity as aggressive, bypassing their culture and ignoring their way of life. Bede, on the other hand, would start a dialogue meeting by reading a paper on a subject of universal concern such as salvation; he would then encourage everyone, academic or not, to ask themselves what salvation meant to them as a Hindu, as a Christian, simply as a person. In that way the discussion could come to life, as people spoke from experience as well as theory.

It was not, of course, as simple as that. The issues raised by the meeting of faiths strike at the heart of the most complex area of theology, as those who had been this way before him – from Robert de Nobili and Brahmabandhab Upadhyaya to the founders of Shantivanam – had already discovered. One issue that threads its way through the tapestry of dialogue is syncretism. Bede was very aware of the dangers of a superficial syncretism that regarded 'all religions as "essentially" the same, only differing in "accidental" characteristics'.[15] That attitude he considered destroyed all serious dialogue and made real understanding impossible. He held to the fact that for a Christian the mystery is disclosed in Christ, for a Buddhist in the Buddha, for a Hindu in the Vedas and for a Muslim in the Quran – each has its unique insights and the essence of dialogue is to share these insights and to see their relationship to the whole. Nothing of the essential truth of each religious tradition must be lost:

> We are not seeking a syncretism in which each religion will lose its own individuality, but an organic growth in which each religion has to purify itself and discover its own inmost depth and significance and then relate itself to the inner depth of the other traditions. Perhaps it will never be achieved in this world, but it is the one way in which we can advance today towards that unity in truth which is the ultimate goal of mankind.[16]

Another complex problem arises from the different concepts of time held in the East and the West. The Hebrew revelation brought a linear concept of time, progressing towards an end, an eschaton; then Jesus comes in the context of this linear time – an unrepeatable event bringing history to fulfilment in time and place. On the other hand, the eastern concept of time is cyclical, as in nature everything moves in circles – the sun rises and sets, the moon waxes and wanes, the seasons give way to each other – to attain liberation is to escape from the wheel of time. This issue preoccupied theologians in India, and Bede was convinced that the meeting of these two aspects of the different traditions was crucial. He felt on the one hand that Hinduism was wrong in thinking that Jesus could simply be taken into its cyclic world, ignoring the significance of the Resurrection, and on the other hand that the West had placed salvation too firmly in time, not sufficiently aware of 'the eternal reality which is always there'. He suggested that the key might be found in the spiral:

> A spiral is always going round in circles but it is moving towards a point. This is where the real dialogue is: we're discovering each other, we are dis-

covering another dimension. It is not easy and not very many of us are ready for it. I think the Church will grow with the discovery of another dimension in the approach to God, and equally the Hindu and the Buddhist will have to discover this dynamic move.[17]

These differing concepts of time lead to a different understanding of God. The Semitic experience is of a transcendent, personal God, revealed in a particular way: God dwells in heaven and looks down on earth. The oriental experience is of immanence, the non-dual reality present in the whole of creation as Brahman, and in the heart of every man as Atman, the Self. Finally Brahman is revealed as Ishvara, the personal creator God, known in the *Upanishads* as 'the Lord of the past and the future'. God is perceived as being not so much above the universe as in it. Where is the meeting point between these two approaches? Christians, of course, can and do see God as immanent in nature, but the emphasis is different, the Judaeo-Christian tradition starting from transcendence and discovering immanence, the Hindu starting from immanence and reaching towards transcendence. How Ishvara, the personal God, is related to Brahman, the absolute Godhead, has long been a matter of debate inside Hinduism itself; how much more complex this becomes when the Trinitarian faith of Christians is brought in. Perhaps, though, the Trinity can be a doorway to understanding rather than an obstacle. Raimon Panikkar suggested that the Trinity 'may be regarded as a junction where the authentic spiritual dimensions of all religions meet'[18] and as Bede's ideas on the subject developed, he came to agree with him. He began to find that Greek theology tended to divide Christ by conceiving him in terms of a human nature and a divine nature: 'The Greek view leads to the idea of the Trinity as something apart. The Father, Son and Holy Spirit are eternally there, and then apart from that comes the Incarnation, time and history.'[19] Bede was drawn more to the understanding of people like Jan van Ruysbroeck, one of his favourite Christian mystics; thus, in seeing the movement of the Trinity as the rhythm of the universe, he began to close the gap between the Hindu and the Christian understanding of time:

> Everything comes forth eternally from the Father, the Ground of Being, in the Son, the Word and Wisdom of the Father and returns in the Spirit. The Father, the ground, is pouring itself out eternally in the Son, knowing itself and expressing itself in the Son, and the Father and the Son return to one another, unite with one another, eternally in the embrace of the Holy Spirit. We are all enfolded in that love.[20]

Bede's thinking on the meeting of religions found its most sustained expression in another book, *The Marriage of East and West*, which was published in 1982. It is subtitled *A Sequel to The Golden String*, and begins with a vivid account of how his discovery of India gave new life to the ideas he had been formulating in England. India, he wrote, 'had been nourished from the beginning by the truth of the imagination, the primordial truth, which is not abstract but concrete, not logical but symbolic, not rational but intuitive. So it was that I was led to the rediscovery of the truth which the Western world has lost and is now desperately seeking to recover.'[21] The main body of the book is not autobiography as it is generally understood, rather it is a distillation of his understanding of the revelations contained in the Vedas, in Judaism and in Christianity. He warned of the disastrous effects of western industrialism, suggesting, as he had been doing privately for some time, that the present era was coming to an end and that the age of the domination of the white races was passing, the future lying with Asia, Africa and Latin America. Yet, optimist as he essentially was, he saw no reason for despair. He argued that it was essential for the survival of the world that spiritual wisdom should be recovered and that this was possible if the Church opened itself to the values of eastern religion and culture and found new forms of expression for its faith. Neither East nor West had the whole truth: the danger of Hinduism was its tendency to see time and history as passing phenomena without any ultimate significance, while Christianity tends to attach too much importance to temporal events and to lose the sense of a timeless reality. Once again he returned to the conviction that had taken him to India in the first place: 'The balance can only be restored when a meeting takes place between East and West. This meeting must take place at the deepest level of the human consciousness. It is an encounter ultimately between the two fundamental dimensions of human nature: the male and the female – the masculine, rational, dominating power of the mind, and the feminine, intuitive, passive and receptive power.'[22]

Just as he greeted every new chapter in his life with enthusiasm and excitement, so he felt that each book represented the essence of his thought up to that moment. Of *The Marriage of East and West* he wrote:

> I feel that everything has come together here – all that I have been working at since Eastington – especially the place of intuition and imagination as distinguished from science and reason. The theme of the book is really the 'marriage' of intuition and reason, of the feminine and the masculine, denouncing the domination of science & reason – the aggressive male – over the feminine intuition & typified by the abuse of nature, the oppres-

sion of the coloured people by the white races, the growth of cities at the expense of the country, of industrialism instead of craftsmanship.[23]

Even he, with his capacity to be unruffled by criticism, had to admit to disappointment that the book received a mixed reaction from his friends, and 'As for public notice it has been greeted with an almost deafening silence.'[24] Writing two months after publication he had seen only two reviews, one in the *Church Times* ('rather good and appreciative') and another in the *Church of England Newspaper* ('superficial and rather snooty'.)[25] A later review[26] considered that though it said nothing very new, it had value in its synthesis of previous scholarship, obviously resulting from years of thought and prayer, and that it conveyed an important message. It is unlikely that Bede was too disturbed by a damning review in which the critic was shocked at the idea that sexual intercourse could have a mystical value and stated that as a result of his involvement with Hinduism the author had been led to 'transcend all denominational limits, and so has ceased to be a Catholic'.[27] Such a misunderstanding of Bede's position makes it hard to take this writer's numerous criticisms seriously.

As happens to many prophetic figures, appreciation of Bede's views came later: sixteen years after its first publication, *The Marriage of East and West* is still in print, widely appreciated and regarded as one of his most important books. Indeed, the distinguished American paper the *National Catholic Reporter* remarked in Bede's obituary that if some of the views expressed in *The Marriage of East and West* sound 'almost commonplace nowadays' it was partly because of 'Griffiths' own prophetic pilgrimage, begun so many years ago'.[28]

One problem resulting from the tightrope Bede walked between Benedictine monk and Hindu sannyasi, between monastery and ashram, had serious practical implications; this was the uncertain position in which the younger members of the community found themselves. It was one thing for Bede himself, for though it placed him in an ambiguous position and left him bereft of an official religious family, he had long pursued a lonely path and had become accustomed to it; in any case, the strength of his convictions and his personal fame protected him. But he was getting old – what would happen to the rest of the community when he was no longer there? How could they become ordained priests without being attached to a Christian order? Though he needed and loved his independence, he needed to affiliate himself with a monastic community in order to ensure the institution's survival.

The question of the status of Shantivanam had always been complex. When Bede arrived in 1968 the ashram was regarded as a foundation from Kurisumala and therefore free from episcopal control. But could a foundation following the Latin rite of the Mass come under a Syrian monastery? Should it have some kind of oblate status, unbound by either eastern or western canon law, free to develop on its own lines? Bureaucratic delays, coupled with the uneasy relationship between Father Francis and Bede existing at the time, stood in the way of an easy solution, and it was not until 1975 that Bede learned that they were officially listed as dependent on Kurisumala with Father Francis as 'superior general'. Under oriental canon law this meant that the ashram had no right to receive novices, to profess monks or to elect its own Superior. Bede was keen to retain a link with Kurisumala, but he also wanted to be free to develop what he called a 'Hindu-type' ashram; in short, he wanted independent status.

In 1977 he wrote to Mar Athanasios, the Metropolitan of Tiruvalla and the 'founding father' of Kurisumala, pointing out that as Shantivanam was financially self-supporting and had ten members, five of them professed monks, could they not now be independent? He was becoming more confident and determined, adding that if this were not possible then 'we should have to seek it [independence] elsewhere, as none of the brothers here is willing to remain in perpetual dependence on Kurisumala'.[29] Receiving no reply, he wrote again, suggesting the ashram might follow the model of Gandhi's ashrams and include not only monks and religious but also lay people, both married and single, of any religion; they would have no strictly monastic or religious status, all they would require would be ecclesiastical permission. Perhaps the lack of response was due to the Metropolitan's health, for in the autumn all negotiations came to an end with his death and Bede had to pursue a different path. It was predictable that he should lean towards the Benedictines, and, though he 'would have preferred in some way to have the link with Prinknash',[30] the choice eventually was to become affiliated either to Mount Saviour, an independent Benedictine house in New York, or to the Camaldolese congregation. The warmth of his welcome when he visited the Camaldolese in Rome decided him, and in 1980 he was formally accepted by them, the ashram itself following two years later.

The Camaldolese congregation was founded at the beginning of the eleventh century by St Romuald, an Italian priest who spent much of his life founding and reforming monasteries and hermitages. Its administrative centre is in Rome, the mother house at Camaldoli, near Arezzo, but there are also houses in America and India, and a house for sisters in Africa. The order combines the solitary life of the hermit with an austere form of monastic life and belongs to the Benedictine Confederation, following the Rule of St Benedict with the addition of St Romuald's 'Little Rule'. This begins 'Sit in your cell as in paradise', and it is easy to see why, with their emphasis on the contemplative life in both eremetical and community form, the Camaldolese should have appealed to Bede, especially as they are always open to visitors and are also prepared to allow for wandering monks, like St Romuald himself. They welcomed the Shantivanam community warmly and accepted them just as they were, anxious that they should not change their way of life. The *nihil obstat* from Father Francis and the Syrian Bishop of Tiruvalla was obtained without difficulty and Bede, to his delight, was once more officially within the Benedictine order.

CHAPTER FIFTEEN

Unity in Diversity

THE 1980S

F irm on the rock of meditation, the dawn and dusk pillars of his day, never ceasing to question, explore and search, Bede's life was full at every level. Though by 1980 he was seventy-four, the decade for him was not one of quiet and retirement; rather it was one of intense activity in the ashram, as the numbers of vocations and the stream of visitors increased. It also saw the publication of books, articles and letters to the press and extensive travel. 'Unity in diversity', the slogan blazoned on the billboards of Indian cities to promote national unity, was never truer of anyone than of Father Bede, both in what he was and in what he sought.

An ashram is a microcosm of society, as prone to the problems of daily living as any other group of people living together. Prone also to the occasional crisis, such as the time when Bede returned from a trip abroad to find one of the brothers accused of having an affair with a visitor to the ashram; or the time when a cyclone devastated parts of South India, causing a flood at Shantivanam, covering parts of the ashram with three or four feet of water and forcing the community to go by boat to Tannirpalli. Some of the villages suffered far worse, many of the mud houses being completely washed away, and Shantivanam helped to rebuild one of the nearby villages.

It is easy to forget that, for all his international fame, Bede was a monastic Superior, responsible for the welfare and training of the young men who had dedicated their lives to the growing community, giving them talks and individual instruction and arranging for them to go to theological institutions to obtain the qualifications necessary for priesthood. He felt refreshed and renewed by 'having so many sons in my old age', rejoicing in the growing community, now a close family who cared for each other, and particularly for Bede himself, with real love and affection. At the beginning of 1986 his efforts were crowned by the ordination of Christudas and Amaldas to the priesthood, a colourful occasion with music and drums, processions, garlands and other Indian rites of welcome, attended by 500 people both from the neighbourhood and from as far away as Kerala. Bede was so moved that his customary reserve collapsed and he wept for joy.

He was also, in effect if not formally, the guest master. He not only gave daily talks to the visitors, preached homilies at Mass and presided over the regular evening meetings, but answered letters by hand from people wanting to come and stay, time and again welcoming them and telling them the best way to travel. When visitors arrived the first person they saw was his tall figure standing at the gate to greet them and many were touched that every day he would hand out the mail himself, largely in order to keep in regular touch with the guests. He was living to the full the Benedictine ideal of treating the guest as Christ himself and this was not just done for duty, but from the heart. Christudas told how if there were difficult guests, for instance if someone was taking drugs, he might suggest that they should be asked to leave but Bede's response was: 'Christudas, you do not know the heart of these people. Everyone is created by God and everyone is attracted to the ashram not by his own power or his own call, but God sends them here to have a change of mind. Nobody is unimportant, because they are created by God.'[1] Christudas had to agree. Bede would also spend hours every day seeing people individually, once saying ruefully, 'people come to see me all the time and I am like a doctor or a dentist with a list of appointments every afternoon'.[2] These appointments he would make, and if necessary change, himself, seeking people out and impressing everyone by the courteousness with which he ensured that the arrangements were convenient for them.

Why did people come to him in such numbers? What were his gifts as a counsellor? It was not primarily the wisdom of his counsel, for he rarely gave advice; in fact, sometimes people were disappointed at not receiving help with specific problems, even complaining that he was too kind, his constant agreement leaving them confused. Nevertheless he was a revered spiritual guide to hundreds of people, and even if they were no wiser about particular situations, people came out of his hut feeling freer, walking more lightly. The way they speak of time spent alone with Father Bede indicates something of the riches they received. 'He doesn't advise or give directions, he just walks with you, follows you with an understanding heart and encourages you,' said one woman, while another told how, when she presented him with her arguments against Christian dogma, 'He wouldn't argue back. He would say with a twinkle in his eye, "So . . . well . . . what can you believe?" By this method he helped me accept many of the things that I couldn't accept before.'[3] The young monks also valued the freedom he gave them: 'He wouldn't say do this or do that, but when you told him your experience he would say "That's something wonderful".' Like any good spiritual director, Bede was never judgmental, rather he was quick to congratulate and was especially encouraging during periods of spiritual aridity; for instance, someone who admitted she didn't feel like meditating remembered him saying, 'That's good. Sometimes we have to go through experiences like that.' The English Benedictine monk Father Laurence Freeman, who knew him well, felt that Bede's success lay both in his ability to listen, enabling people to talk freely, and in his detachment, the mark of a good counsellor: 'You didn't feel he was getting involved or that he had a drum to beat or a theory to impose or a dogma to beat you with.'[4] A New York taxi-driver summed up the feelings of many when he said: 'Leaving him you felt transformed – your whole inner state was changed because of his atmosphere of peace and spiritual power. I always felt changed when I left him after a private talk.'[5] Another American, Chuck Baroo, who became a close friend of Bede's, was impressed above all by his ability to encounter every individual who came to him with unconditional love:

> People, all of us broken or hurt or something, in one way or another, came to him from all over the world – long-term travellers, pilgrims, people who don't even know why they've come, and he accepted them all with great grace and understanding, and again, this unconditional love. And folks walked out of his little hut and after maybe a very short interview they'd experienced – they may not have been aware of it at an intellectual level – but they'd experienced it in some way.[6]

Bede always suggested that people should meditate regularly; he would often recommend books to read; sometimes he would share his love of nature, advising someone to go and sit by the river under the trees. Occasionally, perhaps seeing someone in deep need, he would suggest that they come to his hut in the evening and meditate with him. Not one word was exchanged, 'but I felt the vibrations', said one woman. It becomes clear that Bede's gifts as a counsellor lay not in what he said, but in what he was. Here was somebody who was *being* all that others were trying to be:

> Everybody preaches that you could be compassionate, you should be kind, but he was not only saying this, he was being this, he was always available to anyone who wanted to see him. You knew from the moment he got up to the moment he went to bed, he was available to people, either in correspondence, or in writing, or in the Chapel, or in seeing people, he was

always giving like this, and no strain about it . . . he was always just giving. So this was a revelation for me, when I saw that somebody was actually saying it and living it at the same time.[7]

There is a fable about the wind and the sun competing to persuade a man to remove his coat. The wind blows hard and fierce; the man clutches his coat ever more tightly round him. The sun is wiser – it just shines until the man is warm enough to remove his coat. Bede, like the sun, never criticised, rebuked or even persuaded, but simply radiated goodness. Brother Martin was another who was enriched by Bede's generosity:

> He never told me to do this or read that, I just grew under his wisdom and light somehow, I don't know how, but somehow by being with him and by listening to him . . . he did not interfere with me in any way. My own searching was going on and I would share with him and he used to listen to me. Sometimes I used to argue with him, even contradict him, and I always discovered he was right, but he never felt offended by me or anything. He was completely open and accepted me unconditionally. I think his unconditional love made me grow.[8]

This unconditional love, flowing freely from him, warmed, relaxed and inspired people as no words could have done. On the rare occasions when Bede did give advice, any opinion he voiced was based on the person and their needs, not on an ideological point of view. For instance, though the contemplative life was his own way, he knew it was not for everyone and he saw immediately that an Australian priest, Father Douglas Conlan, was not yet suited to the dedicated contemplative life that he thought he wanted. 'You must act, Father Douglas,' he told him. 'You must be a man of action. But don't forget the need to withdraw into silence and inaction. One day when you've finished all your action you will be purely contemplative, but that day is not yet.'[9] Father Douglas saw that he was right. Nor would Bede let ecclesiastical limitations affect his advice. He had long felt that the system of celibate clergy could not last much longer and that there should be married clergy and ministries for women; in this spirit he would sometimes encourage someone to marry rather than become a priest, even to leave the priesthood to marry.

One area of life in which people frequently found Bede helpful was sex. One homosexual man found the split between his sexuality and his spirituality healed at Shantivanam; another person helped by him on sexual matters was his old friend Raimon Panikkar:

Let me tell you about something which I am not ashamed of. I remember one of my consultations with him as a penitent was on sex. It was a nun who was very attached to me and I was not attached, but had a kind of innocent sympathy which was not too orthodox or too pure. Nothing happened anyway, but I remember having asked him about it and the sane and good advice he gave me. He was liberating and magnificent.[10]

The writer Andrew Harvey was another person who felt that the most profound things he ever heard about sexuality came from Bede, partly because he never felt he was in the presence of someone who had done 'a horrible act of repression upon himself as I did in the presence of certain priests. I think he had a very great capacity for love, which took up a great deal of that sexual energy.' Bede once said to him, 'You can't deny sex – that leads to craziness. And you can't completely embrace it because it has dark aspects which can mislead you. There's only one way and that is to consecrate it.'[11] The sexual struggles of Bede's youth were over, it was no longer a personal problem to him, so he was able to speak about it with gentleness and compassion and a deep sense of reverence. His theology was enriched by a sense of incarnation, integrating rather than rejecting the body. As Laurence Freeman said: 'He treats sex in such an elevated way that it becomes a religious rather than simply an erotic experience.'[12]

Bede's sense of the relationship between sex and spirituality and his ability to discuss it freely still owed much to D. H. Lawrence; the chord struck in him all those years ago at Oxford had never stopped resonating. Shortly before he died, he spoke of the relationship between sex and mystical experience, saying that Lawrence, through his experience of sex, had come to a genuine mystical experience of transcendental reality. He then read an extract from *Women in Love*: 'How can I say I love you when I have ceased to be. You have ceased to be. We are both caught up and transcended into a new awareness where everything is silent because there is nothing to answer. All is perfect and at one. Speech travels between the separate parts but in the perfect one there is perfect silence of bliss.'[13] This is recorded on video, so it is still possible to see the smile of ineffable charm with which he put down the book and said, 'That is *Saccidananda*, the fullness of bliss.'

Being in Bede's presence was comparable to a *darshan*, the word Hindus use for 'seeing', being in the presence of an image of the deity. This experience was beautifully expressed by Chuck Baroo: 'Father Bede had idiosyncrasies, but his ego was almost transparent and you could see the shining of the divine, you could feel it, not at moments in the temple, or moments of sitting before the guru, but at the most profane, ordinary moments, so that you were almost overwhelmed with light.'[14] Sometimes at the end of Mass people would line up to receive his blessing and once, when he was asked what this blessing meant, he said, 'I'm giving my energy'. He did indeed transmit a spiritual energy, his own experience of God, his own peace and deep inner joy; he was giving himself, sharing his long experience and his life-time's search for God. The tension he endured between his need for solitude and his love of people, of communicating and exchanging ideas with them, resolved and bore fruit in these meetings with individuals. It also had wider implications. Andrew Harvey says: 'Bede showed you can live the widest possible mystical life while keeping within the Church, if you want to . . . He had the power to guide souls and I think that as the Christian experience becomes more confidently mystical people will be turning to the great voyagers.'[15]

Bede had indeed become a great spiritual traveller, exploring both Christianity and the essential unity of all religions at a level that led him both to great heights and to dark places – he had learned from harsh experience that crucifixion is the only way to resurrection. In his search for one transcendent reality he was travelling in extreme territory, but he never lost his inner balance, maintaining an equilibrium so delicately poised that Andrew Harvey has referred to him as 'the Mozart of mystics'. There is no doubt that his very English, Edwardian upbringing, together with his long Benedictine training, served as a container for the intense spiritual level at which he lived for so much of the time. But what of him as a person, his foibles and characteristics? How much had he changed from the idealistic young man whom his friends had found endearing, challenging and some-times infuriating?

In many ways Bede had changed little. He was still ascetic, eating sparsely, disliking almost all luxury (though he was known to take an occasional glass of sherry) and admitting that he missed that staple British fare of bread and butter. Like any true sannyasi he travelled light, going long distances with nothing more than a spare *dhoti*, a towel, some soap, a comb and a few books. Wanting to identify with the poorest Indians in the nearby villages, he refused to have a mosquito net, a fan or even a good mattress in his hut. In all this one can see the young man at Eastington refusing to travel by any form of mechanised transport. He still had that appealing quality of innocence: Christudas recalled sharing village news with him – he 'just used to laugh, laugh like a little child'. He was still tidy, particular about details – his morning and evening tea had to be just right – and he could become irritable if things were not just as he wanted them.

This irritability was a characteristic that never entirely left him. It was usually sparked by the smallest things, for instance if he was unable to fold his shawl properly, or if, in the chapel, a cushion, a prayer book or a lamp was not in the right position. He would indicate his irritation with a gesture and a 'Tss'. He was infuriated if the dogs barked during the office, saying, 'Christudas, please get a gun and shoot them all', though one can imagine his remorse if Christudas had obeyed him. Yet it rarely amounted to anger. Philena Bruce, who stayed many times at the ashram, has never forgotten him saying to her: 'I have never been angry with you. I could never be angry with you. If I was angry it would have been my problem. There is nothing you could do to make me angry.'[16] The only two things that made him angry, she added, were when people put books back in the wrong place in the library and religious fanatics. For the most part he was calm and assured, with the radiant simplicity and gentleness of a holy man, these idiosyncrasies merely a sign of his humanity, barely dimming the light that shone from deep within him. Whatever was worrying him, whether in his inner life or in his sometimes difficult dealings inside or outside the ashram, to the outside eye he as unfailingly courteous, gentle and poised.

It has often been said of Bede that he was a poor judge of character, his inclination always to see the best in people impairing his judgement, sometimes with serious consequences. With characteristic humility he recognised this himself, even discussing it with Maarten Turkstra (usually known as Brother John), a frequent visitor to the ashram: 'He said that he had a failing that allowed him only to see the good in people and he had no sense of when they were using him. He saw this as a fault and felt he needed advice and help in this matter.'[17] It is also generally agreed that he was naive and impractical, often allowing himself to be exploited – and there is substance to these criticisms. He was heavily dependent on Christudas, who not only managed the ashram but looked after Bede like a devoted son and protected him from being cheated financially. Christudas accepted this role willingly, recounting how they would both laugh as Christudas said: 'You are not meant for this world, because you are not practical at all, Father. You can't live in the world. You are beyond. So you have to stay living in the kingdom of heaven, not on earth.'[18]

Yet there were some matters with which only Bede could deal, and when they arose his correspondence shows that, when necessary, he could be business-like: for instance, in his dealings with the status of the ashram and his decision eventually to join the Camaldolese; or even with bureaucratic obligations, such as the need regularly to renew his visa. When anything affected the ashram he could be surprisingly stern. He once experienced the property-owner's archetypal problem, the new alignment of a boundary fence. 'I have no objection to it', he wrote, 'but I think you should have consulted us, or at least informed us, before starting work on it.'[19] He then went on to explain their legal rights to the property with a clarity that would put many lawyers to shame.

Another possible threat to Shantivanam came in the form of Ananda Ashram, which was built so close to Shantivanam that they could hear each other's dogs barking. Sister Marie Louise spent a year in Shantivanam in the 1970s and became devoted to Father Bede. Some years later she raised enough money to build an ashram for women on land adjoining Shantivanam, soon being joined by other women, mostly nuns, and receiving guests. The two ashrams shared a common ideal and regularly prayed together in Shantivanam's chapel, but they were separate ashrams, and Bede wanted this clearly recognised. On Easter night 1982 Sister Marie Louise made a remark which prompted Bede to write her a formal, typed letter, in which he made this point, adding that Ananda Ashram should not use the name Shantivanam – he had heard, for instance, that their electricity bills were made out in the name of Shantivanam. 'If this and all similar uses of the name could be avoided I think that it would remove one of the main causes of conflict between us.' The letter, presumably delivered by hand, ended: 'I feel that if these two simple points are accepted it would be possible for us to enter into a new and better relationship . . . not only now but in the future when I am no longer here.'[20] The gentlest mother can be firm if her child is threatened.

It is astonishing how much Bede managed to squeeze into every day. Apart from at least two hours of meditation and the regular offices in the chapel, running the ashram and looking after the training of the young brothers, seeing visitors, giving daily talks and homilies and keeping up an extensive correspondence, his passion for books never left him and every day he found time for reading, re-reading old favourites and, discovering a new book that particularly impressed him, reading it two, three or even four times. A browse through the letters he wrote to Martyn Skinner in the 1980s gives an idea of the range of his reading. Poetry remained a passion and he admitted that though Dante's *Paradiso* had not impressed him when he first read it, it now seemed to him to be 'the summit of all poetry'.[21] He still especially valued poets such as Wordsworth, Shelley, Hopkins and Eliot for the way they fought to maintain a sense of the sacred in a desacralised world. He continued to read and re-read the classics, such as *David Copperfield*, find-ing in Dickens something of the mythical imagination he valued in Tolkien and in C. S. Lewis's *Narnia* stories. In the areas of theology, philosophy and spirituality he read all twelve volumes of Coplestone's *History of Philosophy*, but for the most part favoured the controversial and the esoteric – he had, after all, already consumed pages of traditional theology. He admired John Hick's *Death and Eternal Life*, Avery Dulles's *Models of Revelation*, and a study of Eckhart, *The Way of Paradox*, written by a fellow Benedictine, Cyprian Smith, which he felt reached the heart of religion. His interest in Jungian psychology never left him, and he found Joseph Campbell's *The Masks of God* 'Perverse in its way, but fascinating'.[22] He frequently acknowledged his debt to Aldous Huxley's *Perennial Philosophy*, recom-mending it to others as a book which opened people's eyes to the wisdom of the East, though he admitted that the book was rather immature, finding the most comprehensive exposition of the perennial philosophy in *Knowledge and the Sacred* by the Islamic theologian Seyyed Hussein Nasr.

As he devoured books, so he never stopped writing, contributing dozens of articles to religious periodicals and publishing three books in the 1980s, though now he presented the material first as a talk, then had it taped and transcribed. So *The Cosmic Revelation* was based on talks he gave in America and *River of Compassion*, a commentary on the *Bhagavad Gita*, originated as talks given at Shantivanam. Constantly developing as he was, he constantly had more to say. In 1985 he wrote to Martyn Skinner: 'I feel a constant urge to get everything completed, to sort out all my ideas and write one last book.'[23] This, again based on talks, was eventually published in 1989 as *A New Vision of Reality: Western Science, Eastern Mysticism and Christian Faith*.

This book, and the profound interest he developed in the meeting of science and religion, owes much to four younger people whom he was not too proud to consider his mentors. He greatly admired the writings of Ken Wilber who, he felt, had opened up western psychology in a new way; Fritjof Capra's *The Tao of Physics* gave him his first insight into the new movement in modern science, and Capra's later book *The Turning Point* impressed him so deeply and so personally that he wrote to Martyn Skinner:

> It is the final justification of 'our' philosophy. His starting point is the revo-lution in modern physics, but he shows how this is leading to what he calls a new 'paradigm', a new conception of the universe not only in physics but in psychology & medicine & economics & politics. His critique of the imbalance of modern civilisation is the most comprehensive I have seen, & it is all the more impressive as coming from a scientist.[24]

His prejudice against science gave way to excitement that bridges could be built between science and religion. Through Capra he had absorbed holistic ideas in physics, then he met the British scientist Rupert Sheldrake, who became a close personal friend and whose thinking, Bede wrote, 'completely demolishes the mechanistic theory of biology which is the current orthodoxy'.[25] Sheldrake lived at Shantivanam for eighteen months in the late 1970s, writing a book* which he discussed with Bede page by page, Bede giving 'remarkable insights into the philosophy of form, the scholastic understanding of the soul, and other metaphysical matters, sometimes pointing out where the writing was obscure or confused; sometimes asking simple but profound questions, rather like a child.'[26] Sheldrake introduced him to the work of David Bohm, whom Bede regarded as his 'authority for whatever science I know'.[27]

A milestone in Bede's growing interest in the meeting of science and religion was a conference held in Bombay in 1982 under the title 'East and West: Ancient Wisdom and Modern Science'. Bede was initially doubtful about going, persuaded only by a pressing invitation with all expenses paid; he was then horrified to find that the conference was in Bombay's most glitzy hotel and that he was staying on the twenty-eighth floor, with break-fast – a glass of milk and some toast – costing 25 rupees, a prodigious amount by his standards. However, the conference turned out to be an event of major importance, showing that physics, biology and psychology were now open to the spiritual dimension and that the eastern experience of medita-tion and mysticism must be seen as an essential element in human exis-tence. Bede had met individuals who were working on the relationship between ancient wisdom and modern science; now he saw that there was a movement of people concerned to build that bridge. The conference attracted some 800 people: psychologists, spiritual leaders and scientists; Jews, Parsees, Hindus, Buddhists and Muslims. Fritjof Capra and Rupert Sheldrake were there, representing the breakthrough in physics and biol-ogy, the Dalai Lama was supposed to come but was taken ill, and on the last day Mother Teresa spoke, deeply impressing Bede with 'a pure message of love. I have never seen anything like it.'[28]

Apart from Mother Teresa, Bede was the only Christian there and his talk on Christianity in the light of modern science and eastern thought was received with an enthusiasm that amazed him. Many of the delegates had never before heard the new science or eastern thought related to Christ and the response was overwhelming. Rupert Sheldrake remembered everyone's

*A New Science of Life (London: Anthony Blond, 1981).

delight that 'The perspective he brought to bear was not just from the East, he brought Christianity into the picture. Here was a man of palpable holiness. They saw they were in the presence of a great man.'[29] Bede's success at the conference not only led to invitations to visit America, but to so many people wanting to visit Shantivanam that he feared they would have to expand the guest houses and the refectory even further. However, his delight at the people he met and the ideas that were exchanged outweighed such concerns; at last a new culture was being born from the meeting of East and West: 'I got a feeling of *convergence*, both of science and religion and of religions among themselves.'[30]

Bede was in all senses a traveller, not only exploring the depths of mind and spirit with an insatiable curiosity, but travelling all over India and indeed much of the world. There is no doubt that he was ambivalent about travel, but once he had torn himself away from his beloved Shantivanam he took an almost childlike delight in discovering new countries and seeing the underlying unity in the diversity of people he met. He even risked Martyn's disapproval by admitting to finding some aspects of modern technology acceptable, for instance while flying for long distances could be boring, 'there is also the thrill of soaring above the clouds and looking down on a marvellous cloudscape and seeing the earth at your feet. I must say that it added a new dimension to my experience of the world.'[31] Though he knew he had everything he wanted at Shantivanam and was content simply to stay there, to be 'alone with God', he could not resist any opportunity to keep in touch with what others were thinking and to exchange views with them. As his reputation grew, so the invitations became more and more frequent. Between 1978 and 1985 he not only travelled widely inside India, but visited Pakistan, Sri Lanka, Jerusalem, Spain, Israel, Egypt and Australia. He drove along the valley of the Danube to Vienna, up the Rhine valley to Cologne and Bonn, then on to Denmark and Sweden. He also went twice to Italy and three times to America, usually taking in a visit to England on the way.

His reception in all these countries was so enthusiastic that he never ceased to marvel. For instance, on one of his visits to Italy, where he addressed 100,000 young people at a 'Vigil for World Mission' day in Milan, he wrote: 'I was solemnly embraced by the Cardinal, so it was all quite impressive. I am rather amused at the way I seem to go down in Italy – which is generally either very sceptical or very conservative.' He also had a public audience with the recently enthroned Pope, whom he found 'a very impressive person – very humble, very warm hearted, a strong character'.[32] Three of these visits have particular significance for the evidence they give of his impact on a world hungry for the spiritual message he brought: they were in 1978, when he visited Osage Monastery in Oklahoma, his trip to California in 1983, and a three-week tour of Australia in 1985.

He had been invited to the States by American monasteries who wanted him to teach Indian spirituality, but his visit to Oklahoma was primarily to see Sister Pascaline, a member of the Benedictine Sisters of Perpetual Adoration, who had spent a year at Shantivanam in 1976 and found Shantivanam 'heaven on earth', soon forming a deep friendship with Bede. Indeed, such was her admiration for him and for his vision that she determined to found a monastery on the same lines as Shantivanam, her energy leading to the foundation of Osage Monastery, Forest of Peace, in Oklahoma, one of America's first Christian monastic ashrams and the one which most fully reflects Bede's ideals. (The name derives from their discovery that they were in Osage Indian territory, coupled with the realisation that Osage Monastery would give the logo OM.) The timing of Bede's visit could hardly have been more auspicious, for just two days earlier the nuns had completed their purchase of forty acres of wooded land near the Arkansas river, deep in the countryside of eastern Oklahoma. He offered Eucharist in the grounds, everyone sitting on a large plastic dust sheet as he blessed all who were entering into the ancient and sacred tradition of forest-dwellers. He also brought a statue of Nataraja, the Lord of the Dance, the four arms symbolising the continuous cycle of life. As he presented it to the nuns, Bede said that Christians must begin to see Nataraja as the symbol of the risen Christ, and at Osage Monastery they do, for the statue is honoured by being placed in one of the two side chapels. They are a truly Christian community, yet they recognise that God has many faces, and there are symbols of Jewish and Buddhist traditions as well as the sacred circle of the American Indians.

This visit to America impressed Bede deeply. With Brother John acting as intermediary, he saw for himself some of the spiritual communities that were springing up all over the country; some Christian, some Zen Buddhist, some Vedanta. During a visit to the Ojai community in California, where the members are interested in the American Indian religion and live in tepees, Brother John remembers Bede sitting in a chair and watching while Stan Groff from Esalen led a group using hyperventilation and whale music to achieve altered states of consciousness. As at the Bombay conference, many of the people he met were surprised and delighted that a Christian should take an interest, and though Bede did not write of his reactions to the details of what he encountered, he was clearly not only excited by the spiritual revival that was happening in America, but, with his life-long ambivalence about civilisation, interested in the ability of these young seekers to combine an undoubted commitment to a life of prayer and meditation with the uninhibited use of modern technology. He felt that they were engaged in an experiment comparable to his own with Martyn and Hugh at Eastington.

Bede felt that this spiritual revival, often referred to as the 'New Age', had its roots in the new understanding of physics and in the advance of Transpersonal Psychology, whose centre is at Esalen, the community which had organised the Bombay conference. He found the most interesting person in this field was Ken Wilber, whose books had fascinated him and whom he visited in San Francisco, surprised and delighted to find that he was moving nearer to Christianity. Esalen is near the Camaldolese community at Big Sur in California, so he combined a visit to the monastery with giving some talks to the Esalen community. Many of his audience came from Jewish or Catholic backgrounds but were completely alienated from western religious tradition and Father Bruno Barnhart, a Camaldolese monk from Big Sur, was interested by Bede's approach to his mainly non-Christian audience:

> The first part of his talk was full of references to the Hindu tradition and spirituality, and I think he won them over, first with his appearance and manner, and then with this thoroughly Eastern presentation. But then after a while it seemed to me he was giving them pure orthodox Catholic doctrine, as it might almost have come from the catechism. They seemed to listen to that with about the same receptiveness.[33]

Bede's ability to make Christianity acceptable to people who had wandered far from its embrace was perhaps his single greatest contribution to twentieth-century spirituality, and this was what he did on all his travels, not least in Australia. His first trip, in 1985, started badly, nearly cancelled when Air India lost the tickets, and Bede arrived exhausted and ill, vomiting so violently that he lost his dentures. It was also unfortunate that he was in Australia at the same time as the controversial and eventually disgraced Indian guru Bagwahn Rajneesh, for initially Bede, also coming from India, was seen in the same light; the advertisements to which he had unwillingly agreed resulted in letters of complaint to Father Douglas Conlan, who initiated and largely financed the trip.

Once the Australians saw and heard him, though, they took him instantly to their hearts, a typical reaction coming from a religious sister: 'I shall never forget the moment Father Bede came into the room, the silence was electrified by his presence. My heart stood still as this tall, gaunt man of God with silver hair, beard and blue blue eyes, dressed in the loose flowing robes of a religious person from India, came into our lives.'[34] He spoke to packed audiences in Melbourne, Sydney, Canberra, Adelaide and Perth – on two occasions there were over a thousand people present; he was interviewed on radio and television and there were numerous articles in the press, who were enchanted by both his appearance and his message, namely that Australia, as a multicultural society, had to come to terms with eastern culture and religion and that now there could be a real meeting between western science, eastern mysticism and the Christian faith. Most of all they were drawn to his conviction that all faiths are manifestations of one fundamental truth, with Christ as the centre and fountain head. 'Here was a contemplative Catholic' wrote one reporter, 'who believed it was not necessary to be a Christian to be saved.'[35]

In both America and in Australia, Bede was captivated by the outgoing and friendly people and their kindness, but he disliked the dominance of technology – he was horrified on more than one occasion to be offered an electric blanket – and the ubiquitous skyscrapers, making it hard to distinguish one town from another. 'California is really today a kind of promised land', he wrote, 'but of course the serpent is there as much as anywhere.'[36] Though he felt at home in the American countryside, finding it marvellously beautiful and admitting that it was the most civilised country the world had ever known, he felt 'the whole system is insane and obviously cannot go on . . . It is all fantastic & unreal & the moral, psychological and physical effects are disastrous. As I was leaving New York, it was half shrouded in a mist, & I could see it as a vast city of ruins, like ancient Babylon, & that is probably what it will be like in 100 years time!'[37]

Likewise in Australia, he loved the people, but not their technology: 'There is always the sense of living in an artificial world, & I found myself longing to get back to my hut. No one is really happy – there is a tension everywhere and a feeling of insecurity. It becomes clearer every day that it can't last & there will have to be a return to a simpler way of life.'[38]

Bede often returned from these trips both physically and psychologically exhausted, aware that he could not stand much of western life and promising himself that he would retire into solitude and leave the running of the ashram to the brothers. He had frequently promised never to travel again, and after he returned from Australia he was as good as his word. For the next four years he stayed at Shantivanam, feeling he was 'back in a holy land. Everything here seems sacred',[39] and assuring his friends, 'I never go out now, not even to Kulittalai.'[40] Perhaps at last he was going to enjoy the solitude which, in his own ambivalent way, he had sought for so long.

CHAPTER SIXTEEN

Controversy

Even in those years in the late 1980s, when Bede hardly moved from Shantivanam, he was rarely alone for long, for when he was not travelling the world, then the world sought him out. Wherever he went he had been finding that a spiritual revival was taking place both inside and outside the churches, that materialism was driving people to seek God; and they came, from all five continents, to Shantivanam. Many of the people who found his person and his message so compelling were those who were seeking a spiritual path but who could not find it in organised religion – people on the margins of their religious communities, people in search of a mystical way for which they had so far found little support. The Christians among them were often those who were disappointed in the lacklustre liturgies they found in their parish churches; shocked by the Vatican's silencing of outspoken theologians like Hans Kung and Edward Schillebeeckx; they included those who could not understand the emphasis on dogmas in which they were told to believe, who were shocked by the banning of contraception and the refusal even to consider ordaining women as priests, who felt that other religions were owed more than a condescending tolerance.

Bede often commented on the reasons people came to the ashram: 'of all the young people who came to our ashram in search of God in India, 60 per cent are Catholics, who tell me that they gave up the practice of their faith when they were 15 or 16, because the way in which the faith was presented to them seemed to them meaningless or irrelevant.'[1] He even found that the very institution founded to preserve and promote the Christian faith seemed to be having the opposite effect: 'For most of them Christianity is deemed to be identified with a formal, dogmatic, moralistic religion, which is a positive obstacle to their interior growth.'[2]

Understanding so well that people were seeking an interior religion, a religion of the heart rather than the head, Bede was able to feed this spiritual hunger as few have done in the twentieth century, his integrated approach, his ability to shed the light of eastern scriptures on Christianity and his emphasis on meditation combining to bring many people nearer the experience they sought. Inevitably, the same things also caused conflict with many who did not share his views. For the most part these were serious people who admired much that he stood for and loved and respected him as a holy man who practised what he preached, but who none the less had serious reservations about some of his ideas.

As an old man, more confident in his thinking, he spoke out more and more, publicly airing views that he had previously shared only with close friends. His attitude to controversy showed both his interior balance and his ardent pursuit of truth. He had a tough skin, often unable to let an argument go, though avoiding the trap of taking criticism personally, but he was never confrontational – he was simply arguing for the views he had spent a life-time developing, trying to awaken people to a deeper dimension of life. Laurence Freeman saw him in action at an age when he expected him to need protection:

> In 1991 I was with him when he was ambushed by a hostile evangelical fun-damentalist; he was attacked with a stream of theological invective. Thinking to spare Father Bede the upset of the conflict, I intervened to lead him away. But he stood his ground and began to engage the hostile invec-tive with his own fervent and reasoned arguments. As I saw the reaction, I soon realized it was not Father Bede but his opponent I should be protecting.[3]

How, then, in his eighties, after some thirty years of living in India, was Bede thinking? In particular where did he stand in relation to the Roman Church, the institution to which he belonged and from where he might most expect criticism? He loved the Church, but he had long been aware of its shortcomings and daily he met people who were leaving it, or at the least ignoring official teachings they could no longer accept. He often agreed with them, disliking the repetition of outworn formulas and feeling that the best way to defend the Church was rather to show how old truths can be translated into contemporary language.

The 1980s saw a spate of letters to *The Tablet* as Bede argued that the medieval conception of the papacy, widely questioned today, 'appears to be fatally flawed'[4] and that its 'inordinate claims'[5] must be squarely faced. With an impressive command of historical detail, he pointed out the times that the magisterium had been proved wrong, writing that there could be no real hope of Christian reunion, 'until the Roman Church publicly acknowledges its past errors and admits that it does not have the answer to all the difficult problems of sexual morality and other matters which trouble humanity today'.[6] He had no fear of the power of Rome and, in a letter the editor called 'A Smack at Ratzinger', he reprimanded that scourge of liberal Catholics: 'Perhaps the "scandalous pessimism" which Cardinal Ratzinger finds in the Church today can be reconciled with what others call the "scandalous optimism" of Cardinal Ratzinger, if one considers that what is collapsing today is the old system of Roman Catholicism and what is taking its place is a new understanding of the Catholic Church.'[7]

Often he took up his pen to respond to something he had read in the paper, for instance challenging a priest who claimed that Roman Catholicism was the only supernaturally revealed religion in the world and that all other religions are false. On nuclear deterrence he chided the Catholic Church for being 'hopelessly divided and incapable of giving the moral guidance which is needed'[8] and, dipping a toe in the troubled waters of sexist liturgy, he deplored the fact that, because the words for Father, Son and Holy Spirit are all male in Latin, we have nothing but male images of God. When Lord Hailsham entered the ring, pointing out that the word for Trinity in both Latin and Greek is feminine, a delighted Father Bede suggested we might refer to the Trinity as 'she': 'In other words, while we conceive of the Persons of the Godhead as masculine, can we conceive of the nature we all share as feminine? This would be a breakthrough beyond our present concept of God as wholly masculine.'[9]

Often his letters were in response to some official publication, for instance, agreeing with the bishops of the Vatican Council who had previously voted against it, he found the plans for a universal catechism unacceptable, assuring one of his critics that he was not questioning the need for propositions expressing the Christian faith, simply asserting 'that the object of Christian faith is not a proposition or a series of propositions but a divine mystery'.[10]

His critics, however, did not come from Rome; he was not silenced, or even warned. He was not a theological dissenter and was not regarded as one, though he was once described as 'by far the most radical of these interfaith prophets';[11] his views were simply those of one slightly ahead of his time. To some extent his universally accepted sanctity protected him, but the area in which he met controversy was the very area to which he had given his life: criticism came from theologians engaged in similar work, the children of the marriage between East and West. Oscar Wilde once said that 'when the critics disagree the artist is in accord with himself', and perhaps Bede could have taken some perverse comfort in the fact that his work was and still is criticised from both eastern and western standpoints, from both conservative and radical churchmanship.

Westerners criticised Bede from a variety of different positions. Some did not understand his point of view at all, even feeling that he could no longer be called a Roman Catholic. Others simply could not agree with him, like William Rees-Mogg who found 'the idea of a cosmic, universal religion a poor substitute for Christianity, or indeed for any other of the great religions'.[12] He was sometimes taken to task by fellow priests, for instance by the Jesuit Father Peter Milward with whom he became untypically confrontational. Seeking to end their correspondence he wrote, for what he hoped was the final time, to clarify his position: 'I am not opposing the teaching of the Church but your theology of the Church, which is a very different matter. Your theology is static and unhistorical which leads inevitably to contradictions. I follow a historical theology, which, as I wrote in my last letter to the *Tablet*, recognises that every doctrinal statement is historically conditioned.'[13]

One of the problems Bede's critics had was that he did not fit any category; anyone trying to put him in a particular box, to give him a label, found it rather harder than trying to contain an octopus in a string bag – one aspect of him always eluded classification. One thing is certain and that is that he was not a missionary: he had come to India not to spread the Gospel but to live the Benedictine life in dialogue with Indian life, spirituality and culture; he often said he had come as a pilgrim. Equally, there is no doubt that he was the superior of an ashram and a Christian sannyasi.

Many other claims have been made for him. He has been called a New Age guru, a prophet, a sage, and a mystic. Did he fit these categories? In the 1980s he became quite apocalyptic as he prophesied wars and disasters, writing to Martyn that 'our present civilisation is on the verge of ruins, whether by an atomic war or by other means'[14] and, the following year, 'I expect that there will be a catastrophe soon, but the powers of renewal are present . . . Maybe the second coming is at hand!'[15] His basic optimism never left him, and in his conviction that a new age was dawning he certainly reflected his time and was able to meet the spiritual needs of young people as few Christians in the twentieth century have done. But to associate him with the expression 'the New Age', that umbrella term that includes so much that he did not stand for, is misleading. Much of what he said was prophetic and if not ahead of his time he was certainly at its cutting edge, but does he fit the definition of a prophet as 'One who speaks for God or for any deity, as the inspired revealer or interpreter of his will'?[16] Was he a sage? He was wise, discreet and judicious, but somehow the noun distances him, places him in a fixed and remote position, not allowing for his insatiable curiosity, his humble desire to know, his constant quest for the truth. Was he a mystic, that word used so indiscriminately and often disparagingly? The key to understanding Bede lies here. He was, in the best sense of the word, a mystic, a man who sought, by contemplation and by his painful search for self-surrender, to find union with the divine and to find it not in theory but in experience.

Theological criticism should be made in that context. Bede was a mystic who had come to India because he found the West too masculine, too concerned with reason and too rational, yet to communicate his ideas he had to use the language of theology. To what extent was he a scholar, a theologian or a philosopher; how skilled was he at using theological language? He was frequently referred to as a 'Scholar-Monk', a term justified by a lifetime of reading and study and by his considerable intellect; the Jesuit David Brigstocke referred to him as 'the supremely intellectual Oxford academic', having 'the thirst of an exceptional mind, and the thirst of a wonderfully loving heart'.[17] Andrew Harvey, himself a former Fellow of All Souls, Oxford, went further, talking of 'his extraordinarily sophisticated mental equipment. Here was a man who could have done and been anything.'[18] Laurence Freeman gave a cooler assessment, feeling that: 'Bede's choice of monastic rather than academic life affected the development of his intellectual gifts, channelling them into spiritual insights rather than an academic style of thought . . . He was sapiential rather than scholastic, monastic rather than academic.'[19]

Bede could be regarded as a theologian in that, as a monk, he had studied the subject and theological questions were part of his mental and spiritual bread and butter, but he was never in the theological fraternity and did not talk the language of academic theologians. Nor was he taken seriously by philosophers, generally being considered philosophically naive since C. S. Lewis first chided him for being 'no philosopher'. In fact, it has been argued that it was because he was a poor philosopher that he was a poor theologian. Further, the vast range of disciplines that he covered in his thinking – history, literature and science as well as theology and philosophy – meant that he could not qualify as a specialist in any of them and could therefore often be faulted by the experts. His great gift was for the overarching synthesis, his vision spanning many different disciplines in search of the truth he was seeking. This, though considered impressive, even breathtaking, by many, has been dismissed as superficial by others.

What do western theologians make of him and his ideas? With a few notable exceptions – doctoral theses written by Wayne Teasdale[20] and Judson Trapnell[21] – there has so far been little significant critique of his work and the reason given is that he is simply not taken seriously by theologians. In the light of his international fame and the impact he made on so many lives, this fact demands an explanation.

The explanation, at least partially, lies in the nature of theology. The job of theologians is to assess challenges made within a religious tradition and to try to articulate new developments. For Christians, theology is a response to God's word and presumes the prior initiative of God, who enables us to speak not only *of* him, but *to* him. Theology comes out of prayer and worship. How do theologians deal with someone like Bede, who was challenging the tradition from within it, who was an innovator in that he was developing new insights, but who insisted on the importance of experience over reason and by-passed the distinction between theology and spirituality? How can a profession that uses the rational mind deal with someone who longs to transcend it and who constantly affirms the need to 'go beyond'? Further, the mystical territory is dangerous: is the experience of God or of the devil and if, as all mystics assert, it is beyond words, why do they try to talk about it?

So, too, the theologian is concerned when people who have had a mystical experience avoid theological discourse by claiming to be operating on a different plane. This charge could not be levelled at Bede, but he did largely agree with the assumption behind the perennial philosophy that all religious and mystical experiences are essentially the same – this again is something that worries many theologians. They do not like, for instance, his frequent use of the analogy of the hand, when he would suggest that the fingers and thumb represent Buddhism, Hinduism, Islam, Judaism and Christianity, separate and different, but follow the lines towards the source, the palm of the hand, and they become more closely interrelated, until, at the centre, they are one. Nor does his appeal to the advaitic experience, the state of consciousness where all reality is one, satisfy them – that, they say, is merely stating the problem in different terms, not solving it. In the end, like so many human exchanges, it comes down to language and how language and experience interact. Is experience formed by language or is the experience shaped by the language and culture in which the mystic lives? And once in the realms of language there is a particular problem in Christianity: on the one hand the mystic has had an experience beyond words, yet he is committed to a tradition which claims that it is the revelation of God as Word.

So perhaps it is no surprise that, in so far as Bede has received attention from professional theologians at all, they tend to find him too undiscriminating, too prone to generalise, too vague, even simplistic. Professor Ursula King, reviewing *The Marriage of East and West*, acknowledged the stature of the author but judged it 'an example of "soft thinking", lacking the very union of critical analysis and unifying synthesis it wishes to propound' and considered 'the terms of this marriage proposal simplistic, if not to say myopic'.[22] A Swedish scholar suggested that 'he seems to have too easily accepted ideas which to others are impossible to reconcile. Monchanin would have regarded his thinking as muddled, I think.'[23] Such charges are by their very nature hard to refute but there is another way of seeing vagueness; for instance, Raimon Panikkar, while agreeing that Bede was neither an original philosopher nor a thinker who had broken new ground, qualifies the accusation:

> It all depends what being vague means. If vagueness means the non-Cartesian mind, black and white, yes and no, good and bad – well, blessed vagueness, because things cannot be classified in such dialectical terms, so it would be a very good thing if he was vague. Again he was not a man of harsh judgements – blessed vagueness. He didn't speak in the clear langauge of the Cartesian philosopher, certainly. So I would take the stigma out of vagueness and say, 'Yes, thank God.'[24]

Accusations of vagueness apart, did Bede make a theological contribution? Certainly he made no such claims and the South African theologian Felicity Edwards was quite clear that he was not a theologian, nor was he trying to speak theologically. It is, she said, unjust for theologians to judge Bede as if he were a theologian, though quite reasonable for them to assess what he said from a theological perspective. She also pointed out that if Bede is accused of making no theological contribution, 'that was exactly the same as Our Lord, he also made no significant theological contribution. He actually didn't say anything either that was original. What he was was in his being and what he taught and what he did, at a very, very subtle level . . . changing the way in which a person comes into being at this deep level of reality, so that person is different. I think that's what he's doing.'[25]

If criticism from western theologians is unfocused, rarely reaching the printed page, it was a different story in India. It is generally agreed that he made little impact on the Indian church, nevertheless the criticisms he received, both from Christians and Hindus, were precise and occasionally very outspoken. One accusation was that he was selling Christianity short by allowing the Hindu influence to penetrate too deep. This must have caused him great pain and can only have been made by people of a conservative churchmanship who did not understand his passionate desire that Christianity should be enriched by Indian spirituality. Bede was concerned with dialogue rather than mission, with the complementarity of religions rather than with a competition between them, but that he himself remained a Christian and that Shantivanam was a Christian ashram was never in doubt, the numerous people who returned to their Christian roots after a visit to the ashram bearing testimony to the truth of his instinct that the West could profit from the spirituality of the East.

It was also said that he was guilty of cultural elitism, especially in pre-ferring the Brahmanic tradition of Hinduism to the popular culture of the tribals and *harijans*; further, that his thinking was divorced from Indian reality, not taking sufficient account of socio-political conditions. Numerous social projects, very efficiently managed by Christudas, were run from Shantivanam and give the lie to this accusation. They built houses for poor people, provided a shed and some eighty looms in a project designed to liberate the weavers from the landlords; they ran a tailoring institute for poor girls; projects for spinning and gem-cutting; a 'Self-confidence project' for thirty of the poorest children; free education centres; and when Bede received the John Harriott Award in 1992 he spent the money on a house for old people. However, it is claimed that this work did not spring out of his spirituality and that the social work done by Shantivanam was secondary to the pursuit of the interior life. One man cannot be all things and in the ten-sion between social activity and interiority, Bede's work was indeed primar-ily the latter, he himself being very aware of the tension between the two. He knew as well as anyone that God is found in how you treat your neigh-bour as well as in the esoteric – it is a question of balance: 'The mystic has to learn to see how the transcendent is present in every human situation, in struggle and conflict & pain, & the social activist has continually to strive to see beyond the struggle & conflict of the world to the transcendent Reality.'[26]

That he was drawn to favour the Sanskrit tradition over the popular tra-dition was unquestionably true and this led to a serious disagreement with his old friend Jyoti Sahi. Bede, in discussing one of Jyoti Sahi's books, admit-ted that he simply couldn't see the matter in those terms:

> Surely the marvel of Hindu culture is that the Sanskrit tradition through the temple worship, poetry, music, drama, dancing and pilgrimage has pene-trated to every level of Indian life. It may be that tribals are rather outside it,

& to some extent harijans, but 80% of India is steeped in it. For this reason
I question your saying on p116 that the Brahmanical tradition is 'foreign' to
the ordinary tribal & peasant. Surely they should be encouraged not to
'hate' it but to see it as part of their own culture of which they have been
unjustly deprived.[27]

The argument rumbled on for some years, but Bede was not to be
swayed. For him the Sanskrit tradition was the core of India culture:

I can't understand how you can call the Sanskrit tradition the culture of an
elite minority. The Ramayana and the Mahabharata have penetrated into
every nook and corner of India and have been to India what the Bible has
been to Europe. The temples in which this tradition is enshrined and
which are served by Brahmin priests are visited by millions every day all
over India. You might as well call the cathedrals of the Middle Ages the preserve of an elite.[28]

And there, in the last sentence, it is. Bede's background and temperament remained a product of the middle-class, intellectual, Oxford-educated
Englishman that he was; like any man he had his limitations and he knew
it. But even if the accusation of elitism stands, it never led him to fail in
compassion or in love.

In this disagreement with Jyoti Sahi, Bede was in dialogue with someone who, as an Anglo-Indian, understood both Christian and Indian traditions from the inside, someone of whom he was very fond and with whom
he was in many ways in sympathy; both correspondents were seeking
mutual understanding. It was a different matter when he came into conflict
with Hindu fundamentalists. In 1988 he became involved in a correspondence of such acrimony that it is hard to understand why he engaged in the
dialogue at all.

It started when a number of people took exception to a lecture about
Shantivanam given by Dr Wayne Teasdale, an American theologian and a
great friend of Bede's. Talking of the colonial period, when Britain took
from India and gave little in return, Wayne Teasdale referred to Bede as
'Britain's appropriate gift to India'. Not so, wrote a Swami in the *Indian
Express*, Britain's best gift to India was cricket and Shakespeare, Griffiths
was a mere experimenter, guilty of confusing and insulting both Hinduism
and Christianity by placing the sacred word *Om* on a cross.[29] Another correspondent leapt to Bede's defence: Bede was no experimenter, he was 'an
international theologian of great reputation'.[30] The fire was laid and another
Swami, Swami Devananda, lit the match: 'As these priests know our rites

and traditions and are aware of our sensibilities, by what right or authority do they wear the ochre robe? . . . Bede Griffiths has no grasp at all of the Indian psyche . . . he is meddling with the soul of a very old and sophisticated people by continuing his experiments at Shantivanam.'[31] Bede replied immediately, saying that the saffron robe was the sign of renunciation, of the transcendence of all social bonds, whether social or religious, and that in over thirty years in India he had never known a Hindu sannyasi object to him wearing it. He also pleaded that they should go beyond mutual hostility and work together for peace. His appeal unheard, the Swami returned to the attack: 'There is no unity of religions on the level of religion, each being a distinct entity', he wrote, accusing Bede of misappropriating the sacred symbols of Hinduism and of holding himself above the Indian people. The letter ended with a diatribe: 'By trying to justify your position as it is now, you impugn Hinduism, slur sannyas, rout reason, ruin meaning, mutilate categories, transpose symbols, deny sacred convention and usage, profane principles, philosophise, and generally present an argument that is oxymoronic.'[32]

Bede responded with his characteristic gentleness; he respected the Swami's position and saw the value of the principles he was defending, but:

> I have known many Hindu sannyasis, visited many ashrams and had many Hindu friends, but no one before has ever objected to anything I have done. You are anxious to establish Hinduism as a separate religion with its own unique doctrine and symbols which differentiate it from other religions. But most Hindus hold the opposite view and maintain with Ramakrishna and Vivekananda that all religions are essentially the same and differ only in accidental characteristics.[33]

Enraged, the Swami showered his invective on Christianity in general as well as on Bede: 'I am convinced that Christianity's advent is one of the great disasters in the history of mankind.' Some Christians, he granted, might be excluded, but not

> that soul-sucking, carnivorous, leviathan the Church, and by extension, her ideologues . . . If you were remotely serious about the spiritual ideals expressed in your letter, you would renounce the Church forthwith and humbly place yourself in the hands of God . . . You stay married to the Scarlet Woman when it is the Divine Cow of Hinduism who produces the *amrita* [immortality] you hanker after. If your Woman were not barren and dry, you would not have come to Hinduism in the first place. I am surely a Hindu chauvinist, but you are the very worst kind of spiritual colonialist.[34]

The worm was beginning to turn and Bede responded that the Swami was clearly a fundamentalist, 'one who clings to the outward forms of religion and loses sight of the inner spirit'. He would no longer continue the correspondence. But the Swami could not control himself and wrote again: 'It remains that you abuse and pervert our symbols and traditions to your own motivated missionary ends . . . You have not transcended religion and you have no intention of doing so, whatever your pious declarations. You have an overriding ambition to subvert and subsume us with our own spiritual concepts.'[35]

For some five months, the arrows flew, the Swami accusing Bede of merely seeking public acclaim and wilfully causing grave offence, and returning regularly to his outrage that the syllable *Om* should be used on the 'imperial' Christian cross and that a Christian should wear saffron robes and call himself a sannyasi. Bede tried to deflect the attacks, to call a truce, indeed to terminate the correspondence, but at intervals he would return to the fray. He remained controlled and polite, for instance suggesting that just as great Hindus like Ramakrishna, Vivekananda, Gandhi, Sri Aurobindo and Ramana Maharshi, remained firmly Hindu while being open to the truth in Christianity, so he considered himself 'a Christian in religion but a Hindu in spirit'.[36] He reminded the Swami that *Om* is not confined to Hinduism: 'Would you like to write to the Dalai Lama and tell him to stop the Tibetan people from using their most sacred mantra: Om mani padma hum?'[37]

Why did Bede engage in so fruitless an exchange? Many of the accusations, such as the suggestions that his use of Hindu terminology was a cover-up for proselytising intentions, are so clearly unjust that he would have done well to ignore them. Yet, despite their biased and offensive language, despite the tone of a precocious four-year-old in a tantrum, there were real questions hidden in the invective and Bede was struggling to answer them. Abhishiktananda had been similarly, though more politely, challenged by the spiritual head of the Ramakrishna order. Why was he trying to be a Hindu monk, the Hindu asked? Why not just be what you are, a Benedictine? If a Ramakrishna monk were to live in Rome, should he dress like a Benedictine? Christians do not need to imitate Hinduism to show their appreciation of it; all the Hindu wants is that Indian symbolism and tradition are accepted as a way to reach God.

Bede's defence against onslaughts such as that made by the Swami took the argument back to the area that still worries some western theologians, and that is Bede's overwhelming conviction that there is a vision of reality common to all the great religious traditions of both East and West:

But it is only realised when we pass beyond the external forms of religion and encounter the hidden depth in each religion, the mystical tradition, which is at the heart of all genuine religion. As long as we remain on the level of external religion with its dualities of time and space, of subject and object, of good and evil, of truth and error, of God and Man, we shall never overcome the conflicts of religion, or even of politics. It is only in the mystical tradition of each religion that we can rise above the dualities, neither confusing the opposites, nor separating them, but recognising the mystery of the transcendent non-dual Reality, in which alone the answer to all human problems can be found.[38]

Perhaps the reason why Bede could not resist the Swami's diatribe lay in his personal search rather than in any objective reasoning. Apart from his genuine desire that Christianity and Hinduism should meet, should understand each other and learn from each other, it quite simply was in accord with his own spirituality that there should be the *Om* on the cross, that he should wear saffron robes and adopt Hindu traditions and symbolism. He had in the first place worn the robes of the sannyasi to identify with his lifestyle, and he became so accustomed to it that to wear it was as natural as breathing; he was also aware that in India Christians were regarded as worldly and that wearing the saffron robes was a truer indication of his real identity as a contemplative monk than western clerical dress. Further, he was intensely loyal to his predecessors and as Monchanin and Abhishiktananda had worn saffron robes, it was natural that he should do so too. But this exchange with Swami Devananda upset him deeply and though he had little option but to agree to the publication of the letters in book form he cannot have taken any pleasure from it.

Bede was also taken to task in a crucially important area which led him into troubled waters with some of his fellow Christians: that was the place of the Eucharist in the life of an ashram. In 1988 he aired these thoughts publicly and explicitly for the first time in the Ashram Aikya* news letter. He suggested that although the Eucharist is at the centre of the monastic tradition and though the Second Vatican Council called it 'the source and summit of the activity of the Church', in the context of ashram life this tradition needs to be questioned. However precious the Eucharist is – and he himself said Mass daily – it is still a sacrament and a sacrament of its very nature belongs to the world of signs:

*The Ashram Aikya was established in 1978 through the initiative of Fr Amalorpavadas, the first director of the NBCLC in Bangalore, as a support group for ashramites.

214

In the sacrament of the Eucharist the divine Mystery, that is Christ himself, is made present to us under the signs of the words and actions of the rite and in particular of the bread and wine, which symbolise and make present the Reality of Christ. But that Reality is present to us without signs in its intrinsic being through the gift of the Holy Spirit. The primary mode of the presence of Christ among his disciples is that of the indwelling presence of the Holy Spirit.[39]

So, he argued, the Holy Spirit is to be found in contemplative prayer, in which union with God beyond all signs and images is sought and which is the heart of the life of an ashram. Further, he maintained that this is particularly important where people of other religious traditions are involved, because the Eucharist excludes them as it can even exclude Christians of different denominations, while contemplative prayer unites people of any religion or of none.

Disagreement came swiftly from an Indian Jesuit, who did not think it was possible to meet the needs of the followers of all religions, and by Sister Sara Grant, who had lived in an ecumenical ashram community for sixteen years and who could not accept that a community which has its centre in the Eucharist was necessarily excluding members of other religions – they expected the lives of Christians to be centred on Christ and therefore on the Eucharist. She admitted to finding Bede's letter rather illogical, as he had ended it by saying that 'Christ himself is the sacrament of God' and also because she had so often heard of the great impact made on people by the reverence and beauty of the Eucharist celebration at Shantivanam. Bede's response to this was that the presence of Christ should not be confused with his presence in the Eucharist. Jesus had promised that he would send the Holy Spirit to his disciples and his presence in the Eucharist 'is secondary and is scarcely ever mentioned in the New Testament'.[40] Once again he came back to the theme that so much concerned him – the particular needs of twentieth-century man:

> The danger of sacraments is that they can easily obscure the hidden Mystery by focusing attention on the outward form. For many people to-day this is the reason why they reject Christianity, because they see in it a system of rituals and dogmas which have lost their meaning in the present world . . . It has been our experience in our ashram that many people who had given up the Church come back to their faith and to the Eucharist when they realise the hidden mystery which alone gives meaning to the doctrine and sacraments of the Church.[41]

Another heartfelt reaction came from Jyoti Sahi, who felt that Bede was suggesting that a commitment to Christ cannot be the basis for an openness to other faith traditions, 'so he wants to go beyond the specific cultural, historical, symbolic limitations of what is physical to an experience of God beyond Name and Form'.[42] He goes on to open up a crucial and difficult area of Bede's thinking, which is essentially the balance between an incarnational and a mystical theology. Every time an artist faces a blank canvas, he argued, he is presented with the nameless and formless, but that does not mean he leaves his canvases blank. So giving a faith name and form, far from being an obstacle to dialogue, actually becomes its basis. But Bede could not be moved. Sad that they should differ he wrote to Jyoti personally:

> We both share a certain mystical vision, but you as an artist are concerned to embody that vision in your art, whereas I as a contemplative monk seek to go beyond all signs and images and experience the mystery in itself . . . I appreciate your 'incarnational' theology and all that it implies, but I am driven all the time to go beyond it to a mystical theology. I don't think these theologies are opposed but rather they are complementary. I celebrate mass every day and Christ is very much the centre of my life, but both alike lead me to a contemplative experience which is beyond all sacramental signs.[43]

Perhaps the key lies in the words 'I am *driven* all the time to go beyond . . .' The springboard to his life-long search was that overwhelming experience when he was a schoolboy. He had to follow that experience wherever it would lead.

216

CHAPTER SEVENTEEN

Friendship

Alove of solitude and a deep need for it are not incompatible with a capacity for friendship; in fact, it could be argued that those with the greatest gift for friendship are those who can best tolerate and enjoy their own company. Despite his reputation as a loner, Bede had always formed close friendships, even the invisible 'Harold' of his childhood revealing his life-long need for people. He was intensely loyal, keeping in regular touch with Hugh Waterman, Martyn Skinner and C. S. Lewis, the great friends of his Oxford days, until they were parted by death.* Hugh remembered Bede saying that 'his idea of heaven was a state where each of us knows everything about one another, and all was forgiven'[1] – a remark which gives an insight into his ideal of friendship. Certainly the stormy days at Eastington strengthened rather than weakened the bonds between himself, Hugh and Martyn, and though Lewis's refusal to discuss their differences when Bede became a Roman Catholic and he became an Anglican led to 'a certain reserve in our relationship',[2] the friendship lasted for nearly forty years. Bede was, in fact, regarded as one of Lewis's closest friends, and when, after Lewis's death in 1963, he was invited to contribute to a collection of reminiscences about him, he wrote that it was through Lewis that he really discovered the meaning of friendship and 'There are not many things in my life more precious to me than that friendship'.[3]

Monastic life, he found, increased rather than diminished his capacity for friendship, even though as a Benedictine monk in the days before the Second Vatican Council personal friendships (known with schoolboy non-

*C. S. Lewis died in 1963, Hugh died in 1984, Martyn outlived Bede by just three months.

chalance as 'P F-ery') between monks were frowned on. However, Bede, in common with many of his fellow monks, took little notice, making friend-ships which easily survived his exclaustration and long years in India. Many of the monks regularly remembered his feast day, as he did theirs, but one who deserves special mention was Dom Michael Hanbury, for many years the editor of *PAX*, the Prinknash review. Though it was Bede's contributions to the magazine that ensured their regular contact, it is clear that there was great affection and trust between the two men, Bede sharing his more con-troversial views at a time when they were slowly evolving and for the most part he was keeping them to himself.

Initial contacts were easy for a man of his charm, sensitivity, tact and good looks; even when middle age was becoming a memory Hugh Waterman wrote to Martyn Skinner: 'At 65 Dom Bede would leave me (I won't answer for you) at the starting post for "looks." I don't mean this cyn-ically, but he is a charmer isn't he?'[4] He was indeed, and throughout his life there were many who were captivated by his charm and charisma, even by his physical beauty, though he was perceived as immensely reserved and curiously asexual. Some people, though, found him so unworldly that it created a distance between them. For instance, Peter Bentley, some twelve years younger and a new Catholic convert when he met Bede in the 1940s, felt very much on his wavelength, but:

> The great difference was that he was an ascetic, disciplined man. He lived, for me, on a 'higher realm.' There lay his charm, I suppose. He was some-one to look up to, a marvellous projection for idealistic Catholic seekers. He was so very progressive and open to a new Church that has not yet hap-pened. I was swept along by his idealism. But for me he was not quite human enough. He was solidly installed on 'Cloud 9'.[5]

More and more, as he grew older, it was the quality of unconditional love flowing from him which captivated people, but there is evidence that even in his thirties he was inspiring strong feelings. A young monk who was dispensed from his vows and was leaving his monastery, expressed his powerful emotions thus:

> My dearest friend,
> What can I say to you dear Dom Bede. Nothing can express all I feel towards you. You are my dearest friend. I have never known anyone like you. And our friendship has always been so good – nothing could have been purer or holier. You will always be my friend – always love me in our Lord.

I love you very, very, much. Pray for me. I know there is no need to ask. I will never, never forget you, and someday God will surely let us meet again. Good-bye, dearest, kindest and best of friends.

Brother Gerard.[6]

Bede's pastoral gifts gave another dimension to his relationships. Soon after he arrived in India he received a letter from the principal of a school in Bombay, who wrote: 'I was ailing in health and broken in spirit, but your Christ-like touch has revived the health of my body, soul and spirit.'[7] Another man, after appalling experiences in a mental hospital, found that Bede was the only person who understood his problems and was able to sustain him in his urgent need for a religious faith. He became aware, 'almost to the point of tears, what a beautiful friendship ours has been'.[8]

There is, of course, a world of difference between the love and admiration received from people who have felt helped and supported and the intimate friendship between equals. As far as this sort of friendship was concerned, Bede, during his early years in India, experienced periods of intense loneliness; apart from rare exceptions like Raimon Panikkar, Father Alapatt – though even this was more a relationship of loyalty and a shared monastic purpose than of close friendship – and his sometimes strained relationship with Father Francis at Kurisumala, he had no close friends and at these times he relied more than ever on Hugh and Martyn. Hugh recalled that when he was first at Shantivanam, Bede had said that he and Martyn were 'the only two people left with whom he has an intimate and what you might call "on the same level" friendship'.[9] Gradually he began to form new and important relationships, three of the closest being with Americans. These were Sister Pascaline Coff, the writer Wayne Teasdale, whom he met in 1973, and Judy Walter, a nurse who first came to the ashram the same year and who was to become his intimate confidante. He also had close intellectual friendships, particularly with the British biologist Rupert Sheldrake, and his prolific correspondence kept him in touch with many from whom he was separated by distance. And there were some of the permanent members of the community, the family in which he rejoiced: in the early days his friend the artist and theologian Jyoti Sahi was living at the ashram and, from 1970 till the end of his life, he was warmed by the devotion of Christudas, for whom he had a deep love.

It was perhaps predictable that, as a monk, Bede should never have experienced mutual love at its most profound, but in 1984 a young postulant, Russill Paul D'Silva, arrived at the ashram and the relationship between the two, later including Russill's wife Asha, was to introduce him to realms of friendship of a depth he had never before encountered.

Russill was only nineteen when he came to the ashram, intending to be a monk; Bede was seventy-eight. It was nearly three years before he told Martyn of this friendship, saying that Russill was 'closer to me than anyone I have known in India'. He described him as an Anglo-Indian from Madras, 'a fascinating blend of English and Indian culture', who spoke and wrote English like an Englishman and at the same time was deeply attracted to Indian culture, particularly to the study of the Sanskrit, and who was also a talented musician: 'Above all, he has an extraordinary attraction to contemplative prayer & spends hours in meditation. So I feel that I can share everything with him . . . For me it is as though God has given me a son in my old age who can make me live my youth again!'[10]

This cool account gives little idea of the intensity of the relationship that developed between the two. Russill did not immediately perceive Bede's quality, but as he saw him, every day as the sun rose and as it set, sitting outside his hut praying, he became aware of something so powerful that he was sometimes more interested in watching him pray than in praying himself:

> It really fascinated me, because I was so much aware of his deep communion with Nature and with God. Every time he moved away from people I sensed that deep communion with God, with reality, whatever. It was really then that I began to feel a kind of awe about him, his presence as a person. I realised I was in the presence of an extraordinary being. Somebody who was not just the Abbot of a monastery or somebody who had become a kind of spiritual father to me, but somebody who was far more than that.[11]

Russill began to pray for a similar experience of communion, that he should be in touch with reality in the same way and, early one morning, his prayer was granted with an experience so powerful that he could not talk or even write about it. He knew it was somehow connected with Bede, so he went to see him, giving him a piece of paper on which he had written, 'I am not able to speak. This is overwhelming me.' Bede said nothing, simply held his hand. This sense of overpowering emotion rose up many times and each time Russill, unable to contain it by himself, would go and sit in Bede's hut, finding that being in his presence helped to dissipate the awesome inner experience over which he had no control and which was to inundate him for months, even during sleep.

So began a relationship of a depth few people were able to understand; over ten years later Russill himself still found it hard to speak about. He had found a spiritual father, a man who exemplified his ideals, a friend with whom he could share experiences normally beyond communication. Bede had not only met someone who in his very person bridged East and West, uniting opposites in a way which must have felt like a homecoming, but he had found a sensitive and highly intelligent companion with whom he could discuss everything and with whom he could be completely himself, someone with whom he felt a closeness, a resonance, that he had never before experienced, a gentle, compassionate man of whom he later said: 'He has a greater capacity for unconditional love than anyone I have ever met.' He also, for the first time, experienced the full meaning of the guru–disciple relationship:

> This was shown in what is called a 'manifestation of conscience', in which he opened his heart to me and shared with me everything – including several love affairs – which had happened in his life. He came at all hours of the day and night to pour out his heart to me. This led to a deep love between us, a love which is typical of the guru–disciple relationship, which is not normal human love, but an experience of God in the heart.[12]

But seeds of discomfort were sown in the community, especially when Christudas and Amaldas, who had been away, returned to find this new young brother being given special treatment, for there is no doubt that Bede protected and indulged him, giving him a licence not normally extended to novices, such as allowing him to spend hours alone in the woods and excusing him from community prayers and Mass. But what most roused the resentment of the community was the time they spent together, talking, meditating, sometimes even going away together on retreat. It began to look like favouritism and people felt that Russill was being treated like a spoilt spiritual son, though it is important to say that Christudas, who most of all must have felt hurt by this new relationship, behaved impeccably, his love for Bede enabling him to accept the situation, whatever he may have felt about it.

Resentment was still simmering when, in 1986, a young Indian girl, Asha Muthayah, came straight from high school to stay at Shantivanam. Some women have felt that Bede was generally more at ease with men than with women, but this was certainly not true of Asha, for soon after meeting her he remarked: 'I feel that I have found a daughter.' Russill, too, found with her a new and rich relationship. In a small ashram it was inevitable that the two young people should be thrown together and it was not long before Russill and Asha realised that they were in love. So began a three-way relationship, of which Asha says: 'We each had our own relationship with each other, as well as between the three of us, but I always felt that there wasn't anything he [Father Bede] was trying to keep away from me, or that I had come into a relationship and taken something away. He did not see me as an intruder.'[13] They both discussed their relationship with Bede, who appreciated its depth but still believed that Russill should be a monk, or at least that he should try his vocation for another three years. Asha is adamant that at that stage the question of marriage did not arise: she would continue her studies and Russill would continue to be a monk. In any event, they come from different castes and their families would not have approved of their marrying. Russill was pulled in several directions: he wanted to live at Shantivanam, though as a hermit rather than as a monk, he wanted to fulfil Bede's expectations of him, he wanted to continue his music studies and he wanted to marry Asha.

Though it is curious that Bede should not have anticipated the resentment that was being felt in the ashram, it is understandable that a young man of Russill's age was slow to see it, especially considering the spiritual turmoil he was in, but eventually he began to realise that there was a feeling that he was being groomed for a position of authority in the ashram, even though he was not really accepted by the community, mostly because of his closeness to Bede. A two-week retreat together in the mountains and the fact that someone saw him meditating on Bede's bed brought things to a head.

In 1987 two things happened that left Russill in no doubt of the tension, or to put it bluntly the jealousy, that his relationship with Bede was causing. The first was that one of the senior members of the community spoke to Russill, telling him that he was taking up too much of Bede's time and depriving other people of access to him. This intervention, far preferable to the rumours that had been circulating, was entirely appropriate – the community was becoming uncomfortable and something had to be done about it. But the other reaction to the situation was inexcusable: Bede began to receive anonymous letters, postcards and notes. They were written in coloured ink and signed 'The Committee to save Shantivanam' and contained obscene drawings, accusations of 'crude' relationships and the injunction to 'get rid of your faggot lover'. Bede was shattered. Russill says that he had never seen him so hurt before, even his reaction to the diatribes from Swami Devananda paled into insignificance in comparison with his distress over these letters. Bede had no idea who could have been behind them, but though he burned most of them, he did keep one, and later, receiving a letter from someone asking to visit the ashram, he recognised the handwriting. Russill confronted the writer of the letter, threatening to sue for defamation of character, and eventually the truth emerged. Shockingly, the man behind the letters was a monk and, amazingly, a year later, he had the temerity to ask if he could come to Shantivanam again. It is the clearest measure of how deeply Bede was hurt that at first he was refused – the only time that anyone had been forbidden to come to the ashram. Yet such was Bede's capacity for forgiveness that later, when the monk who had caused him such pain asked again if he could come, he was told that he could.

Bede eventually realised that the hours he and Russill spent together could indeed lead to suspicions of a homosexual relationship between them and, not long before his death, in a statement he made to clarify their relationship, he wrote of this possibility with a transparent honesty that could hardly fail to convince the most hardened cynic:

> In regard to this I can only say that in all our relationship I cannot remember a single word or look or gesture which indicated any such feeling . . . For me this has been the realisation that it is possible to experience love in the most intimate sense in the depths of one's being, where we are totally open to God and to his love in our hearts. There is no doubt that it is a human love involving one's whole being – body, soul and spirit – and I have no doubt that there is a sexual element in it, as there is certainly a deep human affection. But the source of this love is in the 'spirit', the point at which we are both open to the love of God and this is the controlling force in our relationship.[14]

However, the anonymous letters had serious consequences for the relationship between Russill and Bede, for Russill's distress and disillusionment that someone who had been a monk for forty years could behave in so despicable a way played a part in his decision to leave the ashram. Bede's reaction to this shows how much he had come to rely on Russill's love and friendship, but his attempts to dissuade him from leaving failed and the time came when Russill had to say goodbye. Bede was sitting outside his hut, and as Russill left he turned back for one last look at his beloved friend. 'He was all slumped in his chair, weeping and I knew that I had broken his heart in some way.'[15] The image of this dignified, reserved man reduced to inconsolable tears is more telling than any words.

Bede's starved emotions were awakened as they had never been before and he spoke openly about his feelings. After Russill and Asha left the ashram he wrote to them, remembering Russill's parting and final prostration: 'I felt that you were surrendering your whole soul and my kiss was a kiss of benediction, breathing out my spirit on you.' He admitted the distress he had experienced as they took the train to Bombay and he was left alone.

I felt your departure very much at first, but already I am beginning to feel that deep oneness with you, which will never change wherever you will be. Still I also look forward to being with you again, where & when God chooses.
With my deepest love for you both,
Your loving father & brother & friend in Christ
Dom Bede.[16]

Before they left India, Russill and Asha had decided to marry and, after a civil wedding ceremony in March 1989, they had spent several months in the ashram, culminating in three weeks in the hills with Bede, preparing for their spiritual marriage by praying, talking and reading from Hindu and Christian scriptures. Bede saw their marriage as part of his own fulfilment – they were living out something he had not been able to do. He later wrote: 'Somehow I feel that I share in your love for one another & experience married love in myself through you.'[17] His reaction shows how his attitude to marriage had changed. In his youth his outspoken disapproval of Hugh Waterman's marriage had caused a temporary rift in their friendship; even in the 1970s, when Jyoti Sahi decided to marry, Jyoti remembers feeling that 'there was a kind of separation between us. I felt that he was somehow disappointed in me, that he thought I had failed in some "higher calling"'.[18] Now Bede welcomed marriage as a spiritual path as valid as the monastic life, once again showing how, even in his eighties, he was able to change and develop.

It was through his friendship with Russill and Asha that he was able to respond to a question put to him by a member of an Australian film crew in a way he could never have done when he was younger. The question was 'What is the meaning of life?' and he replied: 'The meaning of life is love and there are two ways to love. One is through a dedication of the whole of your life to the spirit and the working out of that dedication. The other is to love another human being so profoundly that that initiates you into the divine love.'[19] Bede's vicarious experience of marriage released an avalanche of thoughts, which he later shared with Russill and Asha by letter. He began to distinguish between priesthood as a sacramental ministry to the people and monastic life as consecrated to a life of prayer and contemplation; in that sense, monastic life did not, he felt, necessarily exclude marriage. 'I feel to-day that many if not more people find God in marriage rather than in celibacy. Your own example has had a great influence on me,' he wrote, adding, with impressive honesty: 'If I had had my way, Paul would have been a celibate monk, but you have shown me how much one's spiritual life can be enriched by marriage.'[20]* It was not necessary, he felt, to give up sex and marriage but to transmute them; this was the great work of asceticism and spiritual endeavour today. So too, agape and eros need to be united:

> Agape without eros simply does not work. It leaves our human nature starved. Of course, eros without agape is equally disastrous. It leaves us to the compulsion of human and sexual love . . . in meditation we can learn to let our own natural desires, our eros, awaken & surrender it to God, that is, let it be taken up into agape. It must be neither suppressed nor indulged. It is *surrender* that is called for.[21]

He was not only writing in theory, he was also working out his feelings for Russill and Asha, continuing: 'My love for you is not only agape; it is a deep natural urge of love which draws me to you. Often I feel your presence, especially during these last days, as a tremendous force in my life, making me realise that I cannot experience the divine love, unless it is united with my human love for you.'[22]

So too he reflected on the *muladhara*, the root chakra, the body's connection to the earth and to sex, reading the exploration of the consciousness of the *muladhara* made by Sri Aurobindo's companion, known as 'The Mother'. At that level, as she argued and he readily agreed, all divisions disappear and everything flows into everything else. This state of blissful consciousness is very like that of the *sahasrara* (the seventh chakra, in the crown of the head); indeed, they are fundamentally the same: 'Whether we ascend to the Father above or descend to the Mother below, we encounter the same mystery of advaita, & eventually, of course, there is no above & below, only the infinite radiance of bliss, which is the bliss of love – where male & female & all other oposites are united in the One.'[23] Concerned as always with resolving opposites, he was both recognising and clarifying the distinctions between the masculine and the feminine, yearning towards their reconciliation.

Far from resenting Asha as an intrusion into his relationship with Russill, in Russill's words 'he transformed it in his usual symbolic, synthetic way into a sacred experience'.[24] Bede saw the relationship between the three of them as embodying the deep unity of the Trinity, the relationship between himself and Russill at first mirroring the relationship between Jesus and the Father, then, with Asha's arrival, the Holy Spirit becoming part of the experience:

---

*Bede liked to think of Paul as Russill's monastic name.

We are not fulfilled until we pass over into that state where there is neither I nor you but a oneness which yet contains both the I & the you. That is why I liken it to the Trinity. The Father loves the son & passes over entirely into him & the son loves the father in the same way. And both father and son find themselves in the bliss of love in the Holy Spirit, the third in whom both lose themselves and find themselves. I apply this to myself & Paul & Asha.[25]

As his friendship with Asha deepened, so she became for Bede the archetype of the feminine, helping him to relate to the feminine in a way he had sought for a life-time and failed to achieve. The culmination of this relationship with the feminine was to come in a way nobody could have foreseen.

CHAPTER EIGHTEEN

Breakthrough to the Feminine

E arly in the morning of 25 January 1990, Bede was sitting on the veranda of his hut meditating, when, without any warning, he felt a terrific force, like a sledge-hammer, hit him on the head. It was as if an explosion had shattered his brain and everything became blurred and confused. He felt himself being dragged out of his chair, which seemed to be rising from the ground. He managed to cling to it for a few seconds until, breathing heavily and very frightened, he fell on to the bed, where he lost count of time until Christudas came and found him.

For two days his life was in the balance and for a week he lay motionless and speechless, sleeping for most of the time. The medical diagnosis was congestive heart failure, pulmonary oedema and a slight stroke, but he was too weak and fragile to be taken to hospital, so his hut was turned into an intensive-care centre. There were over a hundred people in the ashram at the time, including doctors and nurses, and Sister Marie Louise, herself a nurse, organised teams of people to give round-the-clock care. Despite the primitive conditions, no patient could have received more constant, loving care. He submitted to this with his usual grace, telling one of his carers that he rather liked being looked after and admitting ruefully to Russill and Asha, 'I have to be taken to the bathroom and washed and bathed and combed just like an old dog.'[1] The whole focus of the ashram shifted from the temple, the refectory and the library to Bede's hut, as those not involved in looking after him gathered round silently praying and meditating.

Over the next few weeks he improved slowly, and by the end of February he was able to take short walks, to pray, to read and write and even to see a few people. Though it was undoubtedly an extremely serious physical illness, those who heard him talk about it were convinced that it was essentially a mystical experience. Within days his ever-active brain was reflecting on what had happened to him and his great friend Judy Walter, who was one of those closest to him, took notes of everything he said. He told her that at first he had lost all sense of time and space and that his immediate reaction was fear, a fear which he compared to the Dark Night described by St John of the Cross: 'I had blown my mind. The ego has collapsed. I feel totally free. All the barriers have broken down. I think I know now what the void of Buddhism is. I am empty, but it is *not* a mystical experience; it is a negative experience.'[2] Then, early one morning, he told Judy how two images seemed to summarize the whole experience: the Black Madonna and Christ crucified. It was not the traditional devotion to Our Lady, but the feminine in all its forms: as the Mother of God, as Earth Mother, as the Black Madonna manifested in rocks and caves, in all Nature and in the Church, in his own mother, in the hidden power in the womb, in motherhood itself. He also saw in her the Hindu concept of Shakti, the feminine aspect of divine energy: 'I feel it was this Power which struck me. She is cruel and destructive, but also deeply loving, nourishing and protecting.'[3]

The other image, of the crucified Christ, was constantly with him, and several times he felt himself with Jesus on the cross, surrendering himself to the darkness of death and, in this self-emptying, becoming one with all. His understanding of the crucifixion had deepened immeasurably as Christ became for him the Christ who had suffered with the poor and the oppressed, who surrendered everything to this dark power.

> He lost everything – friends, disciples, his own people, their law and religion. And at last he had to surrender to his God: 'My God, my God, why have you forsaken me?' Even his heavenly Father, every image of a personal God, had to go. He had to enter the Dark Night, to be exposed to the abyss. Only then could he become everything and nothing, opened beyond everything that can be named or spoken. Only then could he be one with the darkness, the void, the dark Mother who is love itself.[4]

He saw old truths with which he had long been familiar with the freshness and immediacy of experience. He saw anew how human beings are born to suffering and how that suffering leads to anger, self-hatred, fear, violence; how this mass of evil leads to sin and how Christ, in becoming man, entered into the collective unconscious of humanity and took all this sin and suffering on himself. Our love for each other is Christ's love in us, a Christ that is both mother and father, bridegroom and bride, and who does not judge, whose love is unconditional. Bede would talk to Judy of the way the collective unconscious is the condition every person is in before we develop our individual personalities and how we all carry memories of this state of paradise when we were one: 'Our growth in body, soul and spirit is in some sense a return to this original unity . . . The Holy Spirit, Christ in us, pierces through every level of our being and makes us one in this ultimate ground. That is how everything and everyone comes out of unity and returns to unity.'[5] In this holistic vision of the universe he saw the physical, the psychological and the spiritual as inseparable. The three dimensions are present in all phenomena, in the universe itself, which, like the Holy Trinity, has three aspects but is ultimately one. Thus he was able to bring his Christian and his advaitic experience together. He did not see *advaita* as 'one' in the sense of eliminating all differences, but as a state in which the differences are mysteriously present in the 'one'. They are there, but no longer separated:

> Advaita is an insight which transcends logic; it is beyond all dualities of every kind. The rational mind is limited by dualistic thought and is within those limits, but advaita is an insight beyond reason and logic: it is pure awareness, pure light. I am using rational dualistic language, but I am trying to point to an experience which transcends thought. I feel it is this experience of advaita with all its paradox which we have to seek as the very goal of life.[6]

As he became increasingly aware that the breaking of his body was a sharing in the broken body of Christ, as he experienced the power of love behind all the sin and suffering in the world more acutely than ever before, so he began to feel the same love in himself: 'nothing could stand in the way of that love – least of all death. I feel that death is only its ultimate embrace.'[7] Those close to him saw the way he had changed, Judy Walter writing: 'His body is so weak, but his face is radiant, his mind and spirit have never been so clear & active.'[8] Reflecting some years later, she said that before the stroke Father Bede had for her been an ideal; after it he became real, became a human being, a personal friend. For her an important change was that his reserve had broken down. Speaking as an American she said: 'Father was always British to me, but after the stroke he had no nationality.'[9]

Exactly a month after his stroke, when everyone thought he was well on the road to recovery, Bede had another experience in which body, mind and spirit were inextricably woven together. Just after midnight on 25 February he felt a tremendous pressure in his head and was convinced that he was dying. He was quite without fear and decided to prepare for death, saying the prayers for the dying, the Hail Mary, the prayer to the angels, the Our Father and the Gloria. At the same time he experienced again the sense of being with Jesus on the cross and having to surrender to death, but, as he laconically put it, 'nothing happened':

> I had some breakfast and then I felt sort of restless, disturbed, not knowing quite what was happening. The inspiration came suddenly again to surrender to the Mother. It was quite unexpected: 'Surrender to the Mother.' And so I somehow made a surrender to the Mother. Then I had an experience of overwhelming love. Waves of love sort of flowed into me. Judy Walter, my great friend, was watching. Friends were beside me all the time. I called out to her, 'I'm being overwhelmed by love'.[10]

The effects of this overwhelming experience, of being totally engulfed in love, never left him and he was very sure what it meant. Always when talking about his stroke he would stress that what he had felt as a blow on his head came from the left and propelled him towards the right, and this he interpreted as being a violent assertion of the feminine, the right side of the brain. Despite his early experience of God in nature, despite his longing for the intuitive, the feminine and the unconscious, he had none the less grown up in a patriarchal society and all his life had lived in the intellect, developing his rational, masculine, side and suppressing the intuitive and the feminine. Now, at last, in his eighty-fourth year, he felt that 'the left brain and the whole rational system had been knocked down and the right brain and the intuitive understanding, the sympathetic mind, had been opened up'.[11] And this was an experience of love:

> Death, the Mother, the Void, all was love. It was an overwhelming love, so strong that I could not contain myself. I did not know whether I would survive. I knew 'I' had to die, but whether it would be in this world or another, I did not know. At first I thought I would die and just be engulfed in this love. It was the 'unconditional love' of which I had often spoken, utterly mysterious, beyond words.[12]

So greatly did he feel himself loved, so awesome was this experience, that he wept during it as he would sometimes weep when he recalled it. He began to realise that he could choose whether to live or die and that he must live; he also knew that with this discovery of the feminine, he had been healed. As Judy Walter put it: 'On Jan 25th the Mother came and "struck" him & wounded him. On Feb 25th the Mother came & overwhelmed him with love & healed him.'[13] The next afternoon he sprang out of bed and for the first time began to walk without a stick. A psychic had once told him that he would have a death experience in his eighty-fourth year and if he survived it he would live many more years. People around him, seeing the lightness in his step and an energy flowing from him that they had not seen for several weeks, felt they would have him for a good time to come.

Despite this great improvement in his health, on 2 March and 9 March Bede had two more 'death experiences', speaking of them as times when he surrendered to the darkness of death and by that total self-emptying became one with the universe. More and more he began to feel the masculine mind dissolve and the intuitive feminine side begin to take its rightful place; more and more he was finding the union of the masculine and the feminine, those two opposites he had sought so long to reconcile. This led him to a new appreciation of Mary, and he found himself, though it had not been his normal custom, praying the 'Hail Mary' constantly, finding in the Mother of God the channel through which the Holy Spirit comes into the world.

Bede's understanding of what had happened to him grew slowly. From the very beginning he knew that it had changed him radically and later he would say that the process of change went on for months. He even said that he had grown more in the two years after his stroke than in the previous eighty-four. There were still times of darkness, times of chaos, confusion and bewilderment, but even when he was unsure what was happening he was aware of continual growth. He was unwilling to call it a mystical experience, preferring to see it – as indeed he now saw everything – on three levels:

> On the physical level it was apparently a stroke, a bursting of a blood vessel due to lack of oxygen in the brain. On the psychological level it was a 'death of the mind' – a breakdown of the left-brain rational mind and an awakening to the feminine intuitive mind. But on the spiritual level it certainly left an impression of advaita – a transcendence of all limitations & an awakening to the non dual reality. This has left an indelible impression on me. I am seeing everything in a new light.[14]

He was fascinated by this breakthrough to the feminine and frequently talked and wrote about it. 'I was very masculine and patriarchal and had been developing the *animus*, the left brain, all this time. Now the right brain – the feminine, the chthonic power, the earth power – came and hit me.'[15] In hitting him with such force it was taking him to realms of darkness and chaos, to the depths of the divine mystery:

> God is not simply in the light, in the intelligible world, in the rational order. God is in the darkness, in the womb, in the Mother, in the chaos from

which the order comes. So the chaos is in God, we could say, and that is why discovering the darkness is so important. We tend to reject it as evil and as negative and so on, but the darkness is the womb of life.[16]

Andrew Harvey is convinced it was this force, this experience of the feminine, that infused Bede's last years with such extraordinary energy; it was something he often talked about to Bede:

> He believed his stroke to be an initiation by the Mother (specifically in her Kali or Black Madonna aspect as Saving Destroyer and Killer of Illusion). I know too that he felt himself drawn by this new force in his life into a far deeper immersion in the beauty of human relationships (his world-wide teaching and his love for Russill Paul) and into a deeper and richer knowledge of the intricate ways in which the body, sexuality, and mystic transformation are connected. The Mother, in other words, compelled him to take her path into DESCENT, of descent into the world of matter, into human love, so that he could integrate within himself the 'masculine' and 'feminine' powers of his mind and soul and so give birth with an increasing passion, purity and intensity to the Divine Child within him, the Christ-consciousness.[17]

He was undergoing a profound inner transformation, becoming grounded, earthed, in a way that was quite unfamiliar to him. He who had always lived so much in his head was now, using the language of the chakras, talking of his energy moving down from the head to the heart, then down to the *muladhara*. He had no difficulty in acknowledging how sexually repressed he had always been, admitting that only in his old age was he discovering the sexual dimension of life. So too he saw love as the basic principle of the whole universe and came to a new understanding of his life-long concern: the opposites. 'We have to let go of all concepts which divide the world into good and evil, right and wrong, and learn to see the complementarity of opposites.'[18]

So too he felt that what he called his 'advaitic experience' was a revelation of the greatest possible significance. Though he welcomed it on a personal level, he realised that it raised serious theological problems. He saw more clearly than ever how the Church has always been conditioned by dualistic thought and how God and the world, God and humanity, good and evil are all conceived in dualistic terms. Only at the very end of St John's Gospel, he felt, does the Gospel reach to the level of pure *advaita*: 'That they all may be one, as Thou, Father, in me and I in Thee, that they may be one in us.'[19] Christianity comes from a Semitic background, the product of a patriarchal culture interpreted in the Greco-Roman world in dualistic terms; to see it in advaitic terms would demand a reinterpretation of the Bible and of all Catholic doctrine. A great deal was becoming clear to him, but he felt that the Church was not yet ready for such ideas and he did not want to publish anything on the subject. Nevertheless, he did indicate some of the problems he saw in a letter to Sister Pascaline.

Writing on Easter Day to Sister Pascaline, he reminded her that the God they were celebrating drowned the Egyptians in the Red Sea without mercy, massacred their first-born without pity and commanded his people to occupy the land of other peoples. 'Such a God is obviously intolerable. It was concealed before because the Fathers interpreted it all in an allegorical sense, but the brute reality remains.' Equally he was appalled by the violence of some of the Psalms:

> God is love & mercy and grace & truth to the people of Israel, but for those outside he has no pity. He 'hates' the wicked, he judges & condemns, he punishes in his wrath & this extends to all humanity. It seems to me that Jesus came to put an end to this jealous God, & in his final surrender on the cross gave up the God of Israel ('My God, my God, why have you forsaken me?') and in total surrender to death & the void, realised the absolute truth & the absolute love, which alone is God.

He went on to list 'the problems of women in the Church and the feminine in God' and some of the problems of Catholic doctrine, all conditioned by Greco-Roman culture and a patriarchal system of society: 'Scarcely any of it – Trinity, Incarnation, Redemption, Grace, the Church can be properly understood to-day. There are not three "persons" in the modern sense in the Trinity. There is only one divine Person in Christ. There is no change in the "substance" (that is the physical substance) in the bread and wine of the Eucharist. All this has to be expressed in a different way.'[20]

Another matter that concerned him was Cardinal Ratzinger's document on Christian prayer and meditation and this was something to which he did respond publicly. The Cardinal's 'Letter to the Bishops of the Catholic Church on Some Aspects of Meditation' was promulgated on 14 December 1989 and, though it granted that eastern methods of prayer and meditation have positive elements, it stressed the dangers inherent in the eastern approach. Bede had read this document before his stroke and found it profoundly disturbing; in the middle of February, barely three weeks after his stroke, he put his thoughts on paper in an article later published in the *National Catholic Reporter*. It was, he said, an extremely disappointing document, treating eastern meditation as if it were 'a matter of superficial techniques, of "bits and pieces" which a Christian can use if he wishes, but of whose dangers and abuses he must be made aware'. He further deplored the conception of Christian prayer it presented and again pointed out the crisis in the Church today:

> Many Christians are looking to the church for guidance in contemplative prayer and failing to find it. They then turn to Hindu and Buddhist masters for guidance and often through them come to understand something of the depth of Christian mysticism. But for such people, this document offers no assistance whatever. It is, rather, calculated to put them off and make them confirmed in their belief that the Christian church has nothing to offer those who are seeking God in the dark, often on a lonely path and desperately in need of the guidance the church so often fails to give.[21]

His sense of the inadequacy of this document was undoubtedly reinforced by his recent experience.

When he was well enough to travel, Judy and Eusebia, another of the people who had been looking after him, took him to Kodaikanal, a cool hill station near Madurai, to recuperate. He was here for the celebration of the golden jubilee of his ordination, though in fact it was of so little importance to him that he remembered it only when he received congratulatory cards. It was not his ordination as a priest that was important to him, he said at the time, but his profession as a monk; he saw his priesthood simply as a service to the community. His walking was still weak and rather perilous but his spirit was strong and his mind sufficiently active for him to read the recently published edition of Abhishiktananda's letters.* In reading this book he learned more about the beginnings of Shantivanam and the relationship between Abhishiktananda and Monchanin, realising for the first time the extent of the conflict between the two men: Monchanin remained deeply rooted in a traditional Catholic faith, while Abhishiktananda went through deep anguish as he tried to reconcile Hinduism and Christianity. Abhishiktananda, too, towards the end of his life had suffered a heart attack by the side of the road that was the occasion of an 'awakening' which enabled him to write: 'Really a door opened in heaven when I was lying on the pavement. But a heaven which was not the opposite of earth, something which was neither life nor death, but simply "being", "awakening" . . . beyond all myths and symbols.'[22]

*James Stuart (ed.), *Swami Abhishiktananda: His Life Told through His Letters* (London: ISPCK, 1989).

They differed, however, in their attempts to integrate the advaitic experience with Christianity, Bede telling Judy Walter that he felt that Abhishiktananda, despite his agony at discovering that 'the pearl of great price is not the exclusive property of the Roman Catholic Church, as he had previously assumed',[23] did not share his own attitude to the reconciliation of *advaita* with Christianity. Bede could not accept a concept of *advaita* which denies the reality of the world, the differences disappearing into a formless, undifferentiated, void. For him, Christian *advaita* meant not losing the differences, but transcending them. 'In the ultimate reality we find ourselves & God and Christ and other people and the whole created world, not divided in space & time & subject to conceptual thought, but integrated in one eternal, infinite reality, which is a *differentiated* reality, not divided in any way but realised in its total reality.'[24] He was more than ever convinced that

> the lived experience of the mysteries of the faith is the way to final reality, & not the experience of Hindu advaita. This is not to say that many may not come to final reality through Hindu advaita or Buddhist sunyata but for a Christian the way is through Christ & the Church. I should add that for me there is a Christian Advaita in which the mysteries of faith are not lost, but finally realized.[25]

During his recuperation at Kodaikanal Bede asked Judy to write down some dreams he had had during this period, all of which he interpreted as showing the now constant interaction of the right and the left brain. In the first there were three huge men, looking like prize fighters. One of them put his arms around the neck of another, who, in the curious way of dreams, seemed to be Bede himself, then the three men wrestled together in a free fight. This Bede took as a symbol of the masculine struggling to assert itself. In the second dream there was an animal, either a cat or a rabbit, sitting quietly and a little kitten running about, oblivious of the larger animal. Bede feared for its life, and was astonished when it began to hit the other animal. Once again a free fight followed and once again he saw it as a symbol of the conflict between masculine and feminine. In another of these dreams Father Francis was sitting in a cubicle that Bede thought was his own, but which had been transformed into a Cistercian cell; as he saw Father Francis as a very masculine man, this again he took to represent the conflict between the masculine and the feminine. In the fourth dream he had made a clear decision to leave a community, which he thought reflected the decision he had made to leave charge of Shantivanam. He became aware of a darkness outside and people moving about and with great emotion he called out, 'My brothers, my brothers'. Then a huge African-American appeared and Bede called out with great fervour, 'I put my whole trust in you.' Hearing this 'he or she embraced me very tenderly.'[26] He felt this figure was himself, the African standing for the feminine and the American for the masculine and that this figure, who embraced him so tenderly, was a symbol of the union of the masculine and the feminine.

Was there a connection between Bede's dramatic discovery of the feminine and his loving relationship with Russill and Asha? Though the answer to this sort of question can never be proved, it does seem that it played a crucial part in his awakening to a way of relating, a depth of loving, which had for so long eluded him and which was necessary for the reconciliation of the opposites, particularly of the masculine and the feminine. He knew that his whole life had been a struggle to escape from the tyranny of the left brain and that he had been seeking the compensatory balance of the feminine in poetry, art, music, nature, prayer and mystical experience. He also knew that, as he struggled to understand what was happening to him, it was the rational mind that was working; he knew too how great Russill's part in the experience was: 'This is why you have always meant so much to me, because I felt that you were a whole person . . . You have also been able to relate naturally & spontaneously to the feminine. That is why your love for Asha makes me so happy, & why I also seem to share that love, discovering in Asha the archetype of the feminine which I can love.'[27]

It was clear to Judy how dearly he loved them. She recalled how, often, when he was seized with a new insight, he would write to them – sometimes he wrote almost every day. Only a week after the stroke, his usually neat and regular handwriting wandering uncertainly round the page, he wrote:

> One thing I realise. I need your presence very much. It is not only the thought of you, but your presence, which is somehow always with me, as it is part of the presence of God to me . . . For me prayer has always been the practice of the presence of God. But for me you and Asha are part of the presence of God – it is through you that I realise his presence and again through his presence that I feel you near to me.[28]

Aspects of this relationship have a depth which it is hard to fathom; Russill wondered if it had something to do with 'relating in *advaita*'. Through loving them Bede learned that beyond ordinary human love they shared a deeper love, a love which went beyond differences and 'in which we are *absolutely* one . . . I feel that you are in me and I am in you'.[29] He felt united with Russill in soul and spirit, but 'we are also united in this common ground which is really the *muladhara*'. He applied his thinking on the unity from which we all come and to which we will return, in a very personal way to Russill:

> The Holy Spirit, Christ in us, pierces through every level of our being & makes us one in this ultimate ground. I feel it with you as something quite definite, there is a hidden bond beyond our conscious selves to which we have always to return, & this is true in measure of all of us. This is what it means to love with the totality of one's being.
> With my love to Asha. Share this with her.[30]

Through loving one person totally and uniquely, Bede had learned about love itself in a new and more personal way, and that love, which had already extended to Asha, was growing to include others. It needed a way to express itself. His letters to Russill and Asha show the first tentative suggestions as to how this might be realised. He was coming to believe that one of the greatest needs for the twentieth century was the establishment of spiritual centres, which would be open to people of all religions and where there would be, for instance, music therapy and psychological healing as well as meditation and yoga. He was already thinking of possible locations and was not only encouraging Russill and Asha to start such a centre in America, where they were now living, but was considering the possibility of some day coming over himself.

Bede had also had a vision of an ideal community based on the symbolism of the Tarot. He had been deeply impressed by a book on the Tarot by an anonymous Russian writer, considered by many Christian contemplatives to be twentieth-century classic.* It embraces alchemy, astrology, magic, the occult, Hinduism, Buddhism and modern science, but all, as he wrote to Martyn Skinner, within a completely orthodox Catholic system. Once again he had found unity in apparent diversity and he wrote to Martyn Skinner: 'It is simply astonishing. I have never read such a comprehensive account of the "perennial philosophy" . . . there is hardly a line without some profound significance . . . To me it is the last word in wisdom.'[31]

In this fantasy of a 'community of love', each person was to represent one of the symbols of the Tarot, and the way he paired the person with the symbol indicates how he regarded those who were closest to him. Russill was to be the Magician, radiating a love inspired by wisdom; he would be able to discern the unique value of each person and unite them in divine love. Judy was cast

---

Meditations on the Tarot – A Journey into Christian Hermeticism (Shaftesbury: Element Books, 1991).

as the High Priestess, the personification of divine love, offering counselling and healing to the poor, the sick, the handicapped and the dying. Asha, the Empress, was to be in charge of the house, caring for the community as a loving mother: 'She will be a queen whose work is to serve, and will offer her whole life as a sacrifice to divine love in the person of Russill, and receive his love and that of all the community as the response of love for love.' Wayne Teasdale was to organise the prayer and study of the community, bringing all the religions of the world into unity and reconciling religious differences in a mystical philosophy. He would be the Emperor, 'an example of authority which rules by love and not by power – (as the Pope should but doesn't)'. Bede himself would be the Hermit, though he might not stay for long, 'but may depart to another world where I will continue to give light and protection to you all and keep you in the embrace of divine love'.[32] Bede was not normally someone who indulged in fantasy, and this innocent intellectualising of his close relationships, even if it seems out of character, to some even bizarre, is yet another sign of how he had changed, how the hitherto repressed side of his personality was finding expression.

By the end of March, Judy and Eusebia brought Bede back to Shantivanam and, though still physically fragile, he returned to his old routine, presiding in the temple and in the refectory. Everyone saw how he had changed and they were touched by his bearing in the Palm Sunday procession, by his humility and by the way in which he was both broken and strong. On Good Friday he read the Gospel, and when he came to the words 'My God, My God, why have you forsaken me?', he was unable to finish the line but broke down and wept.

An important outer change had also taken place during his illness. On 15 February the Prior General, Father Emmanuel, who was spending a month at the ashram, announced that Father Bede had officially retired and that Father Amaldas was now head of the ashram and that he would take over in October. Bede was happy about this and excited by the thatched hut he was having built a little further down the river, among the pine trees. He planned an eremetical life, living for God alone, first in this hut in the forest and later, perhaps, further afield. Soon after he returned he spent his first full day in the hut. He took nothing – no books, no pen and paper, nothing. For the whole day he said the Jesus Prayer and, according to Judy Walter, 'had such a sense of the Presence in the woods & trees & plants around. He was glowing'.[33] Was he at last to live the solitary life for which he longed but which both his temperament and his fame had denied him? Could he refuse the invitations that were flooding in? Indeed, could he restrain his desire to communicate what he had learned through his overwhelming experience?

CHAPTER NINETEEN

'You Cannot Put a Prophet in a Cage'

Once he had recovered from his stroke, wanting nothing more than to be with God, Bede told everyone that his travels were over and that he was planning to retire to his hermitage and be alone in solitary meditation. But it was not to be. Within weeks of arriving at this decision he was drawn out of his retirement as invitations to speak flowed in and he responded. 'I felt the call and the need,'[1] he said, and these words carry both aspects of his response. Once again his need to communicate and his need to be solitary were in conflict, and once again the desire to communicate won. He felt the call of a new spirituality emerging in the West and the need to share his vision, now even more deeply enriched by his recent experience. How could he resist? A religious sister living at Shantivanam suggested that it was through this stroke that the prophetic in Father Bede at last broke through: 'You cannot put a prophet in a cage. He belongs to the masses, his message has to reach the entire planet . . . He found he had to go, he had to offer it, and he also had to feel the pulse, not of a country, but of the universe.'[2] Or in Bede's own, cooler, words: 'It is a responsibility, I feel, to present a more authentic understanding of Christianity in the light of world culture today.'[3]

So began more than two years of a breathless schedule that would surely have exhausted someone far younger and fitter than Bede; indeed, those who planned his trips were accused of exploiting him, of squeezing every last ounce out of a very old man (though this charge is well met by Bede's constant gratitude for the loving care and attention he received on his travels – he frequently told Douglas Conlan that he had never been so well cared for as on his travels in Australia). Over the last few months he had plumbed depths of anguish and soared to heights of joy; now an astonishing energy was released in him as, in his eighties, soon after a serious illness which had brought him close to death, he spent months at a time in America, visited Canada, England, Germany, Austria, Italy, Australia and Singapore. During these twenty-six months he gave countless public talks, he was the keynote speaker at major seminars, he was interviewed by press, radio and television, saw people privately and continued to write articles and letters to the press. He was also looking to the future, planning ways in which his vision of the contemplative life could be embodied after his death. If, as he himself said, he grew more during these years than in the entire previous eighty-four, so he travelled more and communicated more than he had ever done before. He thought constantly about death and had accepted the knowledge that it could not be far off without fear, but he lived in the present, accepting invitations and planning for the future as if he would live for ever.

In travelling so widely, taking up so public a stance, he was risking criticism. Should he not, in his ninth decade, be living a quiet, contemplative life? And had he not taken vows of stability? Apart from the fact that Bede had never let the opinion of others deflect him in his pursuit of what he believed to be right, he had no problem in justifying his travels in the light of stability. Stability, he argued, was not about place, rather it implies a constancy in prayer and meditation, so that the sense of union with God becomes habitual. His view of stability was that, 'The "place" of contemplation is "the cave of the heart", which we can take with us wherever we go.'[4] He was again caught between opposites, for he had both taken a vow of stability and was committed to the life of the sannyasi, the wanderer, but for him balance was more important than extremes. Nor did he ever go anywhere without the permission of the Camaldolese to whom he had now belonged for ten years.

Though he had now officially retired as Prior, there were also the responsibilities he still felt towards Shantivanam, responsibilities that were intensified when Father Amaldas suffered a heart attack and died before he had even taken charge of the ashram. Nevertheless Bede had a sense that his own work there was completed, that with three solemnly professed monks, three simply professed, two oblates and two postulants, the ashram was ready to ride on its own energy. Christudas often accompanied him on his travels but he had complete trust in Brother Martin, appreciating him very profoundly both as a person and as a thinker and admiring his commitment and his courage; he knew that in his absence Martin would run the ashram with both wisdom and efficiency.

Bede's first trip after his stroke was to America, but on the way he spent some time in Germany, visiting Roland Ropers, a devoted admirer who had translated two of his books into German and was one of the people most active in promoting and often paying for his travels. Roland was the general manager of a private clinic in Kreuth, Tegernsee, and Bede was to visit it frequently on his travels between India and America, finding the clinic a restful place of psychological and spiritual healing 'where people can discover their inner self, the indwelling Spirit, which is the source of healing for body and soul'.[5] On this first visit he began work on a collection of readings from the sacred writings of the world which Roland was arranging for publication.* He felt that Christians must become accustomed to meditating on the scriptures of different faiths and he hoped that it would be used as a prayer book by people seeking to reconcile different religious traditions in their lives. He summarised his intentions to Sister Pascaline:

> I have tried to show how all the main religious traditions, Hindu, Buddhist, Taoist, Sikh, Muslim, Jewish & Christian, all converge on advaita, on nonduality, as the ultimate truth and reality. Christianity culminates in the saying of Jesus 'that the all may be one, as Thou, Father, in me, & I in thee, that they may be one in us.' In other words the end of Christians & of all human existence is to participate in the divine life, which Jesus shares with the Father and communicates to us in the spirit. Everything has to be seen in this context.[6]

From Germany he flew to Montreal, where he spent some time with the Christian Meditation Community, a group founded to spread the meditation rediscovered by Father John Main and which was at the time based in Canada; then he went on to Vermont, where at last he was reunited with Russill and Asha. The three of them, together with Wayne Teasdale, spent over two months together in a house lent to them by a friend. It was in the hills, 6,000 feet high, surrounded by trees, wild deer and running streams, in a climate which ranged from rain and snow to brilliant sunshine, and Bede loved it. It was the first time that Russill and Asha had seen him since his stroke and they were very aware of a change in him, finding him freer, more expressive, less repressed and more in touch with his feelings; he was no longer keeping so tight a rein on his emotions, thus his anger, for instance, could find more spontaneous expression. They were particularly surprised at his need to talk about everything that had happened to him over the months of his illness. Previously he had hardly spoken about such

*Universal Wisdom: A Journey through the Sacred Wisdom of the World.

things, his constant admonition being, in one way or another, to remind people that 'The Tao that can be named is not the eternal Tao'. It is as if, in keeping with the tradition of mystics such as St John of the Cross, he did not want to attribute too much importance to anything that happened on the way up the mountain, but that in his recent overwhelming experience he had reached the top, the experiential knowledge he had been searching for all his life. How could he not want to talk of it? To say, as it were, 'It *is* there. I was right all along. It does exist, this state of unity.' Russill and Asha also noticed that many of the contradictions and paradoxes with which he had struggled for so long rose to the surface. For instance, though he had at last discovered his feminine side and was freer emotionally, he did not cease to use his rational, masculine, side; indeed, it is arguable that this aspect of his personality, no longer resented and resisted, had found its place in his total being and was released to function more effectively. Certainly his expression of difficult ideas now had the qualities of directness and simplicity which are the hallmark of clarity of thought.

The impression he made on people as he travelled was becoming even more powerful. Annabel Miller, an assistant editor on *The Tablet*, had no particular expectations when she went to hear him in London, but 'As soon as he walked in there was something very special and very different about him. I had a strong sense that everything he was saying was true. I imagine hearing Jesus must have been a bit like that.'[7] Bailey Young, an American academic, said, 'I knew I was in the presence of a saint',[8] and another American, Ruth Harring, thought that, 'It was as if Christ was walking the earth . . . Meditating with him was like being in an infinite ocean.'[9] Christiane Ropers met him in Germany and felt 'real peace, joy, and this very lightness of being, not only in a sense like the sun, but of no heaviness'.[10] Bede was apparently unaware of the effect he had on people, the most he would say was that a talk seemed to go down very well or that a particular hall was packed to capacity; sometimes he would avoid situations where he knew there would be so many people wanting to see him that he would not be able to cope. On a more superficial level he was quite untroubled by the way wearing the saffron robes of the sannyasi, the *kavi*, inevitably made him conspicuous. He never wore western dress, feeling completely comfortable in the *kavi*, the outer witness of his life of renunciation. On this subject he was unperturbed by criticism, though the point was made that a Hindu priest visiting the West would not be expected to wear clerical dress. Nor was he put out by the teasing that sometimes came his way. On one occasion in Berkeley, waiting for a friend with Russill and Asha, two African American men approached in what they at first thought was an intimidating manner, but the men simply said, 'Hello, Santa Claus' as they passed and Bede waved cheerfully back. On an earlier visit to England a small child ran excitedly to her mother saying, 'I've just seen Jesus Christ coming out of that house', and on a family visit to the seaside his nephew remembers Bede and Christudas walking along the sea-front in their saffron robes – 'Hayling Island had never seen anything like it.'

As during his 1983 visit, Bede found much that he did not like about America, particularly the speed of life and its dependence on modern technology, but he found there a tremendous vitality and, especially in California, he saw again that new growth was emerging from the all too apparent spiritual breakdown as groups of people investigated every aspect of psychology, philosophy, religion, even drugs. It was this searching spirit that drew him to a country that in some ways stood for all he deplored, yet which he felt was at the centre of the spiritual revolution taking place in the West, a spirituality which he felt was really a return to the old, a renewal of the true tradition of Christianity. Since the 1960s he had been aware that the world was in a state of transition and that a new civilisation was being born; more and more through the 1970s and 1980s he had seen the signs of this new consciousness dawning.* The fullest exposition of his later thinking is found in a collection of talks published under the title A New Vision of Reality: Western Science, Eastern Mysticism and Christian Faith, which appeared in 1989, the year before his stroke. This book, dismissed by some as another example of Bede's vagueness and woolly thinking, admired by others who regarded it as one of the most important books of our time, begins and ends with the author's conviction that we are on the verge of a new age. In the final chapter he asks what the pattern of this new age will be, suggesting that human society must be based on significant changes, all of which were in tune with the thinking of the people he was meeting in America.

His first suggestion was that human society should involve a new relationship to nature, an organic understanding replacing the mechanistic view; thus the exploitation of nature would give way to an awareness of our responsibility to the world and its resources. Then he supported the idea of a new technology, on the lines of Schumacher's intermediate or appropriate technology, building up local economies rather than destroying them, thus 'the sense of communion with an encompassing reality will replace the attempt to dominate the world'.[11] Third, he looked forward to a new type of human community, based on the village rather than the city and using

*See Chapter 13.

energy derived from the sun, from wind, from water. Education should be concerned with the integrating of emotions, imagination and reason and with developing individual potential rather than concentrating so much on the rational mind. Medicine should not rely solely on modern allopathic methods but should embrace homoeopathy, acupuncture, Ayurvedic, Tibetan and herbal medicine – all methods concerned with the health of the whole person.

When discussing the place of religion in this new society, he returned once more to his controversial support of the perennial philosophy, 'the ancient wisdom which underlies all religion from the earliest times'.[12] Thus we should, he argued, have more respect for the traditional wisdom of primitive people such as the Australian Aborigines, the American Indians and the tribal people of Asia and Africa; we should learn to appreciate more the wisdom of these people and their profound understanding of how human life is related to the natural world and, beyond that, to the world of the spirit. He goes on to consider the great religious traditions:

> All are based on the perennial philosophy, developed under different situations and in different circumstances, and all embody in their different ways the ancient wisdom and the wholeness of life. These different traditions will all be seen as interrelated and interdependent, each giving a particular and new insight into ultimate truth and reality. In fact, of course, they all grew apart and mostly without contact with each other for many centuries. When they did make contact there was often rivalry, acrimony and conflict, and as a result we have the disastrous divisions of religion today.[13]

So Christians have to look forward to a theology and a liturgy which would evolve through contact with other religions, assimilating the cultures of Asia and Africa just as the early Church grew through contact first with Greek and Roman cultures, then with Europe.

This was the context in which he began, on his trip to America in 1990, to envisage ways of realising his vision. He was sometimes asked if he supported the idea of a 'one world religion', but he was adamantly against such a concept, regarding it as illusory and dangerous. He felt that historical structures and the differences between them are necessary and important and should be respected, though he accepted that the great religions have become fossilised and need to be renewed, both in themselves and in relation to each other, 'so that a cosmic, universal religion can emerge, in which the essential values of Christian religion will be preserved in living relationship with the other religious traditions of the world'.[14] He continued to say that we were living in apocalyptic times and acknowledged that there could be a 'general catastrophe' as present civilisation broke down, insisting that out of chaos new life can be born and that a new world order could emerge from the ashes of the old.

After several weeks in Vermont and a visit to the Camaldolese house at Big Sur, a monastery standing on the sea just south of San Francisco, Bede returned to India, arriving at sunset on 16 December, the day before his eighty-fourth birthday. At the time there were about twenty community members and 150 guests, all gathered at the ashram gates to greet his return. He was tired after the long journey, but it was the radiant joy and peace that shone from him that people remember, the inner peace they felt in his presence. Every member of the community made a deep obeisance to Father Bede, gently touching his sandalled feet, as he spoke briefly to each one. Some of the village women had been working since 4 a.m. and already the courtyard was covered with coloured *kolams*. The next morning more people arrived, cleaning and decorating the temple, making garlands and a flower carpet, preparing food for the celebrations. When Bede celebrated the communal Mass it was as if the entire village was present: 'Many of them Hindus and Moslems, all races, colour and creed became one. There was a tremendous feeling of one-ness. Silence was the hallmark. People greeted and acknowledged each other with a smile or a "Namaste", words were superfluous. Everyone seemed to be aware of a feeling of respect and that respect became a sign of love. On that day we were most certainly "One with Christ".'[15]

So for five months he was back at Shantivanam, living quietly, strong enough to walk two miles every day, spending much of his time in the hermitage in the woods by the river. Already he was planning another visit to America, considering spending half of every year there and half in India, a pattern of living which would enable him both to see more of Russill and Asha and to respond to the need he felt so keenly in America and which was preoccupying him – the foundation of lay contemplative communities.

This idea had much to do with his complex and contradictory feelings about the Church in which he had been nourished and which in many ways he continued to love, for like many others he both needed the structure yet also needed to be independent of it. Brother Martin understood this apparent dichotomy well: 'For him the Church should be like a nest, where we are born and like children we need the protection of the parents. But the day will come when the birds grow and are ready to fly. We cannot simply throw away the Church, but it appears in the present time that the Church is not a nest but it has become a cage.'[16]

Bede's spiritual formation at Prinknash had, for many years, satisfied his deepest needs and fulfilled all his ideals, but now, in the America of the 1990s, he was ill at ease in monastic communities, finding the services too filled with words, too short on silence, the setting and the standard of living too far from the simplicity and poverty of Shantivanam. He had to face squarely and starkly the feelings he had long held, that modern monasticism was losing its mysticism and that the renewal of the Church, particularly of the mystical life within the Church, while never excluding priests, monks or nuns, had to begin at grassroots level with the laity, who were so clearly open to what he was saying. He himself never faltered in his devotion to the Church, but he stretched its tolerance to (in the opinion of many, beyond) the acceptable limit. For instance, when he celebrated the Eucharist:

> I think he went beyond the Church in one way because when he gave com-
> munion it didn't matter to him who received it – it could be a Hindu, a
> Christian or a non-Catholic. He never made the distinction, neither did he
> ask. He could have got into trouble for that and he knew it, but in his own
> way he was breaking the conditioning of the Church – making a statement
> through action.[17]

He wrote about ideas on lay communities to sympathetic friends and drafted several short documents on the kind of life he envisaged, pointing out that St Benedict provided a model for community life in the Church which had lasted for 1,500 years, but that today the monastic ideal needed to be released from its captivity in the cloister and become available to lay people. He suggested that the people meditating in the tradition taught by John Main had set an example, as groups of meditators, usually meeting once a week, were established all over the world. Bede wanted to take this idea further, forming small communities of men and women, married and single, secular and religious, dedicated to a common life of prayer and meditation and supporting themselves both by growing their own produce and by continuing to work in the world.* He envisaged a great diversity of independent communities with no central authority though united in some kind

---

*Sometimes he used the word 'oblate' to describe people engaged in the way of life he was envisaging. The word can be applied to lay people who are offered to God in a special way and who are usually closely connected with a religious community but who do not take full religious vows. Bede made many people oblates of Shantivanam, with a moving ceremony by the river Cavery. He also used the word in a more specific sense, even referring to himself as an oblate, indicating a status in line with the tradition of communities like the Oblates Regular of St Benedict, founded in the fifteenth century.

of network and where possible having a link with a monastery or some other religious institution from which they could receive help and guidance. They would be primarily Christian communities, though they would be open to visitors of any tradition and would have contacts with a wide variety of religious organisations. Most important of all was that the members of these communities should recognise a transcendent reality, which he regarded as the greatest need in the world today: 'Unless human life is centred on the awareness of a transcendent reality which embraces all humanity and the whole universe and at the same time transcends our present level of life and consciousness, there is no hope for humanity as a whole . . . The aim of every community should be to enable its members to realise this transcendent mystery in their lives and communicate their experience to others.'[18]

Bede put his ideas into practice, over the next three years spending long periods with Russill, Asha and Wayne Teasdale. Twice they stayed in the house in Vermont and, in 1991, in the hills above Sonoma in California with Father Dunstan Morrisey, who had heard about Father Bede's plans for a community and written to him. However, it turned out that Father Morrisey wanted the life of a hermit, not a community, so they moved on to Empty Gate, a Zen centre in Berkeley. Russill has written about these 'Experiments in Contemplative Living'[19] and a clear picture emerges of the life they led together. Bede would wake at about 4 a.m. and meditate sitting up in bed, then at about 5.30 the other three sat round his bed, drinking tea, talking about their dreams and discussing thoughts Bede had had during the night. The day was a balance of prayer, study and work comparable both to the Benedictine pattern and to life at Shantivanam and Bede insisted on keeping a regular timetable, for instance refusing to let his young friends stay up late talking or watching the stars lest they could not wake in time the next day. Four times a day they gathered in the prayer room, the offices very similar to those at Shantivanam except that Russill would play the sitar. They chanted sanskrit *slokas*, meditated and read from Hindu and Christian scriptures. During the morning office Bede would comment on the Old Testament reading and at the end Asha offered *arati*, the sacred light, handing round sandal paste to remind them that this day, as every other, was consecrated to God. After *Namajapa*, the chanting of the name of Jesus, they retired to bed, Russill, Asha and Wayne surprised and touched at the way Bede would give them a goodnight hug, something the reserved Englishman they had once known would never have done.

Between the offices they went their separate ways. Wayne wrote, Russill read and practised his music and Asha, when not preparing the meals, studied comparative religion. Bede read or wrote letters. During one retreat he spent many hours studying Judson Trapnell's dissertation on the development of his symbolic theology. 'This fellow really knows my mind better than I do,' he would say from time to time, something he also said of Wayne's doctoral thesis. Breakfast and lunch were very simple and taken in silence; during lunch one of them reading aloud, as in a monastic refectory. At one time they read from *The Golden String* and Bede's eyes would fill with tears as he heard his own words. After supper, a cheerful, relaxed meal with much teasing and sharing of jokes and stories, there would be *satsang*, the daily meeting, when they would watch the sun set and discuss their ideas of community, sometimes disagreeing, but bound ever closer as they struggled to give birth to their vision.

The community was always intended to be small and these retreats were periods of withdrawal. However, the local residents would join them for the Sunday Eucharist, an impressive and rich experience with both eastern and western music for which they prepared long and carefully, and sometimes friends such as Sister Pascaline Coff, Father Thomas Keating and Father Laurence Freeman would join them for a while. And as with any pattern of life, it was frequently disrupted. Once they were completely snowed in for two days, without electricity, running short of food and water. They all slept in the sitting room, the only room with a log fire, and Bede would stir pots of snow to provide water for drinking and cooking. A far more serious disruption was when Bede became ill, at one point so ill that Russill and Asha slept on the floor in his room, massaging him and talking with him if he was anxious. In the morning he would wake them at the usual time demanding tea, not seeming to appreciate that after a broken night they needed extra sleep. Eventually his heart beat became so slow that they called in the local doctor, who suggested he should have a pace-maker as soon as possible. Bede, who abhorred allopathic medicine, was so indignant at this idea that they found an alternative practitioner who put him on a macrobiotic diet: no tea, coffee, sugar, salt or milk products, but plenty of grains, rice, millet and vegetables. He did not enjoy it – one of his few gastronomic pleasures was tea with milk and sugar – but he preferred it to medication and found it was good for him.

Did their experiment work? Would their community become, as they hoped, a prototype for the future? They soon established a strong sense of the kind of life they wanted and found an eager response when Bede spoke about the idea in public. They also had support and offers of help from many people, notably from the theologian Father Matthew Fox, at the time a Dominican priest. The two men had much in common. Both shared Bede's vision for communities as the hope for the future; both were convinced of the need for Christianity to recover its mystical tradition; both felt that the future of monasticism was with the laity. Bede supported Fox, for instance by writing a foreword to his book on Aquinas and by doing a public dialogue with him, while Fox rallied his friends in an attempt to give life to the embryonic community in their midst.

As with any such venture, however, there were problems. For instance, there was some resistance to their wish to mix lay people and monastics; this idea received little encouragement from the religious orders, even the Camaldolese Prior, who had given them qualified support, said that 'you cannot mix apples and oranges'. It was significant, too, that when Bede went to Gethsemani Abbey in Kentucky to discuss lay communities only fifteen out of the seventy monks were present at the talk. Then there were the problems caused by their own sometimes contradictory wishes, for though they needed local support, they wanted the community to be small, self-sufficient and under their own control; people would not be keen to be involved unless they were live-in members with a real investment in the enterprise. They were also very selective about their companions, knowing that their own lives were so busy that they needed to be able to withdraw and that they did not have the energy or the skills to handle the dynamics of living in an open community.

Bede began to feel that they should let go of the idea and simply consider their centre to be wherever they were, their community the people around them at the time. Russill and Asha accept that, though they genuinely wanted to establish a new form of community life, it was the opportunity to be with Bede that most drew them, just as Bede, sincere in his intention, above all wanted to be with them.

In the August of 1991, after their second retreat together, Bede went to Indiana where he had been invited to speak at the annual seminar given in memory of John Main, the Benedictine whose method of Christian meditation with a mantra Bede often suggested to people and which he sometimes practised himself. He greatly admired John Main's writing, saying that he knew no better expression of the monastic ideal today and he talked of both this ideal and of the tradition of Christian meditation John Main had rediscovered, going on to relate it to eastern spiritual traditions and the vision of spiritual consciousness emerging in the late twentieth century.* As always his criterion was experience rather than theology or theory, and he made a great impression, not least on Robert Kiely, an American scholar:

*Published as *The New Creation in Christ*, see Select Bibliography.

Rarely have I seen or heard someone more composed. In expression, gesture, even posture, he focused himself (his intellectual, spiritual, and physical energy) on his discourse . . . So alert was he to the mood of his
audience, to their laughter, puzzlement, assent, that his words always
seemed part of a dialogue . . . In his measured approach, in his moderation,
scholarship, self-discipline, patience, and industry, he reveals at every turn
of phrase and mind the formation of a Benedictine monk.[20]

Laurence Freeman found this great empathy with his audience most
apparent during the question periods:

Now certain of his audience he would delight them with a mischievous
humour on the most serious topics. Responding to a question on women's
rights he teased the bull of feminism by telling the story of the Oxford professor who had confided to them his belief that women received the Holy
Spirit primarily through their feet. Telling this his laughter would build up
until the punchline and then explode carrying everyone with it. And as he
laughed he continued to look lovingly at the people he was leading.
Laughter for him seemed the sound of a joy that transcended all the self-
important divisions that sadden the Spirit. Beyond duality, he was saying,
there is the smile of unity.[21]

From Indiana Bede went with Russill and Asha to stay at Osage
Monastery, a place which so fulfilled his ideas that it is sometimes called the
Shantivanam of the West. While he was there he was taken ill again and had
to visit the local doctor who diagnosed hepatitis and advised complete rest
and the cancellation of as many appointments as possible. Virginia Atwood,
the doctor's wife, came to collect him and was amazed and touched by his
simplicity and humility: 'It was as though the air and the sun shone through
him, he was luminescent. I was not prepared for this ethereal quality. He
was radiant – and all he was doing was walking from his cabin to the main
house. It was like seeing the embodiment of everything sacred. We are all
one – he personified that.'[22]

Later she went to the Eucharist, where again she experienced this
'sacred quality' and had an overwhelming urge to be as near him as possible:
'Afterwards I knelt on the floor and asked for his blessing. I felt I was in the
presence of someone so holy that if I had his blessing somehow I would be
connected with his thought and spirit, which I later realised he gives and
shares with us. He's a saint in our time.'[23]

When he had recovered – and he found Osage Monastery the most
peaceful place to rest and enjoy complete solitude – he returned to Europe,

staying for a while in London with the Christian Meditation Community, with whom he felt a close bond, then spending three weeks at the clinic in Kreuth, where he received more loving care before returning to India.

During this visit to America the time he gave to the experiments in contemplative living meant that at least he had long periods in one place, but it was rather different on his 1992 trip, which not only included a visit to Europe, but another tour of Australia. Whereas in America he had moved mostly among small groups, his trip to Australia was organised to enable him to communicate with as many people as possible. Now aged eighty-five, he spoke to a vast public through radio, television and press and through public lectures (a single talk might be attended by over 2,000 people).

Travelling with Christudas, who as always looked after him devotedly, they stopped first at Kreuth, from where Bede gave talks in Salzburg and Munich, then went on to England, where he stayed again at the Christian Meditation Centre in London, giving talks to the Study Society and to the Cockfosters Benedictines in North London. He also spoke at 'Mystics and Scientists', a major conference held annually in Winchester, and at St James, Piccadilly, which was so packed that people were standing in the aisles and overflowing into the street and down Piccadilly. He also had meetings with Cardinal Hume and the editor of *The Tablet* as well as interviews with the BBC. From London he went to Australia, arriving in the wake of the Dalai Lama. Their initial short meeting must have impressed His Holiness, for he invited Bede to meet him privately and they talked for nearly two hours, discussing *advaita*, Dzogchen (the main teaching of the Nyingmapa school of Tibetan Buddhism) in which Bede had recently became extremely interested, and the mystical tradition in Christianity. Bede wrote of this meeting to Roland Ropers:

It is obvious that he knows little of this [the mystical tradition of Christianity] and was deeply interested. We reached an extraordinary level of understanding and he sat close by me, held my hand and embraced me. I think it meant a lot to him to realise that a Christian could be so open to the transcendent. He thinks always of Christianity as the religion of a personal, creator God and does not realise how we can go beyond God to the Godhead. I suppose that he must have heard something of it before, but obviously what I said touched him deeply. Of course, he is extremely kind and affectionate to everybody, but there was something special in the way he responded to me.[24]

This certainly seems to have been true. Douglas Conlan remembers His

Holiness coming up to Bede, taking his whiskers in his hand, ruffling them up a little as he smiled and embraced him. On another occasion, when Bede was attending one of the Dalai Lama's talks, His Holiness came straight over to him and reached across two rows of seats to embrace him.

Over the next month, under the constant care of Douglas Conlan who had organised the trip, Bede gave some twenty public talks in Perth, Adelaide, Melbourne and Sydney. Once again Australia won Bede's heart and once again the Australians loved him. Even hard-bitten journalists were moved by him. A journalist writing in the *Weekend Australian* described him as 'the living evidence that it is the spirit which pervades human life and overwhelms the physical': 'He took my hands into his own and I found myself overwhelmed with tears. Infrequently in a lifetime do we come face to face with incarnate holiness. It is an experience we never forget. It is to touch the face of God.'[25]

Early in his visit he spent a few days with Joan and Paul Terry, friends of Douglas Conlan's, who had a large property in Albany in Western Australia from where he could see whales in the sea and kangaroos in the bush. Joan Terry remembers their first morning together:

> What hit me most was that in my normal rush and bustle of the morning to walk into Father Bede's presence was like hitting a clear wall of stillness. His quietness and stillness was all pervading. It was impossible to rush round him. The quiet stillness was like a blanket round him which affected all who came near. One immediately quietened and wanted to do nothing but sit still in his presence.[26]

Joan Terry was impressed by the way he 'stripped back all doctrine and dogma and found the same core essence in all religion'. Her response shows she was receiving an important part of the message he wished to convey. He summarised it thus to his friends: 'I try to present an orthodox faith which is really open to both western science and eastern mysticism';[27] 'My message was always to transcend our divisions – religious, social, psychological, linguistic – the fragmented state of humanity – & recover the wholeness';[28] 'The message I am trying to convey is the unity behind all diversity'.[29]

Bede's talks were received with an enthusiasm sometimes approaching rapture. It was a time when, in Laurence Freeman's words, 'his thought soared', and though little of what he said on these trips has been published, much of it has been recorded on tape, while more of his thinking has been preserved among his correspondence. Various themes emerge clearly, particularly this search for wholeness, for unity behind diversity. In America, in

Australia, in Germany and in England he spoke of the human race originally coming out of wholeness, just as every person in their mother's womb
once knew that wholeness; originally we lived in unity, one with humanity
and one with God – he referred to this state as an 'unconscious unity'. Then
came the awakening of consciousness and with it knowledge and discrimi-
nation, but, as the mind separated from the body it brought division: in the
individual this takes place in adolescence, in the history of humankind
Bede dates it from the first millennium before Christ. As we approach the
twenty-first century, the divisions have never been greater and the desire for
unity has never been stronger, so now we are striving for a *conscious* unity:
'We are emerging now into this new consciousness where we realize the
unity of creation, the unity of humanity.'[30] The only way to reach this state
of 'differentiated wholeness' is to go beyond duality; the only way to go
beyond duality, to transcend conflicts, is meditation, 'the art of going
beyond the mind'.[31] This leads to contemplation, the goal of all Christian
life, which he called 'knowledge by love':

> The mystery of Christ is the ultimate truth, the reality towards which all
> human life aspires. And this mystery is known by love. Love is going out of
> oneself, surrendering the self, letting the reality, the truth, take over . . . It is
> not something we achieve for ourselves. It is something that comes when
> we let go. We have to abandon everything – all words, thoughts, hopes,
> fears, all attachment to ourselves or to any earthly things, and let the divine
> mystery take possession of our lives. It feels like death, and it is, in fact, a sort
> of dying. It is encountering the darkness, the abyss, the void. It is facing
> absolute nothingness – or as Augustine Baker, the English Benedictine,
> said, it is 'the union of the nothing with the Nothing'. This is the negative
> aspect of contemplation. The positive aspect is, of course, the opposite. It is
> total fulfilment, total wisdom, total bliss, the answer to all problems, the
> peace which passes understanding, the joy which is the fullness of love.[32]

The source of this unity, the One beyond name and form, he stressed,
'is *not* in a personal God. This is very important.'[33] Jesus always refers us
beyond himself to the Father, saying that he can do nothing of himself, that
everything comes to him through the Father: 'So Jesus is taking us beyond
the personal form of God. *He* is the personal form of God, but we have to
go beyond the personal form to the Father who is the transcendent mystery
beyond. And all our mystical tradition teaches us that we have to go beyond
all images and concepts to this mystery. The great authority is Dionysius the
Areopagite.'[34] Bede never tired of saying that our search today is for this
experience of non-duality, the ultimate truth in all religions. Even God and

the world are not two. During one of his talks in Australia he reminded his audience of the problem Buddhists have with the Christian idea of a creator God. But, he continued: 'The Buddhist – and I think the deeper Christian view – is that God and this world are not two. They are not one and they are not two. This has a relative reality. Its whole being is from and in and through the divine. That is the reality and we must try to reach that.'[35] He was, however, realistic about the difficulty of reaching that understanding, admitting that not everybody can be a mystic, though everybody ought to realise that there is this knowledge, this transcendent mystery: 'The supreme is present among us, and we must be aware that at every moment and in every place, we are in the presence of that divine mystery.'[36]

While his advaitic experience coloured most of his thought, so, too, he longed for the Church to grow and change. 'The Church is still in the nineteenth century, it has not progressed,' he said to an Australian friend. Wayne Teasdale many times heard him say that, 'Just as Jesus stood before the Temple buildings and said "I tell you solemnly, not a single stone here will be left on another: everything will be destroyed", so one could equally well stand before St Peter's and say "Not a stone upon a stone will remain".'[37] Bede felt that 'We have to re-think the place of priesthood & the hierarchy and the Mass in the Church to-day'[38] and that in ten years we would not recognise it. He thought the old liturgy, using only the Psalms and the Bible, was finished; that clericalism had taken over the Church; that communities now should be lay communities, after all 'Jesus was not a priest but a lay preacher and so were the apostles. There were no priests properly speaking in the early Church.'[39] So he looked forward to a monastic life that did not exclude marriage and a liturgy using scriptures from other faiths as well as from Christianity. He saw no problem in having inter-faith communities. He wanted a Church that was more concerned with love than with sin; that had no positive attitude to the body and to sex and that felt, as he did, that homosexual love was 'as normal & natural as love between people of the opposite sex'.[40] A Church that separated the vocations to the priesthood and to monastic life; that realised that God was feminine as well as masculine and welcomed married clergy and ministries for women; that gave meditation its rightful place at the heart of its practice; that recognised that 'Jesus did not preach the Church. He preached the kingdom of God.'[41]

Given his recent stroke and his extensive travels, it is hardly surprising that his body should sometimes have given in and that he had to cancel arrangements to talk or to meet people. Yet on the whole people were surprised at how fit he seemed to be physically. Laurence Freeman remembered meeting him at Heathrow airport, expecting him to be frail and weak, and was amazed to see a strong, energetic, Bede 'striding towards him wearing a khaki army greatcoat and looking like a spiritual warrior rather than an invalid'.[42] To most people his mind seemed as alert as ever, though Bede himself noticed a change. Fritjof Capra went to see him in San Francisco during his last visit to America and, concerned about his health, asked him how he felt after his stroke. 'My rational mind is very diminished,' he said, 'but I must say, I rather like that.'[43]

On the way back to India his heart gave trouble again and he was advised not to give the talks planned in England and Germany and to cut his visit to the Camaldolese in Rome to the minimum. That he kept as well as he did was a credit to the vigilance with which people cared for him and to his 'capacity for resting, which puts me right, however tired I get'.[44] He himself was surprised at how well he felt; for instance, he rather enjoyed a journey from Europe to India which took thirty-six hours, at the end of which he arrived feeling fresh and well. Roland Ropers recalled an incident just before this trip, when they were leaving Chicago together. Wanting to ensure that he was comfortable on the flight, Roland went ahead to make arrangements at the airport. He told the stewardess that he was travelling with 'a very holy person – far more holy than the Pope' and promised her a signed copy of one of his books if she would give him a really good seat. She was persuaded, but when she met Bede she couldn't speak or even touch his hand, but silently bent and kissed his feet. She was so overwhelmed with tears that she could not continue to work and had to be sent home. Bede was then asked to bless the cockpit of the plane. He did so, then went to sleep.

He was back in Shantivanam only days before an Australian film crew arrived to make a film about his life. They had invited Andrew Harvey to interview him and a great rapport developed between the two, Bede feeling he had 'a perfect understanding'[45] with his interviewer and Andrew Harvey's admiration for Bede knowing no bounds. Meeting him for the first time at the end of his life, Andrew Harvey found him the best kind of Englishman, with 'the intellect of a sage and the sweetness and candour of a child' and admired his astonishing equilibrium, his intricate and delicate mind, his precision, lucidity and humour. Their encounter, A Human Search, is available both in video and book form, so Bede's last thoughts have been preserved, for within weeks of the completion of the filming he was to have another stroke, one from which he would not recover.

CHAPTER TWENTY

Death

On 20 December 1992, everyone was assembled in the temple as usual for the midday office. When it came to Bede's turn to read he just sat there, his head slightly bowed; people thought he had dozed off, so Father Augustine, who had been at the ashram for some years, gently touched his leg to remind him. There was no response. Bede stayed motionless, though upright, so Father Augustine nudged him again, rather more vigorously. It was clear that something was seriously wrong and several people went over and tried to carry Bede, still in his chair, out of the temple. The side door he always used was too narrow and they had to abandon the chair, one of them picking Bede up bodily and carrying him to the hut. Sister Marie Louise and Sister Valsa rushed to Bede's hut with medical equipment and, after a short consultation between two of the priests present, the service continued, though the atmosphere was understandably subdued.[1]

After a while Bede regained consciousness, but he didn't seem to realise what had happened, insisting that he must go to the refectory for lunch, that everyone would be waiting for him. They told him he had had another stroke and must go to hospital. Despite his protestations, he was taken by taxi to the City Hospital at Trichy, though knowing the rough road and the speed of the traffic they wondered if someone so ill could survive the hour-long journey. In fact, Bede was reacting to everything that was going on, refusing to lie down on the back seat of the taxi, and sitting upright in the front. On arrival at the hospital he said: 'This is an awful place, I don't want to be here.' He was treated by a very sympathetic doctor and, as is normal in Indian hospitals, four people from the ashram, Sister Marie Louise, Christudas, Sister Lydia and Chuck Baroo, arranged to care for him in shifts.

The medical diagnosis was clear. Half of Bede's right brain had shrunk, his left side was completely paralysed and his heart was damaged beyond repair: his case was confirmed as hopeless. The doctors said that, physically, his body was that of a man bedridden for many years; they could hardly believe he was still walking and were confounded when they heard of his travels and activities since his first stroke.[2] They were equally surprised that during his short time in hospital he gained a little movement each day.

Bede was told he must have blood thinners and anti-coagulants and that he would have to lie flat on his back for three days, so that his heart and his head would be level. Chuck Baroo remembers vividly how restless a patient he was and how for a full sixteen hours he asked to be moved this way and that way, complaining that he could not pray lying down. Eventually a curious change of relationship took place as Chuck became counsellor to his guru, explaining firmly that if he did not stay flat he risked having another stroke and being crippled for the rest of his life; he must simply accept the situation, and surrender:

> He looked at me and he started to cry, and he held my hand and I held his. I started massaging him to help him relax and he took the arm that wasn't paralysed, the right one, and he started massaging me, and he said, 'I don't mean to be such a trial,' and I said, 'I understand what's happening,' and he said, 'I don't, but I know it's happening, and I'm not accustomed to living in this way'. I said, 'Well maybe you need to surrender some of it', and he said, 'I'm trying to. I know I have to surrender all.' He said it with such a transparency that here was a moment of clarity, and he wanted to surrender it all, even that comfort one gets from being in a different position. And for the rest of the night he was quite alert, and was trying to serve us. We were just trying to enable him to be quiet.[3]

The next morning Bede began to realise how much the stroke had affected him, for when he was offered a cup of tea he could not move his hand to take it. Later, when he tried to read the newspaper he found his eyes would not focus. He who had spent all his life learning to surrender said, so quietly that hardly anyone heard him, 'I can't read', and put the papers to one side.

Worse, far worse than not being able to read, was the total disruption of the intense prayer life which had been going quietly on in him for months. 'I wasn't doing it, it was going on in me,' he told Christopher Venning, a long-term friend of the ashram. Often tears overcame him as he continued:

> Suddenly the whole thing ceased. In the hospital I felt I was in a place

where God was not present and all they were interested in was my body and
the blood and the brain . . . I felt the absolute disappearance of God. It was
a terrifying experience. It was as though I was in prison and if only I could
get back to Shantivanam – that was the one thought in mind.[4]

Once again, as after his first stroke, he shared in the experience of Christ
on the cross, the abandoned Christ who said, 'My God, my God, why have
you forsaken me?'

Frailer than ever, his left arm lying limply by his side, Bede was back at
Shantivanam for Christmas. It was a strange intense Christmas, everyone
moving very quietly, gathering each evening round his hut singing
Namajapa and occasionally quiet carols. Christopher Venning wrote: 'We
were all living in a state of heightened awareness . . . The intensity of prayer
was so great that it was almost tangible.'[5] So too they were living in great sus-
pense. At one level they all knew how precarious his health was: in their
hearts they must have known that he was dying, yet letters and messages
between people at the ashram and their friends clutch at every sign of hope,
claiming that there had been some improvement, that his mind was clear
and his spirit unimpaired. Bede himself, in a barely legible letter written to
Sister Pascaline just two weeks after the stroke, said that the doctors had
assured him that he would be able to walk normally again. Even after
another stroke on 24 January, when fears that he was dying were openly
expressed, people who knew him assured each other that though his mind
had been affected, he was physically better and had some very clear
moments.

In these moments he was able to rejoice in his friends and the people
who gathered round his bedside and all speak of the profound and peaceful
times they shared with him. Judy Walter had to leave before Bede died and
Russill could not stay for long as he was looking after Asha, who had been
taken ill and was in hospital; in any case, he could not forget the allegations
surrounding his departure from the ashram and endured his private crucifixion, fearing to spend too much time with his beloved Bede, not able to
express his love lest it prove an embarrassment. But Bede's was not a lonely
death – he was surrounded by loving care every minute of every day. One
unexpected English visitor somehow brought his life full circle, for he came
from the Cotswolds and Bede was moved to the depths of his being to be
able to talk about Eastington and the countryside that had been so important a part of his youth. 'I never thought I would ever meet someone from
there,' he said. 'How good God is.'[6]

The changes in Bede were not only physical; the contradictions in his personality became apparent as never before – it was almost as if everything in him was undergoing a final catharsis, a purification. Though sometimes he was able to transcend his suffering, it was a hard and painful death. When Christudas asked him how he was bearing so much suffering he said, 'No, Christudas, I am not suffering. I am okay. This is only a passing sickness. If God wants I will get up. I do not know.'[7] But anyone who nursed him knew that often the pain was as much as his physical body could bear – hearing that someone claimed that Bede did not suffer, one of his carers wrote, 'he was not there to hear his screams'.[8] Those who loved him suffered with him, Judy Walter writing that 'Father has been in hell & those of us caring for him have been there with him'.[9] Andrew Harvey, who stayed on at Shantivanam for a few weeks and sometimes sat with him, spoke movingly about this time:

> I see the dying as the final shattering open of the heart. He was assaulted in the heart by divine passion. It broke him, it shattered his body and it shattered a lot of his mind. It took away the intellect, it took away the last vestiges of the patriarch and left this extraordinary, tender, sweet, amazing being. I saw him at this stage, and it was a birth, this dying. The dying was a very shocking, terrifying, extremely painful, extremely beautiful birth of the Christ child, the sacred androgyne. He had loved Christ so much that he was given the grace of this long, strange, terrible, beautiful death which was his mid-wifing of a new reality and I'm convinced he is in that reality now.[10]

So what did he endure? As he lay dying, how did he seem to all those round his bedside who knew and loved him? On the one hand he was irritable, restless and petulant. This is hardly surprising: he was in great physical pain, he had a terrible cough and burning pain from a urinary infection in addition to all the weakness and discomfort caused by the stroke, pneumonia and the violent fever that followed it. He was confused and agitated, frustrated by paralysis and the loss of his memory and his mental powers, humiliated by his total helplessness, the complete lack of privacy and the need for help in washing himself and going to the toilet. This feeling of being invaded is the lot of any invalid but it must have been particularly painful for so private and reserved a person and sometimes he would behave in totally uncharacteristic ways, shouting at his nurses and telling them to leave the room. On one occasion, when a doctor tried to put a tube down his throat he became so violent that they had to give up.

So too he had moments of delusion, unaware of the present moment, unsure where he was. His longing to see Russill and Asha was so great that every day he would ask for them, sometimes thinking he was on his way to see them and saying, 'Are we on the plane? When are we taking off?' Occasionally he spoke with a simplicity amounting to naivety, as when, on Good Friday, he told Russill he felt ready to die and asked, 'Would you die with me?' In the early hours of the morning, just six days before his death, Sister Marie Louise was startled when he suddenly said, 'I must go to the Camaldolese!' When Sister Marie Louise gently pointed out that this was a long way away and that arrangements would have to be made he replied, 'I must go now. I don't need the booking. The car is here; I want to go by car.' He was so insistent that two of the brothers lifted him into a wheelchair and took him to the temple, but this was not what he wanted. 'I have resigned from this place. I must go to the Camaldolese.'[11] His concern for the community he was leaving behind him showed in almost surreal ways, as when he wanted reassurance that he would be living with Brother Martin, Christudas and Amaldas and, pointing to his desk, insisted that it should be put down in writing.

Moments of delusion are not uncommon in the dying, but what was remarkable about Bede's last days was that at last he was free of any remaining vestiges of the repression that had dogged his life; he had reached his full humanity. Though negative characteristics, previously controlled and restrained, were at last released, on the other hand his capacity for love and affection, already liberated by his first stroke and the experience which accompanied it, found expression as never before. An American Priest, Father John Kilian, arrived with Asha. He wrote to friends:

> I have never seen him so affectionate and loving. He draws people to himself and hugs them. After he greeted Asha with a great hug and tears of joy, he took my hands, kissed them and drew me down to himself, kissed me on the cheek and held me down with a hug and embrace that I shall never forget and always cherish. It was as if the other part of his soul that he had come to find in India broke through the proper English manner like a torrent of love and joy.[12]

There were times of confusion, times of great lucidity; his body was frail and feeble, but spirit and energy poured out of him. Judy Walter saw how helpless and dependent he was, yet saw also how 'from time to time some profound piece of wisdom or intense prayer will fly up from his heart and burst forth in speech and then return to silence'.[13] Perhaps one of his greatest pains was when he knew his mind was confused, as he silently embraced people with tears flowing down his cheeks because he couldn't remember their names. Whenever he had the strength he was trying to communicate, to give, to love. One night Andrew Harvey was stroking his hand and Bede said, 'Are you just stroking my hand or are we every moment going deeper into love?' Another time when he couldn't sleep because music was drifting across from the village, he said to Andrew who was sitting with him, 'Andrew, I think I'm losing the ability to greet people, I want to practise it', so he lay in bed, practising gestures of greeting with the little movement that was left to him.

> It was as heartbreaking as the last scenes of *Lear*, because you saw behind everything in Bede his majesty, this knowledge that he really was this extra-ordinary tender being whose real concern, at the moment that he was being broken apart, was how to make people at ease. It was rather like a rock being split apart by lightening and you could see exactly what has gone into the formation of the rock.[14]

Andrew also remembers him lying for hours, profoundly peaceful, saying the Hail Mary or simply 'Jesus' or 'Bless you' as he rotated his hand in 'a kind of circular ecstatic blessing, as if he were blessing the whole of reality'.[15] But he was not – and anyone who knew him would be aware of this – seeing himself as special. Once Andrew thanked him for the illumination he was giving, the way his dying was bringing people closer to God. 'Andrew, don't exaggerate,' he responded sternly. 'It's not me, it's the Holy Spirit.' When Judy Walter told him how many people round the world were praying for him, he said: 'But not just for me, but for everyone in need.'[16] Nor did his stillness cause him to forget the concerns that had preoccupied him for so long. Often he would wake with some theme in his mind, for instance the union of eastern and western faiths. Judy Walter recalled how, 'Later when I was bathing him I picked up his paralyzed arm to wash it & it was so painful he cried out & said, yes that is just where the breach is between East & Western Church – that we feel the split in our bodies.'[17] When his mind was clear he seemed to see directly into people's minds with an unerring accuracy and Brother Martin was told that this is like the state known in Hinduism as *sahajah samadhi*, a term which eludes precise translation but means a sort of unified consciousness. Curiously enough this was the title of his last talk in England, when he said that after his first stroke, when his rational mind had been knocked down, 'a deeper, intuitive, contemplative spirit had emerged, with a unitive vision. It is still going on, it is not complete at all, but it is there.'[18]

Bede had lived his life fully and, with the humility that had become so profoundly part of him, he was given the grace of knowing it. Shortly before he died, he said: 'I have given everything I can give. I have received everything I can receive.'[19] This humility also infused his response when Brother Martin said to him, 'Father, we will continue your spirit in the ashram,' and Bede replied, 'Not my spirit, but Holy Spirit.'[20] Above all, Bede's dying was about surrender and about love. Forty years earlier he had written that 'the greatest obstacle in life is the power of self-will'[21] and all his life he had consciously sought surrender; now, in these last days, he was being forced to submit yet more totally to God's will. So too did he love more deeply, more constantly – he spoke only of love, love was his entire universe, the central experience of his consciousness. One morning he said to Russill: 'I feel that God has created a love and understanding in us that I have never experienced before and that has completed my life. It is a plan of total love, of total self giving love.'[22] Brother Martin considered that the key to Bede's nature was his capacity for unconditional love and Andrew Harvey talked of the 'totally tender love, which is what he was giving to everyone'. Russill, who was with him at the end of March, wrote of the purity, grace, innocence and holiness that emanated from him: 'His eyes are like windows to the Divine and one feels like one dissolves into them when gazing into their depths. Ever so frequently he would draw us down to him and say "Oh Sacred Heart of Jesus, oh sacred heart of Jesus." . . . He often says, "I am so happy, I am so full of love".'[23]

In March Sister Marie Louise and two others took him to a hospital in Kotakil in Kerala, where he had six weeks of ayurvedic treatment, which he probably agreed to less for his own sake than for the sake of his disciples who were anxious to do everything possible to help him. Laurence Freeman spent a week at his bedside and later spoke of Bede's cries of pain when he was laid on his wooden pallet in preparation for the *dhara* and the *pizhichil*, the treatments with milk and oils that were a last attempt to prolong his life. He remembered too how, after the treatment, he lay in his bed in perfect peace and contentment. Most vividly he recalled Bede's reaction when he read from the Gospel of St John:

> I have never experienced such intense attentiveness. The way he listened and fed on those words forced me to read them in a way that showed them really to be 'words of life'. 'This is too wonderful,' he said one day, 'it is all I can take for now.' He lay in silence digesting the words and then motioned me to continue. 'I believe, I believe. Thanks be to God.' When I read the words 'This is my commandment that you love one another', he caught his breath and lifted his finger with emphasis and said 'That is the whole gospel.'[24]

By the night of 12 May, back in his hut in Shantinvanam, Bede was peaceful and very still, often unconscious. Sometimes he was aware and when his devoted disciple Christudas anointed him he tried to join in the prayers. Then, in a voice so faint and weak that the words were barely audible, he said: 'Let me die in church, just as St Benedict – they held him in his place in choir . . .' A cassette recorder was on at the time and those who listened to the tape later recognised the story of St Benedict, who asked to be carried into the Oratory to receive Holy Communion and who died with his monks holding his arms aloft in prayer. During the next day Bede grew weaker and weaker, eating nothing, seldom speaking and barely able to breathe. Late in the afternoon of Thursday 13 May he said: 'God the Father, God the Son, God the Holy Spirit, I surrender to you.' Then, in the arms of Christudas, with Sister Marie Louise, Sister Mecthilde (another nun from Ananda Ashram) and James, one of the young brothers, gathered round his bed, he slept. After the terrible struggles, the pain and anguish of the last five months, he died peacefully in his sleep as they sang one of the Sanskrit chants he so loved: *Christa jaya jaya, Namo, Namo*, Praise be to you, Oh Christ. Hail! Hail! Praise be to you, Oh Christ.

The next day the body was taken to the temple and Bishop Gabriel of Tiruchirappalli celebrated the Eucharist for the repose of his soul. All that night people prayed and sang, unable to believe that their beloved guru had gone.

> On the 13th of May 1993 all of us suddenly became orphans. Is he gone, to return no more? But no, it was only a painful dream. He is with us, and so we feel him present everywhere and in every one of us. Every morning we are aware of him in the Eucharistic celebration, consecrating and breaking the bread. He is amidst us at the prayer services. You feel him at the heart of the community, sharing our humble meals. He is in and out of the library, on the river bed and in the forest grove. But more than this it is his monastic and prophetic vision and his spirit which constantly reminds us that he has not left us orphans but enriched. He keeps beckoning us not to look backward and moan but to look forward and advance.[25]

On Saturday 15 May, hundreds of people from the surrounding villages, Christians, Hindus and Muslims, gathered for the funeral. Before the funeral Mass began, Russill was asked to play the Purusadic hymn, a song that Bede loved with 'a passion that was overwhelming'[26] and which Russill had sung almost every day while he was with him:

I know that Great Person
of the brightness of the Sun
beyond the darkness.
Only by knowing him
one goes beyond death.
There is no other way to go.[27]

The Vicar General of Tiruchirappalli, Father Xavier Irudayaraj, celebrated the Mass with Christudas and then the coffin was placed between the entrance to the temple and the cosmic cross, the cross surrounded by a circle which symbolises the essence of Shantivanam. There was a long, slow ritual as people from the ashram and its extended community placed flowers at his feet, washed his feet with milk and water and applied sandal paste and red kumkum powder between his eyebrows. Then Christudas placed his prayer shawl in the coffin and everyone present said their final farewells, kissing him on the forehead and on the feet, before he was taken to the grave prepared beside the temple, alongside the grave of Father Amaldas.*

It is tempting to exaggerate events surrounding the death of a beloved person, but there is no doubting three unusual things that happened over these months. The first was the way, during his dying and after his death, Bede appeared in the dreams of people close to him, helping them, even giving messages. The second was that, despite the heat and the humidity of May in Tamil Nadu, over the two days between his death and his burial, his body showed no signs of decay. Though the body was placed on ice and surrounded by fans, nevertheless this was considered at the least very unusual, at the most miraculous. Finally there was, during the funeral, a dramatic change in the climate. As the coffin was being lowered into the grave the sky suddenly darkened and a strong wind began to blow. The coconut trees swayed, everyone closed their eyes and lowered their heads as the dust was blown around them and the leaves and the flowers of the trees poured into the coffin, 'As if the trees of the ashram were giving their last homage to the master of the house.'[28] The ancients have a saying, 'When a great soul dies, the winds go wild',[29] but however these things are interpreted, there is no doubt that those mourning the death of Father Bede had known a man of great holiness. They had seen love made manifest.

---

*The graves of the two founders, Monchanin and Abhishiktananda have since been moved, so all four are now together.

Epilogue

How will Bede Griffiths be remembered? What is the legacy of this man whose youthful experience of a moment out of time was the catalyst for a lifetime's search for union with God? Will his own struggle, his own eighty-six years on earth, affect the future of the Church of which he was so critical yet for which he had such love? Will his vision inspire the lives of generations to come as the holiness of his presence inspired those who knew him?

Some members of the Shantivanam community remember Bede saying, 'Why am I so lonely? Why am I left all alone?' He did not feel that his life had been a success or that he had succeeded in conveying his message. His great pleasure at receiving the 1993 John Harriott Award for outstanding work in religious communication (though he was too ill to be present at the ceremony) was a measure of how seldom he felt publicly acknowledged. So his obituaries would have surprised and probably pleased him. Many saw him as a man ahead of his time; one leading article referred to him as 'a lonely trail-blazer', urging American Catholics to pay him attention, for 'our country is now a microcosm of the world's religions, and thus a perfect setting for the interfaith experience and dialogue that Bede Griffiths pioneered'.[1] The *National Catholic Reporter* wrote: 'Even at age 86 and on the edge of death Benedictine Fr Bede Griffiths was still running so far ahead of the pack that his life's momentum will quicken him for many springs to come.'[2] The American newsletter *Monos*, along with the British *Independent*, saw him as 'one of the great religious prophets of modern times'.[3]

Religious and secular press alike emphasised his personal holiness, the *Guardian* saying that he 'radiated hope in a confused world' and that, for thousands, 'his example and enthusiasm will remain a lifelong inspiration'.[4] William Rees-Mogg, writing in *The Times*, remembered him as 'an entrancing figure . . . a man who seemed lost to everything except truth and compassion, a guru yet still a Benedictine monk and a Catholic priest'.[5] The *Church Times* saw him as 'a holy man of great vision, a Christian sage',[6] while the *Daily Telegraph* acclaimed him both 'for his personal sanctity and for his prophetic vision of the future of religion'.[7] Some obituary writers recognised that his real significance was not yet appreciated, *America* suggesting that his full impact would be felt only posthumously and *The Scotsman* saying that he was spiritual mentor to thousands of people in all parts of the world, a visionary and a scholar, and going further: 'I think that it is not going too far off the mark to say that in years to come, Bede Griffiths will be regarded as one of the great original Christian thinkers of this century.'[8]

Despite his controversial views on the Church, despite having spent so many years as an exclaustrated monk, his fellow Benedictines honoured him unstintingly. Cardinal Hume held him in the highest respect, saying, 'we can only stand in admiration for the way in which, through his life and holding us all in his prayer, he explored the origins of all religions',[9] and Laurence Freeman, preaching at the memorial service held in Westminster Cathedral, said that 'in so faithfully following his monastic call he had become purely and simply himself. No one can do more or is asked to do more with the gift of their life.'[10] Thomas Matus, a fellow Camaldolese writing for a Vatican publication, appreciated the way Bede sought to meet other religions in prayer: 'It was there, at the heart of life, of being, and of love . . . that Bede Griffiths sought to understand the religions of India.'[11] The Camaldolese official statement found that: 'The radiance of his personal presence was the best commentary on his theories of interfaith relations . . . his was an example of the practice of interfaith dialogue and study as a way of realizing the highest Christian ideals of holiness and of mystical union with God.'[12]

As his life was publicly applauded, so was it privately praised. Of all that Raimon Panikkar remembered about his old friend, when asked for a tribute he chose to say: 'His extraordinary gift (and I know how much it cost him) was one of tolerance. He did not judge anybody or anything. Everyone felt immediately loved . . . He seemed unaware of the concrete existential evil which torments so many people, without being blind to the objective evils in the world.'[13] Brother Martin, when asked how Bede should be remembered, said that it should be by his capacity for unconditional love;[14] for Sister Pascaline, 'This monk with a universal heart was an icon of integrity and guilelessness';[15] and countless people remember him as a teacher and as a healer, for ever grateful that his loving acceptance of them had helped them to love and accept themselves. Others recall his openness; how until the last moments of his life he was learning, changing, developing. Many were impressed at the regularity with which, however many demands were being made on his time, he sat, morning and evening, in meditation.

Apart from the thousands of people who will never forget the impact he had on their lives, on a material level Bede left a dozen books, hundreds of articles and scores of videos and tapes, one day, no doubt, to be transcribed and published. Increasingly, articles, books and doctoral theses are being written about him and his thought. It is easy to forget, in veneration of his person, that he was a man of vast learning and culture, 'a rare example of modern liberal humanism and wide culture, bridging the two cultures of science and art';[16] many people who never met Bede revere him through these writings and recorded talks, and their value should not be underestimated.

Though there could have been few men humbler than Bede Griffiths, he was realistic about the importance of his vision and towards the end of his life, he took an interest in plans that were being made to ensure that it could be passed on to future generations. He was involved in the forming of the Bede Griffiths Trust, an international group with eleven trustees who are responsible for the care of his publications, manuscripts and tapes, for ensuring that royalties are used for the support of Shantivanam and similar groups, and for the disseminating of his spiritual vision after his death. They meet once a year, publish a newsletter, *The Golden String*, and have established an archive of Bede's papers and tapes at the Graduate Theological Union in Berkeley, California. They also host an annual Bede Griffiths Lecture, give retreats and lectures and authorise writings about Bede Griffiths, for instance this biography.

While forming the Trust, Bede also approved the Society for the Renewal of Contemplative Life, to be run under the protection of the Camaldolese. He had often discussed this and had drafted several short documents on how such groups could be set up. Though his early dreams had not materialised, since his death organisations have been formed in the United States, India, Germany, Australia and Italy. In Britain the Shantivanam Sangha, a group of people who have been touched by Bede's life and teaching, meet regularly for retreats of sometimes a single day, sometimes a week, occasionally celebrating Mass in the Indian rite.

He also gave shape to his vision of lay communities by drafting some notes on how people could become oblates of Shantivanam, stressing that they would be people who recognised that the eternal reality is made known in different ways, but that for Christians it is through Jesus Christ. One problem in implementing these plans was caused by Bede's ability to make everyone feel important, the only person in his life at that moment, and this, coupled with his wish to please and his willingness, at the end of his life, to sign anything put in front of him, makes it hard to determine his last intentions with any certainty. However, these documents can be taken to represent his wishes, not least because for the most part they correspond with all that he had said during his life.

These groups, even the Bede Griffiths Trust, are only attempts to give a framework for his thought and to ensure its survival. What happens to Bede's vision is now up to others, his spiritual heirs. As a religious sister said: 'What will be important will be for us to see how much of the lustre of the pearl we manage to retain and reflect.'[17] Though in giving some fifty people *sannyasa diksha* (initiation as a sannyasi) Bede ensured that there was a group of people who would, he hoped, witness to Christian relationships with other religions in a very specific way, he did not found a new order or institution, nor did he leave a specific teaching or way of prayer. His insights are read, discussed, recalled and treasured, but he was, first and foremost, a master who taught by his life. And a life leaves memories, but sometimes it leaves more – a mysterious working, an underground fermentation, a development of ideas: 'A silent ripple continuing to spread after the physical energy has been exhausted.'[18] Bede's vision has not died with him, it continues to influence, to inspire, to confirm the tentative thinking of others. When two people meet who knew Bede, either personally or through his writings, often something happens. It might be a retreat, the starting of a meditation group, a lecture or a conference; it might simply be a shared understanding, a moment of recognition of Bede's thought, then, like Easter candles taking the light from each other, the room is filled with light.

'In my beginning is my end' was never truer of anyone than of Bede. With hindsight his life had an extraordinary wholeness, an inevitability. His life's work unfolded from his first experience of God in nature, from his difficult temperament, torn between opposites yet yearning for their reconciliation, from his fine mind, his gift for synthesis, his passion for truth, his longing to be able to surrender. All these elements combined to make an irresistible force, taking risks, seeking wholeness not in compromise but in the reconciliation of extreme opposites. In forging on until he reached this truth, the advaitic experience which was for him the goal of life, he at last found the 'other half of his soul' and in finding it for himself he marked the way for others struggling with the same problems, drawn, sometimes confused and lost, on the same lonely path.

As any prophetic vision does, Bede's sense of a universal, cosmic Christianity made some people uneasy, undermining as it does both intellect and the normal structures of society. But his message was of love and of unity. Karl Rahner wrote: 'The Christian of the future will be a mystic or he or she will not exist at all.'[19] Bede's vision was for all humankind, but it is of special importance to Christians. Through his own great longing to reach the reality beyond the opposites, the mystical union that he was convinced lay at the heart of every religion, he helped today's Christians to realise that it is possible to follow a mystical path and remain within the institutional church. In his humility and in his confidence of the truth of his experience he challenged the Church and left an image of an inclusive Christian for the future, once more his own example, his own courage, inspiring others to follow their instincts. People who feel that there must be one God, one reality, behind all religions, that God did not create a divided humanity (and their numbers increase daily), have found in Bede that their instincts are clarified, developed and, most important, were *lived*. The inspiration lies in the holiness of the man Bede Griffiths became; the articulation of his thoughts in the writings and tapes he has left behind him; the authority, one he constantly quoted, lies in St John's Gospel: 'That they all may be one; as Thou, Father, art in me, and I in thee.' 'This is the final reality – the realisation that we are all in God and God in us and all dualities are transcended . . . each religion has its own approach but we all arrive at the same insight.'[20]

He was like yeast, leavening the flour and water of institutional religion, seeing its point of transcendence where all is one and where all is love. In his life and in his thought, Bede Griffiths eventually found the meeting place between the opposites. His whole life and thought culminated in the knowledge that beyond the opposites, beyond the darkness, was 'that Great Person, of the brightness of the sun'.

Notes

Full publication details of books by and about Father Bede Griffiths are contained in the Select Bibliography.
I have abbreviated frequent references as follows:

BG   Fr Bede Griffiths, OSB Cam
CSL   C. S. Lewis
GS   *The Golden String* (Bede Griffiths)
HW   Hugh Waterman
JW   Judy Walter
LF   Fr Laurence Freeman, OSB
MEW   *The Marriage of East and West* (Bede Griffiths)
MH   Fr Michael Hanbury, OSB
MS   Martyn Skinner
NB   Nigel Bruce
PC   Sr Pascaline Coff, OSB
RP   Russill Paul D'Silva

Interviews conducted by the author were recorded in India, America, England and Scotland between December 1994 and August 1996.

Prologue

1. GS, p. 9.

1. An Edwardian Childhood, 1906–24

1. GS, p. 18.
2. BG, letter to HW, 26 December 1970.
3. GS, p. 19.
4. John Swindells (ed.), *A Human Search*, p. 6.

5. GS, p. 20.
6. John Swindells (ed.), *A Human Search*, p. 5.
7. Ibid., p. 9.
8. BG, interview with Kathryn Spink, 1986.
9. Lord Longford, *Avowed Intent: The Autobiography of Lord Longford* (New York: Little, Brown, 1994).
10. GS, p. 19.
11. BG, interview with Kathryn Spink, 1986.
12. NB, interview with author.
13. BG, interview with Kathryn Spink, 1986.
14. Ibid.
15. Ibid.
16. Ibid.
17. HW, *Answer for Andrew*, unpublished MS.
18. NB, interview with author.
19. John Swindells (ed.), *A Human Search*, p. 12.
20. GS, p. 24.
21. Ibid.
22. Ibid., p. 25.
23. John Swindells (ed.), *A Human Search*, p. 15.
24. GS, p. 25.
25. William Wordsworth, from *Lines composed a few miles above Tintern Abbey . . . 1798.*
26. GS, p. 28.
27. Ibid.
28. Ibid., p. 11.
29. Ibid., pp. 13–14.

2. Athletes and Aesthetes, Oxford 1925–29

1. MS, *Autobiography*, unpublished MS.
2. Geoffrey Hayward, letter to author, 28 May 1995.
3. Geoffrey Hayward, interview with author.
4. MS, *Autobiography*, unpublished MS.
5. HW, *Look, the Dawn*, unpublished MS.
6. GS, p. 37.
7. HW, *Answer for Andrew*, unpublished MS.
8. BG, *The Poetry of Martyn Skinner*, for the Finzi Bookroom, Reading University, c. 1979.
9. MS, *Autobiography*, unpublished MS.
10. Ibid.
11. Geoffrey Hayward, letter to author, 28 May 1995.
12. MS, *Autobiography*, unpublished MS.
13. Ibid.

14. Ibid.
15. BG, letter to MS, 24 January 1985.
16. GS, p. 35.
17. Ibid., p. 36.
18. BG, 'Light on C. S. Lewis', *The Month*, June 1966.
19. CSL, letter to BG, 26 December 1934.
20. CSL, letter to BG, 20 February 1936.
21. Archives of Magdalen College, Oxford.
22. Humphrey Carpenter, *The Inklings* (London: HarperCollins, 1997), p. 36.
23. Owen Barfield, interview with author.
24. GS, p. 38.
25. Ibid., p. 31.
26. Ibid., p. 37.
27. Geoffrey Hayward, interview with author.
28. Ibid.
29. GS, p. 41.
30. Ibid.
31. Ibid., p. 47.

3. 'Like a Man Climbing a Mountain', July 1929–April 1930

1. BG, letter to MS, 19 December 1955.
2. William Blake, *Jerusalem*.
3. GS, p. 63.
4. Ibid., p. 49.
5. Ibid., p. 50.
6. BG, 'Pilgrim to Jerusalem', *PAX*, April 1938.
7. GS, p. 50.
8. Ibid.
9. Ibid., p. 56.
10. Ibid., p. 52, from Berkeley, *Principles of Human Knowledge*, 1710.
11. Ibid., pp.52–3.
12. Ibid., p. 53.
13. Ibid., p. 57.
14. Ibid., p. 61.
15. Ibid., p. 60.
16. Ibid., p. 44.
17. Kathryn Spink, *A Sense of the Sacred*, p. 50.
18. BG, interview with Kathryn Spink, 1986.
19. GS, p. 45.
20. Ibid.
21. BG, interview with Kathryn Spink, 1986.
22. BG, letter to MS, 3 November 1974.
23. MS, *Autobiography*, unpublished MS.

24. Ibid.
25. GS, p. 39.
26. Ibid., p. 62.
27. Ibid., p. 40.
28. John Swindells (ed.), *A Human Search*, p. 26.
29. GS, p. 40.
30. Ibid., p. 64.
31. Ibid., p. 63.

4. Eastington, 1930

1. GS, p. 70.
2. Ibid., p. 91.
3. MS, *Autobiography*, unpublished MS.
4. HW, letter to MS, 21 August 1970.
5. MS, *Autobiography*, unpublished MS.
6. HW, *Look, the Dawn*, unpublished MS.
7. GS, p. 75.
8. Ibid., p. 79.
9. Ibid.
10. *Wisdom*, Chapter 7 vv.22,23.
11. GS, p.91.
12. Geoffrey Hayward, letter to author, 28 May 1995.
13. HW, *Answer for Andrew*, unpublished MS.
14. MS, *Autobiography*, unpublished MS.
15. GS, p. 66.
16. Ibid., p. 70.
17. MS, *Autobiography*, unpublished MS.
18. Ibid.
19. HW, letter to MS, 27 March 1972.
20. HW, *Answer for Andrew*, unpublished MS.
21. BG, interview with Kathryn Spink, 1986.
22. Ibid.
23. HW, letter to MS, 27 August 1934.
24. HW, *Answer for Andrew*, unpublished MS.
25. MS, *Autobiography*, unpublished MS.
26. GS, p. 91.
27. BG, interview with Kathryn Spink, 1986.
28. BG, letter to MS, 30 May 1932.
29. BG, letter to MS, 1 July 1932.
30. HW, *Answer for Andrew*, unpublished MS.
31. Ibid.
32. HW, *Look, the Dawn*, unpublished MS.
33. MS, letter to HW, 27 September 1971.

34. HW, letter to BG, 22 July 1968.
35. HW, *Answer for Andrew*, unpublished MS.
36. MS, letter to HW, 27 September 1971.
37. HW, *Answer for Andrew*, unpublished MS.
38. GS, p. 92.
39. MS, *Autobiography*, unpublished MS.

5. *Dark Night, 1931–32*

1. GS, p. 87.
2. Ibid., p. 89.
3. Ibid., p. 92.
4. Ibid., p. 96.
5. Ibid., p. 97.
6. Ibid., pp. 101–2.
7. Ibid., p. 102.
8. Ibid., p. 103.
9. Ibid., p. 104.
10. Ibid.
11. Ibid.
12. Ibid., p. 107.
13. Ibid., p. 108.
14. Ibid., p. 109.
15. BG, letter to MS, 30 May 1932.
16. BG, letter to MS, 1 July 1932.
17. BG, letter to MS, undated.
18. BG, letter to MS, 1 July 1932.
19. BG, letter to MS, 28 August 1932.
20. GS, pp. 116–17.
21. BG, letter to MS, 29 November 1932.
22. GS, p. 119.
23. BG, 'Pilgrim to Jerusalem', *PAX*, April 1938.
24. GS, p. 122.
25. Ibid., p. 127.

6. *Love at First Sight, Prinknash 1933–47*

1. Fr Alban OSB, letter to Br Hildebrand, 7 November 1990.
2. Fr Alban, interview with author.
3. GS, p. 130.
4. BG, letter to MS, 9 January 1933.
5. GS, p. 134.
6. Ibid.
7. Ibid., p. 135.
8. Ibid.

9. Ibid., p. 150.
10. BG, letter to MS, Easter Sunday 1936.
11. GS, p. 153.
12. BG, 'Pilgrim to Jerusalem', *PAX*, April 1938.
13. BG, letter to MS, October 1937.
14. Fr Fabian Binyon, interview with author.
15. GS, pp. 141–2.
16. Peter F. Anson, 'From Caldey to Prinknash', *The Tablet*, 9 November 1963.
17. BG, 'Dom Wilfrid Upson 1880–1963', letter to the Editor, *The Tablet*, 1 February 1964.
18. BG, letter to MS, 21 November 1954.
19. BG, letter to MS, June 1940.
20. BG, letter to MS, 25 April 1941.
21. LF, interview with author.
22. BG, letter to MS, March 1937.
23. BG, in James T. Como (ed.), *Lewis at the Breakfast Table and Other Reminiscences* (New York: Macmillan, 1962), p. 12.
24. CSL, *Surprised by Joy* (London: Fount, 1977), p. 187.
25. Ibid.
26. CSL, letter to BG, 29 April 1938.
27. CSL, letter to BG, undated.
28. CSL, letter to BG, 26 December 1934.
29. CSL, letter to BG, 20 February 1936.
30. BG, interview with Kathryn Spink, 1986.
31. CSL, letter to BG, 23 May 1936.
32. CSL, letter to BG, 14 September 1936.
33. CSL, *Surprised by Joy*, p. 187.
34. BG, *Lewis at the Breakfast Table and Other Reminiscences*.
35. Fr Fabian Binyon, interview with author.
36. GS, p. 146.

7. *Shattered Dreams, Farnborough 1947–51*

1. Kathryn Spink, *A Sense of the Sacred*, p. 104.
2. BG, letter to MS, 17 June 1947.
3. Fr Fabian Binyon, interview with author.
4. CSL, letter to BG, 15 April (year not given).
5. Fr Magnus Wilson, interview with author.
6. BG, letter to Fr Aelred Carlyle, 9 December 1949.
7. Jyoti Sahi, interview with author.
8. BG, letter to MS, 30 August 1946.
9. BG, letter to MS, 26 June 1938.
10. Ibid.
11. BG, letter to MS, 13 April 1940.

12. BG, 'Integration', *PAX*, November 1938.
13. BG, 'A Christian before Christ: The Sayings of Lao-Tzu', *PAX*, Winter 1940.
14. BG, 'Catholicism To-day', *PAX*, Spring 1950.
15. George Ineson, *Community Journey* (London: Sheed and Ward, 1956).
16. Ronald Seex, interview with author.
17. II Corinthians 5 v. 17.
18. BG, 'The New Creation', *PAX*, 1946.
19. Hilary Seex, interview with author.
20. Fr Magnus Wilson, interview with author.
21. HW, letter to MS, 18 June 1970.
22. MS, letter to HW, 1 August 1970.
23. MS, letter to HW, All Saints 1970.
24. HW, letter to MS, 21 August 1970.
25. Fr Magnus Wilson, interview with author.

8. *Pluscarden, 1951–55*

1. BG, 'Pluscarden: September 8th', *PAX*, Autumn 1946.
2. BG, letter to MS, 21 November 1954.
3. Ibid.
4. Fr Maurus, interview with author.
5. Fr Wulstan, interview with author.
6. Fr Barnabas, interview with author.
7. Fr Maurus, interview with author.
8. BG, interview with Kathryn Spink, 1986.
9. BG, letter to MS, 21 November 1954.
10. GS, p. 11.
11. Philip Toynbee, 'The Cenobites', *Observer*, 1954
12. 'Books of the Week', *The Tablet*, 6 November 1954.
13. GS, p. 187.
14. *MEW*, p. 7.
15. GS, p. 171.
16. GS, p. 173.
17. *MEW*, p. 8.
18. Ibid.
19. BG, letter to MH, 9 January 1955.
20. BG, letter to Abbot Wilfrid Upson, 10 October 1954.
21. Ibid.
22. BG, letter to Abbot Wilfrid Upson, 4 November 1954.
23. Fr Maurus, interview with author.
24. Ibid.
25. Ibid.
26. Kathryn Spink, *A Sense of the Sacred*, p. 96.
27. BG, letter to MS, 21 November 1954.

9. *Discovering India, 1955–56*

1. *MEW*, p. 8.
2. BG, letter to MS, 24 August 1955.
3. Ibid.
4. Raimon Panikkar, interview with author.
5. BG, letter to MS, 22 January 1957.
6. *MEW*, p. 10.
7. Ibid., pp. 10–11.
8. Ibid., p. 14.
9. BG, 'Vinoba Bhave', *Blackfriars*, February 1957.
10. *MEW*, p. 15.
11. Raimon Panikkar, interview with author.
12. *MEW*, p. 16.
13. Ibid.
14. BG, letter to Judson Trapnell, 31 May 1988. Quoted in Trapnell's doctoral dissertation, *Bede Griffiths' Theory of Religious Symbol and Practice of Religions. Towards Interreligious Understanding*, 1993.
15. BG, 'For a Hindu Catholicism', *The Tablet*, 21 May 1955.
16. BG, letter to MS, 20 April 1956.
17. BG, Review of *The Reign of Quantity* by R. Guénon and *The Transcendent Unity of Religions* by F. Schuon, *Blackfriars*, 1954.
18. BG, 'The Transcendent Unity of Religions', *Downside Review*, 1954.
19. BG, letter to HW, 2 December 1972.
20. BG, letter to MS, 14 June 1969.
21. BG, *Symbolism and Cult*. Paper given at Madras Cultural Academy, 6–13 December 1956.
22. Cardinal Newman, *The History of the Arians*.
23. BG, *Symbolism and Cult*, p. 56.
24. Raimon Panikkar, interview with author.
25. BG, letter to Abbot Wilfrid Upson, 22 June 1956.
26. Abbot Wilfrid Upson, letter to BG, 25 September 1956.

10. *A Monastic Experiment, Kurisumala 1956–63*

1. BG, letter to Fr Francis, 20 September 1956.
2. Fr Francis Acharya, letter to Toni Sussman, 27 November 1956.
3. Fr Francis Acharya, letter to Toni Sussman, September 1956.
4. 'A Monastic Experiment', in Fr Acharya (ed.), *Kurisumala Symposium on Ashram Life* (Kerala: Kurisumala Ashram, 1974).
5. BG, letter to MS, 20 July 1958.
6. BG, letter to MH, 9 September 1960.
7. BG, 'Kurisumala Ashram', *PAX*, Winter 1958.
8. 'An Interview with the Acharya' in *Kurisumala Symposium on Ashram Life*.
9. BG, *Christ in India*, p. 24.

10. 'An Interview with the Acharya' in *Kurisumala Symposium on Ashram Life*.

11. BG, *Christ in India*, p. 100.

12. Ibid., p. 25.

13. Ibid., pp. 131–2.

14. BG, letter to MS, 26 July 1964.

15. Quoted in *A Quest of Monastic Inculturation in India: Forty Years at Kurisumala Ashram*, The Harp, Kottayam 1995.

16. Quoted in 'First Growth' in *Kurisumala Symposium on Ashram Life*.

17. BG, *Christ in India*, pp. 199–200.

18. Ibid., p. 200.

19. Ibid., p. 217.

20. BG, letter to MS, 26 August 1962.

11. The Other Half of the World, 1963–68

1. BG, letter to MS, 10 March 1963.

2. BG, letter to MS, 25 December 1967.

3. BG, letter to MS, 20 July 1958.

4. Ibid.

5. BG, *Christ in India*, p. 13.

6. BG, letter to MS, 10 March 1963.

7. BG, letter to MS, 20 July 1968.

8. BG, letter to MS, 9 March 1967.

9. BG, letter to MS, 24 February 1966.

10. Ibid.

11. BG, letter to MS, 7 October 1966.

12. BG, *Christ in India*, p. 165.

13. BG, letter to MS, 19 November 1961.

14. BG, 'The Mystery of Sex and Marriage', *PAX*, Summer 1949.

15. BG, letter to NB, 5 March 1960.

16. BG, letter to MS, 18 February 1965.

17. BG, letter to MS, 23 June 1966.

18. BG, letter to MS, 25 December 1967.

19. BG, letter to MH, 12 July 1964.

20. BG, letter to MS, 25 December 1967.

21. BG, letter to MS, 23 June 1966.

22. BG, letter to MS, 20 June 1965.

23. *MEW*, p. 50.

24. GS, p. 55.

25. Judson Trapnell, *Bede Griffiths' Theory of Religious Symbol and Practice of Dialogue*, p. 225.

26. Karl Rahner *The Theology of the Symbol*, quoted in Trapnell, *Bede Griffiths' Theory of Religious Symbol and Practice of Dialogue*, p. 247.

27. GS, p. 186.

28. Ibid.
29. BG, letter to NB, 12 January 1958.
30. Ibid.
31. BG, letter to NB, 8 November 1958.
32. Matthew xvi. 25.
33. BG, letter to NB, 29 November 1959.
34. BG, letter to NB, 8 November 1958.
35. BG, letter to MS, 19 November 1961.
36. BG, letter to NB, 8 November 1958.
37. BG, letter to MS, 26 March 1959.
38. Ibid.
39. BG, letter to Fr Fabian Binyon, 17 April 1958.
40. BG, letter to MS, 19 November 1961.
41. Ibid.
42. Fr Francis, interview with author.
43. Ibid.
44. Kathryn Spink, *A Sense of the Sacred*, p. 148.
45. HW, letter to MS, 7 March 1972.
46. Fr Francis, interview with author.

12. *Lonely Years, Shantivanam 1968–75*

1. BG, letter to HW, 5 April 1969.
2. BG, letter to Abbot Dyfrig Rushton, 11 November 1968.
3. MS, letter to HW, 11 November 1971.
4. Jyoti Sahi, interview with author.
5. BG, letter to MS, 25 December 1968.
6. Ibid.
7. BG, letter to MS, 15 March 1970.
8. BG, letter to HW, 27 September 1970.
9. BG, letter to HW, 1969 (month illegible).
10. Stephen, letter to HW, undated.
11. BG, letter to HW, 22 December 1968.
12. BG, letter to HW, 11 September 1970.
13. Ibid.
14. Quoted in letter from MS to HW, 16 April 1979.
15. BG, letter to MS, 19 January 1971.
16. BG, letter to HW, 11 September 1970.
17. MS, letter to HW, 18 June 1970.
18. MS, letter to HW, 20 June 1970.
19. MS, letter to HW, 1 August 1970.
20. HW, letter to MS, 21 August 1970.
21. MS, letter to HW, All Saints 1970.
22. HW, letter to MS, 27 March 1972.

23. MS, letter to HW, 1 April 1972.
24. Kathryn Spink, *A Sense of the Sacred*, p. 149.
25. Fr Christudas, interview with author.
26. Fr Christudas, interview with Fr Douglas Conlan, Australia, 1995.
27. Raimon Panikkar, 'A Tribute to Fr Bede', *Ashrama Aikaya*, September 1993.
28. BG, letter to Fr Francis, 5 September 1956.
29. Fr Francis, interview with author.
30. BG, 'Forest of Peace in South India', *The Tablet*, 1969.
31. Norman P. Tanner, SJ (ed.), *Decrees of the Ecumenical Councils*, Vol. 11 (London: Sheed and Ward, 1990).
32. BG: *MEW* p. 23.
33. BG, letter to Judson Trapnell, p. 6.
34. Probably BG, *Saccidananda Ashram*, Shantivanam.
35. BG, 'The Ideal of an Indian Catholicism', *The Examiner*, 20 August 1960.
36. BG, 'The Declaration on the Church and non-Christian Religions', *The Examiner*, 19 February 1966.
37. Quoted in BG, *Saccidananda Ashram*.

13. International Guru

1. BG, letter to MH, 23 September 1976.
2. Sundaram, S. J., *The Examiner*, 3 January 1976.
3. BG, *Saccinanda Ashram*, Shantivanam, 1975.
4. BG, letter to MS, 28 December 1975.
5. Ibid.
6. BG, 'Mission is Dialogue', *Verbum SVD*, 1979.
7. Gavin D'Costa, *Studio Missionalia*, Vol. 44, 1995.
8. BG, letter to MS, 28 December 1975.
9. 'Purhoit Griffiths Consecrates Vimana', by 'A Trichirapalli Correspondent' (source not known).
10. BG, 'Shantivanam – an Explanation', *Vaidikamitram*, Vol. 9, 1976.
11. BG, 'An Open Letter to Anastasius Gomes', *Vaidikamitram*, September 1976.
12. Bishop Thomas Fernado, letter to BG, 4 December 1979.
13. Archbishop of Ernakulam, letter to BG, 9 June 1980.
14. BG, *Return to the Centre*, p. 71.
15. Ibid., pp. 19–20.
16. BG, letter to MS, 21 August 1974.
17. BG, letter to MS, 14 October 1976.
18. Julius Lipner, 'A Pessimistic Journey', *The Tablet*, 2 October 1976.
19. *The Times*, 22 May 1976.
20. *The Aryan Path*, Vol. XLV11, No. 6, November–December 1976.
21. *Church Times*, 30 April 1976.
22. BG, letter to MS, 1 December 1973.
23. Fr Douglas Conlan, interview with author.

24. BG, letter to MS, 25 August 1975.
25. BG, 'The Seekers', letter to *The Tablet*, 28 April 1984.
26. BG, *Christ in India*, p. 13.
27. BG, letter to HW, 22 December 1972.
28. BG, 'The Mystical Dimension in Theology', *Indian Theological Studies*, No. 14, 1977.
29. BG, letter to MH, 25 September 1970.
30. BG, 'The Search for God', *The Tablet*, 30 June 1979.
31. BG, letter to NB, 23 December 1975.
32. HW, letter to MS, 21 November 1971.
33. BG, letter to MH, 12 July 1964.
34. BG, letter to MH, 19 October 1968.
35. BG, letter to MH, 25 September 1969.
36. BG, letter to MS, 23 January 1980.
37. BG, letter to MH, 26 June 1966.
38. BG, 'Spirit as Mother', *The Tablet*, 9 June 1979.
39. BG, letter to MH, 26 October 1977.
40. BG, 'The Priesthood and Contemplation', *Life of the Spirit*, April 1951.
41. BG, 'Indian Christian Contemplation', *Clergy Monthly*, Vol. 35, 1971.
42. BG, letter to NB, 24 February 1977.
43. BG, letter to NB, 6 April 1976.
44. BG, letter to NB, 20 February 1979.
45. Jacob Needleman, *Lost Christianity: A Journey of Rediscovery to the Centre of Christian Experience* (Shaftesbury: Element, 1990), p. 130.
46. BG, *The New Creation in Christ*, p. 16.
47. BG, letter to MH, 31 May 1971.
48. BG, letter to NB, 24 February 1977.
49. Brother Martin, interview with author.
50. GS, p. 177.
51. BG, 'Erroneous Beliefs and Unauthorised Rites', *The Tablet*, 14 April 1973.
52. BG, letter to MH, 23 September 1975.
53. BG, *Return to the Centre*, p. 107.
54. Abhishiktananda, *Hindu-Christian Meeting Point: Within the Cave of the Heart* (Delhi: ISPCK, 1969), p. 98.
55. Ibid.
56. BG, letter to NB, 21 August 1981.

14. The Marriage of Opposites

1. BG, letter to MS, 16 April 1981.
2. MS, *Autobiography*, unpublished MS.
3. BG, letter to MS, 28 January 1978.
4. BG, letter to MS, 27 March 1984.
5. Abbot Primate Jerome Theisen, Statement, 2 June 1993.

6. BG, 'The Monastic Order and the Ashram', *American Benedictine Review*, Vol. 30, 1979.
7. Ibid.
8. Ibid.
9. Ibid.
10. BG, letter to MS, 19 January 1971.
11. BG, letter to NB, undated.
12. HW, letter to MS, 11 November 1971.
13. 'Mission is Dialogue, an Interview with Father Bede Griffiths', Verbum SVD 1979.
14. Ibid.
15. BG, 'Kurisumala Ashram', *Eastern Churches Quarterly*, Vol. 16, 1964.
16. BG, 'The One Mystery', *The Tablet*, 9 March 1974.
17. 'Mission is Dialogue' an Interview with Father Bede Griffiths.
18. Raimon Panikkar, *The Trinity and the Religious Experience of Man* (New York: Orbis, 1973), p. 42.
19. BG, 'A Meditation on the Mystery of the Trinity', *Monastic Studies*, No. 17, 1986.
20. BG, *A New Vision of Reality*, p. 251.
21. *MEW*, p. 47.
22. Ibid., p. 151.
23. BG, letter to MS, 6 October 1980.
24. BG, letter to MS, 22 June 1982.
25. Ibid.
26. Book review signed 'H.H.', *PAX*, Autumn 1982.
27. *Christian Order*, April 1982.
28. *National Catholic Reporter*, 21 May 1993.
29. BG, letter to Mar Athanasios, 15 July 1977.
30. BG, letter to MH, 22 September 1980.

15. Unity in Diversity, the 1980s

1. Fr Christudas, interview with author.
2. BG, letter to MS, 26 March 1988.
3. Patricia Cave, in John Swindells (ed.), *A Human Search*, p. 136.
4. LF, interview with author.
5. Anon, interview with author.
6. Chuck Baroo, interview with Christopher Venning.
7. Jyoti Minor, interview with author.
8. Br Martin, interview with author.
9. Fr Douglas Conlan, interview with author.
10. Raimon Panikkar: interview with author.
11. Andrew Harvey, interview with author.
12. LF, interview with author.

13. *A Human Search* (video) More than Illusion Films, Sydney, Australia, 1993.
14. Chuck Baroo, interview with Christopher Venning.
15. Andrew Harvey, interview with author.
16. Philena Bruce, interview with author.
17. Br John, fax letter to author, 18 June 1997.
18. Fr Christudas, in John Swindells (ed.), *A Human Search*, p. 144.
19. BG, letter to Mr Britte, 9 April 1978.
20. BG, letter to Sr Marie Louise, 15 April 1982.
21. BG, letter to MS, 15 April 1980.
22. BG, letter to MS, 13 May 1986.
23. BG, letter to MS, 31 August 1985.
24. BG, letter to MS, 22 June 1982.
25. BG, letter to MS, 23 June 1979.
26. Rupert Sheldrake, Obituary, *The Tablet*, 22 May 1993.
27. BG, letter to MS, 20 April 1992.
28. BG, letter to Sr Pascaline, 27 February 1982.
29. Rupert Sheldrake, interview with author.
30. BG, letter to MS, 13 March 1982.
31. BG, letter to HW and MS, 29 October 1983.
32. BG, letter to MS, 14 December 1978.
33. Fr Bruno Barnhart, letter to author, 14 October 1996.
34. Sr Carla Curran RSJ, letter to author, 29 July 1996.
35. *The Age*, 4 May 1985.
36. BG, letter to MS, 28 October 1983.
37. BG, letter to MS, 29 August 1979.
38. BG, letter to MS, 20 July 1985.
39. BG, letter to MS, 3 July 1984.
40. BG, letter to MS, 26 March 1987.

16. Controversy

1. BG, 'Two Theologies', *The Tablet*, 12 July 1980.
2. BG, letter to *The Tablet*, 21 April 1984.
3. LF, *Christian Meditation Newsletter*, December 1993.
4. BG, letter to *The Tablet*, 12 December 1987.
5. BG, letter to *The Tablet*, 26 September 1987.
6. BG, letter to *The Tablet*, 17 January 1987.
7. BG, 'A Smack at Ratzinger', *The Tablet*, 27 July 1985.
8. BG, letter to *The Tablet*, 28 July 1984.
9. BG, letter to *The Tablet*, 24 October 1987.
10. BG, letter to *The Tablet*, 27 October 1990.
11. Quoted in *The Fullness of Christ*, William M. Klimon, Crisis January 1994.
12. William Rees-Mogg, 'Old truths for the young', *The Times*, 20 May 1993.
13. BG, letter to Fr Peter Milward, SJ, 7 November 1989.

14. BG, letter to MS, 15 April 1983.
15. BG, letter to MS, 17 August 1984.
16. *Shorter Oxford English Dictionary*.
17. David Brigstocke, SJ, *The Month*, February 1996.
18. Andrew Harvey, interview with author.
19. LF, letter to author, 23 June 1977.
20. Wayne Teasdale, *Towards a Christian Vedanta*.
21. Judson Trapnell, *Bede Griffiths' Theory of Religious Symbol and Practice of Dialogue*.
22. Ursula King, *The Clergy Review*, September 1983.
23. Dr Sten Rodhe, *Vidyajyoti Journal of Theological Reflection*, October 1995.
24. Raimon Panikkar, interview with author.
25. Felicity Edwards, interview with author.
26. BG, letter to Jyoti Sahi, 31 October 1983.
27. Ibid.
28. BG, letter to Jyoti Sahi, 15 August 1986.
29. Swami Kulandaiswami, letter to *Indian Express*, 30 March 1987. In Sita Ram Goel, *Catholic Ashrams*.
30. Ignatius Absalom, letter to *Indian Express*, 10 April 1987. In Sita Ram Goel, op. cit.
31. Swami Devananda, letter to *India Express*, June 1987. In Sita Ram Goel, op. cit.
32. Swami Devananda, letter to BG, 21 July 1987. In Sita Ram Goel, op. cit.
33. BG, letter to Swami Devananda, 23 July 1987. In Sita Ram Goel, op. cit.
34. Swami Devananda, letter to BG, 30 July 1987. In Sita Ram Goel, op. cit.
35. Swami Devananda, letter to BG, 7 August 1987. In Sita Ram Goel, op. cit.
36. BG, letter to Swami Devananda, 31 July 1987. In Sita Ram Goel, op. cit.
37. BG, letter to Swami Devananda, 16 October 1987. In Sita Ram Goel, op. cit.
38. BG, *Emerging Universal Consciousness and the Mystical Traditions of Asia*, ed. Wayne Teasdale, given at a seminar at Guru Kal Lutheran College, Madras (Vincentian Pubs, 1985).
39. BG, Ashram Aikya, newsletter, Pentecost 1988.
40. BG, Ashram Aikya, newsletter, undated.
41. Ibid.
42. Jyoti Sahi, Ashram Aikya, newsletter, undated.
43. BG, letter to JS, 13 March 1989.

17. Friendship

1. HW, *Look, the Dawn*, unpublished MS.
2. BG, in James T. Como (ed.), *Lewis at the Breakfast Table and Other Reminiscences* (New York: Macmillan, 1962).
3. Ibid.
4. HW, letter to MS, 28 April 1971.

5. Peter Bentley, letter to author, 19 August 1997.
6. Brother Gerard, letter to BG (date unknown).
7. Rev. H. O. Mascarenhas, letter to BG, 17 June 1965.
8. 'Richard', letter to BG, 3 December 1960.
9. Quoted by HW, letter to MS, 29 December 1970.
10. BG, letter to MS, 18 September 1987.
11. RP interview with author.
12. BG, Statement, 'My Relation with Russill', 6 September 1992.
13. Asha Paul D'Silva, interview with author.
14. BG, Statement.
15. RP, interview with author.
16. BG, letter to RP and Asha, 18 August 1989.
17. BG, letter to RP and Asha, 11 February 1990.
18. Jyoti Sahi, letter to author, 29 December 1995.
19. Recounted to author by Andrew Harvey.
20. BG, letter to RP and Asha, 4 May 1990.
21. BG, letter to RP and Asha, 15 January 1991.
22. Ibid.
23. BG, letter to RP, Asha and Wayne Teasdale, 22 August 1990.
24. RP, interview with author.
25. BG, letter to RP, Asha and Wayne Teasdale, 3 June 1990.

18. *Breakthrough to the Feminine*

1. BG, letter to RP and Asha, 11 February 1990.
2. BG, quoted by JW in letter to PC, 11 February 1990.
3. BG, quoted in JW's journal.
4. JW, journal.
5. Ibid.
6. Ibid.
7. Ibid.
8. JW, letter to PC, 16 February 1990.
9. JW, interview with author.
10. BG, quoted in John Swindells (ed.), *A Human Search*, p. 89.
11. Ibid., p. 90.
12. JW, journal.
13. JW, letter to PC, 26 February 1990.
14. BG, letter to PC, 15 April 1990.
15. John Swindells (ed.), *A Human Search*, p. 89.
16. Ibid., p. 100.
17. Andrew Harvey, letter to author, July 1997.
18. JW, journal.
19. St John 17 v. 23.
20. BG, letter to PC, 15 April 1990.

21. BG, 'Meditation: Is East Least and West Best?' *National Catholic Reporter*, 11 May 1990.
22. Abhishiktananda, letter to Murray Rogers, 10 September, 1973 *Swami Abhishiktananda: His Life Told through His Letters*, pp. 349–50.
23. Ibid., Foreword, p. viii.
24. BG, letter to PC, 15 April 1990.
25. BG, letter to RP and Asha, 18 March 1990.
26. Ibid.
27. BG, letter to RP, 14 February 1990.
28. BG, letter to RP and Asha, 1 February 1990.
29. BG, letter to RP, 17 February 1990.
30. BG, letter to RP, undated.
31. BG, letter to MS, 22 November 1986.
32. BG, letter to RP and Asha, 26 April 1990.
33. JW, letter to PC, 1 April 1990.

19. 'You Cannot Put a Prophet in a Cage'

1. John Swindells (ed.), *A Human Search*, p. 109.
2. Anonymous, interview with Christopher Venning, 20 January 1993.
3. BG, letter to Roland Ropers, 14 May 1992.
4. BG, letter to PC, 17 August 1992.
5. From BG's entry in clinic's guest book.
6. BG, letter to PC, 26 May 1991.
7. Annabel Miller, interview with author.
8. Bailey Young, interview with author.
9. Ruth Harring, interview with author.
10. John Swindells (ed.), *A Human Search*, p. 135.
11. *A New Vision of Reality*, p. 282.
12. Ibid., p. 286.
13. Ibid.
14. Ibid., p. 296.
15. Sheila Bowler, letter to author, 29 July 1996.
16. Brother Martin, interview with author.
17. Asha D'Silva, interview with author.
18. BG, *A Centre of Contemplative Living*, unpublished MS.
19. Asha Paul, Wayne Teasdale and Russill Paul, 'An Experience in Contemplative Living', in *Swami Bede Dayananda*.
20. Robert Kiely in Laurence Freeman and Robert Kiely (eds), *The New Creation in Christ*, pp. xiv–xv.
21. LF, 'My memories of Father Bede', in *Swami Bede Dayananda*.
22. Virginia Attwood, interview with author.
23. Ibid.
24. BG, letter to Roland Ropers, 2 May 1992.

25. *Weekend Australian*, 22 May 1993.
26. Joan Terry, letter to author, 12 February 1996.
27. BG, letter to Roland Ropers, 20 May 1992.
28. BG, letter to PC, 20 April 1992.
29. BG, letter to MS, 20 April 1992.
30. BG, 'The Light of Wisdom in East and West' re-named 'Marriage of East and West', talk at Melbourne, 17 May 1992.
31. Ibid.
32. BG, 'Prayer', talk at Kreuth, Germany, 7 April 1992.
33. BG, talk at Melbourne, 17 May 1992.
34. Ibid.
35. BG, 'Mysticism', talk at Christchurch, 5 May 1992.
36. BG, 'Integration of Mind, Body and Spirit: Balancing Duality', talk at the Fetzer Institute, Kalamazoo, USA, 9 September 1992.
37. Wayne Teasdale, interview with author.
38. BG, letter to RP, 3 June 1990.
39. BG, letter to Asha, RP and Wayne Teasdale, 2 June 1990.
40. BG, *On Homosexual Love*, unpublished MS.
41. BG, *The Reason for Being*, unpublished MS.
42. LF, interview with author.
43. Fritjof Capra, letter to author, 27 November 1996.
44. BG, letter to MS, 20 April 1992.
45. BG, letter to Fr Douglas Conlan, 14 December 1992.

20. Death

1. Christopher Venning, unpublished MS, January 1993.
2. Patricia Cave, letter to LF, 30 December 1992.
3. Chuck Baroo, interview with Christopher Venning, 21 January 1993.
4. BG, interview with Christopher Venning, January 1993.
5. Christopher Venning, unpublished MS.
6. BG, quoted in letter from John Kilian to friends, 10 May 1993.
7. Fr Christudas, 'My Experience with My Guruji', Ashrama Aikya, newsletter, September 1993.
8. Carol Watson, letter to JW, 19 May 1993.
9. JW, letter to PC, 14 May 1993.
10. Andrew Harvey, interview with author.
11. Thomas Matus, recounted in 'Bede Griffiths, Monk 1906–1993 The Universal in the Specific', *Bulletin Pro Dialogo Rome*, No. 83 3/1993.
12. John Kilian, letter to friends, 10 May 1993.
13. JW, letter to PC, 2 May 1993.
14. Andrew Harvey, interview with author.
15. Ibid.
16. JW, letter to PC, 4 May 1993.

17. Ibid.
18. BG, 'Unified Consciousness', Mystics and Scientists Conference, 10–12 April 1992.
19. LF, Homily at BG's Memorial Service at Westminster Cathedral, 15 June 1993.
20. Brother Martin, in *Swami Bede Dayananda*.
21. GS, p. 135.
22. RP, diary, Maundy Thursday 1993.
23. Ibid.
24. LF, Homily.
25. The Community of Shantivanam, letter to friends, undated.
26. RP, letter to friends, 26 June 1993.
27. *Svetasvatura Upanishad*.
28. Fr Christudas, letter to Fr Robert, 25 May 1993.
29. Quoted in Ken Wilber, *Grace and Grit* (Dublin: Gill and Macmillan, 1991).

Epilogue

1. *America*, 5–12 June 1993.
2. Tim McCarthy, *National Catholic Reporter*, 21 May 1993.
3. *Monos*, June 1993; *Independent*, 15 May 1993.
4. Isabelle Glover, *Guardian*, 18 May 1993.
5. William Rees-Mogg, 'Old truths for the young', *The Times*, 20 May 1993.
6. David Lorimer, *Church Times*, 28 May 1993.
7. *Daily Telegraph*, 15 May 1993.
8. Peter W. Millar, *The Scotsman*, 19 May 1993.
9. Cardinal Hume, statement.
10. LF, Homily at BG's Memorial Service at Westminster Cathedral, 15 June 1993.
11. Thomas Matus, *Bulletin Pontificium Consilum pro Dialogo inter religiones*, July 1993.
12. Camaldolese press release.
13. Raimon Panikkar, *A Tribute* (publication unknown).
14. Brother Martin, interview with author.
15. PC, *Bede Griffiths. The Man – The Monk – The Mystic* (Sandsprings OK: Osage Monastery, 1994).
16. LF, letter to author, 23 August 1997.
17. A religious sister, interview with Christopher Venning, 20 January 1993.
18. LF, letter to author, 23 June 1997.
19. Karl Rahner, *The Practice of Faith* (London: SCM Press, 1985).
20. BG, letter to MS, 4 April 1991.

Select Bibliography

Books by Father Bede Griffiths

The Golden String (London: Harvill Press, 1954).

Christian Ashram (London: Darton, Longman and Todd, 1966). Published as *Christ in India: Essays Towards a Hindu–Christian Dialogue* (Illinois: Templegate Publishers, 1966).

The Book of Common Prayer of the Syrian Church, trans. Dom Bede Griffiths, Monk of Kurisumala Ashram. (Vagamon, Kottayam: Kurisumala Ashram). Initially, private circulation only. Later *Syrian Churches Series*, Vol. III (c. 1972).

Vedanta and the Christian Faith (California: Dawn Horse Press, 1973).

Return to the Centre (London: Collins, 1976; and Illinois: Templegate Publishers, 1976).

The Marriage of East and West: A Sequel to the Golden String (London: Collins, 1982; and Illinois: Templegate Publishers, 1982).

The Cosmic Revelation: The Hindu Way To God (Illinois: Templegate Publishers, 1983).

River of Compassion: A Christian Commentary on the Bhagavad Gita (New York: Amity House, 1987).

A New Vision of Reality: Western Science, Eastern Mysticism and Christian Faith, ed. Felicity Edwards (London: Collins, 1989; and Illinois: Templegate Publishers, 1990).

The Universal Christ: Daily Readings with Bede Griffiths, ed. Peter Spink (London: Darton, Longman and Todd, 1990).

The New Creation in Christ: Christian Meditation and Community, ed. Laurence Freeman and Robert Kiely (London: Darton, Longman and Todd, 1992).

Universal Wisdom: A Journey through the Sacred Wisdom of the World, ed. Roland Ropers (London: Fount, 1994; and San Francisco: Harpers, 1994).

Psalms for Christian Prayer, ed. Roland Ropers (London: HarperCollins, 1995).

Pathways to the Supreme, ed. Roland Ropers (London: HarperCollins, 1995).

A Human Search: Bede Griffiths Reflects on His Life, ed. John Swindells (Tunbridge Wells: Burns and Oates, 1997; and Ligouri, MO: Triumph Books, 1997).

The Mystery Beyond: On Retreat with Bede Griffiths (London: Medio Media/Arthur James, 1997).

Published letters

Catholic Ashrams: Adopting and Adapting Hindu Dharma, ed. Sita Ram Goel (New Delhi: Voice of India Publications, 1988).

A Follower of Christ and a Disciple of Sri Aurobindo, Correspondence between Bede Griffiths and K. D. Sethna (Amil Kiran) (USA: Integral Life Foundation, 1996).

Books about Father Bede Griffiths

Bruteau, Beatrice (ed.), *As We Are One. Essays and Poems in Honor of Bede Griffiths* (North Carolina: Philosopher's Exchange, 1991).

Bruteau, Beatrice (ed.), *The Other Half of My Soul* (Illinois: Quest Books, 1996). (Expanded edition of *As We Are One*).

Rajan, Jesu, *Bede Griffiths and Sannyasa* (India: Asian Trading Corporation, 1989).

Spink, Kathryn, *A Sense of the Sacred: a Biography of Bede Griffiths* (London: SPCK, 1988).

Teasdale, Wayne, *Toward a Christian Vedanta* (India: Asian Trading Corporation, 1987).

Trapnell, Judson B., *Bede Griffiths' Theory of Religious Symbol and Practice of Dialogue, Toward Interreligious Understanding*, doctoral dissertation, Catholic University of America, Washington DC, 1993.

Swami Bede Dayanda: Testimonies and Tributes (India: Shantivanam Publications, 1994).

Glossary

Anglicised Sanskrit is not consistent in its spelling. Where there are variations I have adopted the spelling used by Bede Griffiths.

advaita – non-duality
amrita – immortality
arati – the waving of lights and incense
ashram – a place of retreat where seekers engage in spiritual practices and study sacred teachings
atman – from the Sanskrit 'to breathe', so 'soul' or 'self'
ayurveda – the ancient Indian science of medicine
bhajans – devotional songs and hymns
bhakti – devotion, love
brahmachari – student of spiritual knowledge
Brahma – the name of God, the creator
Brahman – the non-dual reality without properties; the absolute, the ground of being
chakra – one of the seven centres of psychic energy in the body
darshan – lit. 'seeing', being in the presence of an image of the deity
dhoti – the loincloth worn by Hindus
guru – spiritual guide
harijans – 'Children of God', *dalits* or 'untouchables'
Ishvara – Lord of the Universe, the personal God as creator
jnana – wisdom, knowledge
kalasam – the round pinnacle on top of a temple symbolising the four elements
Kali – the terrible form of the goddess Shiva
karma – work, ritual action; the law of causation which ordains the result (good or bad) of all actions
kavi – the saffron-coloured robes worn by sannyasi

kolam – traditional drawings painted at the entrance to a home or temple. They are drawn to invoke divine blessings and are done by women

Krishna – lit. 'dark blue', divine hero of the *Bhagavad Gita*

kumkumum – purple powder placed between the eyebrows, used in rituals

Kundalini – cosmic energy, seen as a coiled serpent at the base of the spine

mandapam – the outer courtyard

mantra – a sacred word or phrase of spiritual significance and power

muladhara – the root chakra, the body's connection to earth and to sex

Nataraj(a) – the dancing form of the god Shiva

neti, neti – not this, not this

nirvana – the final state of being, beyond change and becoming

Om – the sacred syllable, the sound symbol for the ultimate reality

Panchanga pranam – kneeling in veneration with forehead and palms of the hands on the ground

Paramatman – Supreme Self (from *parama* 'highest' + *atman* 'self')

puja – ritual offering

purohita – a Vedic priest

Purusha – the 'primal being' or archetypal man

Rama – hero of the *Ramayana*

rishi – seer

Saccidananda – the Hindu name for the Godhead, from *sat* 'being' + *cit* 'consciousness' + *ananda* 'bliss'

sadhaka – learner, aspirant

sahajah samadhi – unified consciousness

sahasrara – the seventh chakra, in the crown of the head

sangha – community

sannyasa diksha – initiation into sannyasa

sannyasa – renunciation of the world in order to seek God

sannyasi – one who renounces the world and earthly possessions

Sarvodaya – lit. 'service of all', a movement started by Gandhi and taken over by Vinoba Bhave

satsang – lit. 'the company of good people' – a meeting

Shakti – spouse of Shiva, the divine energy personified as a feminine principle

Shiva – the supreme Godhead, God as the destroyer and regenerator

slokas – verses

swami – a title of honour given to a holy man

Veda – the ancient holy books of the Hindus

Vedanta – a school of philosophy founded on the *Upanishads*

vibhuti – sacred ash

vimana – the dome over a Hindu temple

yoga – lit. 'yoke' – union, harmony

The Bede Griffiths Trust

The Bede Griffiths Trust oversees and has care for Father Bede's publications, manuscripts and tapes, encourages the renewal of contemplative life and publishes a quarterly newsletter, *The Golden String*. When it was founded in 1992 it established eight centres throughout the world.

In the USA

Osage Monastery, c/o Sr Pascaline Coff, OSB,
18701 W. Monastery Road, Sandsprings, OK 74063.
Tel: 918 245 2734 Fax: 918 245 9360
New Camaldoli Hermitage, c/o Fr Robert Hale, OSB Cam,
Big Sur, CA 93920.
Tel: 408 667 2456 Fax: 408 667 0209
Incarnation Monastery, c/o Br Cassian Hardie, OSB Cam,
1369 La Loma Ave, Berkeley, CA 94708.
Tel: 510 548 0965 Fax: 510 845 0610
Epiphany Monastery, c/o Fr Romuald Duscher, OSB Cam,
96 Scobie Rd, New Boston, NH 03070.
Tel: 603 487 3700 Fax: 603 487 3020

In India

Saccidananda Ashram, c/o Br John Martin, OSB Cam,
Tannirpalli 639107, Kulittalai – Trichi Dist.
Tamil Nadu, South India.
Tel: 011 91 4323 3060

In Italy

Monasterio di San Gregorio, c/o Fr Bernadino Cozzarini, OSB Cam,
Piazza di San Gregorio al Celio, Rome, Italy 00184.
Tel: 011 396 700 8227 Fax: 011 396 700 9357

In Germany

Shantigiri/Mount of Peace, c/o Roland Ropers, Obl OSB,
D-83707 Kreuth/Tegernsee, Germany.
Tel: 0049 8029 9998 Fax: 0049 8029 998944

In Australia

Christ by the River Hermitage, c/o Fr Douglas Conlan, Obl OSB,
PO Box 35, Pinjarra 6208, W. Australia.
Tel: 011 09 5211 227 Fax: 011 09 5312 480

There are also two informal networks of people who have been inspired by
Fr Bede's vision.

In the USA

The Friends of Bede Griffiths
c/o Nicholas Groves,
604 Judson Avenue,
Evanston, IL 60202.
Tel: 847 492 1275

In the UK

The Bede Griffiths Sangha,
c/o The World Community for Christian Meditation,
International Centre,
23 Kensington Square, London W8 5HN.
Tel: 0171 937 4679 Fax: 0171 937 6790

Permissions

The author and publisher would like to thank the following for permission to quote from their publications:

The American Benedictine Review (*The Monastic Order and the Ashram*, issue 30, 1979). Ashram Aikiya Newsletter. The Clergy Review. Darton, Longman and Todd (*The New Creation in Christ* by Bede Griffiths, published and copyright 1992 by Darton, Longman and Todd Ltd and used by permission of the publishers). The Downside Review. Element Books Ltd (*Lost Christianity: A Journey of Rediscovery to the Centre of Christian Experience* by Jacob Needleman). The Indian Society for Promoting Christian Knowledge (*Hindu-Christian Meeting Point: Within the Cave of the Heart* by Abhishiktananda and *Abishiktananda: His Life Told Through His Letters* by James Stewart). Life of the Spirit. Ligouri Publications/ Triumph (*A Human Search*). Little Brown (*Avowed Intent: The Autobiography of Lord Longford*). Monastic Studies, The Monastery of Christ the King, London. The Month (*The Way of Bede Griffiths* by David Brigstocke). The National Catholic Reporter Publishing Company (*Benedictine Fr. Bede Griffiths, 86, dies in India* by Tim McCarthy, May 21, 1993 issue). New Blackfriars. The Observer © (quote from *The Cenobites* by Philip Toynbee, 1954). PAX, Prinknash Abbey. Sheed & Ward (*Community Journey* by George Ineson). The Society for the Promoting of Christian Knowledge (*Sense of the Sacred*, published in Australia by HarperCollins*Religious*). The Tablet Publishing Co. Templegate Publishers (*Christ in India*). Verbum SVD. Vidyajyoti Journal of Theological Reflection (article by Dr. Sten Rodhe). William Rees-Mogg/Times Newspapers Limited, 1993.

Illustrations: 1, 2, courtesy of Saccidananda Ashram; 3, courtesy of Kathryn Spink; 4, 10, 11, 12, 14, 15, 16, 18, 23, 24, Author's collection; 5, courtesy of the Skinner Estate; 6, courtesy of Kate Nowlan; 7, courtesy of Hulton Deutsch Collection, photograph by John Chillingworth; 8, 9, courtesy of the Abbot and Community of Prinknash Abbey; 22, 25, 27, courtesy of Roland R. Ropers; 19, 20, 26, courtesy of Fr Douglas Conlan.

Every effort has been made to contact owners of copyright material used. If there are any omissions please contact the publishers and corrections will be made at the earliest possible opportunity.

Index

NOTE: This index is arranged alphabetically word by word *except* under 'Griffiths, Bede, life,' where subheadings are arranged chronologically